SKIP AND J. MARIE

R. Mustafa Lucas

Copyright © 2018 R. Mustafa Lucas

All rights reserved. No part(s) of this book may be reproduced, distributed or transmitted in any form, or by any means, or stored in a database or retrieval systems without prior expressed written permission of the author of this book.

ISBN: 978-1-5356-1019-3

Contents

Introduction 1
Chapter 1: First Grade 3
Chapter 2: The Teenage Years 18
Chapter 3: Connie Running the House 32
Chapter 4: Mischief 46
Chapter 5: Opportunity Makes a Thief 62
Chapter 6: Mr. Scruggs 78
Chapter 7: Basic Training 100
Chapter 8: The Magician 115
Chapter 9: Daddy's Gone 128
Chapter 10: Betting on the Ponies 145
Chapter 11: Kenny O 169
Chapter 12: A Step in the Right Direction 187
Chapter 13: Lions and Sheeps 200
Chapter 14: Let the Games Begin 221
Chapter 15: Trouble in the Yard 240
Chapter 16: A Devestating Visit 259
Chapter 17: The Squared Circle 277
Chapter 18: Brothers 296

Chapter 19: The Cut 313
Chapter 20: The Imam 319
Chapter 21: One on One 342
Chapter 22: The Board 362

Introduction

SKIP LUCAS STANDS APART FROM those around him, then and now. From the streets of Anacostia, S.E., Washington D.C., a good-looking boy who learned to use his hazel eyes and enchanting smile to compensate an average intelligent mind. In the early years, he was a larcenous truant, notorious car thief, and threatened with reform school by the juvenile court system and Connie. It would practically kill her that her oldest boy would be put away, but it was not all her decision; he wasn't leaving her much choice. She'd get him away from his stomping grounds, change schools, and…yes, he would go for her proposal, or else.

Using his uncle's N.E. address to be in accordance with the zoning for the school district, Skip found himself in a new environment filled with the same thugs he'd left, except these New Jacks were ostentatious and overblown, all but J. Marie. She was a knockout with a killer body that grown women would sell their souls for. He and she resembled each other in mannerisms, taste, demeanor, and tolerance; some thought they were brother and sister. She was a class act, unlike Skip, and most of all, she wasn't a crook. She didn't use drugs or alcohol and loved Skip despite his own use of the stuff. They fell very much in love. So much so they made a pact, which neither would ever forget…ever.

Skip's criminal career accelerated to new heights as he got older. By then, he'd worn J. Marie down until she was a part-time co-conspirator, and his "rap-buddy" in a pinch; that'd be before Candie, the second of their children. Though their friends and some of their own relatives envied the success they had, and their union, the two were loved and admired by all that came to know them. Skip had a dual lifestyle and was living on the edge, but she would be by his side forever, remaining the faithful wife and partner, for better and for worse, in sickness and in health… that'd be before the murders.

Together since they were fourteen, now adults married with children, their lives and world around them would be turned upside down, changing them as well as their families and friends, once committed to both.

In the coming years what twist of fate will befall this once aspiring and loving couple? And what about the pact… and Mustafa?

Chapter 1

CONNIE HAD JUST JOINED THE small group of onlookers, parents peering through the classroom-door window at their little ones, who were taking the first-grade entry test for the highly-promoted parochial school in the lower-middle-class Southeast Anacostia neighborhood. Actually, the test was nothing more than a faux formality, because gaining entry was all about the money, and if you had the cake ($) your kid was in, straight like that. As Connie smilingly looked for her son among the busy little soon-to-be enrollees, she overheard one of the mothers humorously, albeit sarcastically, lamenting about the boy in the third row looking onto her daughter's page. Connie's smile vanished as she found the perpetrator to be her son. The sight of Skippá obviously copying from the little girl's paper to his own, looking back again, then in the direction of the nun at the front of the class was disheartening to say the least. More disturbing, however, and also perplexing, was how in the world and where, at such a young age, had he learned to incorporate this appalling act. For crying out loud, he was only six years old!

Two dollars, three, four, five is ten, that was the change young Skippá got back from the ice cream man after ordering a banana boat with all the fixings imaginable, and a milkshake. In the early sixties, one could get a heck of an ice-cream extravaganza for a buck. That particular hook-up came to just 85¢ (50¢ for the banana split, 35¢ for the shake). Stealing the ten-dollar bill from his mom's purse was easy, and he didn't see any problems ahead at the time, but when the ice-cream truck driver started counting off the change to him and he was actually holding all those bills in his small hand, well… Now he began seeing things clearer. This was Skippá's first imagery of looking at the bigger picture, and now he had some contemplating to do. He thought the ice cream man would never stop counting off the money to him. It wasn't so much that he was anxious to dig into the cold treat as it was he didn't want to be seen with all that cheese (money)! He was not yet aware of his surroundings, not quite, and he was somewhat oblivious to potential threats in the likeness of thieves or bullies. Skippá was not the sharpest knife in the drawer, but not a complete idiot either; after all, this was Southeast, Washington.

Southeast, Anacostia, in Washington D.C., began actually as Washington's very first suburb; this area, east of the Anacostia River, was provided and approved by Congress in 1854 purely for profit; and for whites only. Congress had built a bridge over the river from the "Navy Yard," giving workers there access to a subdivision they named "Union Town."

Documented records reveal how real-estate developer John Van Hook and his partners subdivided, and put up for sale, a few hundred housing lots in the area. John Van Hook was the first owner of "Cedar Hill," the house Frederick Douglas owned when he moved to what would later be called Anacostia in around 1878. There is information on the history of Anacostia in Louise Hutchinson's book *Anacostia Story*, which was commissioned by the Smithsonian Institution.

After one hundred years, Van hook wouldn't have recognized the place he first settled. By 1940, Anacostia was forty percent black. Over the next three decades under the guise of urban renewal, federal officials forced Washington's poor into apartments and public housing that the government built in Anacostia. The influx of seven housing projects came in the 50s. Many of the people who came to the community were alley dwellers from Georgetown, and slum dwellers from Southwest. By the 1960s, Van Hook's "whites only" section called Union Town was sixty-six percent black. Today, it is ninety-eight percent.

Skippá was a fourth generation "Anacostian." His grandfather, Ralph Waldo Lucas, would come by to ride him around in his 1944 Buick, with a running board. Skippá liked standing on it and leaning in the window, talking to Granddaddy Lucas on the few occasions he'd come by. He would ride his grandson along the old Nichols Avenue (now Martin Luther King Jr. Avenue) and show Skippá the house he lived in as a boy coming up, which was across the street from what's now the Barry Farms Projects. He'd tell stories of how he would go down to the train cars on the railroad tracks to take coal off the cars to be used for heating the house. Skippá's Granddad was a painter, and he also did roofing and carpentry work.

Meanwhile, Skippá was seven years old, he had a pocket full of cheese (nine dollars and some change), he had an ice-cream mega-meal, and he was contemplating thoughts of living large, if only for a little while. Well he knew what to do with the ice cream, ha!; that was the easy part! But about his new-found riches, he hadn't quite figured that out yet. Skippá was living in the low-income apartment complex called, "Parkland," just off a precariously threatening tract – Stanton Road. He attended school on the other side of the Suitland Parkway. The parochial school he attended was on top of one of the highest points in the city, let alone S.E. (Morris Rd.). Skippá was indeed admitted into "Our Lady of Perpetual Help," because Connie could afford to send him, and perhaps he'd copied enough correct answers off the little girl's paper.

That morning, as he got dressed, he stuck the nine dollars in his uniform pants pocket (dark green pants, white shirt, and green tie), all the while trying to concoct a scheme. By the time he got home that afternoon, his father was waiting for him. "Where did you get that money, boy?"

How'd he find out? Someone told him I had a lotta money, I bet, Skippá thought. "What money Da'," he inquired, figuring feigning ignorance was worth a shot.

Whack! "You know what damn money, boy. The money you had, buying all that ice cream; don't play with me."

"I found it."

Whack, Whack, and *double* Whack!

After what seemed an eternity for Skippá, despite sticking with the lie, Paul wasn't done just yet. After a few more minutes of talking while laying the strap on him, his father had given up.

Young Skippá had soldiered up, stood firm on his lie and the whipping had caused only minor damages. Much later on his "side job", he would learn to use the old convicts' catch phrase of "That's my story and I'm sticking with it." Despite all the leather his Dad put to him, he wouldn't crack; what'd be the use now… True, he stole the money. But he no longer had the money, and he was still getting whipped for it. Another terse saying he would hear over the years that would remind him of the tragic event he so ignorantly created at a young age is "Don't crap on the floor of your own house." (Actually it's "Don't shit where you live.")

Skippá learned Anacostia exceptionally well at a very young age. To get to school his mom would drop him off on her way to work at The Department of Health, Education, and Welfare. (H.E.W.) Getting home, he was supposed to catch the 94- Stanton Road; it would stop at a bus stop just a block down the street from the apartment he shared with his mom, dad, and baby brother, M.G. (short for Michael Gordon). Instead, he would walk the mile and a half across Suitland Parkway, up

Stanton Road, and on through the notorious Garfield Projects. Garfield was one of the three most dangerous project dwellings in Anacostia, along with Barry Farm and Knox Terrace. Skippá knew enough to walk fast – real fast – upon entering the portion of Garfield that ran parallel with Stanton Road, despite lugging the bulky oversized book bag. The satchel was purely for show and not included with the hefty tuition fees. It was most unfortunate Connie and Paul did not see their hard-earned money produce anything positive. But the positive thing Skippá got out of it was he got to see his beloved Donna; and acquire a life-long associate.

His father, after whom he was named, didn't have a driver's license, although he could drive well enough to get from point A to point B, provided point B wasn't in Philly. He ordinarily used to walk or use public transportation. A product of 10th and Maryland Avenue, in N.E. Washington, D.C., Paul, which was his middle name, had ties of some sort all over the District of Columbia. Now, living in S.E. Washington, he and his first born would walk together over the area in which they lived. Skippá could barely keep pace, attempting to match his dad's long strides. He would be forced to do a sort of fast step, semi-trot (much like he did going through Garfield Projects) which he learned to master, most times, without tiring.. Skippá would eventually grow to the exact height of his father, 5' 11 ½ - 6 feet tall, as long as he had on shoes. However, he would be much heavier than his Dad.

Paul had a steady diet of beer and bad food; the pig's feet and chitterlings semi-monthly were the worst. His appetite for beer was insatiable. On weekends, he would also treat himself to a pint of Kentucky Gentleman Bourbon, and if the weekend fell on the Friday of his bi-weekly payday from the department of Housing and Urban Development (H.U.D.) then the long-neck bottle distinguishing what Skippá would learn to be a "fifth" would make its way to the Lucas apartment. Paul was not in very good shape physically. He did not take good care of himself and was discharged from the Army because of a heart murmur. Whether it was a fifth of trouble or only a pint, chaos was sure to rock the little two-bedroom apartment on Stanton Road eventually.

Paul would get real ignorant after a while of sipping that sauce. One could see the metamorphosis take effect. Like Dr. Jekyll and Mr. Hyde; he was a nice guy or fairly pleasant during the weekdays especially at work. His coworkers liked him and he was a nice-looking guy – his parents and siblings called him "Buddy." But on the weekends… whew! Lookout! I'm telling you this dude was off the hizzy! Young Skippá would light into Paul at an early age when his dad became obnoxious and picked fights with Connie, trying to rough her up. Connie was adamant about having the last word about whatever it was disrupting her program, especially with Paul. She could be a sassy little something when she wanted to be. She stayed with him God only knows why, despite the emotional and psychological abuse that, at one time, got very physical, putting her in the hospital. Later, after Skippá got older and more protective of Connie, he'd often place himself in the line-of-fire. At times, he'd wish his mom wouldn't have to always try getting in the last word and could just shut-up. Paul later curtailed his assaults to verbalizing with the "threat" of physical harm. Skippá was seven years old. It wasn't all bad, and Skippá enjoyed both their company, separately. The only time he would witness affection between them, it seemed, was when Paul was trying to "Ahh… get busy" when they thought Skippá was asleep.

Connie was from Wilmington, North Carolina, the birthplace of Michael Jordan, and Joann Chessimar, aka Assata Shakur, the former Black Panther Party member and radical. Connie and her two sisters, Lucy and Mattie Vee (Jennie), came up North when they were pre-teens (the girls were a year to a year and a half apart in age). Their mother Mattie

Lee (Madoo) had all but abandoned them. The eldest Smith girl, Lucy, later on resided in Hampton, Virginia, while Connie and her younger sister, Jennie, made homes in Washington, D.C. They eventually caught up with their mother and all lived in the Brookland area of N.E. Thomas Smith, the girls' father, was a mathematician that found an error in a text book and was compensated with cash. He was much older than the girls' mother, and was a teacher of hers while she was a student in North Carolina. Mattie Lee Lowrey was Indian/Irish, born in Spartanburg, South Carolina. She was quite the looker. One could see how the teacher would fall for such a beautiful young pupil. Unfortunately, the union didn't last long and Mattie Lee moved on, alone.

Skippá's brother, M.G., was born when Skippá was five years old; he was the apple of his brother's eye. This little dude was a riot! He was so funny, Skippá truly loved and enjoyed watching him. They were the only two, of the eventually five Lucas children, to experience the Parkland Apartments, though M.G. was too young to remember. The only two things they would know little M.G. to be afraid of were the craters in a full moon when it looks like there's a face in it (the man in the moon), and the lion when a movie comes on that's an M.G.M Production. When that lion roared, man, M.G. would take off running or bury his face in Connie's lap. He'd usually break things…knocking over anything in his path to put space between himself and that lion, and the lions on the Calvert Street bridge on the way to the Washington Zoo. Connie's loving arms were always a welcome comfort to her children, but then that's how it's supposed to be. At the age of two, M.G. was old enough to go on outings with his mom and older brother. Connie called it sightseeing. Being from North Carolina, Connie loved traveling throughout and about Washington serendipitously preparing her children for the world outside of Parkland Apartment Complex. They knew how to act.

The three of them and occasionally a couple kids from the neighborhood, or sometimes Skippá's cousin Chris and Aunt Toni (Toni's was Connie's youngest sister by her moms' second husband, whom all of Madoo's grandchildren called "Papa Earnest"). They'd all jump in Connie's '59 Ford Galaxy and for a few hours were inundated with what they thought to be all the pleasures the world had to offer. They would find themselves looking out of the windows a top of the Washington Monument or climbing over and upon the tanks and other ex-military equipment the Smithsonian Institute displayed. They went in the Capital building, ran up and down the stairs outside, and visited all the museums downtown. Connie particularly liked the botanical gardens and visiting the cherry blossoms in Hains Point during the years when the kids were allowed to climb the trees. They'd visit the relatives religiously, including Connie's in-laws. A most peculiar and yet enjoyable visit the children would go on (this would be after two more additions to the Lucas household. Carlyn and Anthony) was to their paternal grandparents' house on W. Street in Northwest Washington.

Grandma Lucas (her given name was "Otilia Hensley") became germaphobic and agoraphobic somewhere along the way before Skippá was old enough to remember. All he and his siblings knew was she was very light-skinned, old, and would withdraw when one of her grandchildren tried to hug her saying, "I don't hug, germs, germs!...this can ordinarily be confusing for a child, especially when the maternal grandmother is the exact opposite. However, the children took it all in stride – she had that old people's smell anyway.

Grandma Lucas and Madoo were only alike in their complexion and silky hair, only Otilia's was all grey, whereas Madoo's still had a lot of black mixed in and it was much longer. Madoo was Skippá's favorite woman in the whole world; with the exception of his mom, naturally. She showed Skippá an abundance of love and kept him when he was too small for school while Connie and Paul were at work. Every morning for breakfast she made him cheesy grits with toast. He loved it. She would sit at the table with him with a half of cantaloupe and coffee followed by a Kool cigarette.

He loved going to his grandma's house in Suitland, Maryland. It was like going to the country. So many people not far from Madoo's had chickens, ducks, ponies, and you might see a goat or two along the way. Connie would sometimes stop off at the pony stalls on Marlboro Pike, that was M.G.'s favorite stop and if you'd drive anywhere in the vicinity of those stalls you may as well pull it on over so he could get at least one ride.

Once, when Skippá was about nine and M.G. four, Skippá burned up twenty dimes feeding the mechanical horse in the back of Sears and Roebuck department store, entertaining his little brother while Connie was shopping. They monopolized the big horse for over an hour, but M.G. was happy as a fat kid in a cake factory.

Skippá thought his grandparents in Suitland were rich, or at least as close to being rich as he could fathom. It was not that their house was anything close to a mansion, but it was surely the biggest and best he had access to. Actually, Papa Earnest was the one with all the cake, Madoo didn't have squat, but she was a looker in her day so…go figure. Papa Earnest was a cool, smooth, G.Q. type that kept a slick ride and a dominant pure-bred, mostly German Shepherds. Skippá liked dogs but knew he couldn't have one in Parkland and was very well pleased some years later when they moved out of the apartment. Skippá knew enough about dogs to know when you walked up on one or one approached you weren't familiar with, you should call their name if you knew it and say stuff like "Hey boy; Here boy, here boy," and make that kissing sound. He used to see that on *Lassie* and on *Rin-Tin-Tin*.

Connie and Paul rarely, if ever, socialized together. Skippá could only remember once. When his dad was out at his grandma's, Connie used to say Paul didn't know how to act around people. Actually, he knew how to act but around certain people, in certain situations; it all depended on the circumstances, the people involved, and mostly how much "sauce" he had in him. Once when they'd all gone to Paul's brother Jimmy's house, the two brothers got into it because Paul insulted an old family friend, about the friend's masculinity or the lack thereof. Paul didn't like effeminate men and abhorred homosexuals. He must've been one of the few Washingtonians not to know that Marvin Gay, Sr. was a faggy.

Paul graduated from Armstrong High School. He was offered a scholarship to "Lincoln University" for Drama. Unfortunately, his parents were not educationally motivated enough to be insistent or even encouraging, so he resolved himself to a career at H.U.D. He was a likeable guy, had a sense of humor, and not a bad-looking guy. Paul landed the job at H.U.D. via a word from his father who knew someone who worked there. In the 40s and 50s, it helped having the right complexion. It ain't fair but that's how it goes – it is what it is, and you take advantage of the accessories or opportunities the good Lord places before you.

While in Parkland, Skippá and his Dad would go for long walks, mainly on Paul's beer runs, which would be to the "Shipley Terrace" market and liquor mart. One day on the way, to Skippá's surprise, about a quarter mile out of Parkland and into the Shipley Terrace neighborhood (another low-income apartment complex, of the three in the area), he saw a schoolmate, and not just any school mate – it was Donna Hutchinson. She was his girlfriend, only he hadn't told her; the extent of his affiliation with her was that he would see her at school and everyday give her one of the two quarters Connie would give him. In return, little Donna would smile at him; he didn't even remember if the little vixen said thank you.

Skippá didn't much care, all he knew is that none of the other boys in his class better not try their hand, or there might be trouble. When Paul looked back to see what was taking Skippá so long to catch up, he saw his son's attention was diverted, and the object of his son's gaze was the little light-skinned girl playing on the sidewalk.

"Skippá, you know her?"

"Yeah, Da', that's my girlfriend."

Paul was amused now; his beer would be on hold for a minute, because this was funny. Paul fancied himself a ladies' man, and now the "Buddy" in him was coming out. Vicariously, he was for a moment living through Skippá.

"Your girlfriend. Oh yeah, is that so? Go tell her 'hi,' ask if this is where you live. Watch the cars. I'll wait."

Skippá would've been just as contented to leave things as they were, now his dad was about to mess up the whole arrangement. His young rap game hadn't yet materialized, and all this conversation with Donna was scary. At seven years old, he had yet to begin formulating any type of boy-to-girl dialogue. As soon as he got his heart up, starting to step off the curb to cross over, a tall man with a thick mustache came out to call her in. Before leaving, she looked then stared at Skippá standing on the curb. She waved, then the man looked at Skippá and he didn't wave…just looked. Defiantly Skippá matched his stare until Paul's voice snapped him back. "Skippá! Come on, boy."

Like his father Skippá was something of a peripatetic; he would be out of the apartment playing for hours, hide-n-go seek, the pie store game, red light, football, baseball, and sliding down the steep long hills in Parkland on cardboard. He once ripped a gash in his leg on one of the industrial staples and continued sliding down the hill with his friends until blood soaked the cardboard. All this was before he learned how to ride the old bicycle Connie brought home from somewhere.

Skippá wasn't allowed to venture off the grounds of the four buildings that made up that particular court, other than when he was going to school. Still, it was a lot of ground he could cover. There were several boys he befriended during his days of Parkland. He got in just enough fights to teach him what he needed to know about getting along, avoidance, and "standing up" when he had to.

The "Mayhew" brothers were friends with Skippá, although they were a year or so older and a few inches taller. Sometimes Michael (the younger of the two) would lean on Skippá, talking, greasy, and what not. One day, Paul had enough. He was observing the scene from off to the side. He shouted out, "Get 'em, Skippá!" Hearing the command from his dad, he lit into his foe with all elbows and knuckles. The fight went on several minutes; a small gathering had assembled, and at the end, Paul eventually pulled Michael off Skippá. Even though he got his butt whipped, he made his Dad proud for his efforts.

One evening, Paul called him in from playing. However, when he bent the corner of his apartment building, half his family's belongings were out on the sidewalk. Upon further observation, he saw it was all being boarded on a big green truck. Paul let his son ride on the back of the open-ended truck with the movers, he saw his dad go around to get in the front part of the truck, the cab. After riding across Suitland Parkway, on up to the top of the hill past the school he and Donna attended, down the hill past a fenced in basketball court, and into an area with a lot of houses all made the same, two-story apartment-looking buildings, but with two doors and front porches, the truck went up another hill, made a left, and then stopped in front of a place he remembered his mom and Aunt Jennie going to after church one day.

In the apartment on Stanton Road, the place seemed a perfect fit to hold its furnishings, but here in the new house on 18th place, what Skippá would learn was a housing development called "Fort Stanton." It seemed to dwarf their meager belongings. Not that the house was all that big, but it had two floors and a basement, three (3) bedrooms, a back yard, a great big open field right beyond the front yard, and woods and forest everywhere. There was a front porch where Paul would sit with his feet propped on the railing, kicked back, sipping cold ones.

Skippá hadn't given his old parkland friends a second thought, and by the time a couple summers passed in the new house, he had twice as many little knuckleheaded buddies. He was no longer in Catholic School. His grades were a joke, and as one of the nun's told his father when summoned for a parent/teacher meeting, she said … "And his spelling is out of this world!" Oh well, good-bye, Donna; by this time, in the third grade, he'd gotten up to offering her candy too; in addition to giving her a few quarters every now and then. Now that he was in public school with a new crew, and his comfort zone was all over Fort Stanton and beyond, he was a familiar face at the recreation center.

Larry Dunmore live several doors down from Skippá, he was two years older and knew a lot! The second day in the new house, Larry walked by on his way toward the rec center and invited Skippá along. Even though the slight variance in age caused the two boys to gravitate towards their own respective groups, they would forge a perpetual friendship. It seemed as though Larry knew everyone and everyone knew him. He was very respectful to grown-ups, always neatly dressed, and at ten years old, somewhere along the way he'd learned some vicious boxing and fighting skills. Skippá watched him knot a few guys up from other neighborhoods and found him to be patient and calculating. Larry picked his time to strike. He wasn't wild with his punches when he moved in. Larry was one to truly enjoy a good laugh; he was definitely a people person and would later in the years accept the nickname by an old friend, "The Mayor of Fort Station," and "Don Vito."

Skippá by now shortened his name to "Skip," but Connie and Paul apparently didn't get the memo. Meanwhile Skip and his main three new friends: Mark and Jr. (Eldridge) Buchanan, and Tommy Jenkins would become close to inseparable. They would trek through the woods, shortcutting to the stores, or wander off two or three miles sometimes, in search of fruit bearing trees. They'd follow streams and hang out in the woods, or at the rec center all day. They knew where the apple trees were, pear trees, fig bushes, grape vines and mulberry bushes. They'd build tree houses, and also knew where an underground cave was that was used by soldiers in one of the wars. Anyone knowing Anacostia knows it's a plethora of hills and forests; *this is what being a kid is all about*, he thought, man!

The only things they had to worry about in the woods were snakes and wild dogs. The wild dogs would often run in packs and the snakes, well, you wouldn't see many, but you had better be on the lookout while picking mar berries. He would find "box-turtles" in the woods, especially after the rains. He'd take them home and turn them loose in the back yard. Skip once found a grass snake, let it loose in the hedges right in the front yard where it stayed for a couple years. Sometimes one of the boys would swing out over a creek on a "Tarzan vine" only to fall in the two to three feet of water.

The boys' parents reluctantly bought them B.B. guns from Sears and Roebucks; they'd hunt squirrels, rabbits, and a whole lotta birds. Paul came home from work one day to find a dead Cardinal right in front of the house; he went off! He was pissed off to say the least. Skip never harmed another colorful bird again, and later would feel guilty killing any of them.

A while later, afterwards, one of the B.B.s Skip fired at something on the sidewalk ricocheted catching M.G. in the neck. By now Skip had an additional set of friends (the Burwell and Dent brothers); he was next door at Steve Burwells when he fired the shot that caught his little brother M.G. on the neck. Connie found out about it later that evening; took the rifle, beat Skip with it then smashed it on the side of the house, breaking the butt (the stock) off it. The gun wasn't much good after that; the next rifle Skip got, about ten years later, didn't have a butt either, and he also sawed the barrel off it too. It was a twelve gauge, three-in-the-clip bolt-action shotgun.

Chapter 2

THERE WERE TWO OBJECTS OF young J. Marie's desire when she was thirteen. They were both consumable; a bottled Royal Crown (RC) soda and a sour pickle, both of which she would purchase from the little mom-and-pop corner store down the street from the house she shared with five of her six siblings. The Brooklyn section of Northeast Washington D.C. was a fairly peaceful residential, lower-middle-class, and predominately black neighborhood. Semi-detached and some row houses lined both sides of the street.

If J. Marie had a dollar you could bet she would surely be making her way to the little grocer to purchase this unlikely combination of caffeine and spicy hot vinegar. The Kool cigarettes she would sneak back then were not the third of her small pleasures yet. They would not prove to be as financially taxing on her as the sodas and pickles, but would surely become an albatross around her neck long after the others were gone.

The following year, 1970, "Tricky Dick" was in the White House, an ex-actor from Hollywood was the governor of California, and, along with F.B.I. director J. Edgar Hoover, they were giving hell to a black radical group formed by Bobby Seal and Huey Newton called the Black Panther Party. Joe Frazier was crowned boxing Heavyweight Champion (over Jimmy Ellis). The New York Knickerbockers, Cincinnati Reds and Kansas City Chiefs were World Champions in basketball, baseball, and football, respectively. Bob Beamon shattered the long jump record with a shocking 29+ foot leap into the record books. And in that same 1968 Olympic meet in Mexico two black sprinters made a defiant stand during their crowning ceremony by raising black-gloved fists to signify Black Power (John Carlos and Tommie Smith). Jimi Hendrix and Janis Joplin died of drug overdose and thousands of guys were being sent home in body bags from Vietnam; many recording artists were taking political stances via their lyric about the war. Inspired by war protesters at the People's Park in Berkley, California, Marvin Gaye would go on in September 1970 to complete an album that he had to force Motown executives to release. In January the following year the *What's Going On* album eventually made its debut. The album would become the biggest seller in Motown history to date (See Washington Post, G6, 2-25-2001). Also that year, D.C. and Prince Georges County, Maryland's Police Department were experiencing an unusually high spike in car thefts.

Although J. Marie presently lived in the Brooklyn section of N.E. D.C., her heart was tied to, and she would often frequent her, old neighborhood in the N.W. area. The houses were more upscale than those in Brooklyn. The grade school she once attended, McFarland, was one of the historical landmarks in the district, so was Theodore Roosevelt High. It was this high school she envisioned herself attending someday. The school her older cousins Ernest and Paul attended.

The Williams family house was run by Grandma Tia, the matriarch. A once spotless old-fashioned, three-story brick, with a neatly manicured lawn, and an alley-accessible garage was now wearing down from the constant traffic of running children.

Her favorite uncles, Cookie and Hyda, helped to make her and her siblings early years fun and exciting. Cookie and Hyda, along with sisters Jean and Ella, like their father, were big drinkers. Cookie was the neighborhood mechanic, body and fender man. You name it, if it had something to do with cars, he was your man. This was during the time of the ever-so-popular shade-tree mechanic; if he was reputable, he was worth his weight in gold, silver, or a fifth of liquor.

Hyda was a middle-aged man that would race the kids occasionally; causing J. Marie to laugh so hard her side would hurt. He was pretty fast for an old guy, even while he was tipsy. The best laugh they all would get would be when they would see J. Marie's sister Sharon ride her bicycle. She would remind them so much of "Dorothy Hamilton" when she played the part of Elvira Goulch riding her bike before she became the wicked witch of the East on *The Wizard of Oz*. Reflecting back, as J. Marie got older she would often be reminded of the scene, then smile. She was affectionately thinking of her younger sister.

Just up and across the street lived April. April was J. Marie's wild and often meretricious childhood friend. It was her house where all the slick, older popular kids hung out, in part due to April's older brother. He was cool with J. Marie's older cousins Ernest and Paul. J. Marie's mentor, Francine, was Ernest's girlfriend whom J. Marie more often than not took advice from on guys, fashion, as well as other girl-stuff secrets that young and older girls pass on amongst themselves. "A girl's heart is an ocean of secrets," she would tell her young protégé. Every adolescent, preteen, teenager and young adult needs in their life an older person they admire and/or respect for something in their persona; something in them that's positive and beneficial; something in their lives to steer them right. Every man or woman can reflect back on someone in their life that was older and had an influence in some of the actions they took later on, or decisions they made, even thoughts they may have formulated. Whether the affect was unconscious or overt it's usually based on the strength of the mentor's character. These people often have a degree of omnipotent authority over the younger's mind, though they may be oblivious to the power they possess. A young man or woman will often reflect upon an act of kindness perpetrated by an older sibling, cousin or associate whether small or large, long after the senior kith or kin is out of their lives.

April's mom, Ms. Lena was like an aunt to J. Marie and loved her as though she were her own. Ms. Lena secretly harbored thoughts of being willing, if she could, to trade J. Marie for April. Silly me, she thought.

Between the two houses there was enough excitement jumping off to even keep T.M.Z. and the paparazzi both hopping. There was more drama than the *National Enquirer* or the *Star* could ever print. Never was there a dull moment, this was especially true through the weekends. Hanging out around "Grant Circle", and the middle New Hampshire Avenue corridor for a teenager coming up in the late 60s to mid 70s on that turf was like training days and spring break all rolled into one. It was an opportunity for one to hone his or her skills – social and/ or cultural; opportunistic status seeker, 101, class was undoubtedly in session.

The good Lord above was most generous to J. Marie. At age fourteen she possessed physiological features grown women would sell their souls for. Faust would not have been the only one entering into an agreement with Mephistopheles. An adult man would surely be sent to prison had he allowed concupiscence to misdirect him her way.

An amazing feature of the African American race is the variegating colors; from one end of the color line to the other. One could be considered black with skin so light they would be thought white, or, contrarily, a shade so melanistic there would be no question as to their ethnicity. So when J. Marie's light-skinned father consummated the union with her beautiful dark-skinned mother, the six children they produced were of varying colors, with J. Marie and the sister closest to her in age (Sharon) being the lightest. J. Marie also had a brother, although not of her father, Robert, who was very dark and the splitting image of the actor Sidney Poitier, only Robert, unlike Sidney, could sing tenor with the best of them. They all had fairly good pipes and could carry a note, however, J. Marie and Robert had the others beat out.

J. Marie's laughter was infectious, accentuated by the dimples she inherited from Tia, her beloved grandmother. J. Marie was as honest and trustworthy as she was affable. If one was to have a "life-calling," as many people do, hers could have easily been in childcare. She had natural maternal instincts. Children were drawn to her like moths to a light. One was sure Curtis Mayfield had her in mind when he composed, "The Makings of You" …The joy of children laughing around you… Like metal on a magnet she could pull them in. She would sing lullabies of the time, or if a child were in her care she would sing lullabies until the child thought he or she was seeing angels, stars, and fairies dancing in their hypnotic slumber, mesmerized by her physical beauty. The richness of her voice, and a natural scent that lie somewhere between roses and honeysuckle, all combined to give her an edge in life. It may not be totally fair in life that some people are gifted with certain benefits, whether they are physical, financial, or intellectual. A person should take advantage of what God gives him or her and make good of it as best they can.

She was a good student; her family didn't have much money. The car her father had during the early years was the oldest in the neighborhood. Sharon was so embarrassed to the point while riding in the car she would often slouch down so her friends would not see her. However, J. Marie was contented for the most part; she had a loving family and good friends; that trumps money in most cases, any day of the week… in most cases.

She, along with her many girlfriends and cousins would gather in April's basement or on the front porch to socialize and sing along with the hundreds of 45s and albums the kids and young adults collected back then. There were dozens of popular singing groups. J. Marie's favorite girl groups were the Shirells, the Marvelettes, Martha Reeves, and the Supremes. A little later, when the Emotions would enter on the circuit, J. Marie would like them most of all. She would sing along with them ("The Best of My Love", "Don't Ask My Neighbors," and others). If a guy could reach the notes or achieve the style of the Delfonics with "La La Means I Love You" or Black Ivory's' "Don't Turn Around," whew! Then she would be the one mesmerized and seeing stars. Unbeknownst to her a new young artist would enter onto the scene with a number one single "Let's Stay Together" that would forever have a significant meaning in her heart.

These were the days of the "crooners", house parties, and being seen shopping downtown on F Street, anywhere between seventh and thirteenth. For the guys, if you were toting one of those red Caviliers' or National Shirt shop bags, you were up and coming. As far as "players" go; for the girls, if your bank was long enough, you could step into Lord and Taylor's or Garfinkles. Some of the wannabees would get their wear from a so-so store, then get the sales person from a more dignified and acceptable store to give you a bag, an oversized bag for something small like a pair of socks, then make the transfer, you feel me.

Where J. Marie was hanging out, an outsider from across town on the wrong zone couldn't walk through visiting the neighborhood uncontested, let alone attend a party without proper clearance. One of the cliques or gangs up around Grant Circle, the middle of New Hampshire Avenue (The Flaming Eagles) wasn't having it; however, occasionally there would be exceptions to the rule. Usually one needed a relative or strong auxiliary presence to vouch for your presence. The local roughnecks, who were, for all intents and purposes, the maintainers of the block in which they lived, were themselves sometimes ominous and sinister residents. These dudes were very protective and possessive about their neighborhood, especially about their girls seeing outsider "off-brands."

For the girls as well as they guys, fighting, or at least being able to aggressively defend yourself, was as natural for most kids in the D.C. area as skating – notice I say skating opposed to riding a bicycle. Skating is harder. Contrary to what outsiders believed for years as a fact, every dude out of D.C. ain't like that, nor the girls, however, in J. Marie's case, she could throw down with some heavy hitters, but she didn't like to.

Being the eldest Williams girl, of whom there were four, she didn't have the luxury of an older sister to run home to if things got thick. She had to fend for herself. It was fight or take flight. Her slightly knocked knees, which she inherited from her mother, prevented her from ever acquiring that Flo-Jo, Marion Jones on steroid speed. So she had to make a stand. Her older brother Robert was not indigenous to the area and seldom socialized in that part of town.

Kalorama Road Skating Rink was a huge draw for most of the younger crowd in N.W., although many came from the other three corners of the city as well. Even some of the hip parents that were not quite ready to hang up their skates yet would accompany their children there to strut their stuff. The latest boogie-down beat would blare over the P.A. system and everyone would be out on the floor doing their thing; dancing to the funky beat on skates, gliding from side to side, backwards, on one skate, or with their girls or guy. They'd be hand-dancing and outright show-boating; some were there just fronting and really could not skate, not even a little bit. But it was all good.

J. Marie loved to skate, and in her crew, there were some of the slickest, skatinest rollers to ever don a pair of precision skates. They would catch the bus or a ride with a parent or older friend, knowing full well sometimes they'd be footing it back – which was a long hump back up New Hampshire avenue, even worse at dark.

She also liked being there with Slick. They would skate together holding hands for hours, talking and laughing. Slick was older than her and the only one who seemed to have a problem with it was her dad. Dads are like that about their daughters; it's just how they are. Needless to say, she and Slick's union didn't last long and she never shared with her friends to what extent the relationship reached or didn't reach.

It's said that all good things soon come to an end. Whether this was a good thing or not, it came to its end when Slick and her Dad collided. With Mr. Williams moving towards Slick threatening to crush him, all of a sudden, Slick pulled a gun. It could've ended in disaster were it not for J. Marie screaming out to her boyfriend "Slick!" After the tears, pain and heartaches; she eventually got over him. However, there is more often than not a void in one's heart when a relationship ends abruptly and under duress.

J. Marie had good sound judgment early on about most things. It may not be so much as her being able to look at the bigger picture or doing much consequence forecasting, as it was for her a sort of divine intervention, or it would seem.

Francine once imparted upon her that, "everyone is hurt by love at least once in their life. Moving on isn't easy all the time, but when you're young you got a whole life ahead of you. At fourteen if you lived long enough you may have more good times to experience in the future than what you may have lost in the past. J. Marie experienced at an early age that all sickness wasn't the death sentence. Unfortunately, too often, J. Marie would bottle up a lot of what she felt. Sometimes Francine would be the object of her effusions. She couldn't always talk to her mom about these trials because her mom had enough of Mr. Williams's drinking and abuses, so she'd bounced early on in J. Marie's life.

North Carolina, Connie in the house!

Ten dollars! For a pair of tennis shoes?! Boy you have *got* to be kidding; you ain't but ten years old.

Despite Connie's protest, she eventually gave in, taking Skip up to Safeway Surplus, where most all the young guys and teenagers were copping their slick gear. This spot, across from the Saint Elizabeth's mental hospital (where they kept John Hinkley after the attempt on former President Reagan's life), had all the latest wear for guys. After Connie bought Skip a pair of white Chuck Taylor Converse All Stars, she sprung for the hunting socks too, with a lecture. Her last words being, "This is it for you!"

Skip was up on all the gear the boys outta S.E. were wearing in the mid and late 60s; the big-belt-loop khakis, the Lee jeans, big-stripe polo shirts, he had them in all colors. She even got him and M.G. "Peter's" jackets with their names monogramed on the right-side chest.

Connie didn't mind making sure her boys had suitable clothes, even while she was going to buy her own from the second-hand stores (Thrift or Goodwill). The stuff she bought them there, like for herself, was usually name brand. Her thing was quality. Back then the labels to watch for were Saks, Lord and Taylor, Garfinkles, and maybe D.J. Khufmans. Their first few years in the house, although somewhat financially squeezed, they weren't near the poverty level – not by any means. Though they had the oldest car in the neighborhood, and perhaps the oldest furniture, the Lucas's cabinets and refrigerator were "chugged;" they had plenty food, mucho grande!

Skip never in his life saw Connie buy a new dress, coat, shoes, pants, or a blouse for herself from a department store. All her clothes were either from the second-hand store or she made them herself, other than women's personals, you feel me.

She made drapes/curtains for the house, chair and sofa covers, you name it. She'd sew up Paul's clothes as well as the kids. Patching up the knees that boys so often wear out… not a problem. Connie had a sewing machine she all but performed magic on; she could crochet and knit too. When a friend or friend's daughter had a baby, she'd crochet baby blankets and caps, booties and all that. Appliances she would get from the Goodwill, and when one of her friends put her down with the main branch Goodwill store just outside "Georgetown" off M Street… Skip and M.G. rode over there with her. To their amazement, they saw what could only be described as a smorgasbord of second-hand clothes, appliances, even furniture for as far as the eye could see.

Connie had another car by now, a green Ford Falcon station wagon. They came away with a sofa and chair set (Connie was excited; she said it was "wicker," that it was expensive stuff) perfect for the basement. She procured an old waffle-iron from one of those joints, cleaned it up, and would make waffles before the kids went off to school and especially on the weekends. Like straight outta IHOP, or the waffle shop downtown.

Skip would get real sick when his "bronchitis" would flare up. Occasionally M.G. would catch his colds, but when this happened Connie was on top of it. She had most all those down-home remedies on speed dial, potions to mix up, and all sorts of concoctions to brew. Just naturally Connie was a vitamins/prevention person, so from day one the kids would be on vi-daily, or one-a-days. When Flintstone Vitamins came out, the kids knew to pop one before going out the door each morning during or after breakfast.

Connie had instincts unparalleled when it came to healthcare, straight old school.

If, however, you *did* come down with a cold – man it was on! Connie was a one-woman army on a mission. She was a quasi-certified and an official cold/sickness buster. At the second or third cough in the night hours, it was as if Connie had radar zoomed in on particular anomalous sounds coming from the children's rooms. She would bust in the door, flick the light on, observe the occupant(s) in the room for any sign of a malady, and if she determined it was only dust or a little dry mouth, you were fine. But if you had that "sick look," like you were ailing, the next thing you knew she was at the edge of your bed, sitting you upright. One hand would go up your back to see how warm it was while the other was on your forehead. In Skip's case, it was his bronchitis, and then a jar of that Vicks VapoRub would materialize from somewhere like magic. This minty medication would be spread over his back and under his nostrils, followed by a spoonful of Robotussin or a Coricidin pill. She'd check back on you a couple of hours later, wash the Vicks off of your back and chest, put a fresh shirt on you, and then determine after she got up for work whether you'd get a day off from school.

In the more extreme cases, if Skip or M.G. *really* had that mojo on them, and were ailing, sure enough, then the full treatment was in the mix that night before they went to bed. This included drinking Connie's Grandma Lucy's original "hot toddy" hook-up, which consisted of tea, honey, a twist of lemon, onions, and a hit of Brandy. To go with this, you'd be sleeping in a Long John top and sweatshirt, with a towel wrapped around your neck to hold in the Vick's that was rubbed all over your torso; you would also be tucked under one or two of Paul's Army blankets. She would lastly fill a vaporizer with water and some other Vicks stuff so that it sprayed a medicated mist into the air about three to five feet away from the bed. Now, when this particular medical alert procedure was in effect, she would take but about three hours of sleep because she might be in and out of the sick kid's room two or three times a night studying symptoms, changing clothes and bed sheets. In two or three days tops the crisis would be over and the kid back in school.

The only time one of the kids had such an emergency that they had to go the hospital was when Skip and M.G. were playing Billy the Kid and Jesse James in the basement. Billy the Kid (M.G.) robbed the bank and was to leap off the balcony (a high, wooden bar in the basement) onto the horse (Skip). Needless to say the dumb horse moved and Billy the Kid went flying headlong into the corner of the coffee table. Of course the first arrival on the scene was Connie. She was doing laundry in the basement. She screamed at the sight of the large gash and the blood pouring from M.G.'s head like Niagara Falls, but quickly grabbed one of the baby's diapers to absorb the blood and stem the flow. Paul came flying down the stairs from the sound of Connie's scream. He assisted Connie in helping M.G. up the stairs, holding the diaper to M.G.'s head as Connie cranked up the wagon. Paul wanted desperately to knock Skip's brains out – just a few seconds is all he wanted! Skip could see the dilemma all over his father's face, torn between the two choices of jumping on top of him or helping M.G.. The fact that M.G. was in such dire medical attention may have been the only thing that saved Skip, if only temporarily. But his dad's look also told him something else – that it was not over and as soon as he got back, "You are dead!"

The doctor put fourteen stitches in M.G.'s head, while delivering the "boys will be boys" speech to Connie and Paul. By the time they arrived home, Skip was already in bed and didn't see M.G. until the next day. He had on, what looked to Skip to be, a turban because of the amount of gauze and bandaging. All Connie said to Skip was, "The doctor talked to us," meaning Paul and herself. Skip's dad never said anything about it, however, his silence was implicit, and Skip would feel a chill if ever he would catch his dad's eyes go from M.G.'s head back to Skip.

The other time one of Connie's four boys had to be carried out was when the youngest one, Paul Jr., crashed after flying down the street on his Big Wheel. That little stunt amounted to about eight or nine stitches.

Connie graduated from Howard University in D.C. with a bachelor's degree in English; she paid her own way with very little, if any, assistance from her parents. She went on to become a management analyst with H.E.W., where she'd retire as a GS-11.

Unfortunately, Paul was unsupportive of her educational endeavors. He had a "diamond in the rough" and never knew how to make the best of it. Actually, he resented her college education, and was all out just plain hating on her. She looked like the black actress from the 50s and 60s, Dorothy Dandridge, only about five inches shorter. She was just 4'10". and she had one of those little people complexes.

Chapter 3

THE LOSS OF A PARENT leaves the average adult deeply saddened; and it can mortify a child. That the parent is no longer directly involved with the child on a regular basis as he or she once was takes years, sometimes, adjusting to. Although Dickey (Mr. Williams) played down his once beloved "Louise Lorrain" walking out on him, and despite the façade he portrayed as "Life goes on," for all intent and purposes, he was a psychological, mental, and emotional wreck. It's hard enough taking care of children with two working parents, but now he was single-handedly responsible for filling six hungry mouths, as well as a dachshund's name Duke.

All the Williams children were big boned healthy children that could put a hurting on a refrigerator, except, perhaps, the third eldest girl, Cindy. Cindy had always been on the slim side with big, beautiful brown eyes like her mother's. J. Marie kept her younger siblings fed once the food was brought in. She made sure they were neat and off to school on time, at peace amongst themselves, and fairly disciplined at home. The weight was on her shoulders and she handled it well for being so young.

If, with *two* parents, finances were tight, then with only one they were surely in a deep recession. Perhaps things would have been better and more tolerable had Dickey been a more responsible and conscientious provider. Although he did keep a roof over their heads (a leaky roof when it rained), and food on the table, a child needs more than a minimal amount of care to maintain a higher level of productivity and inspiration.

The one thing that was not lacking in the Williams household was discipline; Dickey ruled the house on the 12th Street with an iron fist, or at least the threat of one. He could definitely back up the peril. He was a crass brute whom, on more than a few occasions, J. Marie had observed bringing physical harm to other men over traffic disputes and other social disagreements, as well as her mother.

Although in his late thirties, years of hard liquor and cigarettes caused him to appear in his mid-forties. One could tell that he was no stranger to a once pugnacious life. He only stood 5'9" and weighed about 230 pounds, most of which he carried in his stomach and upper body, from beer and years of boxing and weightlifting. Despite the alcohol abuse and nicotine, he was able to "mack" some of the ladies due to his still somewhat handsome face and well-kept hair. It wasn't so long after J. Marie's mom left that Dickey acquired a steady girlfriend.

In their second and third year, respectively, Sharon and J. Marie began what would be their last year at Taft Junior High. Sharon hated being in the house with her father; she longed for Louise's company. Her life-long mission those days were to reunite with her mother, at any cost. Meanwhile, she'd help J. Marie out as best she could to maintain a somewhere close to normally functioning household.

She would pass most days listening to records, singing along with them while cleaning; when the mood struck, she was on "joke time" with her siblings. All the Williams children enjoyed a good, hearty laugh from time to time, and when J. Marie smiled, just before she laughed, you would bear witness to the most pronounced dimples ever. Sharon and J. Marie looked very much alike. They were just thirteen months apart with the exact same complexion and height; however, J. Marie was more curvaceous. The two could have easily been fraternal twins.

J. Marie had a few steady local suitors since her parting with Slick; there were Kip, Michael Leonard, Vernon Ham, and now a new guy from the "Big V" supermarket was trying his hand. The few that were from around the neighborhood had status; they, along with the Wright brothers and Sharon's beau, Thomas Doze, though they were young and rambunctious, were some of the maintainers of the Lower Brookland area. This guy from the supermarket was an import, a "New Jack," and J. Marie would only keep him interested for her own amusement. Michael, from the Big V, was a good-looking young man, and his family had a couple of stores; he had potential. However, he was an "off brand." She foresaw him having problems with the neighborhood boys and figured that she had enough drama in her life.

J. Marie had easily established herself around her Brookland, N.E., neighborhood. She had close bonds with two of the Barnhart girls, as well as the Ham sisters, Brenda and Linda. These were her ex-boyfriend Vernon's sisters. One thing that was apparent about the majority of the teenage girls in the area, not just Brookland, but Brentwood and the Montana Corridor too, was that the girls had rogue older brothers that were either stickup boys or just straight-up prison-bound thugs.

J. Marie attracted all types; clean-cut guys, thugs and miscreants, the upper-middle class, bourgeois, and some outright paupers. She was an astute young lady who was extremely conscience of others feelings; she knew how to let the suitors down easy without breaking their spirits. Truly a class act, a diamond in the rough.

One of her best friends at school was pretty much the same way, only without the class and vision. Dawelder Rodgers had, all of a sudden and seemingly out of the clear blue sky, caught the sight of a sort of tall light-skinned guy with the prettiest eyes she had ever seen; whether they were light brown, green, or mixed with speckles of *both*, she wasn't sure. He had light-brownish hair that could've had red strands through it, like some older men whose hair takes on a salt-and-pepper appearance as it grays. Dawelder was sure of one thing if nothing else; he was new on the scene, but from where? And where had he been all her life? Could she take him around Montana Avenue? How would her brothers take to him? What would her mom say? Her mind was anticipating all kinds of premature assumptions; *for now though, I've got to tell J. Marie!*

J. Marie was beginning to connect the dots. Just a week or so earlier her dear sister Sharon told her, in her joking way, of a tall light-skinned boy with light-colored hair and freckles insinuating something lewd and lascivious to her and her close friend, Charleen. Sharon told J. Marie how this boy just *had* to be joking with them because the stuff he was saying was only befitting loose women or "trick girls." This precocious boy had, in no uncertain terms, alluded to a ridiculous notion that she and Charleen "work for him." It all seemed in fun to the girls, and somewhat amusing; little did they know, in part, this guy had actually entertained such a thought.

Could it be the same guy Dawelder rambled on and on about? J. Marie thought, "If he is the same guy, he has got a lot of damn nerve pressing up on my sister that way. And if Charleen's sister, Cynthia, found out about it…"

Meanwhile, other problems and more complex issues were springing up in J. Marie's life. Since then, shortly after Sharon told her sister about the light-skinned guy whose name no one seemed to know, she had run away from home. One of the Temptation's hit singles came to mind as J. Marie and her father drove around for hours in search of Sharon. They went to some of her girlfriend's homes, her only boyfriend, Thomas, and finally landed at the Number 11 Precinct in Southeast, Washington. "Runaway child, running wild, you'd better go back home, where you belong – runaway child running wild…"

J. Marie had never been to this part of the city as far as she could recall. A large, red neon sign reading "Anacostia Liquors" illuminated a crowded sidewalk as they turned off Good Hope Road onto a strip called Martin Luther King, Jr. Avenue.

Once in front of the desk sergeant inside the precinct, Dickey was told (after dispatching several calls) his thirteen-year-old daughter was safe and unharmed with the child's biological mother, Louise L. Williams. There was nothing more the police could do. If there were any further inquiries, he suggested Mr. Williams take it up with child services. He gave Dickey several pamphlets, gave J. Marie a quick look-over, and told him to be safe driving back home.

J. Marie was crushed; few people outside of her parents and Sharon ever saw her cry – other than when Lu-Lu sang the song to Sidney Poitier in her all-time favorite classic movie, *To Sir, With Love*. Outside of that, J. Marie was like the Rock of Gibraltar; she was the one her siblings would learn to lean on. She was strong and sympathetic, and now she needed someone. Who'd be her rock?

Something Francine told her years ago came back. "That growing into womanhood can seem so complicated at times." Someone along the way mentioned to her that "young ladies" should shave the hair under their arms, otherwise it's non lady like. Besides, it looks gross. During those years, also, or a little earlier, her aunt Ella took her shopping in the young ladies' department of Sears for a brassiere, and told her it was time to be more conscious of herself while she jumped rope.

J. Marie began noticing certain boys looking at her differently during that time, too. She didn't quite understand all of this stuff going on with her body. She wasn't comfortable with it, and she didn't like it – not one bit!

These thoughts flooded her mind, of how things had changed; and if that weren't enough to contend with, there was still the situation with Sharon all but abandoning her. Now Dickey was drinking more, becoming ignominiously more base and ignorant. He was making her feel self-conscious and uncomfortable lately with his show of affection.

Skip was not limited to his excursions in his own neighborhood, whether it was Parkland or Fort Stanton. When he would stay the weekends, or a few summer weeks at his aunt's apartment, where his cousins, Duke and Michele, lived, he would roam all throughout that area, as well. "Mayfair Mansions" were low-income apartments off Kenilworth Avenue, in N.E., and it was a rough camp; maybe worse than Parkland, but not as bad as Barry Farms or Garfield.

His cousin Duke had the largest model collection Skip had ever seen; hundreds of them, glued, painted, and decaled replicas of pretty much every American-made car you could name. He even had one like the old car his mom used to have (the '59 Ford). Also, one like his dad's present car, a '67 Ford Galaxy, complete with rear fender skirts and all. It was no surprise that Duke would take auto mechanics at Phelps Vocational High School when he graduated from Woodson Junior High. He then went on to become a gas station mechanic; however, his employer told him after a few years of it that there wasn't really a future in "grease monkeyin'" for a bright guy such as himself. Wisely, Duke took heed to the advice, took the test for Metrobus service, was hired and never looked back. However, now he was just Skip's cousin, older by two years, and a few inches taller.

There were three major newspaper distributers in Washington during the sixties, not to include the *Washington Times*. There was the *Washington Post*, the *Evening Star* and the *Daily News*. The paper boy's motto was, "Serve the *Post*, you make the most. Serve the *Star*, you can go far. But serve the *News*, you wear out your shoes." Duke served the *Star* and had the biggest route in Kenilworth. This dude would not only serve and collect for Mayfair Mansions but Paradise (which was later built behind Mayfair), and he served for the Parkside Projects, too. Skip use to help him deliver and collect whenever he stayed over. Duke would take Skip out with him and his delivery boys on the route manager's official *Evening Star* truck, where they'd deliver papers and/or collect right off the truck. Then come lunchtime. They would stop at the Shrimp Boat on Benning Road, or one of the McDonald's.

Skip had a *Daily News* paper-delivery job that he inherited from Donna Hutchinson's older brother, Ronald. He got to ride with the route manager, too, but it was an old station wagon; the *Daily News* was on its way to being bought out by the *Star*. Skip would have to deliver in the dreaded Barry Farms Projects with a few other guys from Mr. Taylor's station wagon because it was too dangerous for the local paper boy(s). Besides that, when it came time for the local boy to collect…well…that was a problem.

Oh, was it mentioned Donna's family had moved to Fort Stanton? Yeah, one street over from Skip; he was eleven years old by now. Though he rarely saw her, he still had a thing for her. They were still cool, but had other interests; and Skip's interests were purely on the streets. Skip was like this – as long as he had his mind and/or time occupied with an alluring interest, he was copasetic. Right now, his inclinations were directed towards trekking through a short patch of woods to get him to the Greenwood Manor apartments where he'd cut into a girl visiting relatives from a section in West Baltimore called Popular Grove. Debbie was twelve and had with her a sister and cousin. This was all the more reason for his new best friends, Chick and Steve, to roll with him. Even if she didn't have her girls with her, there were a few eligible little honeys in Greenwood Manor. Skip, Chick, and Steve were as thick as thieves, and basically that's what they were; petty larceny opportunists.

Meanwhile, Debbie was fast, whether it was because she was from the Popular Grove section of West Baltimore and was used to being around thugs and roughnecks, or maybe that at eleven Skip was naturally two steps behind her. Nevertheless, Skip told her he was thirteen, too, and had developed a little dialogue by then to pull her in. The two spent most of the summer hanging out in the evenings, talking and sneaking kisses until Skip figured it was time to bounce. After all, he was only eleven and still had a curfew.

One day, to Skip's chagrin, not only was Debbie gone back to Baltimore, but before she left Craig Stevens, a little coon-booga that use to hate on Skip, told her that Skip was only eleven. When Skip found this out he stepped right to Craig – although Craig was, himself, thirteen, the two of them fought for three hours. They went up and down the streets of Fort Stanton, from the rec center, down 18th street, past Donna's house, around the corner past Eddie Jordan's (the ex-head coach of the Washington Wizards basketball team), and back up by the rec center again. They continued on until people began to get off work, one of them being Skip's father, who watched for a little while, walked up the hill and around the corner to the house, put his bag down (his daily six-pack of Pabst Blue Ribbon beer), then went back to the corner and called Skip home to eat dinner.

When Skip got home, Paul looked at him and told him to go wash his hands, and get ready to eat. Neither Paul nor Connie cared that their boys would fight; it was the *not* fighting when or if you *needed* to that they would not accept. Craig Stevens went on to fight at the bouts held at the D.C. Armory in the mid-70s. For his weight class, he was fair; he didn't have much discipline, and as he got into his late twenties he developed what some fighters called "encephalopathy," or the "punch-drunk syndrome."

Skip was no Muhammad Ali (Sugar Ray Leonard hadn't entered the circuit, yet), but he was not a lame to the game either. His older cousin,

Duke, while in the company of some of Duke's boys, once found this out while Skip visited him in Mayfair.

Duke and one of his friends were joneing on each other. His cousin's friend made an offensive crack about Duke's mother, who was also Skip's aunt, Jennie. Although the remark was inappropriate, Skip nevertheless found it hilarious. Skip laughed and Duke said something to Skip. That's when things took a turn for the worst. It began with the two of them slap boxing, as was a popular sport among the young guys then. Well, after awhile when Skip was getting the best of his cousin, Duke kicked Skip in the gut. Skip wound up on his back looking up while the world spun around. His cousin's crew helped him to his feet as they nodded their approval of him, as well as a few short words of encouragement.

It wasn't heavy as far as Skip was concerned. He wasn't paying full attention and paid the price; a lesson well-learned – Larry had told him that "fools must be taught by results" – no one would ever catch him this way again, but he would catch others.

The only thing Skip didn't like about visiting his cousin was that there was, as far as he was concerned, wa-a-ay too many cats wondering and meandering their way around Mayfair, literally hundreds, and neither Skip nor Connie were cat people.

Skip was not too fond of "Pinch" either. Pinch was his cousin's bipolar dog, a black-and-white Springer Spaniel. This dog had serious issues, and bucked at Skip on more than one occasion.

By this time, the Lucases had a dog, too, and Skip thought about introducing him to his cousin's dog. Skip's dogs name was Smokey. He named him Smokey because he was black. He wasn't a real big dog; he was about the size of a small German shepherd, and had the features of a shepherd.

You see, way before this pit bull and Rottweiler craze came into effect, the baddest dog in the average neighborhood was a German Shepherd, or maybe a dude might've had a Doberman Pinscher, but Dobies were mainly for show. Mostly they sort of just "looked the part."

But this dog Skip had when he was coming up was, pound for pound, the "fighting-est" dog in the neighborhood, and it didn't matter to him how much the other dog weighed because he'd give away fifty pounds or so. He was just that bad, and he was also smart.

The only dogs in the neighborhood that were able to best Skip's were Bow and Jerry. They were owned by Mr. and Mrs. Manigo who lived several houses down the street from Skip and Larry Dunmore.

These dogs supposedly had gone through the Korean War with Mr. Manigo. Now, however, they were kept by a specially constructed 6 ½ foot fence that, sometimes, they were still able to scale regardless of its height. Eventually Mr. Manigo had to tie their hind legs down with stakes in the ground in an attempt to keep them inside the yard. Miraculously, they *still* went over the fence, stake-tied rope and all.

Bow was a mix; black German Shepherd/Wolf, and *huge*. His m.o. was to come up behind his intended victim, catch them behind the knees with his body – you'd go down easily – and then Jerry would come in for the coup de grace.

Jerry, a bigheaded black and white pit bull, almost the size of a Great Dane, was undoubtedly the most dangerous and feared of the two doges.

On any given day, one could see a small gathering of boys in front of the Mangios' house, trying to peer to the side of their house, hoping to catch a glimpse of these legendary assassins. And the two dogs would watch their crowd of spectators back, as if they relished in their attention.

The two times that they broke loose, news of their escape spread like a wildfire. The whole Fort Stanton neighborhood was like a ghost town; clear of any pedestrian traffic for blocks.

A caller would shout from the corner by Skip's mom's house, which overlooked the recreation center, "Bow and Jerry's loose!" You would see mothers snatching their kids off of bicycles, and someone on the basketball court would make sure the entry gate was slammed shut and a few other neighborhood dogs that were allowed to roam freely, like Smokey, were brought inside until Mr. Manigo had them harnessed again.

Though in their golden years the two of them were a formidable force, alone, as well as together. Mr. Manigo would sometimes take these beasts down to the "old road"[1] to exercise. Wild dogs would be easily spotted there, so Mr. Manigo would let Bow and Jerry loose to catch one of the bitches in heat, relieving themselves of stress supposedly, and getting a chance to unwind. Some of the wild dogs that were born in the dins were the progeny of Bow and Jerry. Skip even suspected that his own dog, Smokey, was one of Bow's offspring, because of the wolf-like head he had. Allah knows best.

The thought of those two getting loose and roaming free in the neighborhood still haunts the memory of many residents in Fort Stanton, as well as those long since moved away. Those old enough to remember anyone walking past the Manigos' house had only to peer into the back to catch a look at Bow and Jerry standing side by side, just watching…

Smokey knew all the major commands, not tricks. Commands like "ssssss-sssss," which was meant to indicate an order to attack someone. And when Skip or one of the Lucases said that, Smokey was taking off after any dog or man in the direction of where the commander pointed. Win, lose, or draw, he was trying to bring something down. He'd sometimes meet Skip on the grounds after school when the bell rung in the afternoons. He would have hung out with Skip or his brother, M.G., all day if he could. He knew about "sit", "lie down", "go home," all of that. If Skip said, "Cat!" he was up for the chase.

[1] A car trail the Park police used to drive down which was surrounded by woods.

He didn't lose but two fights that Skip could remember in the six or seven years Skip had him before he was ---aah, "pronounced."

Anyone that knows about the east side of Anacostia River knows that it has a lot of woods in certain areas, and that's where most the boys used to get their dogs. Those woods in and around Fort Stanton were a haven for wild dogs.

They would run in packs, especially when one of the bitches were in heat. Smokey was a wild dog puppy that Skip and his young crew found with some others in one of the dens of the woods when he was about 8 or 9. His mom and pop told him he had to take care of him; that it was a big responsibility and all that – "no sweat."

Smokey was one to recognize a good thing when he saw it. He didn't stay behind the fence in the back yard, but could be found chilling on the front porch, following Skip or M.G., or somewhere in the vicinity of the neighborhood. He wouldn't bother children, wouldn't sweat the mailman either, and was cool with most of the people in the neighborhood.

Sometimes he would be gone for days at a time, running through the woods with one of the packs. Skip figured it was just something in him that had him going back to his roots, back to that from which he had come. He would come back after one of his periods of absence, bloody from fighting, or found under the porch eating something he had ran down in the woods. That's when everyone would leave him alone for a few hours until he was done and collected again. They never would quite know exactly what it was he was eating. That was *his* business, as long as it wasn't a rat. His father had told him about rats having rabies or something. If he had caught that they may have had to shoot Smoke like they did "Ol' Yellow."

Now, there were these other dogs that used to belong to one of Skip's friends, Kenny. Kenny's father use to work on old cars; their yard was full of them.

So these two dogs (Ace and Duke) were the closest thing to "junkyard dogs," and Smokey used to hate them! He would fight them both together, just for kicks, Skip used to think. He was about three or three and a half, and in his prime, and Skip was about eleven. Smoke would get over on them sometimes, and other times it would end in a draw. This one particular time, however, they got out on Skip's boy when he missed a step and landed on his back in between the curb and a parked car. Man, they were getting in Smokey's ah…tail something awful.

Usually he would regroup and pull out of these situations for a strong finish. This day however, Skip saw that he wasn't up for it and he needed an "out." Recognizing immediately that Smoke was in trouble, Skip told Kenny, "Alright, man! Get your dogs." But Kenny was really into it and wasn't hearing anything that Skip was saying. The paw was on the other foot now and his eyes were wild with excitement and anticipation of the thrill of victory for Ace and Duke.

Skip yelled at Kenny one more time, "Kenny, get your dogs." This time, when Kenny seemed to ignore Skip, he jumped in and started kicking Duke – the larger of the two dogs – in the ribs, underside, stomach and testicles. Wherever he could get them in at; he didn't care. He was trying to get them hounds off of Smoke.

Now this got Kenny's attention. The dogs weren't the only ones in action now; it was now Skip and Kenny rumbling. But Skip was still trying to assist Smoke, who had gotten trapped between the curb and the car, at the same time that he was getting it in with Kenny. So, while he was going blow for blow with Kenny, every chance he got, Skip kicked the crap out of one of Kenny's crazy dogs. Skip had always been leery of them whenever he went over the Kenny's house. Skip could always beat Kenny in a fight, and figured that he wouldn't have too much trouble rumbling him and one of his dogs.

These dogs that Kenny had were natural fighters, and Duke was Smokey's twin – making him a wild dog, also. Kenny was also part of the crew that was in the woods when they found the den that he got Smokey from, and Kenny took Duke for himself. Duke was only a little bigger than Smokey, with a humongous head like Bow's. But dogs don't know anything about kinship after they have been separated from puppies, for some years. Meanwhile, as Skip continued fighting Kenny and putting his black canvas Converse All-Stars to Duke's ribs, Ace was biting holes in his leg that were exposed by the shorts that he was wearing. But it was all good because it had its benefits; it was all the distraction that Smokey needed, as he was able to get back to his feet after a minute or two and get back in the thick of things.

A crowd had formed while all of this was developing. Things seemed to suddenly come to an eerie stop when Connie showed up wearing that old raggedy Baltimore Colts hoodie, with the hood up, and her hand in the front warm-up part. Skip knew she was strapped, and the crowd must have sensed it too, because it had begun to disperse a little, some concerned about Skip's moms with the burner. The heck with the two friends fighting; their lives was more important than that. Some of them were already familiar with Skip's mom and how she could "act out," and did not care to be there in case she decided to go St. E's out there again.

Skip felt Connie's presence though he didn't see her, and he knew somehow he had to get her off the scene because she was about to bust a cap off on one or both of Kenny's dogs.

Chapter 4

I'M TELLING YOU, THE WHOLE scene was total chaos. Skip and Kenny sort of fell off after that and Skip did not go by his house anymore because Smokey *and* Skip were beefing with Kenny's dogs.

A few years later, Skip had become more mischievous, errant and, though gregarious, began to mess up more blatantly. He had three separate groups of rouge friends/associates that he ran with. One group, from his Fort Stanton neighborhood, was still in school and around his age. They were small time petty-larceny-type of dudes, actual "friends" that he got drunk with on the weekends and helped steer towards a life of corruption. There were two other groups that attributed to his own criminal career; these guys were older as well and engaged in everything from grand theft, strong armed robbery, *armed* robbery, and, as was the case today, night-time house breaking and burglary. Skip also had a criminal record by now and was on probation for unauthorized use of a vehicle (U.U.V.) Just last year, he broke Connie's heart by getting picked up in Lanburg Department Store shoplifting with his mentor, Sam Buggs; he had three stolen jackets on, a set of pierced earrings for Connie's birthday, as well as other items.

Today, however, one of his twice-as-sinister and corrupt crime tutors contacted him to incorporate his assistance in one of his capers…him and Fat Frank. All he had to do was to meet his old mentor by the Big Chair, a well-known landmark found in front of The Curtis Brothers Furniture Store in S.E. Washington, D.C. It was only about a half-hour from his Skip's house.

Now Smokey was like this – anybody that strolled out of the Lucas's house, he trailed them. And if they weren't conscious and on the quick look around, he would follow them on the sneak tip, seriously! And that joker would time your "look backs" and duck behind a car or some bushes when he thought he was about to be exposed. So by the time Skip noticed that he was being shadowed, he had arrived at the rendezvous, copped a squat and was waiting for Buggs and Fat Frank when…you guessed it – Smokey!

Everyone pretty much would talk to Smokey like they would another person. He was just that sharp, feeling me? So when he crossed the street to where Skip was, he knew what time it was; he knew what to expect from one of his providers. Skip told him calmly, "Smokey, what you doin' here, man?"

Smokey, since he was a puppy, had the ability to "snicker" just like the cartoon dog, Previous. It was like he was saying, "I'm here, Homes, and it is what it is. I almost got hit by that car over there and I ain't in the mood; so let's not make this any uglier that it has to be. Besides I'm still not over that move your pops made on my peoples. He could've injured her bad. Princess is one of my babies' mothers; why that lame keep hatin' on me, anyway?"

"Which babies you talkin' about, Smoke? You have them all over Anacostia and, besides, that bitch turned over the trash can and then growled at him. Hatin'! Smokey, what do you expect when you have had some mangy mutt tramp under the porch every day this week. And of all days, Friday, when my mom brought the sisters from church to the house after service. You was locked up in the front yard humpin' that three-legged sooner 'Queenie' that hangs in the "Miles long" parking lot, begging for scraps. Don't laugh it off; it ain't funny! Moms was humiliated, embarrassed and talking about 'get back,' or putting your sorry tail on the chain, and you don't want that. What's been up with you lately, anyway?"

Skip and Smokey just looked at each other. There was no longer any need for any more rap because Smokey knew what his owner meant. The bitches were only half of the problem; his pack-crew from the woods was starting to hang out around the house, too. Not only were they drawing heat to the house, but the neighbors were complaining, and rightly so. That bunch of thugs didn't have any cut card. Howling, scaring kids, flashing gang signs…

"Look, Smoke, I don't have time for this right now. I…" Just then, Buggs and Fat Frank pulled up, and in good time to because people were beginning to stare at Skip like he was deranged or something.

Buggs and Frank were already familiar with the relationship between Skip and Smokey, but that still did not account for Smokey's presence there that evening. Skip could see the disgust on his mentor's face, as well as the inferences between Smokey, Buggs, and Fat Frank.

The instructions they had for Skip were clear; he was to go to this place a few blocks down and around the corner. A certain window would be unlocked for him to climb through. He was then to walk to a side door, unlock it and wait for Fat Frank. If Frank wasn't there within five minutes, leave the door unlocked and *leave*. It sounded easy enough.

It had begun to get dark and drizzling. Skip was anticipating the many dead presidents he would have to count following this lick; *mucho grande*, he figured. Proceeding on his way, he thought of sending Smoke home regardless of his protest. Lately, Skip had been beginning to feel that Smokey thought *he* was the one in charge; that Smokey was taking liberties around the house that he didn't use to take nor was entitled to, even trying to ease Princess into the family to be a live-in. "Perhaps," Skip thought, "I don't spend enough time with him like I used to." Skip had *way* too much going on these days to have time for Smokey as he once did.

Meanwhile, when he got to the location he didn't have to tell Smoke to chill for a couple of minutes; he already knew the drill and laid low behind the hedges. Skip could see Smokey was cool with that. Skip reached the designated window; things were copasetic; so far, so good. He took a look at Smoke and thought about how they had first met. The memories caused him to smile as the early years flashed before his subconscious. Smokey winked at him as if he knew what Skip was thinking; he often reflected upon their first encounter, as well as those few years that followed, too. (Before Chick, Buggs, and that damn Steve came on the scene; Smokey hated Steve and vowed to his pack-crew that he would get that bastard if it was the last thing that he did. Steve had shot Smokey in his ass with a B.B. gun once when Smokey was young and didn't know not to crap in the neighbors' yards.) Smokey cleared his head of those visions just in time to catch sight of his master's leg as it disappeared through the window.

When Skip got inside, due to the lateness of the evening, it was darker inside than it was outside. He knew to squat low and let his eyes adjust to this new darkness. In the process of Skip looking around in this darkness, he observed a most perplexing thing; a pair of small red bulbs, not ten feet in front of him. After more study, he decided that they weren't bulbs, as first though, but more like…*cat eyes*? No, this can't be because they were too far spaced (the small, red bulbs – or eyes – were about six inches apart). Man, wait a minute… Skip pulled out his penlight and trained it on this mysterious set "eyes" and froze, losing control of his already full bladder from all the beer that he had drank earlier. He was fortunate not to have had any food on his stomach or, he was sure, he would have lost that too as he stared into the eyes of the largest panther that he had ever seen in his fourteen-year lifespan. Not a poster or stuffed animal, either, but an actual, real life one, with slobber and all!

Thankfully the cat blinked, breaking the speechless grasp that Skip was temporarily held in, and allowing him the opportunity to collect himself. Reflexively he spun around and upward in one motion, crashing through the window that he entered through. Hearing the commotion, Smokey was immediately on point, quizzically looking at his master like, "What the hell is wrong with you?"

Smoke realized that something was definitely wrong and rose to his feet awaiting Skip's command. However, between the crashing of glass and faint odor of his master's urine, he never heard the words, "Come on, Smoke. Cat!" He only caught the last part – cat. After quickly surveying the scene and not seeing a cat, Smokey's next move *should've* been to roll with Skip. Instead, he opted to enter the building through the same window that Skip had just exited through. Well, that definitely should have been the last thing that he chose to do because Smokey was M.I.A. Later on, Skip sent one of his boys from the Fort to discreetly inquire into certain particulars, but all that he got back was that someone was arrested for housing an exotic animal and cruelty; but nothing about a dog being found on the scene.

Afterwards, Skip just figured that Smokey had gotten killed and someone moved or dumped his body; or perhaps he made it out and after thinking that Skip had set him up, went on his own. He was always unconsciously on the lookout for his trusty sidekick; he truly missed him. Later he found himself visiting the very place that he first found Smokey, six years prior. Lamenting over the loss of his friend, Skip released a scream into the air, to no one in particular, "I love you, Smoke. You were a soldier, dog. My bad!"

Paul saw signs of his first born and namesake slipping away from him; the lack of communication is usually a dead giveaway, along with failing to connect with the child. These are among the stratagems that keep parent and child cohesively partnered. It has to be more than D.N.A., sometimes more than love even. When there is little or nothing to attract an offspring to the parent, when respect is lost, contempt takes its place.

Skip now had three brothers and a sister in between the four of them (Carlyn had two older and two younger brothers). Often Paul would leave Skip "hangin'" with his mono-line phrases such as (when education was the issue), "I got mine, boy – you got yours to get.'" (When the streets summoned Skip to hang out), "I got four more in here to worry about; mess up out there if you want." Skip needed more dialogue than that, more elaboration upon some of the complexities teens faced in the world, or rather the street.

Perhaps this is the downside of beginning parenting later in life, and/or being somewhat disconnected with potential "at risk" youth. Skip swiftly became amalgamated to the customs and practices of his environment. Surely by divine intervention, he had yet to be committed to one of the youth facilities; one could only infer it was due, in part, to the nature of his offenses. So far they were non-violent, besides that, his household was occupied by both parents. Sometimes this reason alone is enough to weigh heavily in the reports of someone's "case file."

By fourteen, Skip had his share of unlawful dealings with cars and guns; he was a terrible influence over his friends. Fortunately, his siblings were too young to be directly affected by his delinquent behavior. Connie somehow assumed his friends and older associates were the bad influence on her son. He was a habitual truant at school, so much that, because of his absenteeism, his parents were contacted by telephone and informed he would have to repeat eighth grade. Connie was shocked, "How could this be," she would exclaim. Skip's report card was filled with "A's" and "B's" – but the fact that they were in "red ink," instead of the usual blue, was never questioned.

Though Connie was a substitute teacher at the local elementary school and cognizant of when the semesters ended, Skip still had changed the grades from "F.A." (Failure to Appear) to "A's" or "B's", and, as ridiculous as the alteration looked, no one ever questioned the absurdity of it.

Skip could not stand to see his mom crying as she was now – good *Lord* she could sure make some ugly faces. In between the cursing and fussing out, the ultimatum she gave him was unequivocally crystal clear, "Either you use your Uncle Jimmy's address on Brentwood Road and go to school in N.E., or, I swear, I'll have you sent to that place for boys where Howard's father sent him." Skip knew Howard Ford from Parkland; now he was in Cedar Knolls, a reformatory for hard to control boys, or those that the courts sent there for breaking the law.

Skip knew his mom was not joking; she wasn't just trying to scare him. He was convinced that this bone had some meat on it. He was already on probation for a stolen Lincoln Continental, and there was also an incident about some knives that he had pulled out at the recreation center. To make matters worse, Paul forced Skip's hand while confronting his son about the knives, leaving Skip with no other choice but to defend himself. In the process, Skip caught his father square on the jaw, knocking Paul back and causing him to stumble onto one of the beds in the boys' room. Skip then leaped up onto his surprised dad, not sure what either of their next moves would be. The moment passed and he got off of his dad and stood, bracing himself for retaliation; it never came and Paul left the room. The next day Skip's father and him let bygones be bygones, and moved on.

Skip would use the incident years later, when dealing with potentially volatile situations; the lesson learned was to be very careful when intending to become verbally or physically aggressive. Always try to give a man an out, especially one you ain't sure you can handle.

Connie could really get pitiful in her gloom; Skip thought the transfer to a new school might not be so bad after all. Besides not having to go to reform school, he also would not have to be in a school where his peers would know that he had to repeat the grade because he had flunked the previous year. The people in the new school would be none the wiser. He assured Connie that he would comply and, this time would be different.

Skip and Necie were the reason Iverson Mall hired parking lot rent-a-cops in 1970, specifically assigned to patrol the levels. Necie, for a few weeks, was on a Road Runner, Dodge Charger, and Mustang Shelby fixation. To hotwire most Chrysler products, one merely needed two and a half to three feet of wire, preferably with alligator clamps on each end so as not to lose valuable time before bumping the starter or relay switch. Necie could hotwire *anything* with an engine, within seconds.

As Skip stepped out the front door of his new school, he spied the souped-up orange Road Runner with the short, tight skirt leaning over the passenger's door talking to the car's driver. Necie wasn't outwardly looking for his car-thieving companion directly; he knew if Skip was at school this day, he'd be coming out of that door for lunch on his way to wherever, and he would spot the car. Necie knew his young counterpart was attracted to two things if nothing else; short, tight skirts and slick cars. Necie could not have been more right; soon as Skip stepped from the entrance, he looked right, left, followed by a quick right again at the bright orange flash. "Damn! A double treat," he thought as his eyes traveled up the backside of the young girl's thighs. As soon as Necie saw Skip approaching the car through the rearview mirror, he dismissed the skirt.

Skip would never ask ridiculous questions like, "Whose car?", or "Where'd you get it?" That he got in the car told Necie all he needed to know; that Skip was done with school for the day, and he was ready to bounce.

When they got to S.E., Skip wondered why they were riding through Congress Heights. Necie had cut into some tenderoni, and now he was trying to impress her with the flashy whip. Road Runners had a unique horn sound, and if you ever watched the old Road Runner/Wiley Coyote cartoons, then you would know the sound the horn makes…Beep, beep!

Not surprising to Skip, the young girl, named Robin, wasn't at home but was where most fifteen-year-olds should have been in the early afternoon (school). Nevertheless, on the way out of the Heights Skip saw Necie double-take in the rearview mirror with bulging eyes and clenched teeth as if saying "sheets." Skip had played this scene out with Necie before, and he knew it wasn't "sheets" that he was saying.

Something was wrong, cataclysmic even; Skip needed to know what it was so he could quickly calculate his options. The two had always been pretty much in sync about these sudden revisions. Still looking in the mirror, Necie said, "It's Eddie Hall. I took the car off of his lot."

Now it was Skip's eyes that bulged as he looked at his friend. He knew Eddie Hall was a slick white greaser throwback from the late 50s. he grew up in Anacostia when it was only about 60% black. On sunny days, he wore dark Blues Bothers-type shades, and kept a small comb in his shirt pocket to pull his oil-drenched hair back. He ran a three-truck towing company/body shop that operated behind Curtis Brothers Furniture. He drove a light-purple '70 Cadillac with a white convertible top, and was into black girls just as much as white ones. He was also known for keeping a Saturday Night Special in his dip or glove compartment.

He taught Greg Lipscomb, his brother Louie, Larry, and other guys in the business most everything there was to know about towing and running accidents. Necie, who was Larry's younger brother, was way out of line stealing this car out of Eddie's garage. What made it an even more egregious error was that Necie was pushing it through the streets of S.E. Anacostia. Damn, Necie! What the hell…

For ten minutes, Necie maneuvered through the streets and back alleys of Congress Heights and the Alabama Avenue corridor, trying desperately to shake off the tail. Necie was good, but he was no match for the driving skills of the highly proficient master accident runner. The only thing Necie and Skip had in their favor was that Eddie was in his car and not one of his tow trucks, which would have given him access to his two-way squawk box. He could then be in touch with his drivers, getting them in the immediate area to assist him, literally in seconds – as the towing company was only six to eight traffic lights from the chase scene.

It wasn't long before Eddie coaxed Necie's hot-rod Plymouth into taking a turn he should have passed up; he, himself, did pass it by. Eddie then took the hard cut on the grass between two apartment buildings, cutting the rookie driver Necie off at the alley's exit.

Eddie knew most of the car thieves and hustlers in the area; he didn't quite know Skip, but was sure he'd seen him around. Necie was doing his best to keep his identity concealed because Eddie definitely knew him. When the front of Eddie's Caddy appeared in the exit of the alleyway, both Necie and Skip, without waiting for the car to reach a complete stop, wordlessly bailed out of the hot Road Runner. Leaving the doors open and the car on and drifting towards the front of Eddie's Caddy. The two fleeing friends got low, unconcerned with the imminent collision that they were sure was coming.

Pop, pop! Eddie had quickly thrown the Caddy into reverse, avoiding the battering ram that the Road Runner had become, and gotten out of his car with heat in hand.

As a rule, Necie and Skip never took the same route when fleeing a scene. When they'd split up this way, they usually would have a good laugh about the ordeal afterwards when retelling the story. Most times, Necie liked to joyride around with a carload of his "Garfilian" homeboys, such as the time he was apprehended by authorities and sent to juvenile detention. Skip, on the other hand, chose to drive solo, or with his girl, J. Marie – but that would come later.

This time, however, it was Skip who'd come up short. As soon as he thought he had put distance between Eddie and himself, he stepped from the corner of the apartment building, and would swear later that he heard the shot after he felt the burning in his eye. The shot that was meant for his head caught the brick near his face, knocking the mortar off into his eye. Fortunately for Skip, Eddie wasn't as skilled a shooter as he was a driver and mack.

When one's adrenaline is on high and fear is the preeminent motivator for his actions, pain sometimes comes secondary. The sole intent then becomes getting away. The temporary blindness in his left eye didn't take precedence over avoiding a third possible encounter at the juvenile branch of Indiana Avenue; another episode of juvie court would surely lay him down for a minute. Skip knew he had to get out of this situation and had to get out of it *now*; "by hook or crook," as Connie use to say.

"Plan B," Buggs always told him, as if it were the Gospel. He would say, "Skip, you got to always have a backup plan." Buggs called it a contingency stratagem.

The cogs in his criminal mind began to turn; he could only produce two feasible options; one was his patented "groundhog" move, where he located a safe spot and burrowed in for a few hours until the coast was clear. Gaining a good vantage point, Skip was known to hole up somewhere for five hours and wait out a potential threat. He rejected that idea for option two, though, and took it to the woods. He made his way to the foot of Congress Heights, to the bottom, then across Mississippi Avenue. Just inside of the wood's edge, he made tracks up around the tree line surrounding Parkland to Southern Avenue, then across Suitland Parkway, until he finally exited the wooded area some two hours later into the parking lot of Gransville Village, where his friend Chick lived. He was a mess; a sweaty, dirty, creek-water-smelling mess. That damn Necie!

After the debacle with Smokey and the panther, Skip resolved breaking and enterings (B&E's) just weren't his stick. The few others he had participated in with Chick and Steve didn't net the payday he'd anticipated; not by far. There was too much left to chance for his liking, too many variables.

Right now, however, Skip was "doing *him*," and despite yet another harrowing escape, he was in his element. Stealing cars, and all the perks that went along with it, was more his comfort zone; it was his, ahh… métier.

Hustling tires and car parts, or recovering the spoils of whatever else was sometimes found in people's cars – especially the guns – were an added bonus.

Although J. Marie and Sharon began the new year at Taft Junior High School together, by late October, Sharon found her way back to Louise

(Lou, as her children called her). Surprisingly enough, the two oldest Williams girls didn't roll together in pursuit of their mother, perhaps realizing her siblings needed an older maternal influence in their lives, J. Marie opted to stay – or maybe she simply drew the shortest straw. In any event, her new homeroom teacher this year (Ms. Gilliam) was one of the most pleasant, approachable teachers J. Marie and her crew of girls (comprised of Jackie Frazier, Barbara Floyd, Vanessa Barnhart, and Dawelder Rogers) ever had. Perhaps because they had only to tolerate her for fifteen minutes a day, in the morning, and there were forty other students in the room.

Dawelder was from "Montana." No not the northwestern state which borders Canada, but Montana, the projects on Montana Avenue in N.E., D.C.

Unlike the housing community in the immediate vicinity of Taft's upper-middle class, and not "lower-middle" like where J. Marie lived on 12th Street, in Brooklyn. Montana, like the Brentwood section, was straight ghetto; thug life, for real.

Nevertheless, most of the guys at Taft dressed "up." They wore shadow-striped and shark-skinned slacks, sweater-shirts, Stacy Adams shoes, and a couple of dudes had gators. If they did wear tennis shoes, it was usually with a pair of slacks; even on the basketball court. It wasn't unusual to see a guy hooping in slacks and his low-cut Converses, or Jack Purcells, with his sweater-shirt thrown aimlessly to the ground until the game's end.

Clothes were a double entendre at Taft; not only were they a fashion statement, for some of the guys, it also signified, "I'm 'caked up,' because I'm a hustler and gettin' mine."

Fitting in amongst one's peer group while growing up is *huge* in the eyes of kids and adults alike. Being ostracized has been known to lead many people into despair; it can especially be detrimental to the youth. Depending upon one's "class" or "standing," fitting in can have positive benefits as well as negative detriments. Girls are under just as much pressure, maybe more, to be in-keeping as boys. Each sex can be maliciously cruel to one another, and have been known to bring a fellow classmate or neighborhood outcast to tears; and in some extreme cases, suicide.

J. Marie, though, never mentioned to have been representing Gloria Vanderbilt, Liz Claiborne, or MCM clothing lines, kept her meager belongings clean, pressed, and neat. It isn't always what one wears, but how you wear it. J. Marie was genuinely liked and had that certain *jene sais quoi*, so clothes didn't make her, but she made the clothes.

Through the past few months, an emotionally charged and disturbing dilemma was transpiring at home. This was a funky situation that J. Marie wasn't exactly sure how to handle. At 5'3", she played hard as a child; she was always filled with energy. She was thick built, but not fat by any means. The boy's football coach for the local rec center in Turkey Thicket wanted her to try out for the cheerleading squad. J. Marie often brushed off many of her suitors at school and around the neighborhood; she'd just recently broken up with one of her best friend's brother (Vernon), and wasn't interested in another commitment so soon. Not unless, maybe, the right one caught her eye, or she caught his. She knew exactly what the average one of these jokers had on their minds; they all wanted basically the same thing, and she wasn't having it; not yet. She missed her sister, Sharon, to talk with about boys. Although Sharon often tended to make light of or turn everything into a joke – she could be a regular Phyllis Diller when she wanted to be – she was still a help in dealing with some of these issues.

Eventually, J. Marie reconciled; she would have to give up one of her favorite cheap treats, or at least cut back on them; that junk was taking a toll on her skin. She thought of drinking the smaller bottles of RC and maybe the Doublemint gum was too sugary; "I'll eat or drink half, and then, maybe, give the remainder to Cindy or Tawana," she would reason. J. Marie didn't know her mild case of acne didn't have as much to do with the Royal Crown sodas and sour pickles as it did with genetics and her reaction to puberty three or four years before; and how long would it be before Dickey caught her smoking. She was sure that he smelled it in her clothing. Although when it's also in your clothes, in your car, and your own breath, it's harder to pick it up on someone else, even though the person is in your own household.

The next day, as J. Marie and Dawelder were in route to Mr. Young's third-period math class, deep within her own thoughts, J. Marie was thinking of a possible job Mrs. Gwynn (her English literature teacher) proposed, that she may, at sometime, want J. Marie to babysit her two-year old daughter. "This would be perfect," J. Marie thought. For one, it would be a chance to earn money doing something she truly enjoyed; children were so sweet, especially the toddlers. The fact that Mrs. Gwynn, along with Ms. Gilliam were among her favorite teachers didn't hurt matters, either.

Angela Gwynn was five years out of Morgan University. She was very attractive and had more of a big-sister relationship with many of her girls than that of one of the old fuddy-duddy school faculty members. J. Marie thought this would be ideal! And…

"Did you hear me, girl?! There he is!"

"There *who* is, Dawelder?"

"Damn J., wasn't you listening to *any*thing I was sayin'? The boy I was tellin' you about last week; this is the first time I've seen him since then. I wonder where he's been?" Dawelder introduced herself to the tall, light-skinned boy earlier in the month, but hadn't seen him since then. Now she wanted her friend to walk with her while they approached him at his locker, just across the hall from Mrs. Gwynn's classroom. J. Marie wasn't really up for that at that moment, even though he *was* sort of cute.

"Hi, Skip," Dawelder said as she and J. Marie walked up to him.

"Hi. How are you doing," he responded. It was more rhetorical than anything else. He didn't really care because he too busy looking at her companion.

Dawelder continued on, "This is my friend, J. Marie."

"Hi," was all Skip said.

Chapter 5

"*Occasio Facit furem*" – opportunity makes the thief. If Skip was the opportunist, then Necie (short for Cornelius) was unequivocally the thief. This dastardly duo would create the climate (thrity-some odd years later) for movies such as *Gone in Sixty Seconds* and *New Jersey Drive*, just to name a few. Skip and car-thieving Necie, as they were disparagingly called, were as opposite as night and day. They had one thing in common – they both loved driving other people's cars; Road Runners, Chargers, 'Vettes, Caddies, Lincolns. If it was an eye-catcher, or just a convenience, no model was exempt.

Skip, on more than one occasion, jetted with someone's whip having no more than a safety pin he'd found on the ground, and a piece of a coat hanger. Most of the cars didn't have lock steering then; lock steering for Fords didn't come out until 1970, whereas it came out for Chevys in 1969.

Skip and Necie both began driving at eleven or twelve years old. I'm talking driving good enough to be doing so flowing with daily traffic, nondescript. Skip was shorter than Necie and would have to roll up the car's floor mats to sit higher. Sometimes he had to fold up his jacket or coat, too.

This was one of the several reasons his folks had him transferred to a school on the other side of town. His mom *swore* it was the crowd of guys he associated with that was leading him astray. "They were a bad influence," Connie would say. How naïve they were; it was Skip that was a bad influence and ring leader in most circles he traveled in. Skip was, perhaps, the most corrupt teen in Fort Stanton at the time; although he was courteous and respectful to his elders.

He had done a short stint in the receiving home on Mount Oliver Road, but was never committed to any of the juvenile centers, like Oak Hill, Cedar Knolls, or any training school for long terms. Some of his cronies were not as fortunate, however.

Connie had read the riot act to him while driving home from the store one day. Skip swore to himself, "This lady takes the doggonest times to break down cryin'." This was the second time he'd seen his mom burst into tears in the middle of hanging a sharp turn while driving. The first time was when he was ten years old and her father down in North Carolina had passed away a day or two before. Skip accompanied his mother, aunts, and cousins Jo-Jo and Duke, to the funeral. All of a sudden, while hooking a turn coming off the 295 ramp onto Pennsylvania Avenue, S.E. – on the hard turn! – she just burst out crying and saying, "My daddy's dead!" Connie was barely hanging onto the steering wheel. Skip was watching his distraught mother closely, prepared to grab the steering wheel and help her along, all the while trying to call her attention back to completing the turn.

Now it was like déjà vu; his mother in the midst of crying and bordering on hysteria while hanging a turn, and Skip riding shotgun. At times like this, Skip would've complied or confessed to anything; so here we go…

Taft Junior High School was so named after William Howard Taft, this nation's twenty-seventh president. Sidney Young was Skip's new eighth-grade homeroom teacher, along with an assembly of boys and girls that Skip didn't know or really care to. He was a product of S.E., *Anacostia*, which was the first home that he had ever known. And now he was across town in this spot that he hated being in, but for the sake of his ol' ma…crap!

Every morning Skip would report to Mr. Young before starting his other classes; Young also taught ninth-grade math (he was J. Marie's math teacher). The school itself sat in the middle of an upper-middle-class neighborhood; big houses, some with decorative brickwork, and fancy wrought-iron storm doors, winding walkways with pricy whips parked out front. Skip noticed only a few of the cribs had "driveways," a sure sign these Negroes was fronting, because anyone who's sure enough caked up would be parking that Caddy or Benz in a garage, and not out on the street.

Well, Skip knew one thing for damn sure, you'd better not mess this thing up, Homes, or they'll be sticking a fork in you and turning you over, because you'll be *done*. Connie was serious about this reform school thing.

Skip was making serious attempts to make the best of this new situation he brought upon himself. He was even carrying a writing tablet home each day; some days he'd go to his uncle Jimmy's house on Brentwood Road and catch a ride to S.E. with him. Uncle Jimmy was the recreation supervisor at Douglas Dwellings in Garfield Projects; a rough camp. Most times, however, he would just catch the B-2, Anacostia at the beginning of the line, in Mount Rainier, Maryland, just across the line.

Going to school, sometimes he could get off the bus at Bladensburg and South Dakota and walk the rest of the way; he was used to walking fast and long from his days of walking with his dad in Parkland, so it wasn't no thing for him to foot it the mile from his first bus drop. It was three transfers to get to within a block of Taft from Fort Stanton, actually four.

Every now and then, Skip would see Mr. Young driving his old Dodge up South Dakota Avenue. Mr. Young would pull over for Skip without Skip having to wave him down. Skip was surprised his teacher never asked him where he was coming from. It was a violation for kids to cross school zones, traveling from one school district to another, without living in the district closest to the school you attended. Skip simply would have told his teacher he lived in S.E. and let the chips fall where they may.

Had it not been for Skip's older cousin, Lil' Jimmy, Skip's clothing line would've been wa-a-a-ay under par. Taft was a school for fashion, like Eastern High and McKinley Tech back in the day.

Skip's cousin went to McKinley Tech. He had a few pair of banging slacks he gave to his younger cousin, and some sweater-shirts. A couple of older guys around the Fort (Fort Stanton) gave him stuff, too. Skip eventually began buying his own wear, becoming more fashion conscious as he attended Taft.

Skip could clean up pretty good. At fourteen years old, he had that look that made the average girl in his age range give him a double take; he attracted grown women, older teenage girls, and preteens, the last at which he just shook his head at and brushed off.

When November of 1970 came in, Skip had already hung out with no less than ten of the little N.E. honeys. By the time Dawelder Rogers approached him at this locker with another girl she introduced as "my friend, J. Marie," Skip actually didn't remember they (he and Dawelder) met last month or so ago. Skip had seen Dawelder around; she was definitely cute enough, with long silky hair.

Skip hadn't been to school in a few days; he was up to his old truancy tricks again. He had bailed out of a hot rod Dodge Super Charger a few weeks ago on his way to school. A car he had stolen from Georgetown, and kept stashed in his friend Chick's apartment building parking lot.

Skip was balling up South Dakota Avenue in the car, not paying attention, and the next thing he knew the traffic had stopped. He had to jam on breaks in the rain, causing the car to slide and nose out into the oncoming traffic lane. A patrol car had observed the near catastrophe and called the tag number in as a routine measure and, of course, the license came back on the "hot sheet." Now with flashing lights and wailing sirens, the patrol car was in hot pursuit. The description was a young light-skinned black guy fleeing the scene.

Of course, that'd be Skip, on his way to school in a stolen car. Now, on this November morning, it would be Skip that was the object of Dawelder's desire; handsome, mild mannered, and criminally corrupt Skip. In about fifteen minutes, he would detach her from his memory to pursue her friend.

Maybe, however, it was Skip getting played by the cunning N.E. honeys, and this was the intent all along – well, if that be the case, it worked. Now the wheels in Skip's head were grinding on all cogs and as soon as an opportunity presented itself he would, as long as he had breath in his body, be hollering real loud at this girl with the dark Chinese eyes and killer body… "Jesus," he thought.

That afternoon, Skip saw J. Marie in the newer addition of Taft. He asked for her phone number; it wasn't a whole bunch of extra rap, just simply, "Hi, J. Marie. I'm trying to call you. Can I have your number?"

Skip spoke with J. Marie the next day briefly at school. He didn't call that night, but waited two nights later. Somewhere in the conversation he said, "Look, are you tryin' to go with me or what?" (meaning – be my girlfriend)

J. Marie said, "Yeah," as if she was being asked to get a flu shot or something that she really wasn't too sold on.

For the next weeks, Skip walked her home from school, kissing along the way, and a much longer good-bye kiss before parting at the corner of 13th and Franklin streets.

She wouldn't see him every day because he was still hanging on to his previous lifestyle of cutting school to hang out at A&A Towing on 9th and I streets, N.W., with a group of much older guys who lived next door to his oldest childhood friend, Larry – the Lipscomb brothers.

Their entire life was built around cars and drinking. The youngest Lipscomb brother, Jr., only drank an occasional beer; his thing was reefer. He was the closest to Skip's age, and like his older brothers, Greg and Fat Louie, had also dropped out of school to work with cars in some capacity.

Skip met Necie at A&A Towing; he and his brother, Larry, were closest friends with the Lipscomb brothers, and also worked and hung out on 9th and I Street at A&A Towing.

The Lipscombs, Necie, and his brother, and the nefarious, dirty, rotten, low-down Ricky (Monk) Kingsbury were all products of S.E. – Larry and Necie, along with Ricky came out of the Garfield Projects, and all loved having Skip around. Although Skip and Necie were the youngest of the group, they were all cut from the same cloth.

In time they would all get to know J. Marie as Skip's girl. J. Marie even would have the phone number at the Towing Company to reach Skip on the weekends if he wasn't at home.

Skip's other friends in and around Fort Stanton would come to know J. Marie, as well as his family.

About two months into their union, Skip and J. Marie would take the bus ride to S.E., Anacostia.

As they passed the number eleven police precinct, J. Marie informed him how her and her father had stopped there while looking for her sister Sharon. The cut by the Temptations, "Runaway Child, Running

Wild," she said, reminded her of her sister's departure. Skip could tell his girl was sad, so he placed his arm around her, gently accepting her head on his shoulder.

J. Marie's lips always welcomed Skip, and he didn't press her for anything more. This was, perhaps, the most patient Skip had *ever* been; for some reason he couldn't understand, just being in her company settled his mind and body, and her presence did something to his heart he didn't quite comprehend.

When Skip was fourteen, the last of his siblings was born. Connie and Paul were in their forties when little Paul Emmanuel was born. When Skip and J. Marie walked the last stretch to the house in Fort Stanton, after getting off the bus, they had to walk through Woodland Terrace projects on Anger Place. On the way, Jr. Lipscomb passed them going the other way in his hot rod '64 Galaxy. This may have been the first time seeing the girl his brothers and all the crew said had Skip's nose wide open. (Jr. would be killed by gunshots later that year in a "hit" mistakenly meant for Fat Louie. Fat Louie had robbed the big dope man, Ted, in Anacostia earlier.) Skip had been known to ride with Jr. often; fortunately, he was not with Jr. that tragic night in March '71.

As Skip and J. Marie entered the Lucas home, the first person to meet J. Marie was his maternal grandmother, Madoo. She was there to babysit Lil' Paul, who was only three months old.

J. Marie took one look at the sleeping baby boy, and fell in love with Skip all over again, and Madoo fell in love with her. Madoo reminded J. Marie of her own grandma, Tia, and J. Marie would remind Madoo of someone that had been a part of her offspring for years. The two kids, J. Marie and Skip, stayed for an hour or so, and then bade their farewells to Madoo. Skip had to get J. Marie back home again; it would be a long evening.

Skip didn't enter into J. Marie's home until the third or fourth time he walked her home. They would sit on the front porch of J. Marie's house, where Skip would get to know her siblings. She had told him the bark he'd heard was the families German Shepherd; not knowing Skip was very familiar with the bark of big dogs and that of small ones; she had to laugh when she saw the expression on her boyfriend's face after her lie was exposed. That wasn't the only trick she played on Skip, in which he was good humored about. After an hour or so of their kissing, one evening, while her siblings were upstairs, Skip suggested (because he was getting horny) she should go put on a dress or skirt. J. Marie was a willing participant, and after a short moment, she came back from her change; the only problem for Skip was J. Marie hadn't taken *off* anything. After a few wasted thrusts and her laughter in his ear, he realized how clever this girl of his could be when she needed to be. He respected her for that and learned to control himself in the future with her; "this girl ain't easy," he thought, "and that's a good thing." Skip knew that when the time came for them to take their relationship to this other level, it would be on her time and he was cool with that because he loved her.

One of J. Marie's worse fears came to its apex one evening at home; Dickey had been drinking heavily, but this time his lewd insinuations and improprieties could no longer be tolerated; he'd gone *way* too far, and it was time to leave, immediately!

Skip was at his mom's house when the phone rang; it was J. Marie. She was at Lou's place in S.E. on a strip called "Anacostia Road". Ordinarily somebody's car would be making the hot sheet about now, but Skip wasn't exactly sure where Anacostia Road was, only that J. Marie needed him to get to her – like it was yesterday.

So like Marvin Gaye sang to Tammie Terrell, "Ain't no mountain high enough/ Ain't no valley low enough/ Ain't no river wide enough for me, Baby…" Within minutes the taxi pulled up in front of an apartment building with a lady standing in the doorway of the main entrance. She wore a blown-out afro, big hoop earrings and one of those long, flowing Hawaiian "moo-moos". When Skip exited the cab, walking to the building and closer to the woman, he realized the woman was his beloved J. Marie; she looked great, and all grown up! Lou wasn't there; J. Marie was home alone.

She told Skip all of what led up to her sudden departure; he was more saddened for her sake, for having to go through it all, then angry. The main thing was J. Marie was no longer in that situation, she was now safe and he never wanted to be too long or too far from her again.

Lou's two-bedroom ground-floor apartment was a straight bachelor/bachelorette-type crib. Skip and J. Marie both loved it. Already with two of her seven children living with her, J. Marie didn't actually have suitable sleeping quarters. For now, he and J. Marie had lots of hugging and kissing to do. She was ready for Skip tonight; she would be his, he would be hers. The night and its entire ambiance was theirs, and what's more – there'd be no tricks.

Curtis Mayfield was playing on the stereo in the apartment; the album featuring "The Makings of You." Skip previously never truly paid attention to the words of the song until that night with J. Marie. They let it play over and over again. That was their song on that special night (music and singing, "…add a little su-gar, honeysuckle and a great big expression of happiness./ Boy, you couldn't miss, with a dozen roses/ Such will astound you, the joy of children laughing around you/ these are the makings of yooooou")

Skip didn't get to meet Lou that night, though he stayed with J. Marie until after 2:00 am; Skip had found his second home. He'd meet J. Marie at school then they would ride the bus together for the long ride to where J. Marie had to transfer a short way up Minnesota Avenue.

One day, Skip didn't see J. Marie at their usual meeting spot on the grounds of Taft after school, and about half an hour passed and still no J. Marie. He couldn't understand what could be the alteration in her schedule. He decided to head for the bus stop alone. A few blocks off the school grounds on the way up 18th Street, in the distance, he recognized her headed his way, but something was out of sync. For one, she was carrying her shoes and they were broken. Also her hair was a mess, her blouse was torn, and she had a bruise on the side of her face. "What happened, Baby? You alright," he asked once they met. As soon as he said it, he realized what a dumb question it was; of course she wasn't alright.

"I was fighting Niecie Hamlin, me and Janet against her, her sister, and mother. Janet got her leg messed up; Niecie's mother hit her with a board."

Skip gave J. Marie his jacket to cover her partially exposed brassiere. "Damn," he thought, "this girl's a soldier."

They got on the bus and rode to S.E. mostly in silence. Skip knew his girl was tired. He guided her head to his shoulder, this time riding all the way to Anacostia Road with her.

The next day at school news of the fight on 12th Street circulated, and the word was the girls J. Marie and Janet fought wanted a rematch. Part II.

Skip was in class but stationed himself by a window where he could see outside to where the trouble was supposed to come from. J. Marie was now in front of Taft waiting for her foe, with a few other girls. Skip had instructed a few of her girls to call up to Mrs. Gwynn's room where he'd be if the girls showed. Suddenly he heard, "Skip!" He broke out of class and out Taft's doors to the caller – but it was a false alarm. The girls never showed up; they'd had enough apparently. The crisis was over to Skip's relief as well as to J. Marie's. She didn't like trouble; she didn't look forward to any kind of trouble, but if she just *had* to, well…

Skip especially did not favor being caught up in this "girl vs. girl" conflict because when it becomes boy on girl it most always turns into boy on boy, and Skip would've been greatly outmanned in that case. He would have to bring in reinforcements in a couple of stolen cars from Anacostia to deal with these dudes. No, it would've been far too much drama all for a bunch of buff-head broads – no offense to J. Marie. The rest of the school year passed pretty much uneventfully. J. Marie graduated and went on to attend Eastern High, the same school Chick's gangster brother Cortez graduated from six or seven years earlier.

Skip and Lou hit it off from the start, or so he thought. Perhaps she was just being tolerant. Nevertheless, he thought she was one of the cutest older broads that he'd ever seen. She didn't drink, smoke cigarettes, or use drugs and was hilariously funny in her own subtle way. She wasn't home much; neither was J. Marie's older brother, Robert. Whenever he was, he'd stay in his room, listening to records. Skip had first met him over at the house on 12th Street when he came through to knock back a couple of tall cans of Colt 45s with Dickey, and to holler at his siblings. Skip also found out J. Marie's sister, Sharon, was the same girl he'd cracked on before meeting J. Marie. They'd recognized each other immediately, though neither mentioned the encounter.

Lou was working in the Department of Housing and Urban Development (H.U.D.) too, same as Skip's father, only in an administrative capacity for a contract cleaning company called "Worldwide Services." She got J. Marie an after-school job, as was the in-thing for so many of the teenagers during those times, despite J. Marie being only fifteen – and that was how Paul came to meet Lou.

Paul genuinely loved J. Marie as he would his own daughter; one of the few seemingly bright spots of his day would be when he'd see the big dimples on her face each time she smiled. He nicknamed her "Dimples." Paul and Lou would privately joke that Skip was just plain, outright p-whipped; as strange as it may have been, the two parents didn't have a problem with the kids being sexually involved with each other.

Connie on the other hand was old school and "fit to be tied," as she would say. It was bad enough the streets had partly claimed dibs on her son at a young age, but now he was sleeping over and spending entire weekends with his girlfriend. Although she, too, loved J. Marie – as did all the extended family and relatives, especially the men – this was going too far, in her book. There *had* to be a law against this sort of thing; it just had to be!

"Paul! Paul!!!" Connie shouted one day. Skip's dad never actually shouted an acknowledgement to many people; he'd simply head to the caller. He appeared in the doorway of the kitchen while his wife was rambling on to no one in particular while banging pots and pans around inside of the oven. She was bent over in the oven, so he just stood there admiring the view. It was his little wife's second greatest asset and he was suddenly turned on. She turned around to catch him…

"Oh, there you are. Paul, I don't like this business of Skippá shacking up over there not one bit. The boy ain't but fifteen years old and we could go to jail. What kind of person lets a fifteen-year-old boy stay with their daughter? What sort of message is it sending the rest of the children?" And on and on she went…

Paul sucked in the side of his lower bottom lip like he'd always do when faced with a situation, or about to come up with an answer to a problem. He was actually amused by the entire ordeal. "That damn Skippá," he thought. "Can't much say I blame the boy. The young girl is stacked." He, himself, had a steady girl he was "involve with" when he was about his son's age, maybe a year or two older. Paul had got a case of the crabs and his mom, Otilia, told him, "That's what you get when you hang around them ol' dirty girls." Nevertheless, for the sake of assuaging his wife's moral sensibilities he'd speak with Louise. "Damn," he thought to himself, "always something!"

Lou knew Skip was prone to getting into…stuff. She convinced Paul he was better off there with her and J. Marie than running the streets getting into trouble; she told Paul she'd help keep an eye on him.

Paul relayed the conversation he had with J. Marie's mother. Connie wanted to know something. Later Skip would smooth things over with his mom, if only a little; it would certainly be a cold day in July before they pulled a stunt like that under *her* roof – or so she said.

J. Marie graduated from Taft with little or no ado whatsoever. More than likely Skip would've made it to the ceremony had she mentioned it, or had he realized there was one. School for him was only a place where J. Marie was; if she'd been a volunteer at the old folk's home – he'd be there, too. If church were her thing – then he was going. For the most part he was just trying to be with her, wherever she was.

Skip, on the other hand, repeated eighth grade for the second straight year, once again for failure to attend. When he finally got into the ninth grade he was sixteen years old, with a driver's license and driving to school legitimately. Well, at least he was legit as far as having a license to drive; he was still driving hot cars to school; even selling them with bogus paper work. He was in cahoots with his old friends, Ricky Monk and Necie occasionally, to bid on old abandoned and/or confiscated cars from the monthly police auction at the impound lot in Blue Plains, Maryland. Only buying these heaps for the title, and serial number that was affixed to the driver's door (on Fords before 1969), he would afterwards go into Virginia or deep in Maryland to steal one of the exact same year and body style, change the paint color at "Earl Shyibe" for $29.95, change the wheel covers/hubcaps, then drive the car himself around town, especially amongst his associates as a demo – no one knew he was selling stolen cars, not even Ricky or Necie; all anyone knew was that Skip bought old cars, fixed them up, and sold them.

To get top dollar for the cars, he'd run them through one of the district's inspection stations, and who better to take a car through one of the stations than a little old lady.

Once, when Connie brought the '65 Ford back to her son with the diamond-shaped "rejected" sticker, she told her son the man at the station said the car had a small crack down low on the windshield. That was one that got by Skip, had he known about the crack he never would've snatched it; he took a loss on that one. Well not really; he sold it to his friend over in Fairfax Village, S.E.

Someone must have called themselves, putting a bug in Connie's ear, because one day she popped the driver's side door on one of the Lincoln Mark III's, copied down the serial numbers and mentioned something about "getting to the bottom of this stuff."

The next couple of days when Skip came by the house she told him, "Skippá, I took the serial number to the police station. They said they didn't have anything on it. Look boy, I don't know where you're getting all these cars from, but you'd better watch yourself." Skip was out of control. He was so negligent and unaware of the seriousness of his own corruption, he never gave the incident a second thought.

Skip and J. Marie were living a gloriously contented life as a couple under Lou's roof with the money they both earned. They kept the refrigerator and cabinets stacked with food. Skip was sixteen and starting to get a gut from J. Marie's weekend morning breakfasts. Five scrambled cheese-eggs, a half pack of Hungry Jack tender flake biscuits, hash-brown potatoes, five sausages or bacon strips, and orange juice will take its toll after a while. He was still knocking down beer too, albeit not in Lou's crib.

Paul was not the only one with a few noteworthy clichés in his repertoire. One of Connie's was, "Why buy the cow when you can get the milk for free?" Skip knew that was in reference to J. Marie and his sexcapades, and he not having to marry her. Her terse sayings may have sounded cold, nevertheless, they were always close to, or dead-on, the truth.

He convinced Connie to let him leave Taft to start night school. He was sixteen and asked her to let him handle working during the day and school at night. Connie and Paul thought he was finally getting his act together, sort of. Somehow his old friend, Dunmore, wound up there too. Dunmore was two years and grades ahead of Skip, and was actually about to graduate from Anacostia High; his admission was for extra credits. The night school campaign lasted all of three months for Skip, while Dunmore went on to graduate, and then on to Federal City College.

Skip and J. Marie were going to most all of the shows the various bands and singing groups performed. Skip was never short on wheels to get the two from point A to point B, and J. Marie never questioned him about it. That Christmas they exchanged leather coats; he got her an off-white ivory colored, full-length one from Greta Stevens, and she got him a slick long grey double-breasted one with a belt. He was helping her buy her school clothes because, as when Chick's older brother Cortez went to Eastern, it was all about fashion. It was still that way, and J. Marie fit right in.

When the "wet look" wear was in style for the girls, she had the boots and matching jackets, like Baskin Robbins – in all flavors. He bought her high school class ring, a beautiful piece of gold with a semi-squared-off back where the inside of the finger was, with a small "E" on an upraised centerpiece. The graduation ceremony was at Constitution Hall. She wore the shortest little fling dress ever designed with matching panties, made to be seen at the slightest bend; it was called a "sizzler." Skip was alright with it. Though after the ceremony, when she removed the gown – whew!

Chapter 6

MR. HUBERT SCRUGGS WAS FROM Birmingham, Alabama. He used to tell the story of being run out of town by the local rednecks when he was in his twenties. That would've been around the mid 1940s because he and Skip's dad were the same age. His sweetheart, Ethel, came up north with her man to make a new way in the seemingly up-and-coming section in D.C. called Anacostia. Through his veterans' G.I. home loan he was entitled money for a ten-thousand-dollar lot in Fort Stanton, complete with a finished semi-detached brick house with three bedrooms, for the children they anticipated. By the time the Lucases moved into the house around the corner, in which their backyards connected, the Scruggses were fifteen-year fixtures in the neighborhood.

Hubert and Ethel thought the Lucases were nice enough neighbors, except, maybe, Paul could be a bit forward, and even obnoxious at times; but only when he'd been drinking. The big-headed oldest son of theirs – who everyone called Skippá – seemed respectful and friendly, and he got along well with the other kids in the neighborhood.

The first group of friends Skip had when he moved into the neighborhood (Mark and Jr. Buchanan) lived next door to the Scruggs. Skip and Jr., the oldest brother, would cut the Scruggses' lawn, as well as several other residents around Fort Stanton. Front yard and back for three dollars. Scruggs watched the boys in Fort Stanton grow up; he and Ethel never had any of their own for some reason. So, years later, as the supervisor on his part-time job, when he had trouble getting the offices properly cleaned by his night crew, he left work, drove through Fort Stanton, and rounded up no less than a dozen guys he knew to be good working, respectable young men; Skip was one of them. It was an evening job at the Department of Agriculture just after the government workers got off, just like J. Marie's job, around the corner a ways, at H.U.D. In fact, Lou and Scruggs knew each other well; they had the same corporate managers. Sherman Blagly and Van Plunkett, two middle-aged junior playboys if Skip ever saw any. After six or eight months, Skip switched over to doing services for the company during the days, hustling and just hanging out at night. He also switched to the H.U.D. building, so now he was working in the building with Paul and J. Marie, only J. Marie was on the night shift. Lou landed a job as a Federal Protective Service police officer. She was one of the officers working the government buildings all throughout downtown Washington, D.C.

Although Skip's stint at Anacostia's night school lasted a short time, the day job he had as a helper and parts driver at Flood Plumbers lasted a bit longer. Things were fine until one day an assignment took him in the area of his old stomping grounds around Taft Jr. High during lunch period. Cindy, J. Marie's sister, was in her last year there, and he decided to drop by to see if she was hanging out, and she was. Somehow she wound up behind the wheel of the parts truck to test out her driving skills, of which she didn't have any; the truck ran through a man's fence. Skip took over the steering wheel and beat it out of the area with the quickness; however, not before someone phoned in the name of the company on the side of the truck. Needless to say, Skip was fired a few days later, though it wasn't a complete loss. He'd managed to hustle up a few hundred dollars hauling copper tubing and pipe to the scrap yard.

The first car Skip ever bought outright with the intention of keeping for himself, with no gimmick attached, was a 1967 Ford Fairlane GT. It was midnight-blue with a black vinyl top and black interior; a real street racer if there ever was one. Within a month's time he'd added the extra-wide L-50 back tires and Cragar Mag wheels; it was jacked up high in the back, and it had that hot-rod sound. It had bucket seats with the gear shifter in the floor of the console, a big V-8 engine that was powerful enough to peal the rubber off the oversized rear tires.

With J. Marie riding shotgun, he'd been in several street races and won them all except one – well, two if one included the time he took the car to the race track to compete. A white guy's '57 Chevy beat him by three car lengths in the quarter-mile. That souped-up rod was a head turner, sure enough. It was stocked with 90% stolen parts. It could fly!

Skip was turning 15 seconds in the quarter-mile, which wasn't bad for a kid back then, and J. Marie loved all the attention the car brought them when they catted around the city, especially when Skip picked her up from work at night. He never left her waiting because, come hell or high water, he was putting the pedal to the metal when it came to picking her up. It was ten o'clock sharp! His friends would pan and tease him about dropping whatever he would be doing when it drew near ten o'clock, but they all knew what time it was. Chick and Steve would usually take the ride with him; J. Marie was like part of the crew.

The apartment on Anacostia Road was too small, no ifs, ands or buts about it. Four, sometimes five, people would occupy the little bachelorette pad on any given day; it was time to go.

In 1972 Lou moved her crew into a much larger apartment in the new Edgewood Terrace community in N.E., Washington, just off 4th and Rhode Island Avenue, not far from Dickey's house on 12th Street. This was a four-bedroom joint with two bathrooms, one of which was in Lou's bedroom. Lou had her own little getaway, with a boudoir!

Eventually all her children would make their way back to her; that's just how kids are. A son will sooner or later seek out to reunite with his mother, and likewise a daughter will do the same with her dad. That is unless the father was so deviant or perverse that he caused disdain and destroyed the bond.

The car Skip used to stock his fast Ford with was one he and Steve snatched while the two were out looking for a mark; it was identical as far as the body type and year. After taking the hot rod to one of their many "drop spots" in S.E. they left it, only to come back a couple days later when they had time to truly molest this trick. They would also have the third musketeer (Chick); the three of them together could strip a car down to practically nothing within fifteen minutes. Like a NASCAR pit crew at Daytona, each one had an assignment. Skip got his wheels and pipes that night. He also got an added feature he'd yet to affix to the hot rod; an aluminum high-rise manifold with three deuces (three two-barrel carburetors to give his street machine more power).

That was several months ago, and now he and Sterling had the hood up on Skip's fast Ford about to do some major surgery. Skip knew how to break stuff down well enough, but adding manifolds and carburetors, and hooking up hoses and gas lines were way out of his league. He had Sterling with him to help and oversee it all because, after all, Sterling was the youngest Proctor brother. And everybody in Fort Stanton knew Ronald, Lynwood, and Wardell Proctor, who were the Lucases' next door neighbors, were the car-fixingnest dudes east of the Anacostia River; their skills were legendary. Unfortunately, it didn't trickle down to Sterling. The operation ran into major complications about midway through, and now it was getting dark. Skip wasn't thinking straight. They'd started the operation off with a couple of six-packs and the highest expectations. Three hours later he began to see things going downhill. Sterling's pace slowed, and then there would be the mono-syllabic grunts and reactions. The kicker was, "Skip, I'm gonna have to check with Wardell about why this line won't hook up." Or maybe it was, "where this line goes." Either way, Sterling left. Skip was frustrated, and within minutes he and Chick were stripping off the remaining salvageable parts, to include replacing the Mag wheels and tires with junk rims and onion skins. Next they pushed the once-adored racer onto Gainsville Street behind Chick's apartment building. Two days later it was towed away.

Immediately J. Marie asked Skip, "Where's the car?" He told her the car was having a few "repair complications."

"Repair complications? But, Skip, the car was fine the other day," she went on. "What's the matter with it?"

"J. Marie, you don't understand these things, see. The car was, ahh, misfiring; it just wasn't right." She'd been with him long enough to know when he was stunting. She only took one of her deep penetrating looks that bore through him; the look that said all she didn't care to verbalize. That, "Yeah, Negro, you f'ed up, didn't you? Where's the damn car?" The ride home in Connie's car was a quiet one.

He juggled cars for the remainder of the month. A couple nights he used Connie's car, Steve's at other times, or he asked Steve to give J. Marie and him a lift to Edgewood Terrace. Other times…well, somebody just came up short. To have J. Marie waiting for a bus at night was out of the question; it wasn't even on the table for discussion. Since Taft, or rather, the entire time the two were dating, J. Marie never took public transportation at night. Skip never even imagined it.

One of the angriest times, so far, Skip had seen J. Marie was the night shortly after the catastrophic mechanic job on the Fairlane. He knew J. Marie knew he screwed that racer up big time. She never let it be known what she truly thought of how it all went down; Skip played the entire cover-up down. It began with the botched upgrade, to dumping it on the street like discarded trash, to never mentioning it to her in the first place, at the outset saying, "Ahh, Phats? I'm planning to make some major adjustments to the car, and I don't exactly have a clue as to what I'm doing…"

This was the longest stretch the couple had ever gone without their own wheels. After close to a month, the two, along with several friends from the N.E. area, met up at one of the Duff shows a R.F.K. Skip, J. Marie and a couple of her sisters were dropped off there earlier that afternoon. The others they knew met up in the stadiums parking lot after near rioting and tear gas canceled the bands' performances, the partying, and everything.

The entire group, about seven or eight, decided to foot it back to Edgewood and the Brookland area during the late evening, as it was now dark. The fastest route took the group behind J. Marie's school, Eastern High, across Bladensburg Road, then down and around past Mount Olivert Cemetery's rear on West Virginia Avenue in N.E. In someone's attempt to create a climate of terror, being how they were all a bit apprehensive about passing by the graveyard, a few began expressing thoughts of seeing or hearing…something. When the mood was just right, someone screamed, "Aah! Did you see that?!" Someone took off running. Cindy or Sharon snatched off their shoes for better traction; for more emphasis the guys ran, too. Skip ran to support J. Marie, who stubbed her toe and was now limping. When they finally got past the cemetery they were all out of breath, one or two of the girls sniffling from crying. J. Marie's Chinese-like eyes found Skip's and he could see that she was seething, "Why the hell did you have to get rid of that car?!"

"Here we go," Skip thought to himself. Sooner or later he knew that she'd get around to it. Of all the cars he'd had up until this point, she'd never said anything or much of anything about their sudden disappearance. She wasn't used to walking these long stretches like Skip was; not since her days at the Kalorama Road Skating Rink. Tonight, she was not very friendly.

Skip wasn't usually one to ask obvious questions, so he knew that now would not be the best of times to start, especially now while J. Marie was tired, angry and in her present state of mind. There was no need, although he thought of it, of commenting on ownership of the car, stating whose car it legitimately was in the first place. No, he knew his girl was right and the best thing to do was what that injured little bird should have done when the factory worker found it in the cold; the worker placed the bird in the steamy, warm cow crap. The little bird would've done good to keep his mouth shut, and then he or she wouldn't have gotten eaten by the passing wolf. The story was in one of Maya Angelou's books; one of the few passages he'd read in a book Connie had laying around the house.

Skip let J. Marie get it all out on that long walk back to the apartment, and never said a word. By the next morning, the two of them woke up as they always did when Skip stayed over – wrapped in each other's arms. They'd never stay angry with one another long, not even when she sailed his leather Dutch-boy hat out of the car window (that would be when he had the '69 Galaxy convertible) while they drove down Rhode Island Ave. She thought it was hilarious the way he whipped the car over, jumped out and ducked in and out of traffic amid honking car horns and yelled insults. J. Marie truly let out a good laugh when she and Skip were together, usually at his expense. Skip could be the funniest guy she'd ever known at times. Even after they got back to the apartment following the hat incident, she was laughing as he told her, "Don't do that again, baby. I could've gotten hit by a car, let alone ruining my hat. What's wrong with you?" J. Marie only snatched the hat off of his head and sailed it across the room onto the floor, still laughing.

They would always wrestle in Lou's room; J. Marie was strong and thick. Skip would joke that she was only a big Whopper away from being a fat girl. If Skip would position himself behind her just right, she could body slam him onto the floor. The two would play hard together; and it's how Skip's cap was once dislodged from his front tooth. Once Lou's glass coffee table wasn't pushed back far enough and Skip's foot came down hard on the edge after J. Marie flipped him. Fortunately, it wasn't hard enough to shatter it. Now he wondered what was causing her to take things this far, all in the guise of fun? Was there a line being drawn in the sand?

This would be the first and last time Skip ever slapped her – suddenly and more reflexively, rather than with malicious intent. He didn't regret it though. She took on a fighter's stance against him and just cried convulsively. Skip just looked at his girl, thinking any moment her brothers and sisters would enter in upon him. A few moments later he reached out to place his arm around her shoulder. She allowed him to guide her head onto his chest, while she cried it all out.

Two days after the run down West Virginia Avenue, past the cemetery, Skip had another whip, mysteriously, out of the clear blue like the others.

The big, red rag-top Galaxy that J. Marie sailed his hat from while they rode down Rhode Island Avenue; she took to it like a seal to the sea. He surprised her with it one weekend afternoon when she and Tawanna were in the living room at Edgewood. Tawanna wasn't more than eleven, but loved being around her big sister and Skip. She thought Skip was a good boyfriend for her sister, and that they looked like a perfect match. Tawanna was still living at the house on 12th Street with David and Gary, under Dickey's roof, and she, too, wanted to be with Lou.

Skip came into the living room from the opened balcony door; he thought they had a bad habit of leaving it open. It was on the ground floor and anyone could enter pretty much at will. He greeted the girls as he entered, sat down, and made small talk with Tawanna before asking J. Marie did they want to take a ride through Haines Point. Before she could respond, Tawanna beat her to the punch. "Yeah! I wanna go," she squealed. J. Marie looked at her little sister and smiled, playfully shaking her head "no."

As the trio exited the apartment building, Skip noticed the girls looking to the alley at the pretty red convertible parked in the spot he usually parked in when he just planned to run into the apartment and right back out again; Skip would never blow the horn for her. J. Marie had a feeling the convertible was Skip's all along, especially when she didn't see anything else familiar. As they crossed the street towards the car, she just looked at him subtly, and quietly she said, "Oh yeah!"

"Yeah, after the way you blew up on me the other night, you know I had to get back on track," Skip responded wryly.

The exchange wasn't lost on Tawanna; she, along with Sharon and Cindy, was with them running past the cemetery too, scared and half crying. It was one of the angriest times she'd seen her sister. Poor Skip had caught it that night. Afterwards, she thought the run funny as hell; not that all of us, including the guys, would've fit into Skip's old hot rod anyway, but she would've certainly had a spot and she would bet money on it.

This afternoon, however, was another day altogether; she was about to be on the road again with big sis. She hopped right up front to secure her place, leaned on the armrest and held the seat forward for J. Marie to climb into the rear. It was unfathomable to think that J. Marie would get in the back seat of one of Skip's cars, considering J. Marie was with him, and she made this known immediately. "Girl, get your tail in the back," J. Marie told her younger sister affectionately. Skip looked at Tawanna and smiled, half laughing. Once everyone was settled into their perspective places, Skip and J. Marie each leaned on the armrest as he cranked up the big Ford. J. Marie adjusted the radio finally settling on one the girl's favorite and familiar melodies and they were off.

Skip's first stop was usually at a store that sold beer and wine. Whether he was cruising the parks or not, he was getting himself a tall Schlitz Bull. He knew the girls would want a Royal Crown soda; Tawanna was just like her sister in that regard, and had also begun to get a little acne across her cheeks.

He and J. Marie would go to many of the concerts and shows the latest groups and artists performed at. Skip, J. Marie, and her sisters would most often make their way out to the Capital Centre, Constitution Hall, The Warner Theater, and upon the Wilson Liner cruise ship on the night time runs to Marshall Hall. Usually it would be a go-go band performing onboard. Skip couldn't dance, except for with the slow drag cuts ,where he'd grind with J. Marie; later on he'd learn to do a few moves to blend in with a crowd.

J. Marie, however, along with her sisters and Lou, was a dancing machine, especially Lou. They were all exciting and full of energy.

Skip was selling hot cars outright, hand over fist. It was his best payday ever and he didn't need a gun. Sometimes his friend Chick's brother would contract him to get one for a heist he and his boys had planned, but it would always have to be the fast, luxury type. Chick's oldest brother was a "gangster" with a serious and bona fide bank-robbery crew. He was in and out of the various federal prison facilities in the early 1970s when it seemed like southeast Washington was putting out stickup boys like they were coming out of an academy.

You could tell who most of them were by their dress and the cars many of them drove; they wore their trade on their sleeves, flaunted it, and Skip wanted in.

Oldest friend Chick

COME JOIN THE FORT STANTON FAMILY AS WE CELEBRATE BIG CHICK & SKIP LUCAS.

No matter how hard he tried to get J. Marie knee-deep in his corruption, she'd bend but never break. When Skip started dealing with guns, she didn't sweat him about carrying one, but she'd never touch them. Most times the firearms were left in her bedroom, because there were too many children at his own home in S.E. Besides, he was there with her more. He could understand her not wanting to go anywhere near the sawed-off 12-guage, but he figured the nickel-plated .25 automatic he'd gotten along with cash from a car sale would be ideal for her own personal accessory. She was immutable; she was smart enough not to take part in what Skip was calling her to, clearly going along with her better judgment. He never tried to force any exchange between them; he knew his girl well enough to know when she had her mind made up and settled on a position.

One night, he and J. Marie left one of the movie theaters along U Street, the Republic Theater, after enjoying *Coffee*, starring the buxom Pam Grier. As they walked to the car, to his chagrin, the interior's light was on, suggesting a break-in. He knew what would be missing as soon as he looked to the rear seat; his pea coat was gone. And as an added bonus for the thief, so was the sawed-off he had under the coat. He and Danny Head planned on using it that previous night for a hold up, and he never put it back in J. Marie's closet.

J. Marie knew most of Skip's friends and associates, however, there were several he didn't want her to know, nor them her. These were his top-of-the-list rogue crime partners (Necie, Ricky Monk and Buggs). Chick and Steve were boy scouts compared to these dudes. Skip hadn't dealt with Necie in several months after torching his brother's car; their relationship was tepid these days.

The liquor store robbery wasn't planned; it was a spur-of-the moment idea that Skip and Danny had decided on. They'd been out that evening randomly robbing and mugging anyone they thought had cake, point blank. Later that night, close to closing time, they entered into the 4th Street liquor store. Skip was holding the cut-off butt-end of the sawed-off while holding a brown paper bag up around it, his finger ready on the trigger. The two would-be robbers were in over their heads with this one. Had it not been for the fact that the store clerk was stocking shelves for the following day in the glass-enclosed refrigerator, Skip and Danny would've made the 10:00 pm news that evening. Although the attempted robbery fell through thanks to Danny signaling Skip to abort the mission, Skip never transferred the weapon from the car back to J. Marie's. Now it was gone, and good riddance. Someone did Skip a favor that night by stealing that piece, because he would have made headlines with it sooner or later.

As Skip lay kicked back in Lou's living room sipping a cold one, Lou burst through the front door of the apartment, letting her car keys drop noisily upon the glass table. She was mumbling something about someone being impossible to teach as she walked down the hall to her back bedroom. Then she yelled back over her shoulder, "Skip, you teach her!" Moments later J. Marie came through the door with that dimpled trademark smile of hers, showing her front teeth.

"What's up, Phats?" Skip greeted her.

"Nothin', 'cept Lou don't have any patience. Skip, will you teach me how to drive…and how to park?"

Skip was totally unprepared for this one, caught off guard with this new and sudden juncture in their relationship; he was momentarily stunned. He'd been so engulfed in his own hot-wheel revelry, it had never occurred to him to teach J. Marie how to drive. "Damn," he thought, "I should've thought of this a long time ago."

She proved a most attentive and competent student; Skip would take her to the R.F.K. Stadium parking lot for her to get the feel of the wheel; turning, accelerating, breaking and driving in reverse. He gave her the raw basics. None of that stuff about holding her hands at 10:00 and 2:00 while they were on the steering wheel, and not a whole lot about using the rearview mirrors while backing up. Skip taught Chick and Steve how to maneuver a wheel when the two of them were thirteen and fourteen, and like with J. Marie, it was on one of the larger-bodied cars. Skip's preference was what she used to practice on; Lincolns and Galaxies, and who cared if she tore a few of them up in the process. They weren't actually his anyway. "Collateral damages," he humorously thought.

Of course, she passed the written and hands-on driver's tests on her first attempt with flying colors, and graded higher than Skip when he took the test. J. Marie didn't make a big deal of outscoring her mentor; that's just how she was. But inwardly Skip was mystified and somewhat baffled. He'd considered himself to be "like that" as far as driving was concerned. Besides he had been driving since he was eleven years old, and good enough to drive in traffic since twelve. Connie hated his driving; the fact was Skip was reckless, less focused, and impatient. Later, J. Marie would distinguish herself a much better driver than her boyfriend. At high speeds, she'd be totally concentrated; hanging turns during inclement weather. She was cautious, not easily distracted like Skip, and she was exceptionally skilled turning with the skid during the snow or on icy spots.

J. Marie, now able to drive, was a definite benefit to Skip, as well as herself. Skip was drinking and smoking reefer more often now. Sometimes when he'd pick her up from work at night he'd be tore up from the floor up! She wondered how he ever made it to meet her in the condition he was in to begin with. She would be even more furious at whoever allowed him behind the wheel in the first place.

Whether it was one of the hot rods or a Lincoln Continental, she would take over the wheel when he was in this state of inebriation; she'd be pissed off, too.

On one such occasion Skip arrived, on time as usual, but intoxicated, smoked out, and with a big German Shepherd in the car!

"Get out, Skip. I'm driving," she told him. "Don't make no sense. Look at you," she finished as she shoved him over into the passenger's seat, replacing him behind the steering wheel. "They'd surely have to talk," she thought to herself, about all the drinking, guns, and recreational drugs, and he's only seventeen. Damn, how will he be five or ten years from now? She never asked about the cars – and there were many of them. She didn't worry about him messing around with other girls, but told him if she ever thought he was shooting dope he could kiss her goodbye, because it would be over.

Skip thought, "Hell, if this needle thing is the only thing compelling enough to force her departure, then we must gonna be hangin' out *forever*." Skip had a phobia when it came to syringes, especially being injected in his veins. Of all the faults or negative vices he had – needles were not one of them; nor would they ever be. He was also astraphobic – fearful of being out in lightning.

No sooner had his probationary time expired from juvenile family court, he was jammed up again. His probation officer, Mr. Blue, had an office on Martin Luther King, Jr. Avenue, S.E., right across the street from the main gate of Saint Elizabeth's Mental Hospital. After meeting with Mr. Blue one evening, and on the way out, his probation officer began wrapping things up for the day and wound up walking out with Skip all the way to the parking lot, where Skip had his latest means of transportation parked.

Skip made a major faux pas; he walked straight to where he had his latest car parked. Another Galaxy, this one was sky blue and looked like an unmarked police car (the transmission went out on the convertible that he had, so he dumped it in a cul-de-sac just outside Fort Stanton).

Mr. Blue noticed the fifty-cent-sized hole in the trunk of the car before he seemed to see the car itself. Skip would change the ignition switch in these cars so he could have keys to start it; however, the trunk and door locks weren't exactly his forte. He could never lock the doors of these cars and had to open the trunk with a screwdriver through the lock he'd knocked out. Except on the Lincolns, where the trunk release was in the glove compartment, as well as on the trunk itself. Nevertheless, Skip knew he'd made a huge mistake this time.

"Whose car is this?" Mr. Blue asked Skip.

"A friend of mine is selling it and I'm thinking of buying it," Skip responded.

"Oh yeah, is that right…okay. See you in two weeks," Mr. Blue finished as he departed, and that was it. Skip breathed a sigh of relief as he thought to himself, "Had Blue questioned him further in the matter or asked to see some paperwork, as he should have, Skip would've been like a fish too long out of water. Instead, Skip was allowed to proceed on his way, his probation officer going on his.

This was one of the cars Skip kept for several months. He'd picked up a single Maryland tag for it out on the highway where it had simply fallen off someone's car. These tags would be good for the rest of the year; in most cases, they wouldn't be reported stolen, if they were reported at all. In Maryland, one could get away with displaying only a single tag, unlike in D.C., where they wanted you driving with both.

Skip and J. Marie were seventeen, had enough money to be comfortable with, mainly because they were living at home or at each other's homes sometimes, and were the envy of most of the young people they knew. J. Marie was a financial wizard with the meager amount she made working part-time after school; Skip, on the other hand, was never any good with his money. He would run through it like it was water.

Though he was getting money from various endeavors besides working, he didn't keep it long; he often thought of his father's patent one-line phrases: "A fool and his money are soon parted."

Skip knew he could not continue on as he was. He desired something better, even at seventeen he felt this menial multitasking was far from *apropos*. He was working in the same building as Paul and would occasionally run into his old man. Paul was basically just glad to know his son was working and enjoying himself while he was young; he figured the boy would get himself together sooner or later.

Ironically, Skip and J. Marie worked for the same company – he full-time during the day, and her part-time at night. Paul would see them both from time to time. Skip's dad was sporting a new look these days. He now wore his hair in the afro-bush style and he was getting most of his clothes from his son's collection of cabaret and concert gear, which were mostly double-knit flared slacks, leather boot-type shoes, and the larger collar colorful matching shirt; Paul had turned into a pretty hip old guy.

Skip and J. Marie probably smoked more reefers during those days then in their entire life, especially Skip. J. Marie wouldn't indulge much unless Skip was on the scene, and even then, unlike him, she knew how far she wanted to go. With Skip and some of his "get-high crew" … they'd have to be all but passed out before they would tap out.

No one could hang with the McRaven Brothers (Joe and Al) when it came to smoking reefers. These dudes wouldn't take any hostages when they cranked up the special miniature-bullhorn bowl they used for a pipe. Joe and Al had their own crew from mostly Fairfax Village that Skip and his boys knew from the days at Douglas Jr. High, and who J. Marie had just gotten to know from working part-time in the evening at H.U.D.; they worked there also.

One day Joe, the eldest brother (to whom Skip had just recently sold one of his cars), mentioned he would not be working with Skip much longer because he'd joined the armed military service – specifically the Army. He told Skip there was a recruiter out on Suitland Road that made a good case concerning some interesting points, as well as talked about some lucrative benefits.

That July Skip was in Fort Dix, New Jersey; he turned eighteen in basic training the same day his drill sergeant came to him with the company's flag telling him he was the "guide arm barer" for Charlie Company. Sergeant Dubose gave him the company flag with explicit instructions on how and when to lower it. He also told him that he should learn how to spin and twirl it while they ran during drills, and "if you ever drop it, Private Lucas, me and you have problems, and it won't be pretty." Drill Sergeant Dubose was only 5'5", and the blackest, meanest son of a gun Skip had ever encountered; more so than even Bruce James, and he was about 6'4", two sixty. (The James family was, by far, the toughest family in Fort Stanton; there were two boys and three girls. Their house was directly behind Connie's, with a fence bordering the two yards. They'd all liked Skip since he was a small kid, and treated him like family; especially Mr. and Mrs. James, and the middle girl, Linda.)

While Skip was in basic training, catching hell, J. Marie was spending most her days thinking about him being so far away. This was during the end of the Vietnam era, and the United States had begun pulling troops out in 1973, so she wasn't to overly concerned about him getting injured or killed in combat.

She'd play many of the sad tear-jerkers she used to listen to when she was younger. She would sit out on her friend April's porch listening to these records and singing along with her closest cousins Kool-Aid, Wonda, Beverly, and Gwynn. The more she sang, the more miserable she got. She was back to running the household, over her sisters and brothers like she did over on 12th Street, only now she was grown. How long before she could be in her own place, just her and Skip like they used to talk about on the playground at Taft?

She'd write Skip often and he'd write her back, sending her money from his military pay. He was getting two hundred eighty dollars per month and didn't have much planned for it, so he'd send most to her.

He didn't have a car to keep up any more; not that upkeep was straining him to begin with, because as soon as something went wrong with one of his rides, he'd dump it on the street somewhere and get another one.

The car he had just before he joined the Army he gave to Al McRaven; it was, perhaps, J. Marie and his favorite of all, and the two of them pushed it to the limit for about ten months. A four-year-old Lincoln Continental Mark III – fully automatic, everything! Eyeballs were on the young couple like nobody's business; they relished in the attention, too. Skip would've left the car with her if he didn't fear reprisals from the authorities. Al might be able to deal with any unforeseen calamities a little better. Besides that, if the big monstrosity had mechanical problems

J. Marie might put it in the shop to spend a fortune in repairs, whereas Al would dump it. Skip's old crime partner and counterpart Necie had picked the Lincoln out for himself one night. A few days later he gave it to Skip while he, himself, took a hold of a brand-new blue Cadillac El Dorado with a white convertible top. Yes, Skip was sure he couldn't leave the Lincoln with J. Marie, even though she was driving like an old pro by now. Man, if she got jammed up with it – it'd be catastrophic. He shuddered at the thought.

Basic training was eight weeks. After the fourth week the men were allowed home on furlough for the weekend. Not so with Skip. He failed to qualify on the rifle range and couldn't leave until the following week. While most of all the trainees took leave, Skip stayed around the barracks perfecting and honing his skills with the flag. He carried it out in front of the company everywhere they marched, and he was good. Spinning it overhead as they ran, twirling it in front, you name it and he was able to pull it off. Drill Sergeant Dubose liked the choice he made selecting Private Lucas for the job. Once, when Skip got caught by the captain doubling up in line for an extra piece of cake, he had to do fifty-five pushups with his full pack, rifle and all – and without putting the flag down. Skip clamped onto the flag with his teeth, but only managed to do fifty.

The first place he directed the cab driver from Union Station was Edgewood Terrace apartments, still in his dress-brown khakis (Army summer dress). His face was clean shaven, his stomach flat, no more soft beer gut. After he pulled up in front of her apartment building, J. Marie almost tripped down the concrete stairs running to meet him as he stepped out of the taxi; she was crying.

There's something surreal about a service man coming home, or anyone coming back to their loves ones after spending time away, for that matter. He had two days home leave with his baby. She looked as sexy as ever and he was trying to "get with her" in a real big way. This was the longest they'd ever been apart. She cried hysterically in June when he explained he would be gone for at least a month. Skip was the object of her desire, *numero uno,* despite the drinking, stealing, guns, foul liquor-smelling breath, and cussing. Skip couldn't stand to see the black eyeliner running down her cheeks when she cried. The stuff would never totally wash out of his T-shirts; she had stained up a many of them through the years.

They were so much alike in their demeanor, taste in clothing, music, recording artists, and family history, although her family was larger than his. She had, by far, way more relatives than he did. J. Marie was soft spoken, unlike skip, at times; they complimented each other beautifully.

When Skip and J. Marie were as young as fourteen they'd talked of having children and a house somewhere with a fence. Back then, though, they just appeared to be the innocent dreams and musings of the youth; of two people that some inquired as to whether they were brother and sister. Skip would often get annoyed at the question from strangers. He thought of her as his better half and trusted her unconditionally; however, he doubted if she trusted him as much. Since they'd been together she was the only girl he'd been with. After all, she *did* have a traffic-stopping body. He needed not seek out the comforts of another; anytime he extended a hand to her, she responded immediately by freely falling into his arms. She never gave him reason to seek out another girl – like her mother had told him for years, "Skip, you're pussy-whipped." How right she was!

Paul and Connie were very proud of their first born all of a sudden. He was in the Army; it was the best move he could have made at the time. They showed their coworkers and the neighbors the waist-up photos that the military provides its servicemen. Those photographs stay with families years after the person is dead. Skip remembered seeing those same 8" x 10" framed pictures of his uncles on the mantle of Grandma Lucas's house up on W Street in N.W. His father was discharged early from the Army because of a bad heart. Skip's recruiter, Sergeant Warren set up an appointment where Skip was to go to his father's old alma mater, Armstrong High School, to take the high school equivalency test; amazingly Skip passed the test and received a diploma… Go figure.

Chapter 7

GRADUATION DAY FROM BASIC TRAINING was three weeks after Skip's first trip home on furlough. J. Marie wanted to be there when he carried the company flag at the front of Charlie 1-3. Connie and Paul expressed to her they didn't think it was a good idea, a young attractive girl traveling alone on the train up to New Jersey. Though Skip wanted desperately to see her, he agreed with his parents and resolved to see her the following week after the ceremony. Had he been thinking, or had fully assessed the situation, he could've sent enough money for Lou, or one of her brothers Gary or Robert to accompany her.

He was sure the proudest his parents had ever been of him was when they first saw him home from boot camp in his khakis, complete with shiny brass insignias, a couple of ribbons, and a marksman's medal. After boot camp and A.I.T. (training for his military profession – eight weeks later) he would be stationed in Fort Eustis, Virginia, just outside Williamsburg, not far from his Aunt Lucy (Connie's eldest sister).

She lived in Hampton, and the last time Skip was there, he and a few of his rogue friends (Chick, Steve and Nooks) rode there supposedly to the Hampton Jazz Festival in one of his stolen cars (two years ago). Not only did they not make the show, but took the longest way possible coming from Washington. By the time they arrived it was daybreak; they had no gas and no money. And all that was left for them was to make it to Lucy's house to rest up and hopefully acquire provisions to make it back to D.C.

His dearly beloved Aunt couldn't have accommodated the boys better, she fed them fresh fried fish, gave them a pitcher of ice lemon tea, she let them camp out in lawn chairs in the front yard to rest up, and then gave them gas money and directions to put them on the route they should have taken in the first place (I-95). She had no idea the car in her driveway was hot.

In Fort Eustis, Va., Skip visited his aunt once or twice a month; she worked as a civilian in the records/administrative offices on the base. He'd trained at Fort Dix to be a tractor trailer and other large truck operator. He was still young and immature, and he never fully acclimated himself into Army life. Perhaps an older, more settled man would've found a setup like this easy. He also missed J. Marie like one would miss their own breathing.

Although Skip was close to several guys on post, he would seldom stay through the weekend to hang out with them. A new apartment complex opened up in Edgewood Terrace, called Edgewood Section II. Skip thought it a good idea to put J. Marie up in an apartment so that, for one, when he drove up on the weekend they would have their own place; another thing was, at nineteen, they were old enough to start living an adult life. Another plus was, the place wasn't fifty yards from her mom and siblings. They needed to go furniture shopping to lay out their new crib, and somewhere along the way Skip picked up a brand-new Buick convertible, it was gorgeous! Ruby red (Skip's birthstone) or maybe it was Garnet (J. Maries birthstone); nevertheless, it was indeed the couple's prettiest means of transportation yet. It had a white convertible top with matching white interior, AM/FM stereo with Bose speakers. Skip was able to fly up and down I-95 each Friday after morning formation. He'd put the cruise control on sixty and the car would practically drive itself to J. Marie.

He and J. Marie were doing okay. They had a new car, new crib, and kept the car's convertible top down. Skip would pick up J. Marie and her sisters for rides like he had keys to the city. He was spending more time at Connie's too. He'd take the Buick there occasionally to wash it in front of the house, and run store errands for his mom. Not saying he was totally legit by any stretch of the word. After all, the car was of dubious acquisition. He'd fanazzled a set of tags to keep the authorities unaroused, and yes, all in all, he was up to his old tricks again.

Opportunity would knock in the form of the unsuspected servicemen trying to make big impressions on their kith and kin folf when going home on leave, to South Carolina, Maine, Tennessee, Oregon, wherever! The further away from the District and Maryland the better for Skips "revamped" whole-sale car operation. Skip stumbled upon the new venture by pure accident; one of his servicemen-friends inquired about how he'd sure like to take the Buick home to impress his hometown homies, and would Skip care to rent it, or even sell it to him (that's when the larceny Skip had within him came out).

"Man, you know what, actually the car belongs to a repo man I know. And if the woman don't make the payment on it, it's gone, for real cheap"

"How cheap, Luke?"

The car that was initially for his and J. Marie's pleasure was on the market after only several months.

"But look," as was his opening pitch, "there's a process in getting the paperwork finalized, sometimes it takes a while."

Skips days were numbered as a serviceman, once again living on the edge. He was staying in D.C. almost as much as he was at the base. On Monday mornings, he would still be lyin' in bed with J. Marie, instead of in formation. He'd call the company clerk with tales of flat tires, stolen batteries, and once, that his Aunt died suddenly. "I'll be there shortly." After a few more car sales, and a year of "failure to conform," the United States Army determined Private Lucas eligible for one of two options, either he would take a "General Discharge" with close to full benefits, and under honorable conditions, or he would be subject to a "Chapter 13" with very little or no benefits at all.

The only reason Skip joined the Army in the first place was for the benefits, now if these people were willing to give them to him in less than the required time of 2 years active, 2 inactive, all well and good; as far as he was concerned it wasn't a bad trade-off.

On one of his last trips to visit J. Marie from the base, while she was using the bathroom at Lou's, she came out looking pale and dizzy. She informed Skip she thought she may have miscarried, but did not have to go to the hospital or anything. Otherwise, she seemed okay, despite being a little upset. He didn't quite understand it all, but comforted her as best he could; sometimes Skip was at a total loss at what should be the best of most logical response, so he wouldn't say anything, and instead would look to her for the next move.

Around the same time he was early released from the Army, he and J. Marie were asked by the super intendant of Section II, to move because of reports of marijuana smoke constantly filtering into the hallway coming from their unit. This was a new high rise and they weren't having it – in no uncertain terms. To Skip and J. Marie, fortunately, it was not a big deal to have to move out. J. Marie was back with Lou, and Skip was in the house at Fort Stanton; he'd redone half of the basement to suit his taste with the look of a bachelor pad, albeit an efficiency bachelor pad, and some of the perks. Connie had her boy back. Skip and his old friend "Dunmore,' down the street, drove to Georgetown one day; they found a little "head shop" of sorts selling all types of paraphernalia, and water beds.

He bought a few odd and ins to accessorize the place, including several yards of see-through "sheer" to encircle the water bed, which he'd built a platform for to raise it off the floor a foot. After dropping a blue light inside the curtain, and throwing a thick white fur piece on the bed, the joint had the look of a "harem" straight out of an Arabian palace.

J. Marie fell in love with the cozy little getaway, especially the waterbed. She wasn't hard to make happy given the right atmosphere, and people involved. They never really had a whole lot to this point, but they had always had each other since they were fourteen, and ninety percent of the time they had a car…a nice one.

Lou passed the test to become a Federal Protection Agency officer. She was lovin' it! A big shot government police officer carrying a .38 and handcuffs, the whole kit and caboodle. Sharon was off to Job Corps in West Virginia somewhere; no one heard much from her.

One day as Skip and J. Marie headed out Branch Avenue in Connie's little Colt wagon, she confided in him as to the stunt her father tried to pull. Again, she cried while Skip listened, plotting.

Again, he regretted not having the right words to console his other heart, the love of his life, especially when she needed it most. The only thing he knew that soothed her, usually, in such situations was to hold her and tell her he loved her. Later, he'd take a ride over to Dickey's new place and torch his car, for starters.

While Skip and J. Marie lay on the water bed one evening in his folk's basement, just kickin' it about everything and nothing in particular, he was called from upstairs by Paul. Only to find his old adopted uncle (Mr. Scruggs) having a drink with his old man, and spitting those little tobacco leaf flakes that come off cigars on his mom's carpet. Mr. Scruggs kept a cigar in his mouth, lit or unlit. This one wasn't lit, not in Connie's house, even though she smoked too.

Mr. Scruggs loved the fact that Skip went into the armed services, got a good discharge status, and wasn't a miscreant as far as he knew. Mr. Scruggs knew J. Marie and her mother Lou, and liked that they were all, in some regards, one big family. This filial affection he had for the young couple compelled him to help Skip help himself via of a gainful means of employment. He informed Skip if he were to go to the Civil Service Bureau downtown, fill out an application for a particular slot in the hospital, where Mr. Scruggs himself worked, he assured Skip the position would be his. However, before he concluded, he asked, "you don't mind working with dead people do you?" Although blindsided by the question, without giving it much thought, Skip said, "no." Skip quickly assessed the question as well as visualized a scenario and surmised Mr. Scruggs could, at most, be talking about moving bodies from one place to another. A month later after the paperwork, job clearance, security clearance, etc., Skip was an official government employee, GS-2. Job title: Autopsy Assistant.

Scruggs was the supervisor over three people that worked in the chemistry department at the Veterans Administration Medical Center in D.C. He an Lemule Woodfork, from the now-defunct Woodfork Funeral Home, assisted the resident pathologist performing autopsies; now Skip would join the team, after a lot of on the job training. Barbara Smith was under Scruggs's supervision also, but her duties were limited to the sterilization room. The men would help her out if things were slow in the morgue. The glassware from the laboratory's chemistry department were sterilized in the sterilization room by soaking them in a five-gallon heat-resistant plastic bucket of soap and water, then setting them in an autoclave, which, after the pressurized door was sealed, could reach temperatures of two hundred degrees or higher. Some test tubes were acid washed; this process was a potentially dangerous one. The highly corrosive liquid could splash, burning any vulnerable material in its range. It's how Skip almost lost his eye.

For the first few days on Skip's new job, things were slow, and he still wasn't totally clear on his morgue responsibilities, where exactly he fit in with relation to the pathology staff, as far as their working relationship. One afternoon, he returned from lunch to find Mr. Scruggs elbow up in a cadaver's abdominal cavity. A resident doctor pathologist was next to him, taking lung cultures, blood from the exposed heart, and speaking into an overhead recorder. Scruggs, Woody, and Ralph (Skip's government name) were to take the entire insides (the post) out of these old veterans using a specific procedure that keeps all the organs intact. The entire gross organ removal pulls out as if an obstetrician were delivering a new-born baby by a vertical cesarean section. Sometimes the family would give consent for the brain to be removed, or the eyes would be donated to the National Institute of Health. In that case, a physician would come to execute the removal, meanwhile, Skip was not prepared for this function of his job. When he walked into the morgue, thinking he'd just pass through as a casual observer, Mr. Scruggs instructed Skip to put on an apron and grab one of those surgical masks.

Inside what could only have been a minute of looking down at the heart, lungs, liver, and fatty tissue, smelling a mixture of bile, fresh organ, antisepsis odor, not to mention the blood, Skip began to perspire, despite the cool temperature from the air conditioner. He also felt himself becoming lightheaded and told Scruggs that he needed to step out to get a drink of water; actually, Skip was going down. He was about to pass out right on the tile floor amidst the blood and other body matter, probably cracking his head on the stainless-steel autopsy table on the way down. Scruggs, as did the physician that he was assisting, assessed Skip's state quickly, and asserted, 'No, no, once you come in, you have to stay."

Skip would later find this injunction to be an untruth. Scruggs only wanted to test the mettle of his new protégé. When Skip learned that he was stuck there, he had no choice but to stand strong or fold up in the corner like Paul thought he'd do the night Skip was caught with knives at Fort Stanton rec center with Paul raining blows upon him. Skip didn't fold then and he wouldn't fold now. Instead he willed himself to stand strong and begin looking at the organs, tissue, and blood all as a learning experience, as if he was in a special class. Observing the second autopsy was easier, the third even more so, with Skip being comfortable enough to ask a question or two. Connie always wanted Skip to work as a male nurse. Now that he was working in a hospital, he would occasionally wear the white pants, scrub top, and hair cover home from work; and if this was as close as he'd get to her dream for him, it'd have to do.

After Scruggs or Woody would remove the organs and set them on another autopsy table for the physician to begin dissecting and diagnosing a cause of death from, the two would then pack the empty cavity with paper and sew the body cavity in the shape of a Y. In order to achieve this Y shape, an incision was placed from each shoulder to the middle of the lower chest, then straight down and around the navel to stop at the pelvis. Skip sewed up two bodies before Scruggs turned him over to his first doctor to assist. He did well, the physician had no complaints, he washed the body off after sewing it up, put it back in the refrigerated cadaver box, logged it in as completed and cleaned up the mess on the autopsy table. Skip felt good logging in his first solo assist. Where the initials go in the logbook for the autopsy assistant who assisted the pathologist, Skip put his given name initials…R.L.

Skip truly learned to like his job, he wore white pants and a white buttoned shirt – this was the uniform. Sometimes he, Scruggs, and Woody would wear the scrub top the doctors wore. He joined the Medical Center's credit union and was saving a few dollars every two weeks from his check. Scruggs and Woody were very pleased with the help they were now getting in and around the morgue. Barbara, the test-tube washer was pleased because Skip was a great help to her too. She had a son that was around Skip's age, Earl, that was in some prison up in Hagerstown, Maryland, and four other children. Skip helped her out a lot, maybe because her physical stature reminded him of Connie. While washing tubes one day, rushing and not paying as close attention to what he was doing, the forceps he was removing the basket full of tubes with slipped only to drop the basket back into the porcelain crock pot. There was a small splash of acid and one of the droplets went in his eye, he immediately began flushing the eye with cold water from the nearby sink for several moments before rushing upstairs to the otolaryngology department. Skip was fortunate, for this was the same eye Eddie Hall shot mortar into from the apartment building brick, and the same one that was injured during a fight in which Craig Stevens hit him with a piece of brick all because of Debbie (a chick from Baltimore). This time Skip had to wear an eye patch for several days. This time he was afraid of losing it. The tissue was scarred but there was no nerve damage.

Scruggs and Woody had other jobs they held down. For Scruggs, it was house painting. he had more than enough work throughout D.C., Maryland, and Virginia to keep him busy. The doctors and chemists throughout the VA's laboratory and research department would hire him to paint their homes, exterior as well as interior. He actually had more work than he could handle and needed help. That's where Skip came in. Scruggs trusted Skip, and knew how fast the young man picked up what was shown him. He began taking him out on jobs after work hours, especially on the weekends. Skip proved be as proficient and skilled painter as Scruggs himself, with his draw back being Skip wouldn't be comfortable going over three stories. However, he had an extremely steady hand and wouldn't have to waste time taping up windows, nor other delicate areas, and, at first, Skip's help was limited to sanding and all the "cut work."

To Woody, this job in the morgue was only something to help him make due until his funeral home business picked up. Woody ran a newly opened small scale funeral practice that he not long ago graduated college in Ohio to perfect. Scruggs and Woody were fifteen or so years apart, with Skip fifteen years younger than Woody. Scruggs and Woody could knock a fifth of "sauce" down like it was soda, though Woody couldn't hold his liquor well. He wouldn't get irritable and/or belligerent like Paul, but obnoxiously playful.

Connie taught Skip years ago, when she learned he was drinking with his young friends at only thirteen or fourteen, and there were about a dozen of them, to first put something on your stomach. This was the key, she said, so you won't become falling-down stupid drunk, because food acts as a sponge and will absorb much of the liquor. He found out her advice to be true – it usually was – and as long as he had something on his stomach an hour or so before he drank, Skip could hang out with all the average old timers. Except for J. Marie's uncles Cookie and Hyda. Those dudes could put it away, sure 'nough.

A few years ago, J. Marie thought, *I'd have tore the fur off this B___ for pulling a stunt like this.*

The woman she had issues with was a shorter-than-her big-breasted heifer that had caught Skip's eye, and before this thing went any further, and she wasn't 100% sure it hadn't, but something was going to give. This B___ was gonna' crap or get off the pot.

J. Marie hated that she had to clean her office. *Of all the floors in HUD, of all the rooms, why did I have to be assigned this area of the building?* To make matters worse Linda knew J. Marie was Skip's girl, and she took a sinister sort of twisted gratification watching her clean the office she shared with several other girls during regular work hours (at H.U.D.).

All the employees for "World Wide Services" wore opened-front light-blue smocks that could be closed and adjusted by long cloth wrap-around ties. J. Marie used to let hers hang open, letting the ties hang down. Occasionally she'd wrap it loosely around her waist. This time, because Linda was obviously tryin' to "get her thing off," J. Marie stopped in the middle of what she'd been doing, to adjust her smock ties to draw it in tight. Linda now looked at J. Marie as though seeing her for the very first time; her jaw dropped, her eyes grew wild and large as saucers, as they stared at the expecting mother's stomach.

With that, J. Marie's cold dark eyes locked in on Linda's as she made her way to the door never once blinking. Linda learned something else about J. Marie she hadn't known – she had the deepest dimples she'd ever seen, when she smiled.

She was five month pregnant, and planned to work until her seventh, maybe her eight month. Skip was doing a great job up the street at the VA, and painting on the side. He'd bought a black-on-black Gran Torino Elite through the credit union. These past few months he'd been very attentive to the mother to be, and he was as legit as he'd been in years, except for the guns.

Cindy had given birth to a cute little girl she named Tamika. Skip went to visit her in D.C. General Hospital while she was in the maternity ward, bringing her several magazines. He got a few laughs out of her with a few of his weak jokes and genuine good humor. Surely Skip liked all of the Williams girls, maybe a little too much. He could be a rotten scoundrel at times with the thoughts he would harbor.

Sometimes he would bring Chick and Steve to Edgewood to hang out with him and J. Marie as well as her sisters and brothers. They all got along well. Just for the fun of it, J. Marie would often hit Steve with a gut-wrenching body blow when she'd see him. He'd be folded over like an omelet until he caught his breath.

They were just as cool with Lou, as well they should be for getting them out of jail a couple of years ago. She'd gotten skip out on more than one occasion when he dared not call Connie. Now she, like others were glad to see him looking like he was settling down and trying to be responsible, Scruggs had helped him out in a real big way. The apartment on Edgewood Street was always jumping, with the siblings all camping out there, as well as some of their friends at times. There was never a dull moment. When Lou was out, which was most of the time (who could blame her), J. Marie and Skip held the fort down, if they were there. J. Marie was getting bigger and bigger each day, obviously. Skip gave her the phone number to the secretary's office where he worked. When she got close to the ninth month Skip was hanging closer to the apartment –he would shoot over there on his lunch breaks – and sleeping with her in her room more often.

Paul and Connie were tickled to death. This would be their first grandchild. Skip had never seen his old man smile so much. He explained to Skip, the fact that "there were all various complexions through the generations of our family, so boy don't you get all simple and stupid acting if that baby come out a few shades darker than what you think he or she should be."

Skip understood. He knew complexions could jump back two or sometimes three generations to match a kin folk's color. Both Skip's grandfathers were brown skinned, and Lou was darker than anyone in his family he knew of. If J. Marie delivered a baby Lou's complexion, he'd have to roll with it, no matter how anomalous it might seem to him. He knew that he loved her truly, with more love than words could adequately describe. They'd been hangin' out a lotta years, and she had stuck by him when she could've easily moved on to a dude that had more than he, and one that was better looking…maybe, and with a less complicated life during those tumultuous years.

The only edge Skip knew for sure he held over anyone else was that no one in the world could ever love her as much as he did; not if they lived to be one hundred years old, and that he knew was undoubtedly true. Skip would bring her bunches and bunches of seedless grapes, mostly the green ones, other fruits too, but mostly grapes. J. Marie and his cousin Duke's wife were pregnant at the same time; in their eighth month and some. They saw each other at Madoo's house. Compared to Dukes wife, "Windy," J. Marie looked like she was having twins. She was getting that waddle to her walk pregnant women get, and having the time of her life basking in all the attention. It was as though all of D.C. knew she was carrying Skip's baby, at least half of Anacostia, Edgewood Terrace, and upper New Hampshire Ave., N.W. She would laugh all the time, she thought Skip was making her laugh to maybe speed up the labor. Her doctor told her to continue having sex. This would help with the delivery. This was fine with Skip. He loved being with J. Marie in every capacity, especially for the kissing, hugging, and sex. They made love all the way up until the night before the day of the delivery, and it would've carried on to the next day if he hadn't jetted to his mom's house for a few hours for whatever reason. The next thing he knew someone called telling him Lou drove her to Howard University Hospital.

Michael D'Angelo Lucas was born in February, two days before Connie's birthday. Skip saw J. Marie each of the three days she was there. On the day she was to be released, he whipped the all black elite with "Skip" on the tags to the main entrance of the hospital. J. Marie and baby stepped from the wheel chair into the car she thanked the nurses, and they were off.

Days earlier, Skip brought his painting equipment to her bedroom with a gallon of baby-blue paint, and white gloss for trim. He moved everything out of her bedroom, and painted all night until it was done. Skip by then had painted on the side after work and on weekends with

Scruggs long enough to know a thing or two about house painting. He knew a professionally done job when he saw one, and he had to admit – the job he'd done for J. Marie to come home to was "like that."

Despite the cold temperature outside, he left the window open for the room to air out, after first clearing it with Lou; after all, it was her crib.

The next morning he came back to put in the finishing touches; stuffed animals (J. Marie loved stuffed animals), a couple soft baby-type posters, and he put up the white crib his mother gave him that belonged to her last one, Paul.

When they stepped into J. Marie's room from the hospital, she was awe-stricken, overjoyed, and vivaciously delighted that Skip had taken the initiative. He was still the opportunist, and every now and then he would take advantage of a good opportunity.

The name they decided on came from a combination of both their brother's names. Skip's next-youngest brother's (M.G.) first name was Michael, but Skip wasn't so much naming him after his brother as he had decided that Michael went good with his last name – Lucas. J. Maries brother Gary's middle name was D'Angelo, a name he actually appointed upon himself. Nevertheless, Skip thought it was slick, and Skip also knew something of the artist that had painted the Sistine Chapel, his name sounded something like that too.

They didn't stay at Lou's apartment long after their baby was born. Skip wanted them both at the house in Fort Stanton with him, even if it was in the basement. That was his domain, and it was cozy.

Paul was able to regularly see and be near his first and only grandchild. He and Connie seemed to get along better with little Mike D'Angelo on the scene. It was good to see them smiling at each other as one would hold their grandson, and him occasionally spitting portions of his dinner on Paul's shirt or pants, or both.

Each weekend, Skip would leave out the house early, jump in the black Ford, while J. Marie and the baby slept, and return an hour or so later with a case of Similac and a jumbo case of pampers, sometime it'd be two cases of each. Paul would be standing in the door smiling at how his son was doing what he was supposed to do, providing as best he could. What Paul didn't know was that Skip was boosting it all from the local drug stores, or sometime he'd drive out to Marlow Heights. Once he came back with a couple space heaters; the basement was getting a little chilly.

His old mentor Buggs – a boostin' *magician* would've been proud, Skip was now back on to something he hadn't done in years. He thought about what Buggs was up to these days. The last he heard, Bug was robbing banks solo, and – he was getting high.

Chapter 8

Samuel Buggs, was a product of the Trinidad N.E. area of Washington, who, like Skip and most other career or seasoned criminals, started his errant and deviant lifestyle young. Unlike Skip, however, Buggs was not able to duck reformatory training school for boys, and by the time he had hooked up with the young and impressionable Skip, he was on his way to bigger pay days, and was simply trying to add some discipline to the wild and ill-fated Skip's life. He liked the kid as soon as he'd saw him pop the door lock on his friend Cortez's car when he'd accidentally locked the keys in them. Skip couldn't have been no more'n twelve and was in that car in less than twenty seconds.

Buggs had shown Skip a few of his patent signature "cuff" moves, and put him down with certain aspects of the law. When to keep your mouth shut, intimidation strategies cops use, and even encouraged him about his school education. That Skip had made it out of that house in S.E. on the burglary caper a few years ago, and the only loss was that damn dog – well it was time for Buggs to move on.

Now Buggs and Fat Frank were still hangin' out, and had teamed up with a couple broads that use to work for a nefariously psychotic cross-dressing lesbian pimp named "Fee-Fee." Someone you would definitely try avoiding if you were with your peoples, especially if they were church-going God-fearing folks, you feel me...

Buggs, Frank, and the two girls worked in teams, coupled up, entering big-money stores minutes apart through different entrances. For several-month stretches, Buggs was bringin' down three hundred to five hundred dollars. Cashing in proceeds from some impressive establishments; Circuit City, Woolworth & Lothrop, and rolling out with Cannon cameras, component sets, leather coats, and some jewelry. When one of the team got snatched, Buggs made sure the bond was paid, the court date was made so the security wasn't lost, and an attorney was present, even if it was no more than a public defender, which is usually more like a public *pretender*. Afterwards, the team would move on to another location, or county, and sometimes another state for a few weeks.

In 1973 (three years after Skip), Buggs and Nicole got jammed up coming out of Circuit City. Buggs took the weight on this one, because it wasn't that heavy, surprisingly though, unbeknownst to him, a cross was in effect. To his dismay, he was sentenced to twenty months. After doing fifteen months at Lorton Young Center, Sam Buggs was back. Most guys that get "close to the door" (nearing their release date), and then actually make it out of the prison doors, or the front gate, have the exact same mindset – that "this is the last time, I'll never come back!" However, a man or woman that has been through it, having recidivated once or thrice, will tell you – unless you are willing to change people, places, and former actions (things), you will become a recidivist, or you will be killed.

Sam Buggs was off to a great start after he was released. He began spending time with his two little girls, and their mom, doing all the father/daughter fun stuff. He was driving for a messenger service and all the right things.

In 1976 Muhammad Ali fought Jimmy Young at the Capital Centre. Sam was there with Beverly, and he could've sworn he saw his young understudy Skip down close to ringside with some red-bone that looked like she could be his sister.

He did see Stink and Dave, of that he was sure. Though they'd been cool for years – at this junction in his life, he could fair better without them, either one. Sam and Beverly had a good time, not a great time, because the fight was only so-so. Young kept ducking his head out of the ropes, and trying to be elusive, instead of going toe to toe with Ali. Sam had seen better fights, especially in Ali's heyday.

Two weeks after the fight, while Sam was out front washing the Thunderbird he and Beverly purchased, Stink and Dave came calling. They were just in the neighborhood. As fate would have it, they'd seen him and Beverly at the Ali fight, but chose not to intrude upon him and his lady.

Hustlers, ex-cons, and dudes living on the dark side know just what dialogue to use, ever so subtly, when attempting to lure one of their own. Sam had two things going against him upon his release; he was a closet thrill seeker, that is to say he'd get a "rush" given certain situations, and he was experiencing a depleted cash flow, now this Robert Young routine, and this "father knows best" roll were becoming a tad mundane, so he listened, that's all – he just…listened.

Sam Buggs was in excellent shape, he played sports, ever since he was a kid comin' up in Holbrook Terrace (Trinidad), on through his training school days, and in Lorton's Youth Center he played running back for the flag football team. If there was anybody to jump over a countertop unabated it was him; in the register, in an opened safe, or both and back over, and out the door, with a burner in his hand in under two minutes.

All he wanted was someone by the door who knew what he was doing, and someone behind the wheel who could not only handle a whip, but wouldn't panic if the plan deviated a little from what was the norm given this situation.

Stink and Dave were outta that mob. They knew what time it was out the gate! And the only thing Sam had to be concerned about with them was greedy larceny.

They were all on the same page for the most part. Even though Sam was putting in the most work, and it was his face or build and clothes more likely identified, he didn't sweat his crew for the lion's share of the breakdown. Each job, same routine, no deviation, meshing like the gears on an old clock.

Friday, the day before Christmas, the following year after his release, he and Beverly had yet to complete the shopping for the girls. They had bought several nice things for them the previous week at the Toys-R-Us, but Sam wanted Lisa and Chrystal to have a Christmas morning they would never forget. He only knew to do what he did best; boosting or banks. *Take your pick*, he told himself. He was pressed for time, so boosting was no longer an option...

The day before Christmas and he was in Citizens Bank, the take was so-so, he had only hit one teller, and was without his regular crew. Ten minutes earlier, he had Beverly to pull into the McDonald's a block down and over from the bank. He instructed her to order a small meal for the both of them, but be sure to get an oversized bag. When Beverly came back, he took the food out the bag, folded the bag up, and put it in his coat pocket. He told her, "Take your time and enjoy your meal, real slow. I'll be back."

Buggs entered Citizens Bank, hopped the counter, gun in hand, and was out the door in under a minute this time, because he was by himself. He cut through the shrubs on the side of the bank walking fast with the "Citizens" stamped bank satchel under his coat. He started a light jog as one would when trying to catch a bus; just before reaching the McDonald's parking lot, he slowed it down to a casual stroll. He walked to the restroom, where he transferred the loose cash he snatched from the register (he avoided taking stacks of wrapped currency for fear of the explosive dye packets) into the empty McDonalds bag. He exited the restroom just barely looking around, then got in the car, where he and his unwitting accomplice drove off.

Sam didn't tell Beverly about the robbery. The less she knew the better. All she did know was they had enough money now to make more than just their girls happy. Sam got thirty-five hundred dollars from the teller. He gave two G's to Beverly, and kept fifteen hundred. That evening the dope man got three hundred dollars for two 8-balls. The bigger the purses, the more daring and brazen Sam and his crew got, and the more Sam was beginning to use.

He had acquired a vast amount of cake in the three years since leaving the Youth Center in Lorton, VA.; what he had to show for it was the clothes his children, nieces, and nephews had on their backs. Looking to that part of his past made him smile. The smile would quickly vanish when he reflected upon what else he had to show for his toil… A hell of a "habit" by then.

In 1979, the feds, acting on a tip from an anonymous caller (crime solvers), found out Sam was in a treatment center. They entered the facility late one afternoon and arrested him on the spot. He was charged with six bank robberies and on a plea agreement sentenced to thirty years with the Division of Corrections, in Maryland, he was twenty-seven years old. At the sentencing, Beverly and his two girls tearfully watched Sam look over his shoulder to acknowledge them as well as say a temporary farewell. The next time he saw them would be in the horse-shoe shaped visiting room of the Maryland Penitentiary in Baltimore.

The next weekend Skip went out. He didn't come back at the usual time. Later, he'd call J. Marie from upper Marlboro County Detention Center. She would in turn call Chick to pick her up at Connie's, and then they'd go pick up the Elite from where Skip left it in the Marlo Heights parking lot, and lastly, they'd go bail Skip out of jail.

All Connie knew was that Chick picked up J. Marie from the house. She wasn't sure what that was all about, only that it didn't look right. She wondered what kind of games they were playin'. She didn't like this one bit, no sir! Unfortunately, J. Marie couldn't tell her they were going to get Skip from being charged with theft from upper Marlboro.

Skip chilled awhile after that. He went to court and had to pull six weekends "road crew." For six consecutive weekends that winter he would report to the state/highway department for whatever assignment the foreman had that day. No one but J. Marie knew where he'd be going early in the morning for the next month and a half; Connie and Paul assumed he was going to work overtime at Veterans, or he had a paint job lined up somewhere. This was the end of his short boosting career, again.

Connie and Paul couldn't believe Skip had spent so much money on fight tickets, even if it was to see Muhammad Ali. Sure enough, Paul saw the tickets with his own eyes, and mentioned to several coworkers, "That damn boy must think he's related the Rockefellers or somebody – two hundred dollars! To see a fight! Actually, Paul was partly bragging on his boy for being able to attend such a gala, he and J. Marie.

Skip had personalized license plates on his car, and Paul thought his son could go a bit "over the top" sometimes, but all in all he was "doing his thing," as the young folks say, and he didn't blame him. Besides, he'd made Paul and Connie grandparents, and for some older people a grandchild or two is the coup de grâce of their twilight years.

J. Marie was all smiles as she stepped from the freshly washed and waxed black Ford Elite. You would think she was stepping from a limo. Skip loved to see her this way, her dimples would grow deeper than usual, and her cheeks would rise, pushing the corners of her eyes to an even higher slant.

The seats were seven rows from ringside. They saw several celebrities. Skip was surprised that "John Amos" was the same height as he, and not much taller, the way he looked on *Good Times*. He was friendly towards the young couple, and shook Skips hand before posing for a picture. They had as good a time just being there caught up in all the hoopla as the weak exhibition of the fight itself. Even still, the fight was big news for the town during the next few days. Skip was glad he and his lady were part of it all.

J. Marie now had to consider what she would do for a full-time job. She certainly couldn't clean offices all her life, and Skip couldn't take down enough money to support the three of them. Eventually they'd need another spot of their own. She decided to go to secretarial school to become certified or something or the other. She began Washington School for Secretaries (WSS) on K Street in N.W. Washington; Skip footed the bill. He made sure he picked her up each night just as he did when she had the after-school job at H.U.D. He picked up a Mach I Mustang, four in the floor too. This joint was five years old, fast, and more a choice of convenience than of necessity. Skip had yet to teach J. Marie how to drive a stick shift; perhaps he should have just for the sake of it. Meanwhile, there was no great urgency to get her bangin' gears and tearing the transmission out of this hot little number, not yet.

Whenever Skip had to abandon these vehicles for whatever reason, he'd snatch up whatever belongings he had out of the glove compartment, take a couple quick brushes with his hand under the front seats, give it a halfway decent print wipe down, then pull over somewhere out of the way, perhaps an apartment building lot, and bounce. J. Marie never left anything behind. It was extraordinarily strange, Skip thought, as much as she smoked, not so much as a butt in the ashtray.

He often thought how it would've been for them had she ever gone over to the "dark side" as he had so many years ago. The thought of Faye Dunaway and Warren Beatty's last scene in the old 1967 portrayal of *Bonnie and Clyde* flashed through his mind. He shuttered, *whew!*

Secretarial work would be fine, given the right employer and firm. She worked for a few small businesses, and Kelly Girl Appointments, drawing a fairly acceptable salary for a new employee with only a high school diploma and no prior experience.

She was young, attractive, pleasant to be around, and she knew her stuff. She was settling in as a secretary, but not all the way sold on it as a life-long profession.

Skip knew J. Marie was a class act, he wasn't overly jealous, and though he trusted her to the max, he thought about the stigma attached to some male bosses that looked upon their female employees with an ulterior motive. Especially the buxom pretty ones.

In the six years skip had J. Marie there were only two dudes (older heads) she told him about, that he didn't confront for pressing her, no matter how insignificant it may have or may not have been; he still had a sour taste in his mouth years later. He reflected back on Sharon, ducked down behind the bar in the Ham's basement the night of a party when he caught Bodie in the stomach coming up the stairs with a kick the way Duke did him when they were young. Right in the gut full force. That guy was folded over on his knees at the bottom of the stairs every bit of two minutes. That night could've been bad for Skip. He was glad Bodie and his boys weren't liked by the lower 12th Street boys. (That was J. Marie's clique. Skip was way off his turf again.) As it stood now, with J. Maries boss, if he had to bring him some drama on her job, well c'est la vie, it is what it is.

At the behest of Connie, she began showing interest in nursing. Skip was more than happy to see her make the switch, and didn't mind in the least to pay her fees entering nursing school. She would be wearing those cute little white uniforms, shoes, and all the appurtenances. She could have continued on with her education in nursing for several years, but stopped short, and Skip didn't have the foresightedness to inspire her further – after all, he'd been stopping short his whole life.

In this regard, he and J. Marie lacked the same strong motivational personality in their life. Although Skip had several of these people in his life at various times, they were all, unfortunately, negative motivational inspirations.

The house in Fort Stanton was too crowded for the three generations of Lucases under one roof. With Skip working at Veterans Medical Center, and J. Marie done with nurse training and working at the hospital where she delivered their son, the young couple moved into the "North Bridge" apartment complex just across the Maryland line.

Two bedrooms, the place had a balcony, a countertop seating area in between the dining room and kitchen. North Bridge Apartments were not far from Eastover Shopping Center. Paul liked the new place, he came over with Skip one day while J. Marie was at work to "check the joint out," as he said. He had a few drinks under his belt, and before Skip knew it, he was knocked out on the chaise lounge. Skip couldn't help but smile at the sight of him sprawled face down on the low-built recliner. He wished he had a camera. It was a nice little spot to call home, Michael D'Angelo, who was not quite a year old, had his own room.

Earth, Wind, and Fire put on the most awe-inspiring, entertaining displays of the 70s; certainly skip and J. Marie thought so. At a concert at the Capital Center one summer night, once the lead guitarist was raised over twenty-five feet in the air while playing fervently, and still dancing, if that weren't enough, when he came down, the pianist, with piano and bench, were raised to the same level while he was playing, holding on albeit for dear life. Skip could've sworn they were flipping over (the piano and bench he sat on while he played). Of course, Skip was blasted off reefer and wine, but not so much he didn't notice the hoisting apparatus; nevertheless it was another great memorable time for the two.

Afterwards, on the way back to the apartment, and after stopping by Connie's or Cindy's to pick up Michael D'Angelo, they proceeded home.

As usual, Skip would take J. Marie and son as close as he could to the apartment building then go find a parking spot. After clearing out the car of whatever was to go into the apartment – Michael D'Angelo's overnight bag, his beer, etc. – he then walked towards the building to join his family at the door. He never would permit them to enter first, not at night. He was glad to be finally settling in for the night. He imagined capping the evening off with a cold one, turning on the eight track, and listening to a little Whispers – ("Just Say Yes") while lying back next to J. Marie. After Al Green's "Let's Stay Together," The Whispers' "Just Say Yes" was their second favorite choice, for sentimental reasons. *Yeah, that's the plan and whatever comes after that it's on her*, Skip thought. He was just smiling to himself thinking about her and the baby when he saw them in the same spot he left them. They never made it to the foyer of the building, and the closer he got to her, he noticed her eyes locked in on his; Skip fingered the .380 semi-automatic he kept in his dip these days. He looked closer to her and tilted his head for an explanation as to why they weren't closer to the door. She said, while looking Skip in the eyes, "Go see Skip." Now he pulled the burner out of his dip, keeping it down low along his right leg, anticipating the strong possibility something funky was surely about to kick off.

When Skip peered into the open built foyer of the building, he saw the most beautiful pure-bred boxer he'd seen in a long time. The dog was lying stooped down on all fours like he was on guard. Skip had trained

Smokey the same way – when he was "on point." So maybe that was indeed the case with Cujo here, and there was someone inside. The next move was on the dog, Skip hoped he wouldn't nut-up on him when he quietly called him away from the door.

In Skip's friendly dog-calling voice of lip smacks/the kissing sound and a couple "here boy, here boys" (Skip: *more lip smacks/the kissing sound…*) The dog got up, trotted to Skip (Skip thought, *here goes dog, act like you know.*) Skip still had the burner in his right hand, so he patted his leg with his left – for the dog to do what most dogs would do in these situation. The dog complied, giving Skip that "pet-me look," Skip complied, then shook the dog off so he could go to the next phase of getting into the crib. Fortunately, the dog went opposite from where J. Marie was holding the baby and on his merry way. J. Marie was not overly frightened of the average mutt, but this was a boxer, and they have a natural menacing look. Skip would've hated to spill the pretty dog's brains all over the sidewalk, but this was neither here nor there at the present moment. Right now, he was making his way to the door, listening for strange sounds coming from there-in – nothing, nothing but silence. He paused a few more seconds before inserting the key, and when it was inserted he wasted no time swinging it open and getting low, gun up… searching, scanning, moving from room to room, hoping his eyes hurried adjusting to the darkness. He had been in this situation before – slipping into darkness. Nothing. Good. He cut the lights on, put the burner back to his side and quickly walked out to get J. Marie and Michael D'Angelo, then he put the piece back in his dip.

That night after putting the baby to bed, J. Marie listened to Skip singing along with the Whispers tape he'd placed in the player. She smiled and shook her head most every time Skip sang – he couldn't sing a lick. She began singing along with him nevertheless. She put on her nurse's uniform, even though tomorrow was Sunday and she was off work, while Skip smilingly looked on. Skip had a thing for nurses, and loved seeing J. Marie in her uniform, complete with the little white half-hat she wore pinned midway across her head.

Several months had passed since the dog incident. As usual J. Marie and Skip were enjoying parenthood. Life was good, especially when you know sometimes you'll have to take the bitter with the sweet. J. Marie was a perfect mother and nurse to her boys. When they were sick she knew just what to do. Skip would be sick more than anyone in the family, he still had bouts with "bronchitis," and was not taking care of himself as he should. J. Marie would tell him the bourbon and beer were no help for his sickness. He would tell her, "But it makes me forget about being sick." Once J. Marie went to check on Michael D'Angelo, and he was a deathly shade of blue! She knew just what to do. Skip hadn't the foggiest.

Skip awoke from a restless sleep and asked, "J. are you tryin' to get married." Still half asleep, and not sure she was hearing him right, because if she wasn't mistaken – it was, as far as she could recall, the same way and tone he asked her, over six years ago, when he'd called her on the phone two days after they'd met, "…are you tryin' to go with me or what?" (to be his girl). Now, after years of being with him, after having his baby, the crime sprees, the money, or lack of it sometimes, she understood him; he was crass that way, unrefined. No one had ever taught him soft, timely, and poetic words to swoon a lady with. Edgar Allen Poe or Langston Hughes he was not. She doubted seriously if Skip ever heard of them. How could he have? He'd practically dropped out of school in the seventh grade, and from a substandard school in S.E. Anacostia… "Douglas," for God's sake. He never really gave Taft a chance.

She never gave it a second thought; despite his flaws or shortcomings there was more good about him that she loved than there was about him she didn't like. And just like when they were fourteen, when he'd so tactlessly and abruptly asked her to "go with him" (meaning; be his girlfriend), she responded to this question of marriage now the same way.

"Yeah, Skip."

And that was that; no down on one knee, no surprise proposal in some ridiculous but timely setting, no ritz nor glitter, no imagination.

By next week, miraculously, like the way Skip acquired his High School equivalency diploma, he had the necessary documents. The legal attendant notarized for them to be married. All she had to do was sign it. She saw his name was already signed. "But Skip isn't the notary seal supposed to be stamped on *after* we both sign it?"

The three-card monte slight-of-hand card game she used to see came to mind. She squeezed her eyes closed and quickly shook away the vision from her head.

They were married on the second of July 1977. Greg and Fat Louie's father Reverend Leon George Lipscomb performed the ceremony. He was only too happy to do it for them. He'd known of J. Marie since Skip first began bringing her around his mom's house. He'd been glad Skip was not in the car with his youngest son Junior that dreadful night he was killed execution style while sitting with the Hopkin's boy.

It was a small ceremony at Reverend Lipscomb's Allen AME church on Alabama Avenue, SE. Connie and Michael D'Angelo were there. Later, after Skip thought about the seriousness and significance of the occasion, he deeply regretted not having the foresight to have his mother-in-law there. He thought about something his oldest friend Dunmore told him about his fighting skills, and protecting them: "Skip you're too damn impatient." Forgive me, Lou, my bad.

Chapter 9

PAUL LAY IN HIS BED dead for at least a day before Carlyn discovered him. Two days before, Connie's job sent her to Arizona to handle some kind of management analyst affair. For three days, the kids (Anthony, Paul, and Carlyn) were staying with Skip and J. Marie; all but M.G., because Connie was planning to leave Paul as soon as she returned. He was becoming more obnoxious and verbally abusive than he'd been since Skip was younger, when they lived in Parkland. Skip was hardly ever around to keep him in check, and now that the children were older, she could get her own place. It was the 70s, and a lot of women were doing it, and doing just fine on their own. Silva (Steve's mother) just left her second husband, Eddie. Then there was Lou, who had been faring her way for years!

Carlyn told her older brother that she had to go back to the house to retrieve whatever personal items it was that twelve or thirteen-year-old girls needed. So he obliged her and off they went. He'd hit his dad up for a couple of cold beers while he was there. While Carlyn ran upstairs to her old room, Skip headed for the refrigerator. He heard her calling him from upstairs. As usual, he ran to her to find her standing in the doorway to their father's room. Paul and Connie slept in separate rooms. Despite having the stature of a midget, Connie snored like a human chain saw. Paul was on his back, neck slightly crooked. He was stiff where rigor mortis was obviously setting in. First Skip called Woody, since he was the director of his family's funeral home, next he called the police, and finally his grandfather. Paul was prone to drink "boiler makers" when he was dispirited, he never exercised, and had a horrible diet. Often he'd try to get Skip, M.G., or one of the other kids to try some of his pig's feet or chitterling. Twice a month, he would stink up the whole house cooking them. M.G. probably tried them once or twice – you know the old saying, "Give it to Mikey…" Paul was only fifty-three and would have been fifty four that August 10th, and had a bad heart. The medical examiner concluded that Paul died of arteriosclerosis (hardening of the arteries in the heart).

Connie's sister Jenny rode with Skip to pick his mom up from Washington National Airport on her return from Arizona. Neither of the two mentioned Paul's death until they were off airport grounds. Skip simply stated, "Daddy's dead." Skip's Auntie Jenny, as he would affectionately call her sometimes, was silently looking to her middle sister. Connie began to cry, tears, snot, running eyeliner, the whole nine yards. Skip couldn't comfort his ma because he had the wheel, but he could only reach out his hand to hold hers. He thought of their previous frightening encounters while driving and reflected how glad he was that this time *he* was driving.

Usually, Skip would go by the funeral home to pay Woody a social visit and help with the embalming as well as observe. He was taking classes at the Washington Technical Institute (Washington Tech) through the Veteran's G.I. bill to someday become a mortician like Woody and his cousin Jo-Jo in Hampton. Since Skip's father was being prepared for the viewing, Woody deemed it best that this time his friend and protégé stayed clear of the operation for a day or so. Truth be told, Skip was not tryin' to see Paul like that, in the preparatory state anyway.

The body lay in rest for the wake at the funeral home, which went on, for the most part, the way wakes go. The place was small by larger funeral home standards, barely accommodating the large turnout to see Paul laid to rest. There were just as many people from his job at H.U.D. as there were family and old friends. Paul didn't have many new friends, and most of those from Fort Stanton were there more so on the strength of Connie, who was well loved by mostly everyone she ever came in contact with. The people from his job conversed on how liked Paul was, he could be so funny, they would miss him, and what an all-around nice guy he was. Skip and Connie couldn't help but stand aghast in total amazement…Will the real Paul Lucas, aka Daddy, please stand up. Another striking moment was when some younger woman, only the people from the job seemed to know, was being consoled by her coworkers. She was crying uncontrollably. Connie, perhaps reading more into this than what was there, nevertheless looked at Skip as if to say, "Who is this woman?" or some other word she may have referred to her as. A day later the funeral was held at Our Lady of Perpetual Help Church – the church that Skip and his family came up in. Skip didn't cry but felt a severe knot in his chest. Connie sensed it and pulled his head over to her shoulder the way he'd do J. Marie's when she needed it.

From several pews back, J. Marie saw Skip's distress and knew he needed her. For now, Connie's shoulder and mother's love would have to suffice. Later, she'd calm and relieve the stress he was now feeling. J. Marie knew she and she alone possessed the cure-all remedy to soothe Skip's ills, and it never failed. Several days after the funeral, Connie wanted to see her eldest sister, Lucy, in Hampton, VA. Skip put the black Ford on the road. He, J. Marie, Michael D'Angelo, and Connie. If the baby wasn't along Skip might've offered Connie a blast from one of the half-smoked joints in the ashtray. (One had calmed and soothed his ole ma just a year or so ago when her aunt Florence (Madoo's sister) died and she was going by Trailways to Richmond. That morning, Skip encouraged her by saying how it would help put her at ease as they were about to take the 14th street Southeast/Southwest Freeway, taking them downtown to the bus station. Connie didn't have a problem with Skip smoking "them reefers" as long as her grandson wasn't around. She knew how it made Skip forget everything he had to do in the near future – like the very next minute! He convinced her to just take one puff; of course after the one he edged her on to another longer pull…"Go on, Ma." After three or four more draws, Connie gave it back to Skip. He finished it off and put the roach in the ashtray for hard times. The window was open so as not to have his ole ma getting on the bus lighting the place up. He asked Connie, "How you feel, Ma?" She looked at him, eyes glassin', and said, "You know…I do feel more relaxed." Skip asked did she want to take a couple sticks with her for later, she declined his offer, and they rode on.

Now, in Hampton, Skip watched his extended relatives console Connie and attempt to comfort the grieving widow. The Briscos had come up for Paul's viewing and had a chance then to also see the newest addition to the Lucas clan, Michael D'Angelo. Skip reflected upon the omnipotence of the Creator; that his father lived just long enough to see and enjoy a grandchild. When the time comes, God willing, he too will be a grandfather. God gives life and He takes life, everyone, everything has a fixed time limit. Aunt Lucy and Skip's cousins swore Michael D'Angelo was the cutest little fella, they'd ever seen. "That boy looks like you two spit 'em out." Someone snapped a picture of J. Marie and Skip sitting in Lucy's living room watching their son playing on the carpet.

Connie got the pick-me-up big-sister talk and decided to stay on another day or so. Skip and J. Marie had to be to work, so they drove back to D.C. with Skip's cousin Duke and his girl. Along the way, just out of Williamsburg, not too far from where Skip was once stationed at Fort Eustis; the big Ford blew out a front tire. They'd have to pull over. In addition to this, Michael D'Angelo had "a stinky" in his diaper that smelled worse than his old departed granddad's beer farts. Skip and J. Marie thought it funny, funky beyond words, but nevertheless conversation worthy, calling little man all the teasing names parents call their little one in times like these to make fun. Duke's girl however, not only found it offensive, but made an off-handed disparaging remark that implied reference to an inadequate diet the child was receiving or something.

First of all, a phrase like this can go over either way – it's all on how you put it out there. In this case, her delivery was all wrong. She had ventured onto thin ice, and if that weren't enough, she was skating! Before she could get another word completed, J. Marie cut into her like a new Schick razor, and then ended with the "stare game," until her foe looked away in submission. With the flat fixed and Michael D'Angelo washed and changed, they were on the road again. All was well, just a little quieter.

Mike D'Angelo was on the downside of those "terrible twos," and Skip was no longer pushing the big whips he and J. Marie were known to cat around the city and suburb in. No more drive-in theaters stretched out in the sofa-like leather six-way seats of the Lincoln Continentals, sometimes getting so comfortable that they would fall off to sleep before the movie ended.

Skip no longer sought out the attention he once craved. The big Ford with personalized plates was gone, traded for a new smaller whip with a sunroof and rear spoiler kit. And they were now living in Skip's former stomping grounds, another low-income apartment complex one street over from Parkland called Savannah Terrace.

Working at the morgue for four years and J. Marie nursing at Howard University, the couple were deeply ensconced in their jobs and not working very far apart from each other. After leaving Mike D'Angelo at Mrs. Lynsey's, the two would proceed on to work. Skip would swing by to pick up J. Marie when he got off, then head over to Fort Stanton where Mrs. Lynsey's house was to retrieve Mike D'Angelo. Skip's son would grow up playing on some of the same grounds Skip, himself, played on.

There was always something going on in the apartment on Savannah Terrace. Once, while J. Marie was cleaning, somehow her Eastern High School ring wound up in the trash. To her chagrin, Skip had emptied the trash into the complex dumpster in the late afternoon and it was now nightfall. She attempted to beseech Skip's assistance in retrieving this prized possession, and could not believe what she heard in reply. Skip explained to her that not only was he astraphobic, and disliked cats – he felt that they were far too sneaky - he was also terrified of the nest of rats that was sure to live in that dumpster. Unlike their suburban or laboratory counterparts, project rats are the most aggressive and scrappiest rodents known to man, these beasts will relentlessly attack, sometimes unprovoked. Skip had been chased out of the alley by them on more than one occasion. He was telling her that not even with his gun, nor with one of his thug friends with a gun, would he intrude into their domain. "It's just too many of them, baby," he said.

"But, Skip," she protested, "you could get the flash light and you wouldn't have to actually go into the dumpster, but get a long stick and sort of move the trash around to see if perhaps it was in eye sight. Then we'll at least know it's there and could get it in the morning when the rats are asleep or something."

Skip looked attentively at his beloved wife, the mother of his child, his rap buddy on no less than two capers before and after the fact. He especially noted the "We will…" part of her argument, and, just for a moment, thought of telling J. Marie something real foul. He then just as quickly was very ashamed of himself at thinking such a thought. He loved this woman tremendously, would kill or be killed for her. "No, baby," he said. "I'll just have to get you another one." The last thing that he had the intention of doing was climbing into a dumpster that could possibly have a rat in it. Even during those days on the run, trying to evade police pursuits, he would never think about hiding inside of a dumpster – or the sewer either, for that matter. The next morning, he did go out and peer inside the dumpster; there was too much trash and garbage. "That ring could be anywhere. For all I know," he thought, "a male rat could've carried it home to his woman… Yeah, I'll get her another one someday."

Skip won a few dollars in an Acey-Deucey game with friends one night at Connie's house; Skip and J. Marie both made out, but especially Skip, despite Mary's cheating. The next morning was Sunday and J. Marie had to work; Michael D'Angelo would be staying home with dad today, but first they had to get mama to work. Skip never liked dropping J. Marie off at work on the weekends with Michael D'Angelo in the car. She would kiss Skip goodbye, then spend several moments mollycoddling Michael D'Angelo, preparing him for her departure, which he never took at all well. Sometimes the little fellow would look to his road buddy and father in something in-between disbelief and horror that Skip would let her leave.

At two and a half, Michael D'Angelo was the coolest kid Skip had ever been around. The two were inseparable at times. Others seemed to think he was cool too, and handsome. He'd been in several weddings as a ring bearer.

With some of the winnings from the previous night's card game, Skip had a treat for his main man; they went to Toys-R-Us. Skip intentionally steered him to the section with the tricycles and peddle cars where that dude's eyes lit up like last year's Christmas tree. He went for a new-styled Big Wheel, not the ordinary yellow and red one that was popular for a time with the kids. This one was slightly bigger and black with gold simulated mag wheels. It was called "Cobra." It reminded Skip of the hot rod Fairlane he and J. Marie fell out about that night near the cemetery, and of the black Ford he just traded in. Skip wanted to get on it himself after he lifted it off of the platform. After Michael D'Angelo took it for a test spin up and down the aisle a couple of times, the only thing left was to get him off of it and explain that he couldn't get that particular one because it was for display purposes only, the stock clerk would bring him one from the back. At first Skip might as well have been talking to the floor for all the good it did. Eventually, even though his son didn't quite understand the jargon of "switching and trading," he trusted dad and somehow put it together that within the next few minutes they would be leaving the store, and his brand-new whip would be leaving with them.

The salesman reappeared with a large box with the Cobra inside which let Skip know that some assembly was required. Michael D'Angelo was cool with that though. Having seen the picture of the trike on the side of the box, he was reassured, if only for the time being. But as Skip continued walking throughout the store, collecting other items and accessories prior to reaching the counter, Michael D'Angelo began to get a little impatient. He didn't have a clue as to the relevancy of these others items. All he knew was that his dad was wasting valuable time that could be better spent racing around on his new whip.

Finally back at the apartment and a quick assembly job. Skip's son was in awe; those new added items that Skip had purchased were tight! Now Michael D'Angelo better understood…a chrome horn with a black hand-squeezer, gold streamers that sprouted out of the hand grips, and a small personalized tag with the letters "MIKE" on it.

Michael D'Angelo would ride down a portion of Savannah Terrace in front of the apartment for hours under Skip's watchful eyes. He was so proud to show it off to J. Marie when they got home from picking her up from work. "Look, Ma, bike," he exclaimed. "Ma, ma…"

Once, while on one of his longer rides on his Cobra, Skip found a long staff, which he would position behind the seat and rear frame of Michael D'Angelo's trike, and then push him all over Savannah Terrace. One day Skip pushed his son from the beginning of the complex, all the way to the store on the intersection of Wheeler Road and Southern Avenue. Michael D'Angelo would take off on his own when they got to hills, sometimes traveling so fast that he would get too far from Skip, leaving him frantically running after him in an attempt to catch him, calling out to him, "Drag your feet, Mike! Slow down!" Michael D'Angelo was totally focused on the road. Skip thought about how J. Marie was when he taught her how to drive, not easily distracted, and zoned in on the road ahead.

Sometimes on Sunday mornings, when J. Marie would drive herself to work, Skip would push Mike D'Angelo on his Cobra to Connie's house, because she was known to make waffles on the old secondhand waffle iron she got from the Goodwill. The thing looked to be ten or twelve years old when Skip was a kid, and now she was feeding her grandson on the same iron.

The Feds kicked the door in on Skip early one morning when he and J. Marie were getting ready for work. They took Skip out in handcuffs from the apartment complex, with his wife and son looking on helplessly. They briefly searched the apartment feigning to be there for a legitimate reason, apparently only wanting to take Skip out. He was glad that the search was only a half-hearted effort. Skip's mind was racing. It could have been about any number of unlawful activities Skip had partaken in within the last few weeks. His main concern was the string of robberies and assaults with Kenny and Black on separate occasions, never the two together. Skip was still living a double life, in which the details of the second life were sketchy to J. Marie even.

Just last year, she and Lou had to drive all the way out 270 to one of the counties to try to get Kenny and him out of a jam involving a gas station and bogus credit cards. When they arrived, the county police were going through Skip's car, a Monza. To the horror of the women, from under the driver's seat, the officer pulled out the longest barreled gun she had ever seen, except on the old Clint Eastwood movies.

They locked Skip and Kenny up on the spot, holding them for two days at the detention center, and only after a court appearance was Skip released with a sentence of five year's probation for the gun.

Now, whatever this latest arrest was about, J. Marie knew one thing for sure – her husband's probation wasn't expired, and if this has anything to do with Maryland, well…

Studies show the last part of the brain to mature is the prefrontal cortex – the CEO of the human brain, also called the area of sober second thought – which may be why teens and sometimes young adults, and especially males, get into so much trouble. (*Time* magazine, May 10, 2004).

It would explain Skip's behavior in the early years, and something of his plight as he grew older. Contrary to what some professionals and researchers accept, accumulated evidence clearly indicates that alcoholism is hereditary. The weight of evidence on the link between alcoholism to heredity in a study by psychiatrist and researcher, Donald Goodwin (*New Yorker*; Oxford University Press) provides clear and strong corroboration that alcoholism is indeed passed form parent to child through genes. Physiology not psychology determines whether one drinker will become addicted to alcohol and another will not.

From Under the Influence by Dr. James R. Milam and Katherine Ketcham, Skip's brain was never allowed to become fully developed because of the constant use and abuse of alcohol and drugs at too young an age. A young brain needs time to recuperate, cells need to be uninhibited for years until maturity. His prostate and bladder were far too underdeveloped to contaminate with such high levels of alcohol at such a young age.

By the time Skip was twenty-three, after being predisposed to alcoholism and "at risk" as a child, he and many friends and/or associates tried and abused every class of drug, alcohol, and hallucinogenic chemical imaginable in the homes, dens, and alleys in the Washington and metropolitan area(s). It would all seem innocent enough at six or seven years old, sipping the suds off his father's beers, as many children coming up do. Parents, and uncles, family members, or friends look at this as a rite of passage, that "See, my son is all boy," or "That's my boy, a chip off of the old block." Skip was brought up in a family – a clan – that leaned heavily on alcohol. If, however, that family or relative was an abuser of another substance, then chances are high that the child would gravitate or be prone to that preference.

Not all kids of course. Unfortunately, in Skip's case, he had a Goliath of a nemesis. Most every negative vice he was exposed to that he developed an affinity for he'd overindulge in: alcohol, drugs, theft, auto grand larceny, arson, robbery, firearms sales, and felony assaults. Skip would take them all to the extreme measures; he had an addictive personality.

From A to Z, you name the poison, and nine times out of ten, Skip had consumed the substance capable of being abused, however, he still stood firm on his unspoken but accepted pact with J. Marie – no needles. That wasn't to say he didn't do cocaine, heroin, or even a little raw bone occasionally, because nothing would be further from the truth, it just wasn't used intravenously. He wouldn't be done just yet. With the wave of a new inhaled hallucinogenic drug, Love Boat, in the Prince George's County/Washington, D.C. area in 1980, the alphabet chart would be closer to completion.

Skip and J. Marie | 139

The fact that he was capable and would seek to procure gainful employment could be attributed to a number of variables. Until one is endowed with the academic fortitude, or the knowledge of the work involved he/she must utilize the talent(s) God has so graciously bestowed upon them. Skip exploited his to the limits.

From a dazzling smile upon the first encounter to a firm hand handshake upon departure he had his bases covered. He counted largely upon his looks, his brownish-green eyes would draw people into his world like an illusionist when he captivates his crowd. Skip knew some of what to say, but more so when to say it as conversations are often about timing and attentiveness to the listener. <u>He exuded confidence and moxie…he was full of it.</u>

While weighing out the pros and cons that governed his life, it came out even-steven. Had J. Marie recognized and assessed all the "con" parts of his life, she may have long since boarded another ship; though only twenty-three, she had close to a decade invested with him. Up until the detectives burst in on them that morning, the thought of abandoning ship never crossed her mind.

Riding downtown to the main police headquarters on Indiana Avenue, N.W., Skip played over no less than a dozen capers he'd pulled in the last two and half months that this thing could be about. Most were random street robberies, but those that concerned him most were the planned establishment setups, the inside jobs. There were too many people involved, too many payoffs, and for what, two or three grand?! Skip was disgusted with himself for never getting the payday the big boys were getting. Chicks brother Cortez was taking down! He and his crime partner Batman from Benning Heights, Turtle Wells, and Sonny (although both were now doing life in Maryland's Penitentiary) had taken off Baltimore-Washington International Airport several years ago, or rather a bank out there by the airport, for four hundred thousand dollars. Whew! And even his old friend, Sam Buggs, was taking down big numbers, going in banks, but then he'd taken a fall too – thirty slices (years)... Ouch!

Skip, though, if he somehow made it out of this mess, he had to get another crew, because these little leaguers he was now dealing with would probably *never* get to play in the majors. *Running with them*, he reasoned, *I'll be forever relegated to nothing more than being a petty-larceny, nickel-and-dime-type hustler.*

Meanwhile. Skip was playing back in his head the scene on Georgia Ave. last month... Jack gave him the low; the guy would be pulling into the rear parking lot of the bank. Skip knew the type and color of the car. He'd be carrying a small satchel-like zipper bag. He had the kid's description and approximate time to look for him. Jack was explicit about being sure to take him off when he went into the bank as opposed to coming out.

Black drove as Skip road shotgun with the big Magnum in a breakaway shoulder holster. Skip would wear his signature top-coat and Knox Fifth Avenue dress hat when he was going gangster. After the job, he would shave his beard and buy a new skimmer. That was his m.o.

As Skip grew older, he became more reserved and laid back. He was no longer the impatient novice rookie. He was about getting the job done and over with, whatever it was. Sometimes he welcomed the comfort from a swig of the shorty MD 20-20 flask he kept in his liner pocket. Though he didn't need it. It was more a psychological crutch than a dependent.

As soon as the boy stepped from the described car. Skip did a quick visual reconnaissance while stepping from his own vehicle. He was on the guy before the guy knew what hit him – he never saw it coming, which in this case wasn't exactly a good thing. Before exiting the car with Black he removed his hat and replaced it for a ski mask folded up like a regular crew cap. By the time he approached his target, the cap was pulled down to reveal it was indeed a mask. With gun in one hand, he grabbed his man with the other to take control of the situation, and to prevent the guy trying to bail. Skip was in his grill when he told his victim in his most convincing street thug voice, "Don't make me kill you, bitch. You know what it is."

As panic seized him. The dude tried to swat the big gun away from his face. In the process, the money bag fell to the ground, spilling its contents. He then backed up to the car in a hysterical frenzy in which Skip held the gun on him while collecting as much money as he could before fleeing to the get-away car.

Black calmly put the car into gear and they were off, no witnesses in sight – or so they thought. Despite the meager payoff, the only real flaw in the plot was the get-away vehicle. It was one of their own, and not one of Skip's usual ill-gotten methods of transportation.

Skip thought of another setup, an inside job he'd gotten away from. But it, too, had a glitch…that damn Steve. Skip had told Steve, "Look, park on that street right there and position the car where you can see that spot where the alley pours into the street. Keep your eyes locked to that spot because that's where I'll be as soon as I take this cat off."

The heist went off sweet, with the precision of a clip straight out of *The Sting*, starring Robert Redford.

Skip was eating a bag of chips as he and his target walked towards one another. He was eating from the bag to put his man at ease. At twenty feet away, Skip had to match steps so that the money bag would be on the upswing to match the rhythm of the carrier's stride.

This guy was so relaxed and far removed from his main priority that he should have had to pay his company back from out of his own pocket. Skip didn't use a gun on this one, what was intended to be a strong-arm robbery wound up being a robbery without force; theft at the least.

As planned, when Skip bolted through the alley, he began walking slowly out onto the street. As he exited the alley, he noticed that he didn't hear a car engine being turned over, or any motion of a car headed his way, nothing! Skip got a sick feeling in his stomach. Here he was – a bag of money held up under his armpit inside his jacket, just coming off a snatch robbery and stranded a street over from the crime scene.

As Skip looked to where his soon to be ex-friend was supposed to be coming from, he saw the car but Steve wasn't looking in his direction. Instead he was looking off to his left, with his foot resting on the instrument panel. Skip knew this, because he could see his knee propped up, and it was bouncing as it would if someone were listening to music. Skip could also make out smoke streaming from the driver's side window.

Skip couldn't dare risk calling out to him because it would draw an obvious tip on them, and he couldn't break to the car either. It was just too far away and time was of the essence. All that was left was for Skip to try to attract his attention by waving his arms. But even that was not enough to get the joker to look in is direction. He frantically began waving his arms again, this time jumping up and down in hopes of getting his attention, the whole time doing his best to clutch the purse-sized bag under his arm.

Finally…after about 30 seconds (which was way too long to be left hanging after what had just transpired), Steve acknowledged his pickup. Skip, by now, was as his old country-girl mama would say, "Fit to be tied." He was literally smoking! Steve was one of his childhood friends since they were eleven, who, along with Chick were a small group of errant youths in the making. Skip was the youngest of the trio, but always had the biggest money scheme. Now he was trying to put his boy on to something that would surely fatten his pockets a little, but he'd messed that up.

Skip gave him an R-rated tongue lashing instead of a Rated X version. He peeped in the purse to check out the spoils before crossing town. It looked to be about three grand. He peeled off seven hundred dollars and gave it to Steve. After they got back to the apartment on Savannah Terrace, he gave J. Marie three hundred. He'd give the setup man a grand, and be left with a little over a grand for himself.

There were several more robberies Skip considered this ride may be about, and a few stolen cars he'd sold that may have come back to bit him. An old associate, Raymond, was pissed with Skip about a car he'd put in the shop to have some work done; a lady came into the shop and claimed the car was hers. It was one of the old Fords Skip just happened to have papers for that he could use as a match. Maybe, Skip thought, this whole thing is about cars, and these detectives are with some kind of car-theft-ring task force…but there were far too many Feds for this to be all about stolen cars. Skip willed himself to relax for the rest of the ride in. They'd be at the Municipal Center any minute, and then he would find out what this was all about.

Skip was elated to find out that this whole thing was about the A&A Towing Company getting robbed. He had not been to the new location in over five years, not since before he torched Necie's brother's car.

Someone (Danny Watkins, he found out later) gave up his name as a possible suspect. Perhaps if Skip would have thought about it, he would've gotten a young crew together and knocked the joint off, but the thought never crossed his mind.

Later that week at work Mr. Scruggs wanted Skip to take him out to Rosecroft Race Track if J. Marie was fine with it. It would be just long enough for Mr. Scruggs to put a few dollars on a couple of picks. That was Scruggs's thing, one of his hustle's. He'd study the horse racing section of the local newspaper for hours on end when there weren't any autopsies to perform. His old friend, Lonnie, was a big "Trotter" fan too.

Lonnie Perry was Ricky Monk's uncle via marriage; he married into the Kingsbury family. The two old cronies would accompany one another to play the horses, sometimes every day of a given week if one or both of them were hot – on a real roll.

Chapter 10

THIS ONE DAY, LONNIE COULDN'T roll with his road-dog. Skip was like Scruggs's adopted son and didn't mind doing him a favor of most any kind. Nothing short of murder would have been a problem if Scruggs asked Skip. He was just that cool with his mentor and supervisor.

Skip had Scruggs in the car when he swung by to pick up J. Marie from work at 4:00. She was glad to see old Mr. Scruggs since she had not seen him in a couple of years. Like Skip's father, Scruggs genuinely liked J. Marie and was overjoyed that his two favorite young folks were still married and had a "Little Skip" together. Now, however, he hoped his adopted daughter-in-law didn't have plans for this evening, because he had some horses to feed out at the track.

J. Marie said she didn't have anything to do, so when Michael D'Angelo was picked up from Ms. Lynsey's, the group proceeded home so Skip could drop his family off at the apartment. It was on the way to the track anyway.

True to form, old Hubert Scruggs was "on like popcorn." Skip learned enough under his tutelage over the past few days to know which jockey runs which horse the best and a few other things. Skip collected a couple hundred that evening just from hanging out with old Scruggs.

J. Marie was so happy her man had made a few extra dollars with Mr. Scruggs instead of those shady characters Black, Phil, and even Kenny. She knew as long as Skip was with Mr. Scruggs, at worst he'd coming back smelling of liquor, but nine times out of ten, he'd have some money in his pocket, and it would be lawful. The downside to Skip's winning on the horses was that *now he was hooked!*

The race track bug bit Skip and he had the fever, as addictive as any substance can be, gambling can be just as habitual. Skip was studying the racing section of the sports page like Scruggs.

A few days later, Scruggs thought for sure that he had a couple winners picked. Skip thought he himself had a win or two also. Scruggs couldn't get away from the morgue because the six-slab refrigerator was full. There were three permissions signed from the families, which meant a "post" had to be done on half of the bodies there.

Skip asked his supervisor if he wanted him to stay back for overtime, but all Scruggs wanted his young protégé to do was take the money he gave Skip out to the track and put the bets down.

Skip had a few dollars of his own to place too, and assured Scruggs he'd handle it. "Don't worry, Mr. Scruggs. I got this."

That evening when Skip swung by to pick up J. Marie. He told her what the deal was. They picked up Michael D'Angelo from Ms. Lynsey's and carried him along with them to Rosecroft Raceway. J. Marie was a bundle of excitement. This was a whole new arena for her, and she was delighted in all the commotion.

Skip and Scruggs were going in half on all bets, the horse that just so happened to win was one of those Skip picked. The payoff was more than seven hundred dollars. Skip and J. Marie were cool, calm and collected about the win. They didn't make a big show of the win for fear of drawing a tip to themselves.

Skip loved seeing his wife smile when he had something to do with it. That was a payoff in and of itself.

Skip took the money and J. Marie, and Michael D'Angelo, and he bounced. There was no need to stay around for another race as far as Skip was concerned. "Let's go, J."

He put Scruggs's three hundred fifty dollars in an envelope to give him the next day, gave J. Marie one hundred fifty dollars to buy food and whatever, and kept two hundred for himself to settle a few debts and a blast from something.

The next day, Skip went out there with thirty dollars, lost it, and had to walk back because he had someone to drop him off there. He was thinking he had another hit and would pay someone out there to bring him back, but after losing the thirty dollars, he never went back again.

Skip admired, respected, and truly loved his mother-in-law. he'd gone so far as to assist her in retribution against Dickey late one night. They both could've gone to jail easily.

Once, without much forethought, he told her in front of J. Marie, "I hope J. Marie doesn't grow to be like you." Regardless of whatever truth may lie within a statement, some are best left unspoken.

Lou supported Skip like she would have one of her own. The two never had a cross moment – other than Skip's Freudian slip that one time. She would chalk some of his crap up to unbridled youth and ignorance, she allowed room and time for him to grow.

Given the period of her life in question, perhaps she understood why her daughter's boyfriend would feel as he did. Though ignorance is no excuse for breaking the law; it can, however, be worthy of a pardon in social settings.

Skip was, for years, unequipped to give much thought to his statements and actions. It goes back to that underdeveloped pre-frontal cortex in a teen's brain, and in some young adults that have had their brain cells stunted and retarded by hallucinogenic and alcohol.

It's why, after we're older and more mature, we will look back at some of our teen and adolescent activities and say, "What could I have been thinking? I could have been killed, or killed someone else."

The thing is, we were not thinking with a fully developed brain. Over the years since Anacostia Road, during the time in the Edgewood Terrace apartments, Skip would get to know Lou, her mother, and siblings intimately. He would, as J. Marie had become with his family and relatives, get to be an extended family member to them. Unions between a man and woman are often that way. They can unite families to become strong alliances and powerful clans, given the families are united.

Skip saw his own now-mother-in-law do an 180° turn since the earlier years; though she was still outgoing and might give one a thorough rated-X tongue lashing, those closest to her could tell she was beginning to mellow out with the passing of the years.

J. Marie, Skip, Robert, Kenny O, and another brother or sister would occasionally accompany her to a cabaret, or the girls would ride out to Quantico in Langley, VA to the NCO club with her. Skip didn't particularly like that, but he knew enough not to keep his girl reined in too tight. He wasn't a complete idiot.

Skip couldn't dance. He was rhythmless at first, but enjoyed watching the rest of them have a good time. As long as he had a few cold ones and a shot of…something he was alright.

When something slow played however, he and J. Marie would make their way to the floor to relax in each other's embrace.

J. Marie was always a lady, and dignified. He never saw her dancing too close or acting unscrupulously with anyone – though he probably would have pulled a "Paul Lucas" on her and the lame.

Skip didn't learn to do anything close to an acceptable step until the "bump" dance came out. Given the right beat, all one had to do was lean into your partner with the beat then back off, and repeat it. Though he would never be another M.C. Hammer or Fred Astaire, he began to find enough rhythm to blend in with the rest of the partygoers.

Lou on the other hand, could shake that thing with those half her age without missing a step. Skip was still wrestling with accepting how someone could be as much fun to be around and enjoy themselves as she did without any alcohol or drugs. J. Marie was the same way, pretty much. The two of them were on the natural – "THE NAT-CHOO-RAL." For years, Louise was definitely "doing her."

When a coworker of Lou's with the Federal Protection Agency began dating Lou, it seemed to give her even more stability. James Hinant was a serious dude, an ex-military man from the South. He kept things up front and real. He loved Lou without question and loved being around her. How else could one explain tolerating a four-bedroom apartment that was full of lunatic teenagers and young adults? With no less than five of them, and a toddler or two in the crib at all times, running around and tearing stuff up (they nicknamed Michael D'Angelo and his cousin Tamika "Bam-Bam and Pebbles," after the two toddlers from the *Flintstones*), things were at a constantly frantic pace there.

On any given day, the smell of marijuana would be ever-so-present coming from under one of the closed doors. Other than Lou's back room, that was off limits.

The joint was sometimes like National Lampoon's *Party House*, seriously! It was a stash house for stolen property, guns (mostly Skip's), and a fugitive or two might be camped out there until the heat died down – Kenny O. mostly.

Skip was shocked that the place was never raided, or at least the housing authorities didn't ask Lou to please leave… "with all your kids, the guns, marijuana, babies…everybody get OUT!"

James had to be the most patient and tolerant man Skip ever saw. Occasionally, he would go out with Lou, J. Marie, and Skip to one of the more civil shows where there was arranged seating, like an oldies but goodies production at the Warner Theater or Constitution Hall.

Surprisingly, the only fights or assaults that took place the whole six years there were between J. Marie's sisters Cindy and Tawanna. Skip once had to subdue J. Marie's brother, Gary, but that was more of a wrestler's take down than anything else, and things were back to normal after a few minutes.

There were some funny times as well as potentially dangerous days at Edgewood too.

Everyone in the apartment knew that Lou, as a rule, did not authorize the smoking of marijuana in the apartment, though she knew it was going on to some degree, but who exactly, or when, she wasn't sure. Nevertheless, during some of her extended periods of absence everyone was smoking…something.

Sharon and Cindy had been beefing all day about someone not cleaning up the living room, or somebody's turn was skipped on the wash or whatever. When Lou came home, before she broke the plain of the threshold, the two girls rushed to argue their side of the story. Which, when all was said and done, ended with Sharon blurting out… "And, Lou, Cindy was smoking reefer in the house."

Skip saw no less than five jaws drop from everyone that witnessed the exchange between the girls, including his own jaw. Lou shot Cindy a look of resignation and disgust. Cindy, on the other hand, looked at Sharon with disbelief and shock that her sister would rat her out this way.

Looking ahead, years later. it would be a great clip for that commercial… "Feel like you need to get away?"

One night, while alone in the confines of J. Marie's bedroom, and in an intoxicated and drug-induced stupor (after dropping a half or three-quarter tab of Purple Haze, smoking a joint or two, and nursing a fifth of Red Ripple), Skip, in a hallucinogenic state, looked at the poster-sized panda on the backside of the door in J. Marie's bedroom. He himself had placed that poster there to decorate the room when J. Marie and Michael D'Angelo arrived home from the hospital. Now Skip saw this once friendly and smiling bear looking at him with his mug broke down.

The bear, after a minute or so, slowly stood up and threw the red ball he held down. Meanwhile, Skip's mind began to race. He was thinking, *I've got to get to my piece.* During these days, it was the bolt-action, one-in-the-chamber, three-in-the-clip sawed-off. Skip would blast this joker, but he needed to get to the closet where the joint was stashed.

The bear was slowly making his way upon Skip. *There's no way,* he thought, *that I can make it to the closet before this bear mauls all the hell out of me.* So he opted for Plan B. Just as fast, he was out the bedroom window. Fortunately, the apartment was on the ground floor. He walked around to the front entrance, knocked on the door of the apartment where everyone was congregated in the living room. When Robert came to the door, he asked Skip, "Man, weren't you just in the bedroom?"

Skip told him, "I was, but I had to leave. I thought I saw something. Where's J. Marie?"

In 1979 sometime, Lou and James decided they'd had enough of the Edgewood Terrace complex. Lou told Skip to get a few friends. Along with the rest of the family, they would be moving everything to a new townhouse development out in Temple Hills, a suburb of Washington, D.C.

Skip, Chick, Steve, Gary – everyone helped out. Steve had a van, Lou borrowed a pickup truck with sides from a friend of hers, and after several trips, everything was in the new house – nothing broken or lost.

The street was kind of new to Skip, even though it wasn't too far across the Anacostia, S.E. line.

After the initial accolades heaped upon the new house, now occupied by her mother and James, Skip was surprised J. Marie had not said anything later about it. New house talk and house hunting can be contagious sometimes, especially if a couple is able to afford one. J. Marie thought about her own occupancy of the little house her and Skip talked about as teenagers. They both liked hanging out at the new house, it had two floors over a spacious basement, Lou and James had a bathroom with a shower, and Tawanna and Gary each had a room. Cindy had a place in Congress Heights not too far from Skip's old friend, Dunmore. Dave, the youngest of the Williams siblings, wasn't doing too well finding his niche.

Skip had to pick his wife up from her mother's one day. On the way, as he was about to turn up a steep hill and just before the turn to Lou's, he saw a "For Sale" sign in the yard of a modest little semi-detached rambler-style brick house. He didn't think much of it at the time until he spoke to J. Marie once he got to Lou's.

Before he could get all the words from his mouth, J. Marie was smiling while heading for the door. J. Marie loved the little place, a two-car driveway, nice-sized front yard. It was within walking distance from her mother's (what young bride doesn't want that), and the hole-in-the-wall they were now living in just wasn't getting it done. Especially not with another baby on the way – J. Marie was pregnant.

Although she said nothing to Skip, J. Marie thought maybe they were getting ahead of themselves with all this talk of a house. Skip had not so long ago wrecked the car, that wasn't quite three years old. And what made matters worse, the fool had let the car insurance run out. Now he had to piece it back together, part by part, thanks to the help from her uncle, Cookie. (Skip was involved in two other accidents prior to this one. The first one was when he was fifteen years old, zigzagging in the rain, playing and trying to scare his friend Chick. The car went out of control and crashed into a tree, temporarily dazing him. However, he still managed to get out and run behind his friend, escaping. The second accident occurred when he was cutting lanes in the parking lot of Landover Mall, driving Steve's old Dodge; Chick was also in the car. Skip broadsided another vehicle that had the right of way. J. Marie was following in a car behind them. Skip never paid the damages to the other driver, nor helped to fix Steve's car.)

Lately, he never seemed to have enough money for anything other than the basic necessities. J. Marie wondered what on earth he could be doing with his money. She knew he made good money working at the VA as an autopsy assistant. He was painting on the side and doing God knows what else with Phil and Kenny. She knew whatever it was, there were guns involved.

Skip had a knack for being able to put his hands on a nice piece of cheese in an emergency if he really needed to. Most times, he'd come through with whatever amount it called for.

Besides, as far as the house went, he still had eligibility on the Veterans G.I. bill, the home loan part of it. The only thing he'd previously used it for was for going to school.

Skip took the information down off of the "For Sale" sign, then called his real-estate-agent friend and coworker at the VA. Joan Penn got right on it. After she found out the Veterans Administration would foot the bill, she told Skip and J. Marie all they would need would be about two thousand dollars to cover the closing cost.

Skip was flat broke, the few dollars that he had lately was going towards fixing his car. He never knew exactly how much J. Marie had, for as long as he could remember she always had something stashed away for hard times. She'd always been good at managing her money even though it was only a little. This time she had a few hundred dollars in the bank, or her bra, or someplace. Together they would make it happen.

The closing cost wasn't due until the day when they went to settlement, which was five or six weeks away. No sweat, whoever Skip and J. Marie owed simply was not getting paid. Skip took his entire salary from two straight paydays, as did J. Marie, along with a couple of paint jobs with Scruggs and Dunmore.

Skip's old friend, Phil, was a crud-ball sleazy-type crook if there ever was one, but he sure enough went for Skip and his wife, and he was a house painting son-of-a-gun. He and Larry Dunmore were two of Skip's best painting partners. They both were two serious brush slingers!

The day of the settlement, Skip and J. Marie had well over what they needed for closing. The contracts were signed and the cozy little brick rambler on Chadwick Street was theirs! They celebrated with champagne.

In August of 1980, Skip and his junior high school sweetheart were living in their own home. They were married with a son, and a child on the way. They were loving life and each other.

Before they got the furniture moved in, Skip had some preparations to make. He was a professional painter now, no longer working in the morgue. He was still with the VA, although in another department. He was in the engineering department with the painters and wallpaper hangers, making a real nice piece of change for a young blue-collar-type working class. Skip didn't like the color of some of the rooms, and wanted to show off some of his painting skills again to J. Marie.

She was smiling a lot these days. Skip knew it was a woman thing. J. Marie's status had been brought up a notch, just like Lou's was when she became a homeowner… Come to think of it, Lou was looking at Skip differently these days. Lou thought Skip came a long way, and despite whatever negative vices were attributed to him, all she was seeing was this guy, whom she had known since he was a kid, who had given her two grandbabies, and placed her eldest daughter in a house, and they seemed to be very happy together. Lou was happy that, at least one of her daughters, so far, had excelled to exceed her own accomplishments when she was her daughter's age, and that of her siblings.

Skip was doing something he truly enjoyed, he was a naturally gifted painter. He was good at it and he knew it. He had jobs lined up to do for several doctors where he worked. He needed a vehicle of some type to put his painting equipment in, a station wagon or small truck of sorts.

J. Marie ran the house. It was hers now. Skip only paid the note on it, worked in and around the perimeter, and maintained security. He had one request from J. Marie, whom he had affectionately nicknamed "Phats"…that he be able to get a dog. "More so for the boy, you understand," he informed her. "Every boy should grow up with a dog," he finished.

J. Marie was never anybody's fool. She understood all too well about man's best friend and all that carrying on. "Oh yeah…Well as long as you and "the boy" understand I don't want to see dog crap and pee stains all over my carpet, and the first time I do see it, somebody's getting me a new one."

J. Marie had wanted a new carpet for some time now. The mixed black and red one, they'd had since the first apartment years ago. Another one was *long* overdue as far as she was concerned. Now was the perfect time to set the wheels in motion.

For Skip, it was like déjà vu. He was hearing every word, but wasn't seeing her. Suddenly it was Connie's voice he was hearing. He had temporarily traveled back into the past. He was eight years old again, with one of the little black wild dog puppies he and his friends found in the woods. He'd brought Smokey into the house to show his mom. Connie scolded Skip for bringing the little mangy mutt he'd just pulled out of the woods into the house. "That dog has *fleas*, Skippá, you can have him, but take it outside until we clean him up, and… Skip! Skip! Are you listening to me?"

Skip snapped out of the trance he'd been temporarily caught up in. "Yeah, yeah, Phats, I heard you." Skip searched the papers at work that next morning on his break. He located an animal shelter not far from where he worked. That afternoon, leaving work, he stopped by the place, found what he was looking for, took it home to introduce the little fellow to his new friend, and the warden of the property where he'd be staying. As soon as she saw the puppy she thought about her first trip to Southeast with Skip, about Madoo sitting on the sofa watching soap operas with the sleeping baby stretched out next to her. When her and Skip emerged from the house, there was an older black dog running towards them. J. Marie shouted a warning to her boyfriend while sidestepping, strategically placing Skip between herself and the potential threat. The dog playfully jumped on Skip, throwing his ears back to be petted. She noticed one of his ears had a piece missing from the tip and he had several old scars on his face. Smokey paid her no attention.

Just then Michael D'Angelo entered the kitchen area where his parents stood over a puppy on the floor. Michael D'Angelo was four years old. He knew this dog was his at first sight, so he stooped down to let his new puppy jump onto him and lick him.

While leaving his son and the puppy to get better acquainted, Skip said, "His name is Smokey. Don't let dogs lick you in the face," and then left the room. J. Marie looked after him as he left. She wondered if it was just like old cars and tools that are lying around – it was a "man thing." Although this time it was hitting close to home for her man, and for her.

The rest of the summer at J. Marie's was like Grand Central Station. The fact that they were only twenty-four spoke volumes in their circle of friends, as well as with the couple's families.

Ownership was an amazing phenomenon; all the cars Skip and J. Marie jetted around in during their lives together were easily and understandably attributed as "Skip's cars." The apartments were "J. Marie and Skip's" place. Now with the new house, when someone spoke of visiting the couple, they would say, "Let's go over the J. Marie's house."

Skip loved it. They'd shared the spotlight for years, but now it was all about her; after the years of her, as well as her sisters, having to alternate their outfits, doing without, putting up with the crap on 12th Street while living in the house their father rented, as well as the short time living with Skip in Connie's basement – all that was behind her now. J. Marie was a homeowner!

The place was perfect for them, though there were only two bedrooms, there was a room in the basement that could easily be used as a third bedroom. Now, however, it was the couples "music room," that had a door leading out to the drive way. None of their parents, or grandparents as far as they knew, had such a propitious start. Skip and J. Marie had come a long way since the days of having sex in one of Skip's stolen cars.

Somewhere in the seventh or eighth month of J. Marie's pregnancy, Tawanna and her friend Randy, the community angel dust distributor, organized a house party to be held at her eldest sister's new crib. Skip and J. Marie had several of their own friends there as well, as no less than seventy or one hundred young adults and teenagers from the neighborhood were there. Skip was still on probation from the gun charge he caught a few years prior, and the last thing he needed was a contributing to underage drinking and drug charges.

There was enough loud, blaring music, wine, beer and reefer for everyone to get tight. One of J. Marie's and Gwynn's old friends from New Hampshire Avenue and the skating rink was there too. Skip knew Dexter Lee and his cousin, Terry, also.

The first encounter Skip had with the newly arrived hallucinogenic "love boat" was at the behest of Dexter. Fortunately, Skip thought the small amount of flakes the small aluminum foil wrapper held were too expensive, telling Dexter, "Fifteen dollars for this! Man, you have got to kiddin'."

Randy and Tawanna stayed back after the party to personally help clean up. Skip helped and oversaw it all while J. Marie and Mike D'Angelo lay sleeping; Skip was up and alert until the last person left. Skip was high during the party, but knew the protocol; no one upstairs, especially in the back bedrooms – only select guests could occupy the living room and dining room areas (these places were, more so, for J. Marie and a few of her personal friends to temporarily get away from the madness). That's the benefit of having a bathroom and running water in the basement. One has to also be mindful of loud, raised, vulgar language – it could easily escalate into a fight.

Priority number one protect J. Marie and Mike D'Angelo, and know where J. Marie is *at all times*. Although Skip was high, he could've sworn he saw his mother-in-law in the crowd of young partygoers. He decided that he would ask J. Marie about it later.

Seven months pregnant, J. Marie was getting huge fast, and as happy as a fat kid in a cake factory about her situation. Skip made sure that he supplied her with plenty of fresh fruit, as he did during her first pregnancy. Whereas during the first pregnancy, it was as much grapes as she could stand, now he was on an orange campaign. She was getting fat, slow, and clumsy. Skip knew he had to keep a sharp eye on his beloved fat wife.

One of J. Marie's childhood and best friends found out where her longtime friend was holding up, and contacted her. Skip had always heard of Gwynn, but had never met her up to that point. When he did, though, he understood how the two of them got along so well. One reason was probably the fact that they favored each other a great deal. On the weekends, Skip and J. Marie would go by where Gwynn lived, pick her up, and let her hang out with them all day.

Once, while the three of them were together in the music room at J. Marie's house, J. Marie all of a sudden got an urge for her favorite butter pecan ice cream. Skip would have to make a run to the High's in the nearby shopping center, and the girls wanted to go as well. On her way up the small staircase leading to the driveway, J. Marie took a misstep halfway up and fell down backwards and landed on first her rear, and then her back. Skip and Gwynn rushed to her side to assist her to her feet and/or take her to the hospital for a checkup, if necessary. J. Marie, however, thought that the situation was the funniest thing. She laughed endlessly at her own clumsiness as both Skip and Gwynn exhaled sighs of relief.

As J. Marie's due date drew near, Skip was expecting a phone call from the secretary down the hall from his work station, possibly informing him that his wife was on her way to the hospital, which was just across the parking lot from the V.A. hospital.

The second edition to the Lucas family would be later than expected. J. Marie's physician, Dr. Chumpahtizi, would have to induce labor, which he would do on December twenty-sixth. Skip ardently tried talking him into delivering the day before so his wife could have a Christmas baby (at the time Skip knew nothing about Kwanzaa); however, the good doctor was resolute in his position. Skip was allowed to enter into the delivery room to hold J. Marie's hand and attempt to keep her relaxed during the birth of their next child.

This was the closest Skip had ever been, and probably will *ever be*, to an actual delivery. He heard of fathers being allowed to be able to see the baby coming out of the womb. That would've been fine with him, but it was better at her head, just holding her hand.

Newborns all looked close the same to Skip. They didn't begin taking on a distinct look until about a week or so old, other than complexion, having or having no hair, and some have wrinkles, others are smooth. There was one feature/characteristic Skip was looking for in particular – he had it, Michael D'Angelo had it, and now he was looking for it on his daughter.

Skip was born in July at the old Freedman's Hospital on, what had been, the hottest day of that summer. Connie was a very small and petite woman. This pregnancy had pushed her body to a limit she had never endured or imagined possible. There was no air conditioning then, and with only ceiling fans and ice rags to keep her cool, she was hot and uncomfortable beyond words. She desperately wanted the delivery over and done with.

By infant standards, Skip had a large head that caused Connie excruciating pain. The pain was close to being unbearable, and, for a few moments during the birthing, she honestly thought that she would die. Immediately following the delivery, before showing Connie her baby, she noticed the doctors conferring and examining the hand of the infant, and then continuing to talk amongst themselves. "What's the matter?" She asked. Then, with more urgency, "Is something wrong with my baby? Let me see."

"Nothing's actually wrong, Mrs. Lucas. Calm down, please." Then they asked her, "Does any member in your family have six fingers on one of their hands?"

"Hell, no," she exclaimed. "Bring me my baby!"

The doctor brought Skip to his mother, extending the left hand for Connie's observation. At the base of Skip's little finger, and growing separately next to it, was an extra boneless appendage the size and shape of a regular baby finger. They assured her that, though it was anomaly, it wasn't unprecedented, and a specialist could easily excise the malformation before either of them left the hospital. Following the procedure, all that was left was a barely-noticeable lump of flesh where the little sixth digit began to grow. As Skip grew older and into adulthood, he'd learn to involuntarily protect the sensitive little lump from direct hits, because of its sensitivity.

As the doctor brought Skip and J. Marie's daughter around for the new parents to see, and before cleaning her and giving her a thorough examination, Skip marveled at his wife with tears of joy running down her face. He looked at the dimpled smile as she looked at their daughter. Skip's eyes seemed to split because he was seeing mother and daughter simultaneously. His baby girl had slick, dark hair – and a great deal of it, too. She was red like he was and, what's more, she only had five fingers on each hand. *Oh, well,* he thought to himself, wryly, *we can't all be imperfect.*

Skip stayed with J. Marie until the nurses took her for her post-delivery examination and then prepared her bed. When they brought her back to her room – though, Skip was supposed to have been off the ward by then – he was in her room when she returned.

She was drowsy, and Skip knew that she needed to rest. He kissed her goodbye and told her that he'd see her the following day. On his way off the maternity ward, he stopped by where all of the infants were for one last peek at his daughter before he split.

The way little boys are about playing with toy cars, trucks, and playing cowboys and Indians, or cops and gangsters – little girls are just as enthused about dolls, tea sets, playing house, and dressing up like mommy, complete with lip stick and high-heeled shoes.

When boys get older, most of them still have a car fetish. They're just as enthusiastic about guns, the fights, and tool boxes. Little girls become big girls, then grown women, and become enraptured and giddy over cute babies, sometimes not just any baby will get them "there," either. Candie Renee took them over the top. She was gorgeous.

By J. Marie's birthday that January, people were coming by the house in droves. They were getting rides from friends, dropped off at the nearest main street, and walking the rest of the way, even hitchhiking in some cases. They wanted to see the house, or baby, or Michael D'Angelo and his little sister together, or J. Marie and Skip, or just hang out.

Another good thing about the house on Chadwick Street was the location. Though not exactly close to the couple's job sites, It wasn't far from a hospital, their parent's homes, and a main park the families began to gather in named "Oxon Run." Cookouts and picnics were big with the Lucases and Williamses. The kids from both sides, as well as their many friends, would get together to take advantage of holidays. No park was exempt: Anacostia Park, Fort DuPont, Hains Point, Oxon Run, even Fort Stanton's park. Occasionally they would be invited to a gathering at Rock Creek Park or Fort Washington out on Indianhead Highway. Someone, usually Skip and one of the girls, would drive to the Waterfront in S.W., also known as The Wharf, to buy a bushel of crabs. Along the way back, they'd stop for beer and wine, too. Someone would have gotten to the designated area early to stake out a good spot while the others would be home preparing their special contributed dishes.

Lou would hook up the potato or macaroni salad, with the help of one of her daughters. Robert was always good for a six pack or a case of beer. Michael Gordon (M.G.) was the crab cooker. Sometimes he'd put in too much beer for Lou's or J. Marie's taste, though. Most of the time it wasn't anything planned, but J. Marie would always find time to make deviled eggs, which were mainly for Skip, although all were welcomed as long as Skip was able to get his first. Connie would kick out some cash to help things along, especially when it came to the crab divvy.

A couple of times, when they had watermelon, Phil and Skip injected it with vodka from a fifty-gauge syringe Skip took from the lab. The first time the two dumped *way* too much liquor in it. The thing tasted horrible; one a sure-enough alcoholic could have appreciated.

Bee-Bee was an old Taft Jr. High School friend of Cindy, Skip, and J. Marie. Bee and her boyfriend, Joe, had been together about as long as Skip and J. Marie. The two of them had a son, Lil' Joe, who was about Candie's age, not quite two yet, and the girls were all saying how cute this little fellow and Candie were together. To Skip's annoyance, he looked to see this boy holding his daughter's hand. Skip figured he'd keep an eye on this joker through the years, even if he was a second generation "Wright." He was Sam and Charlie Wright's nephew. They helped Skip out when he was having trouble with relatives of Mike at the Big V Supermarket for smashing him after pressing up on J. Marie ten years ago.

The families and friends played baseball together while Gary's supersized sound system cranked out the maximum amount of tenor and bass; quality and quantity of whatever it was he could draw out of a speaker system. Gary was Skip's and J. Marie's generation's "Uncle Cookie." He got to where he could fix whatever was brought to him; if he could study it long enough, and had the right tools… it was done.

The years he'd spent visiting his uncle paid off for him; he was well adjusted socially with exceptional work ethic.

Skip drove home from work to find J. Marie in one of the back rooms; their habit from their days in junior high on through J. Marie's high school years was to give a short kiss when it was clear that they wouldn't see each other until the next day or so. As they grew older and began living together it turned into a greeting as well as a departure kiss – except for the very first thing in the morning when Skip had that "dragon" in his mouth from the previous evening's or night's drinking and smoking; she never said anything about it, however.

Skip was also in the habit of wearing his green engineering uniform around the house a few hours after he was off of work. He'd come in, find J. Marie, kiss her, and then have a brief chat about whatever; Skip would play with his son for a while, kiss Candie, and talk a little of that baby stuff just to see her laughing. It was so funny to him to see little Candie Renee laughing with the baby drool dripping from her mouth, showing nothing but gums.

There was a window in the kitchen looking out into the driveway; while J. Marie made her way to the kitchen, he expected to hear her voice calling out to him at any second now…5,4,3,2, "Skip, whose car is this is in the driveway?"

Walking to join his wife, he said, "It's yours, Phats. Happy Birthday."

She was all smiles and dimples while stepping onto the back porch and towards her new whip. Though used, it was new to her, and she loved it – who wouldn't love a red '67 Mustang with white interior, white walls, and original wheel covers? It was an 8-cylinder 289; it was fast and tight!

Skip was getting a lot of smiles out J. Marie lately. He thought his old dad would've been proud. He thought a lot about his dad these days, and how unfortunately Skip didn't begin understanding him until it was too late. He regretted never telling his father he loved him. However, most of that was due to the way he treated his mom. Skip thought that old saying was meant to be a "double entendre" about "the fruit not falling far from the tree," but was a load of crap; the only meaning to it is the literal one. Skip couldn't imagine ever treating his beloved J. Marie that way, like his father treated his mom, or how he'd heard Dickey treated Lou. Madoo and Papa Ernest had even separated by now – Skip really had a problem wrestling with that one. Skip couldn't understand how an old couple could grow into their seventies together only to throw in the towel. They didn't want to hang out any more. The problem was two words: SUBSTANCE ABUSE. Alcohol drove Papa Ernest and Madoo apart, point blank.

Skip had a substance-abuse problem too, though he didn't understand it. He knew he had something wrong with his way of thinking, but didn't have a clue as to what steps should be taken to fix it.

In the meantime, the driveway was getting far too crowded, something would have to go. Skip had the new car he bought a few years ago, and wrecked, towed away. An old family friend and his former crime partner, Kenny O, came by the house one day broke and busted, and hating not having transportation to take care of his affairs.

Skip let him take the newest thing in the driveway, the one Necie or Greg had snatched off the street for him to pass off as the wrecked one. Skip gave Kenny explicit instructions, saying, "Don't be riding around dirty, or drawing a tip on yourself, and you'll be fine, and try to get the ignition fixed." Kenny understood.

Seemingly things were shaping up. In a matter of days, Skip and J. Marie's transportation situation had improved dramatically. It was a far cry from the days when the couple was basically just "doing them," with only themselves to be accountable to. They were a family now, a team, even though Skip wasn't playing fair, still making some of his own rules as he went along.

It wasn't just the alcohol Skip was having problems with; one of his oldest and best friends began dallying in a little heroin, sometimes heroin and coke mixed, and he felt obliged to put his main man on front street. He began coming over once a week until Skip would sometimes slip him twenty dollars or so to help out. The next month, Skip was finding the sources himself on the strips of Martin Luther King, Jr. Avenue, 14th and T Streets; Skip began doing 40s (brown tape, Mexican mud, and bone) by himself. He started letting "bills" go. It was to the point Skip knew if it was not for his disdain for needles he would be "firing" like his other childhood best friend, Steve. And like *all* of the older brothers of his closest friends.

Skip was slipping, he was hustling backwards and wasn't bringing the cheddar as he once was. Time was, when he made a sting or got paid on a paint job, J. Marie would get a chunk broke off for herself and/or for the crib. Now it was all about Skip, and he was starting to get cruddy and sneaky. J. Marie noticed it, and she wasn't surprised when, while the couple was sitting in the living room one evening, Skip sat on the arm of the chair next to her and tearfully told her, "J…I need help. I don't know what's wrong with me. The thoughts I'm thinking… I need to stop this drinking and getting high – I need some help."

This was an experience J. Marie wasn't equipped to handle. Not in her wildest dreams had she seen this one coming. "Where was Francine now, when I could use some of that big sister and mentoring advice," she asked herself. "Maybe I should tell Lou."

J. Marie knew her mother saw Skip nodding while he was supposedly watching TV the other night. Maybe she thought he was only dozing because he was tired. "Hell," she rationalized, "I thought he was dozing, too – or did I?"

Skip usually had an answer for most everything all through their lives. Right or wrong, that dude was coming up with a plan for himself if not for the both of them. When he got up to go into the bedroom, J. Marie figured, *He'll be okay – he'll be okay by tomorrow.*

The next morning Skip had forgotten all about his breakdown the previous night. It was business as usual. A week later he had another Mustang, a green one – they had his and hers Mustangs. There was a big race, Skip and J. Marie had both of their cars over at Connie's one night. It was time for them to head home. They knew two ways to get home from Connie's house in Fort Stanton, to Skip both ways were of equal distance. However, J. Marie knew for a fact that her way was faster. Skip told J. Marie, "The only thing that you know is faster is your car over mine, but you can't open it up on these short streets." Skip knew J. Marie could handle a wheel like a pro, but was convinced that the way she was taking was no faster than his way, which was cutting across the Suitland Parkway from Gainsville Street, up, then down Stanton Road, left on Mississippi Avenue, then left on Southern Avenue.

Connie heard the friendly banter that was exchanged between the two; Mike D'Angelo and Candie were with Tawanna at Lou's, so she wasn't worried about the little ones being with them. She knew that, although Skippá (as she still called him) had been driving since he was stealing her car at night when he was twelve, he was reckless sometimes. She only told them both to be careful, and to call her when they got home.

As fate would have it, both of their cars were facing the way they wanted to go, with J. Marie's facing the swimming pool. She hung a hard right at the corner, peeling rubber and leaving smoke to fill the night air. Skip was facing down towards Dunmore's grandparents' house, so he had to be a little more careful as he was still in a slower zone. He made ground up once he made it onto the long strip to the Parkway. After the left on 15th Place, he ran a traffic light as he crossed Suitland Parkway, and continued barreling up Stanton Road!

Thirty yards before the corner where they both would have to take the turn entering into Maryland, and the Oxon Run Shopping Center, J. Marie saw Skip hanging the turn off Mississippi Avenue onto Southern, she was of an equal distance coming head on from the opposite direction. She stomped it, getting everything out of the 289 cu. All it had, and reached the point with seconds to spare before Skip. J. Marie hung the left on two wheels!

Skip couldn't believe the nerve of his woman as she cut in front of two cars before he could, he thought to himself, biting his bottom lip and shaking his head, *Damn!* He smiled.

Kenny O had not spent too many of his birthdays out of prison since the age of seventeen when the juvenile court system waved the "Youth Act" on him. He planned on spending this one quietly, if it was at all possible, and he couldn't think of a better way than with his friends from his Edgewood Terrace days. He knew Skip had been on laid-back time for the past year, other than getting high and still running cars.

Chapter 11

Kenny was down from his crib in Montgomery County just for the weekend. The last time he was at J. Marie's new crib was when he needed a set of wheels, which he eventually got jammed with. It was his own fault. Skip told him to be cool with it. Now Kenny was on probation for accessory to grand theft; of course he took it on the chin.

Skip's probationary time had expired a few months ago for the gun charge that he had caught back in '77. He was fortunate that time. If it had not been for Kenny talking him out of it, Skip was about to make a tragic mistake. Skip had his .41 Magnum drawn, but down low, and only a few heartbeats away from squeezing off a few rounds on the cop. The cop could see it, he was only several yards away. Instead the two allowed the cop to call for backup. Skip wound up charged with the gun. The police never checked the glove compartment, where they surely would have found several sets of credit cards that were left over from various armed robberies and assaults that had occurred throughout the District, Maryland, and Virginia.

J. Marie, Skip, and Kenny had a lot to talk and laugh about when they got together. Kenny used to hang out with the Williams family since Edgewood. He would club and party with them when they rolled with Lou. While he was on the run, he once camped out there until he could find a better safe house. He was theirs and Skip's adopted kin folk. Skip trusted him like no other.

Sometimes Kenny could have some of the worst luck, Skip saw. Like the time at Jimmy's Golden Cue on T Street, N.W., when he got into a beef with a guy that carried over from when the two were in Lorton. The guy cracked Kenny across the eye with the fat end of the pool cue, splitting it wide open. Kenny went to break out of the door and into the street, only to get hit by an oncoming car. He was fortunate to come away with only a broken arm and a concussion.

Skip wasn't feeling any pain when the knock came at the back door. It was his sister, Carlyn, and her best friend, Sonja, rushing a story out about George pulling a gun on Carlyn in an attempt to get back an engagement ring that he gave her. He wanted it back now that they had ended their relationship.

Carlyn wasn't having it, though. As far as she was concerned, the dude had given her the ring, so it belonged to her now, especially since he owed her some cheese! Until he straightened out his bill she wasn't giving him naythin'! Nay-thin!

All that about the ring and the money was irrelevant to Skip. To him *and* Kenny – Kenny had a crush on Skip's younger sister, even though she was only eighteen. When Skip left out of the house to confront George, who was just outside in his parked car. Kenny was on his heels.

Skip didn't know his sister's ex-boyfriend personally, but had seen him and his brother around Woodland Terrace Projects in the early years. He was a year or so older than Skip, and Connie had told this joker before that Carlyn was too young for him.

When Skip approached the car, George informed him he didn't do what the girls claimed, that he loved Carlyn and would never do anything to hurt her. Skip looked back at the girls and Sonja said to him, "I saw the gun. He's lying!"

Skip was disgusted with himself for leaving his burner inside. Now he couldn't snatch this lame out of his car. Nevertheless, when Skip turned back around George sped off.

Skip looked at the rear of the car until it disappeared into the night. The cogs were spinning inside of Skip's head – whether George was guilty wasn't in question any longer; "A guilty conscience needs no accuser."

Skip and Kenny were from a generation where a man just didn't throw down on another man's sister, not with a gun, and not with bare knuckles. It wasn't done like that. To him there wasn't a lot of deliberating that had to be done. Kenny wanted to deal with him too, though maybe not to the extent that Skip had in mind.

"What's up, Skip?"

"I'll be right back," Skip told him before departing for his house. When he came back out, he had on his traveling gear. J. Marie was standing in the doorway of the kitchen when he told Sonja to take him to where George lives.

"Skip," J. Marie called out to him. She began to continue but Skip cut her comments short.

"I got to make a quick run, I'll be right back," was all he said as he left the house.

Surprisingly enough, the foursome rode over to where Skip first cut his teeth. "Parkland." When Sonja pulled into the parking lot area in front of the building he lived in as a boy – back when it was only him and M.G. – Skip couldn't believe it. "What apartment?" At least it wasn't the same apartment number.

George's car was nowhere to be seen. He didn't come straight home. Skip told the girls to go home. As he was stepping out of the car, he noticed that Kenny was doing the same. Although he didn't ask his friend to join him, Skip knew Kenny wouldn't lay back.

If George never showed or took too long to return home, Skip and Kenny would walk back to the house, no sweat. The two were used to walking. It wasn't exactly a hop skip and a jump, but it wasn't like going from R.F.K. to Edgewood Terrace either. Kenny was with them when they walked that stretch too.

They sat on a short set of concrete steps off to the side of the building where Skip had a clear view of what he needed to see, but where he himself was not easily discernible. While he sat on the little staircase he'd sat on twenty years ago as a boy and waited for the blue Monte Carlo to show up, his mind went back to a few years ago to his sister before she started dating…to 1978 or somewhere there about.

It had to be after their father's death, because he never would have stood for a couple of the jokers that Carlyn was starting to kick it with, not in front of *his* house. Skip regretted not being on the scene more with his younger siblings. He was so preoccupied with what was going on in his own life. Well, at least they all knew who to call if and when things got thick. He thought how, when he was coming up, he had to fend for himself, to make his bones on these very streets of Anacostia. He thought about throwing Carlyn into the living room one night to get her off the street, and away from the punk she was hanging out with when she was only fifteen.

The first time Skip ever saw first-hand the aftermath of a violent encounter was on this very sidewalk in front of 3410. There were blood stains all over the walk. There'd been gun shots late into the night. Connie told Skip not to go by the window and she moved M.G.'s crib. A few minutes later there were a lot of flashing lights. It was only then that Connie allowed Skip to look out of the window while she held little M.G. so he could see too.

"Look, Ma, lights, lights! Ma, ma…" Skip thought if he looked up instead of down and saw that "man in the moon" M.G. would be done for the night. Skip thought he'd be a policeman one day.

The next morning, when Skip and his friends met outside to play, there was blood where Evelyn used to jump rope. Also, in front of this building he lost his first fight to one of the Mayhew brothers. He was seven years old. One thing about losing fights, Paul would tell him, people don't remember much or talk about the ones you lose while you're young. It's just when you get older and lose that they talk about them. Skip's dad was right. The next couple of days it was all but forgotten.

Skip thought of simply beating the crap out of George whenever he showed up, right there where he lost to Michael Mayhew, right on the sidewalk at the corner of 3410. The only flaw was that George couldn't fight and would use the gun to defend himself. Skip knew he'd eventually have to kill him, if nothing more than because of not wanting to have to look over his shoulder for the next few months. And it didn't help that he now knew where Skip's crib was. Thanks, Sis…

When Carlyn was a little girl, somehow she got a kidney infection. The doctor told Connie she would have to make sure her daughter's kidneys were properly flushed out with water. For the next two days, she was drinking no less than six cups of water a day. That was on a Saturday, and on Sunday Connie and Paul made sure the water was consumed. On Monday Skip had to stay home with her with explicit instructions to make sure Carlyn drank the water. Throughout the day, Carlyn only managed to take in four cups – she was short two – and told Skip that she couldn't drink anymore. He reminded her of the instructions their mother had left him, however, his sister had taken a stand on her position and even got defiant about it. Eventually, Skip put his sister in a headlock, forced her mouth open, and dumped in three more cups – the extra one to make up for what had gotten spilled on the floor.

When Connie took her to the doctor's, the infection was gone. Skip felt that the end results justified the means. Carlyn never forgot the water incident. It would stay with her for the rest of her life.

"Skip! Ain't that the car?"

George found a parking spot in front of the building that he lived in. Skip was there to meet him; George looked like he's seen a ghost once he realized that Skip was there. He had a bag in his hand from some store that he must have stopped at.

"We got to finish that talk that we started, George," Skip said.

"Okay," George said. "Let me get this bag inside. it's something for my mother."

When George came back, he had his brother with him. Skip knew he had to lighten up the moment. He suggested talking over a few beers. "Run us down to 51 on the way to my house. We can kick back a minute in the basement," he suggested.

When the four of them came in through the kitchen door, J. Marie was still up. She was in the living room looking at her and Skip's favorite nighttime TV program – *Hart to Hart*, with Robert Wagner and Stephanie Powers.

Skip led the group to the music room where he passed them beers. Skip was the only one standing, that's why he noticed the bulge in George's dip. "George, y'all don't have to come into my house strapped. You and your brother take them joints out to the car. I got kids in here. Man, we just talkin'."

George and his brother went out the side basement door, leading out to the driveway. When he came back he supposedly was to have left the burners in the car. Skip excused himself, went upstairs, kissed J. Marie, and on his way back down the stairs, he was pulling the small-caliber revolver from his waist band.

Chick pulled the burgundy Buick Regal into the Eastover Shopping Center parking lot on his way to a deal he thought would raise his financial status. He was selling weight; the wet hallucinogenic known as "angel dust," an ounce of it. Unfortunately, the operation was a setup from the word go; the buyer was an undercover drug enforcement agent. Skip's childhood friend was sentenced to four years with the Maryland Division of Corrections for possession, manufacturing and distribution.

Because he graduated from Howard University a few years prior to this conviction, with letters of character reference from relatives, friends, coaches, and several faculty members, the sentencing judge was lenient on him.

This six foot ten inch once-promising athlete was caught up in drug trafficking and its use, like Skip was trapped in his own self-destructive lifestyle. Though the two were the closest of friends, Chick had his own crew of drug accomplices, as Skip had his car runners and small time stickup and mugging mob, among other things.

J. Marie had known Chick and Steve almost as long as she'd known Skip. Chick was Michael D'Angelo and Candie's godparent; he nicknamed their beautiful daughter Dirty Reds.

After sentencing, Chick was transferred from the Prince George's County jail to the Diagnostic and Reception Center, in Baltimore. He wondered what was taking his main man so long to pay him a visit. He knew Skip was spreading himself thin these days, and when he last hung out with him the two of them did a forty of raw bone. He was concerned Skip was developing too strong an urge for that stuff, and was glad he never started firing (shooting up). Skip and Chick, along with Steve, all went back since they were eleven and twelve years old. Skip was the youngest of all the dudes he ever hung out with, and always the risk-taker, the most daring, the most unpredictable.

That crazy Skip almost got me killed – twice, Chick reflected, back when they were younger. Skip was twelve years old when he gave Chick and one of Chick's older brothers, Ellis, a ride in the first car he ever took; a 1964 Chevrolet Impala. Skip was taking Ellis to Garfield's basketball court just across Suitland Parkway.

During the entire ride Ellis kept saying, "I can't believe I'm letting this little nigga give me a lift in this hot-ass car!"

The day before Skip and Carlton visited Chick at the Diagnostic Center, Chick heard it on the news as he and the other inmates looked at the dayroom TV, of a double homicide that hit close to home. The bodies of twin brothers were found off the side of a road in Prince George's County with two gunshot wounds to the head.

The visit was very relaxing for the three men; they truly enjoyed themselves while talking about a little of everything. That's the way most one-hour prison visits go; talking about all you can think of, to get it said before the time is up. The hour goes so fast among friends. Depending on how far you journeyed to get to the prison, you may be able to get two hours for a visit.

Chick wondered how come Steve didn't come up to see him. How were J. Marie and the kids… He commented on the possibility of an earlier release provided he kept "his nose clean."

Skip told him he was starting to sound like Paul (Skip's dad). That was one of his sayings, "Keep your nose clean, boy!"

Paul was a huge Nat King Cole fanatic – not just *fan*. This dude was *fanatical* about Nat. He would tell Skip's friends, when they'd come to see Skip, "You boys better straighten up and fly right," after one of Nat King Cole's pieces. Skip was glad to get a laugh out of his friend; he always could.

Later that evening, after Skip was dropped off at Connie's, he found out from her that Carlyn's old boyfriend, George, was found dead, along with his brother. She said his sister didn't take it well at all, and that she was hospitalized. Skip and Connie visited Carlyn; she was very upset and an emotional wreck. Skip pulled her off to the side and out of their mother's earshot, to put her down with a few things.

When Skip finally made it home to J. Marie, she told him some people were by the house looking for him. "Who," he asked, and she gave him the card that they had left with her. It was from the Detective's Bureau of Prince George's County Police Department. Skip was overconfident in his ability to persuade; he tended to be cocky sometimes, relying too much on the first impression he made on others, and shooting from the hip.

When Skip made his way to the police barracks in Forestville, he forgot one of his first rules imparted upon himself almost twenty years ago: "Get your story together, then stick with it."

If that wasn't enough, Skip forgot his second rule, which was perhaps the most important: "When you find yourself in the crap, keep your mouth shut."

Perhaps the biggest, most costly mistake the average criminal makes about law enforcement is underestimating their intelligence. Skip thought that because he could outtalk many of his friends coming up, and was most convincing with J. Marie, as well as gabbing it up with the people on his job, for this reasoning he construed he could overwhelm and dazzle the detectives. Oblivious was he to the fact these people go to colleges and universities for *years* to learn how to outthink men and women of Skip's caliber.

The investigating detective called Skip to join him outside the interrogation room, where he took Skip to the door of another such room. Skip looked into the room only to see Sonja sitting at a desk, crying, and signing several pages of documents.

When the signing was over, Skip was charged with two counts of murder, robbery, and weapons charges. Before he was taken to Upper Marlboro lockup to be arraigned, J. Marie showed up at the police barracks crying like he had not seen her crying in years. He had time to hold her, kiss her tears, and console her as best he could for a minute or so before the officers led him away.

The next time he saw her was with Connie and their children through the glass in the visiting room of the lockup facility at Upper Marlboro, Maryland.

Skip was processed into Upper Marlboro's Detention Center after three days of being in a room designated to hold twenty men, which was packed with no less than fifty. He was sent to another section of the jail (3-C-D) where he would await a court appearance, then sentencing.

Kenny O was arrested three days later, the day of his and Carlyn's birthday. He was taken to another part of the jail, but would eventually see Skip when several friends came to visit them. Skip and Kenny would see old faces throughout Upper Marlboro they'd not seen in years.

New detainees entering the processing station are stripped naked, sprayed for crabs, and/or lice, and then given a set of "greens" (the two-piece uniform that is issued to the inmate population).

Skip was in terrible shape; years of physical neglect, internal as well as external – not to mention the voidance of any mental or spiritual aptitude. Though he was optimistic about his current predicament, he was keeping it real, and the reality was he could be a while on this thing. He was not about to sit on his hands or twiddle his thumbs while waiting for release papers to drop from the sky.

The first thing he had to do was hire a lawyer. Connie was on top of it; at his behest, she hired Sanford Berman from the Annapolis law firm of Hulaum, Pickett, and Berman. The firm wanted twenty G's to defend Skip on the charges, ten thousand a body. Skip could contribute a few grand from what the credit union at his job took out for retirement and social security. Connie would pay the rest on installments. People from Fort Stanton and on his job collected money to help with his defense. Skip and his family deeply appreciated all the donations they could get; his Aunt Toni donated a grand!

Kenny was not as fortunate. A public defender would handle his charges of accessory before and after the fact. Those awaiting representation in the bullpens refer to public defenders as "public pretenders." Although not all court appointed attorneys, like used car salespeople, are shysters.

Skip tried to cut Kenny loose from this jam he'd gotten his friend in. However, Kenny had been under scrutiny from the Maryland Police Department, as well as the district, for years. Now that they had him on charges that could possibly lay him down for a while, they were not giving him up without diligent and relentless efforts on his part.

The second order of affairs on Skip's agenda was to get his body back in something close to the shape it was in when he came out of basic training eight years ago. He regretted the shape he'd let his body fall to. He started doing pushups and cardio workouts for his heart and gas; on days his cell block had gym he lifted weights, mostly back arms, chest work, and light squats. The power of a person's strike has a lot to do with the force from the back arm; the legs will hold you up even though your brain might signal the rest of your body to go down.

Skip found out several guys in the cell block of approximately twenty-five men had ties to him through mutual third party relations, in one way or another. One was Ronnie Garnett, who was Ricky "Monk" Kingsbury's half-brother; Skip had eaten at his family's home on a few occasions. Steve's cousin Tony was there on drug possession charges; later, when Skip went to the gym, he saw his old car-thieving friend Necie coming back from a visit. To get to the cell block Necie was on –

they had to escort the inmates through an area of the gym. Skip enjoyed the few minutes he had to kick it with Necie two times before Necie was cut loose; he was in for a minor violation. Necie gave Skip a few packs of cigarettes he had on hand. Skip had developed a five- or six-cigarette-a-day habit before he was arrested. He smoked more when he drank or used drugs. J. Marie, however, was up to at least a half a pack daily; now she'd been addicted to the nicotine going into her eleventh year... and she was only twenty-six.

He missed his wife and longtime friend tremendously. He knew she missed him, too, but somehow understood his past finally caught up with him. She knew her mother-in-law could have had him sent to reform school years before she met him, but he was the first born. She couldn't bear throwing in the towel on him.

J. Marie found out Skip let the house note slip a month without paying it, besides that, he'd taken two hundred dollars from her account without her knowledge. At her first visit to the detention center, she told him, "Skip, it's a good thing you *are* in jail, because if you weren't, I'd kill you!" She said it all in good spirit; she could never stay angry with Skip very long.

The two quickly patched it up, to go on to the business at hand about the children, the affairs of the house, and the two Mustangs. Skip told her, "Phats, I might be while on this thing. I messed up big this time, but you already know that. Look, make sure I have at least one of the Mustangs when I come off this bit someday, okay." He also told her of the love he had for her, the good years under their belt together, and that he didn't want her putting her life on hold because of him. "You're a beautiful, young woman, Phats. If you think you'll move on, well...I don't like it but I understand."

"Skip...?"

"Yeah, Phats..."

"Shut up."

J. Marie never used much profanity, if any at all, except one little vulgar phrase she would mockingly quote from her cousin Kool-Aid. She was an old-fashioned girl with old-fashioned ways and old-school principles. Skip suddenly realized the prize he had. She was definitely a diamond amongst a yard of coal. He thought about the old adage of "not missing the water until the well runs dry."

In the music room in their house was the latest Teddy Pendergrass album with a cut on it, with the lyrics… "Yeah, I had your love right there in the palm of my hands/ and I lost it, I lost it… The whole town's laughing at me, silly fool how'd you lose such a good thing…"

Skip stayed in touch with his family by way of the only phone on the cell block. Though it can be an arduous task for some first-time guys coming through Upper Marlboro, especially obtaining use of the phone, he made out. Through his ties with some main Southeast thug players on the outside, he was considered one of the "regulars" now that he was on the inside. Sometimes guys made a few calls to the street from the cell-block phone to get the "low" of a newcomer's status while he was out there. Ricky Monk hadn't seen Skip in three or four years – the last time being when Skip and Steve rode through Garfield Projects to "cop." Ricky's face always lit up whenever he saw Skip; Skip had that effect on people. Ricky knew Skip from when he was young and used to steal cars with Necie. Besides, young Skip was breaking law with older heads for a couple of years even before that. And now he's sticking up and copping smack. To Ricky that was a rite of passage; Skip had come full circle.

Ronnie got off the phone one day to tell Skip, "My brother told me to holler at you, real loud." (Ricky had told Ronnie that Skip was facing some heavy shit. This was Ricky's way of letting Skip know that he'd told his brother to look out for him in any and *every* way that he could while they were there.) Skip was glad to hear from Ricky, and even happier that Ronnie had said it in front of others.

Friends and relatives came to see Skip each week, or at least, semi-monthly. Michael D'Angelo started kindergarten at Wilkerson Elementary School in S.E., down the street from where Skip went as a boy. Skip knew going to public schools in that area would toughen his son up and give him mettle. His uncles would have to lend a hand raising him, too; that's what uncles were supposed to do. Candie Renee was almost two, and as beautiful a child as Skip ever saw in his life; she had to be lifted up to stand on the countertop before the thick counter-to-ceiling Plexiglas partition.

J. Marie brought them on a regular basis to see their father, and Skip was grateful for that. He'd heard guys cursing their children's mothers out on the telephone about not bringing the child to see them, as well as about other things.

Skip wrote them separate letters, once, sometimes two or three times a month. He also wrote J. Marie love letters and poems like he did while he was in basic training, up in Jersey.

Skip found out this was a way to pass the time amongst many guys locked up and who still had wives and girlfriends on the outside. They would write letters, exercise, get into their legal cases, read books, or soon develop some type of mood or anxiety disorder. It all depends on the person involved, the situation, and the period of confinement.

The cell block was so close to freezing, the men were huffing cold-air vapors to prove the point that the corrections officers (COs) should meet their requests for extra blankets, portable heaters, or to raise the thermostat. The COs were sitting in heated booths, some with uniform coats on, while monitoring the units.

After it became clear to the inmates nothing was going to be done anytime soon, they began taking matters into their own hands. It started when a guy would leave the block to go to the medical unit, on a visit, or another appointment. When he returned to the unit his blanket was snatched from his bunk. The more aggressive inmates wouldn't allow the new guy to inspect the premises of their area, so he was… "beat." This went on until someone snatched Big Hawk's nephew's blanket. Hawk's solution was simple; he told his nephew to go get his blanket. In actuality, he was telling John to "go out and make a name for yourself." Win or lose, John picked a combatant that threatened the least likely resistance and two blankets, and popped him. Naturally, the two began fighting, leading to the "10-10" code being called, and summoning the jail goon squad, whose job it was to restore order whenever there was a disturbance. Miraculously when the smoke cleared, extra blankets were sent from the property room. That's all it took…a near riot for a change to occur.

Skip was thankful no one tried their hand with his blanket or any other property that he owned. Skip realized, after witnessing several fights over the months that ensued, that he wasn't in the shape he preferred to be in, given the gravity of his present situation. These guys were not just in shape, but they were in go-hard-combat, Red-Cross-ready, and *Ford-tough* shape. He knew that sooner or later, somewhere along the way, a joker was going to jump out there, and when he did, Skip knew that he'd have to make him pay, or die trying.

Later that night, they watched on the news where an airplane that was departing Washington National Airport clipped the 14th Street Bridge, leaving dozens of its passengers in the freezing Potomac River.

At last, the fans of the hometown football team, the Washington Redskins, finally received something to cheer about as the team's head coach, Joe Gibbs, took them to a Super Bowl victory. Skip thought about the gatherings in Lou's Edgewood apartment on Sundays to see the games. How, during a halftime break, he rushed to the complex's mini-mart for beer, only to see a big young kid wearing the quarter-length blue leather jacket stolen from the back seat of one the cars he was pushing that year. It was all over in less than two minutes. Skip told the kid, "Main man, I don't know where you got that jacket from or how, but it's mine, and I want it." He then took an aggressive stance and watched as the guy slowly peeled off the jacket. Skip took it and continued on his way.

J. Marie was managing to take care of the house and kids with little or no help from people outside of the two grandmothers helping with the raising of the grandchildren.

The two grand Skip gave her from what he didn't give to Connie towards the lawyer's fee would not go far at all, not with two small children and a house note.

He was glad now that J. Marie held off from having another baby like they planned. The couple agreed a few weeks prior to Skip's arrest to have one. Fortunately, J. Marie had yet to conceive.

It was bad enough that the family and many of their friends were all talking about how "it was a cryin' shame Skip left that poor girl out here with children and a house payment." He wondered how many of them sorry-ass niggas kicked out a few dollars to help her along, while he was gone.

One day, J. Marie told Skip about some of his "so-called" friends trying to press up on her. Skip knew exactly what she meant by the term "pressing up."

"You ain't talking about Chick, Steve, or Dunmore…" he inquired. Chick had just recently been released. When she told Skip that it wasn't any of his long-term regulars, and who it was, he was relieved to a degree. But when or if he ever ran into "Slim", he would be sure to punish that lame, in a real foul way.

By winter's end, Skip's lawyer visited twice; a plea agreement was set up at the sentencing hearing. The police had Skip dead to rights. Berman didn't see an out for his client, despite Skip's protest of taking it to trial. Through Skip's ignorance of the law at the police barracks, as well as Sonja's signed statements, Skip copped out to a thirty and a fifteen-year sentence, to run consecutively – a total of forty-five years. He would be eligible for parole in a fourth of the time. Kenny was given 30 years, also eligible in a fourth. At the sentencing hearing, Connie spoke briefly before Judge Blackwell of how she told George that her daughter was too young for him, and how Skip was a good son, and so forth and so on, until she began crying. Connie clutched tightly to the rosary she held in church on Sundays. It broke Skip's heart to see his mom this way, even if it *was* on his behalf.

Everyone in the courtroom was a blur, except Connie, his dear little, sweet, country-gal mother. Leaving the hearing, he heard his sister scream out. Carlyn broke down. Reflexively, Skip made a move in her direction only to be quickly restrained by the marshals of the court and then ushered back into the bullpens.

There would be no more rushing to his sister's aid for Skip. He thought back on the first time he heard her scream out; she was only eight years old. Skip was unloading groceries from Connie's car when he heard it coming from the direction of the back yard. Skip quickly set the bag on the side walk, rushed to the backyard to see his sister's little Beagle locked up with the big Sooner from around the corner. The big dog was still humping, and Carlyn was hysterical as she watched in horror as her dog was being deflowered by the neighborhood's most hated hound.

Skip picked up a brick from Connie's garden, and, as soon as he raised it to get a good hit without harming his sister's dog, Paul called from the kitchen window telling Skip to let the dog be. Carlyn wouldn't touch the dog afterwards. She didn't want it, and asked that someone take the dog away. She'd never seen anything she thought to be so despicable.

Two weeks after sentencing, Skip was taken to the Diagnostic Center in Baltimore. A seven-story, new-era, security-designed building with dark-tinted windows, carpeted tiers – or pods, as they were called – and air conditioning.

On the first floors were offices for administrative affairs, the visiting room, a gymnasium, as well as access to an outside recreation area. The meals, like in Upper Marlboro, were brought up on "hot boxes" and heated carts to each tier. There were approximately one hundred double cells on a unit. The upper level had recreation in the morning, the lower in the afternoon or evening – for two hours.

Skip continued his calisthenics routine; he also began to read the novels that Connie would send him through the mail some eighty or ninety pages at a time, because books as large as three and four hundred pages long were not allowed to be received at one time. Before going to prison, sadly enough, Skip had only read one book to its completion – a Donald Goines book.

Now that Skip was in Baltimore, J. Marie could not get to see him as often as she did while he was in Upper Marlboro, still she made the trip often. The visits were better because now the two could have full-body contact. J. Marie looked great; the children looked well kept, and happy to see their daddy, and smiled when they'd see mama and daddy kissing each other for long moments.

Chapter 12

ALTHOUGH SKIP MADE GREAT STEPS towards bettering himself, there was still much work to be done. He didn't have access to the drugs and alcohol he once did; that was clear. For fifteen months, he only had two encounters with substances; once in Upper Marlboro when J. Marie and Chick got together and, upon his request, placed a small quantity of marijuana in the sleeve cuff of a sweat shirt, and sent it to him to exercise in, along with a pair of tennis shoes.

Recently his cell was searched. The shakedown officers discovered a gallon container of fermented plums. Skip was charged with Category III, Rule 302 – Possession of material used in the manufactured of alcohol, and Category IV, Rule 40 – Contraband. He was given thirty days on segregation, a special unit for lockup guys that was located on the seventh floor. There he saw several guys from Upper Marlboro he had not seen in over a year. They gave Skip books by authors he had never heard of. He never saw so many guys become obsessed with books; he became one with them. Through reading, he was able to find a way of escaping, traveling to different parts of the country, and the world.

He was still smoking cigarettes, but the regular cigarette brands were not being smoked like what was smoked on the streets, or in Upper Marlboro. The preference, due to accessibility and cost, was towards the loose tobacco, what could be rolled up the way Skip use to roll marijuana; they were called "roll rites."

Skip became so engrossed in a book by Jackie Collins entitled *Chances* that he couldn't put it down. In less than two days he completed it – seven hundred pages, which was record time for a guy who actually just started "absorbing himself" in the last year. He figured he'd better get a dictionary to help him along with the meanings of some newfound words, some of which he never imagined were words at all.

Going into his eighteenth month, he had received two infractions, or tickets, as they were called. He was charged with assaulting a corrections officer, which was a Category I, Rule 101 offense – Assault on staff. It was an accident; he pushed his cell door into the officer when the rookie cop attempted to close the door on him while receiving a book from another inmate. The hearing officers could have made a bigger deal out of the situation than it really was. However, at the adjustment hearing, they were lenient on Skip. He was given another thirty days, after which he was transferred to the Maryland Penitentiary – just across the street.

Much talk went on about the Maryland pen while Skip was at the Diagnostic Center. That it was a very dangerous place to be was not in question; it was the most ominous and treacherous prison in Maryland.

In 1984, when Skip put down his two boxes of property in the receiving area of the Pen, it was on record as the second or third oldest functioning state prison in the United States. The huge granite stones were positioned by ex-slaves and day laborers toward the end of the 19th Century.

A compound the size of a long city block with gargantuan gray-stone buildings at each end, with thirty-foot walls on the sides designed to keep in eleven hundred of Maryland's most dangerous and errant prisoners. The Pen's hospital was juxtaposed with C-dormitory, which faced Madison Street; it's where Skip would obtain his first prison job.

While Skip was on his last lockup bit, just across the street at the Diagnostic Center, he occasionally passed time kicking it with a guy from Baltimore called Horsey. He left for the Pen two months before Skip. A week later he was violently attacked with a knife all about the neck and head. He didn't die, although word of the assault reached the guys that knew him at Diagnostic. He was laid up at the University of Maryland's Intensive Care Unit.

Each of the four main buildings – comprised of A-block, B-block, C-dormitory, and the infamous south wing – were five tiers high. There were twenty-six cells to a tier, most of which were two man or doubled cells. The ground level, or "flats," as it was called, was all single cells, most of them reserved for the handicapped or infirmed in some way. The fifth tiers were singled also, but those were for a selected few, guys with tenure, or those specially connected, or considered by the wing sergeant or above. The second tier of A-block was for men the death sentence was pronounced upon; it was called "Death Row."

For the brief time Chick came through the Pen. He was housed in E or F building, for short timers, and minimum-security status. There were about one hundred or so of these guys in the entire population.

After Skip was processed in, he was given a "bedroll" and a temporary housing location, which was on one of the two receiving tiers; both were located in the south wing. The administration area, just under the visiting room, was between and connected to A-block and the south wing. There were basically three or four social standings of men in the Pen, three of which involved geography. They were either from Baltimore, D.C., both of which included surrounding counties, or somewhere else, which meant you were considered neutral. The sixty Muslims were in a class by themselves for the most part. Their allegiance was usually exclusive for one another, although their ties of kith and kin complicated their position with the brotherhood. As far as gangs went, the Pagans, a notorious motorcycle fellowship, was the only thing resembling such.

Kenny O was sleeping in one of the open annexes in C-dormitory on the other end of the compound. There were three annexes in C-dorm, each with twenty-six guys. The bathroom and shower area was to the rear, and shared the same water supply system with the toilets. So whenever one flushed the toilet, they had to shout out a warning to any unsuspecting bathers or they would find themselves suddenly doused with scalding water.

When Kenny found out Skip was shipped in, and was now sleeping on the receiving tier, he had a sort of welcoming committee check up on him, bearing a few provisions, and the information that Skip had some people looking out for his health and well-being.

One-eyed Herb was on the tier Skip had moved on. The two of them went back to Upper Marlboro and were cool with each other. Herb had his eye knocked out with a baseball bat around his neighborhood in Capital Heights, MD. The story was that he did something foul to Shorty Long's sister, and paid the price. Skip didn't know the entire story involving Shorty Long and Herb, so, therefore, didn't hold it against him. But he would never trust him around any of the women nor small children in his family. That's the way it was with most dudes in the joint, even women for that matter; trust has to be proven and earned. As it stood, Herb was alright to walk to the chow-hall or lift weights with. Skip would go to Sunday service with him occasionally, too.

One particular Sunday morning, when the two of them just wanted to get off of the tier because of their limited-movement status, Skip and Herb signed up for Church service. Reverend Tilman would sometimes invite outside guests from surrounding parishes to sit in during the sermon.

This particular Sunday, a woman preacher came in with a host of others, including six or seven kids, all dressed up, singing, clapping, and carrying on. Skip admitted to himself that it was one of the most relaxing, surreal feelings to ever come over him. Of course, this whole scene was about to change, because Frog and Melvin were there too. The two had fought while cellmates on segregation, or the "hammer," a few days prior, and the beef was still fresh.

Melvin and Jimmy Walker were in the pew just in front of Skip and Herb. It was a time during the service where everyone was standing when Frog came up behind Melvin from where he was in the back of the chapel. He had to partially step into Skip's aisle to reach his intended victim, Melvin, who didn't handle the assault very well at all. Skip learned a valuable lesson that morning about being the victim of an attack, especially if it is a knife attack and the perpetrator is hell-bent on taking his victim out.

Skip reasoned that an attacker would get about one or two good hits in – that was a given. After that *you* had to somehow become the aggressor with hopes of subduing him or her, or maybe until help came. Either way, you could not allow yourself to become docile or submissive; like the saying goes, "A soldier dies only once, but a coward dies a thousand deaths over."

As Frog proceeded to plunge the homemade knife into the back of Melvin's neck, the woman preacher began yelling, "Stop him, stop him!" Frog was not deterred by her shouts, though. He was committed to carrying out his mission to the best of his abilities. Frog continued his vicious assault until Jimmy reached across Melvin and reached for the knife, grabbing at and deflecting some of the blows away from his traveling companion.

After snatching away from Jimmy, Frog futilely attempted to discard the knife, at which point the woman then began yelling, "There it is, there it is. Get the knife, get the knife!"

The entire scene was like something out of the prison movies on TV Skip used to watch as a kid. Skip was probably more startled (he'd never admit to being scared) than the children that witnessed it all. Finally, the correctional officers rushed over, converging upon Frog, and restoring order to the chapel.

Skip was not a deeply religious man, but figured if there was anyone standing before him in the line going to Hell, then this one who committed this stabbing – this attempted murder, for that matter – in the Lord's House would surely find that destination his resting place!

After the COs got a hold on Frog, he was body slammed, searched, and lifted upright to be taken to south-wing lockup; his feet just barely, if at any time, touched the floor as they escorted him out.

The next couple of weeks were much the same routine. Kenny and Skip got together when they'd meet on the compound to talk about the family, as well as getting back into court somehow.

Skip knew Kenny would do his utmost to get out of this fix. Skip would help to clear his friend first, and then work on himself; there was no point in both of them being in this hellhole.

Kenny assured Skip that he would try getting him pulled down to C-dormitory, maybe in the annex where he himself was; Skip would like it much better. Kenny was more in his environment with the prison scene; it was all new to Skip, however. A major component of getting through prison in one piece has to do with being aloof to a degree, not becoming too familiar with guys, giving respect and expecting it in return, not accepting things but from a very select few, and learning how to do without what you can't pay for up front.

There were several buildings within the Pen's confines where the inmate population would go to conduct various activities. Two such buildings were A- and G-buildings. A-building, not to be confused with A-block, was a three-story granite fortress-like edifice which housed the library, barbershop, appliance repair shop, and four religious groups under the banner of Islam; the Sunni Muslims, Nation of Islam (NOI),

Moorish Science Temple of America, and a quasi-Islamic affiliation that was somewhere between the Sunni community and Nation of Islam. This last group was headed by one of Baltimore's most dangerous sages, an implicated hitman serving life, named Dennis Wise, or Brother Hakeem.

G-building was lined with thirty telephones on the first floor, pool tables and several other tables for whatever the inmates chose to use them for. Everything in both buildings was run by certain inmates. Located upstairs in G-building was a State Use Industries (SUI) Sewing Shop, where they made all the jeans for the Maryland Division of Corrections. That, however, was run by outside contractors.

Reflecting over the past week's events and J. Marie and their children led Skip to thinking maybe, just maybe, paying three dollars for a quart-sized plastic jug of jailhouse wine, or "jump," from the resident Ernest and Julio Gallo dream team wasn't such a bad idea. Within three months of penitentiary life, he had developed a liking for the jailhouse "sauce," not to the degree he had on the streets, but a liking for it nonetheless.

One afternoon, he was standing on the third floor of A-building, looking out the window over the back side of the compound, a view revealing one-yard's basketball and handball courts, south wing's lockup gate and A- and B-block, in the distance.

With a fresh forty-five-year bit, Skip was under the impression that with the good-credit time the Division of Corrections gave, plus being a model prisoner, the parole board might be compelled to give him parole on his first hearing. Skip fathomed he'd be out in about another dime tops! He would be thirty-seven, thirty-eight years old, and maybe J. Marie and he would have another baby. If it was another girl, they would name her "Cookie." He laughed at the thought. "Ha! Candie and Cookie…"

Suddenly, off to the right, in the distance, he heard the sound of a gate crashing open. He looked to see inmates and officers alike carrying one of the orange stretchers used for transporting the injured or infirmed to the prison infirmary. On their way to the other side of the compound they had to pass under the window where Skip was perched, and he could see the dark-skinned guy agonizing on the multi-manned conveyance. Skip could clearly see what was the source of the guy's discomfort, too; he was extremely burnt up, toasty in some spots, even. And his clothes were still smoking, those that were still on him. Skip began wondering, *What in the world have I gotten myself into, winding up in this place that has to be hell?!*

Skip had seen enough. The stretcher crew had turned the corner of A-building and the show was over as far as he knew. He decided that he'd had enough excitement for the day. Now, without a doubt, a jug from his homeboy Short Legs, specially brewed, fermented raisins would calm his nerves. Skip swore the stuff tasted like Brandy. When it was made from plums, then it took on the flavor of Richard's Wild Irish Rose.

On his way to see Short Legs in C-dorm, while walking through Sawdust Train (or Dead Man's Alley, as it was also known as) a stretch of pavement in between E-building and the main dining hall, there was a crazed-looking muscular man with a flat piece of steel in his hand that looked like it could've come from the kitchen department of Home Depot.

Unfortunately, the intended victim had his back to the alley's exit, totally oblivious to any impending danger coming from the rear. His attacker was suddenly upon him, hanging every inch of his short sword in his targets head, neck, back, and arms. This was the second time Skip witnessed the victim responding in a way Skip thought he, himself, might do differently, even though it all kicked off with no warning. Skip thought he would begin to be more conscious while in the open yard, and perhaps keep his back to a wall when he was in closed confines… for starters.

There was a yard officer present, however, when the victim was being attacked, and the man attempted to run to him for refuge, the officer scurried to distance himself from the prey.

Skip noticed another thing about these brazen attacks; neither time was the perpetrator trying to conceal his intent; both were unrelenting, ruthless offenses.

These two, Skip later learned, were brothers of the guy on the stretcher and the one who put him there – a tit-for-tat sort of thing. The victim, Johnathan Byrd, was a tall, lanky kid that didn't hassle any one, and was on laid-back time, sure 'nough! His brother, Francis, though a few years older, was a seasoned, prison-hardened terror. It was Francis, along with Hakeem's brother, Kid, who had an unresolved and long-going feud with the Bennets, years before Skip came onto the scene.

This was only one of the disputes going on between factions in the Maryland Pen; these petty beefs between neighborhoods, zones, or cliques have gone on throughout the prison system for years. In the mid 60s, following the death of Malcolm X, aka Malik Shabazz, it was the Sunni Muslim community in opposition with the Nation of Islam, and again in 1975, following the death of Elijah Muhammad, when Warith Dean, his son, took the movement in another direction that didn't sit right with the previous doctrine.

By the time Skip entered into the pen, the main conflicts going on were with overzealous Baltimoreans versus guys from Washington (D.C.). Sometimes it would be simply East versus West Baltimore.

Following this melee, the drink and anything to go with it were secondary on Skip's list of things to do. Right now, he was headed to G-building to place a call to Connie, an emergency call, if need be.

When he got through, he could tell, like always, that she was genuinely happy to hear from her oldest boy. He was sure glad to hear her voice.

Skip told his mom, when it was possible, to please place a call to the lawyer, Berman. He explained that there just had to be a mix-up somewhere, and that he had surely been sent to the wrong place. After the conversation, and on his way back to his cell on the receiving tier, he repeated, more to himself than anyone else, a phrase Connie used to lament over when she'd get into it with his dad real bad. She would say, "Lord! What'd I do to deserve this?" Then Skip thought back to a couple years ago when he perpetrated this offense, and said, "Oh, yeah."

Kenny O was true to his word; he got Skip moved down the compound to C-dormitory into annex one with him.

There were all double bunks in the three annexes when Skip first moved in. He had the first bunk by the main door, a heavily trafficked area, but he didn't care. At least he was out of that dreaded south wing!

Each annex was strategically placed off the side of the beginning of each tier. As one goes up the stairs, an option was to go straight to the annex, or at the landing, hook a right onto the tier.

Early on, there were twenty-five double bunks jammed in each annex. Out of approximately fifty guys, fifteen or so were from D.C. Overall, its occupants tried to get along. Annex three was for men over fifty years old; it was called "The Old Timers" dorm, or "Old Man's" dorm. Other than a few conflicting attitudes, bad hygiene, and bathroom etiquettes to include leaving blood from syringes on the porcelain occasionally, and vomit, it wasn't a bad spot to do a bit. The larger percentage of all guys from Washington, D.C., throughout the Maryland correctional system came through Upper Marlboro, at one time or another.

A month before moving to C-dorm, while still on receiving in south wing, Skip wrote his case manager in the classifications department, attaching a brief résumé with hopes of landing a job in the prison's three-story hospital. He also listed his experience with Worldwide Services as an operator of various cleaning machines and apparatuses. By prison standards, his résumé was most impressive; he was hired immediately to work in the psychology department/crisis clinic keeping the place clean. This smaller annex to the hospital was accessible from the larger recreation yard (number-four-yard), staffed with four psychologists, and a knock-out secretary named Valerie. She and Mrs. Hargrove were black, but as different as night and day. Mrs. Hargrove was professional in every sense of the word, and knew her stuff. She was average height, petite, dark, and lovely. Valerie was the reason most guys in the population would put in "request slips" to be called to the crisis clinic for bogus psychological problems. She was brown skinned, big-boned, yet very well proportioned, and wore pants exceptionally tight to accentuate a voluptuous rump. She was also a rather tall woman with so-so clerical skills and average intelligence for a prison employee.

Many guys in the population were shocked Skip landed the highly-touted job so early after arriving into the prison. Other staff at the crisis clinic included a full-figured middle aged white woman, Barbara Welch, who was the senior psychologist, and two psychiatrists, both white men, mid to late thirties, that were easily approachable, and easier to talk with.

The D.C., or "District" crew as it would often affectionately be called by its residents, were glad to see one of their own land such a sought-after position; to them, Skip could be their "inside man." Skip's hours began when the eight-am-to-four shift started, until any time after 1:30, but not later than when "count" started at 3:00. He had his own little sanitation closet where all the equipment he'd need was stored. One of the first things he checked out in the closet was "stash spots," of which there were a couple nice ones.

Skip got off on excellent footing; though the staff was permanent, the officer assigned to work the crisis clinic rotated from day to day.

After a few weeks of falling into a routine, he eventually worked his way into visiting the hospital. There were four COs to work the hospital. The officer in charge (OIC) ran the administrations and records department on the second floor.

The gas chamber was on the second floor, though it hadn't been used since Nathaniel Lipscomb in the early 60s, as was the officers' dining room (ODR), which fed the nurses and other hospital staff. The inmate workers could sometimes grab a bite from there, too, but couldn't use it as a hang out or lounge area.

With Skip's affable and agreeable nature, he wasted no time befriending the five inmate workers, especially Tyrone, who ran the little dining area.

Since Skip was, by now, affiliated with the hospital, he was legit to maneuver his way onto the floors. All it took was a bit of ingenuity and exercising a degree of his people-handling skills with the first-floor grill officer.

At first, he used his position as the new crisis clinic sanitation man to gain access. He would ask the crisis clinic officer, or Valerie, if they wanted something from the hospital ODR – he didn't mind taking the walk. Or did they mind if he went over, right quick, to a grab a piece of cake, or whatever they had on the line (short for chow line) that day.

Later, it got so when he appeared at the hospital grill, the officer immediately recognized him, let him through, and leave with whatever food he could carry. He learned Tyrone's clean up routine, and volunteered to breakdown the food car, and sweep and mop the floor if Ty wanted a break. If Ty wanted to leave early sometimes when Skip made his rounds, or just kick back on one of the other floors, he felt confident Skip could hold the fort down.

Occasionally, one of the officers would observe Skips cleaning the ODR and would be impressed with his diligence and hard-work ethic. So when it came time for Skip to leave, they didn't mind if he was traveling a little heavier going out than when he came in. As long as it was only food, what did they care; it's the way the Pen was back then.

Skip got familiar with the outside employees, the girls in medical records, the pharmacy technicians, secretaries, and the nurses, many of them on a first name basis.

Chapter 13

TIMMY POOLE AND HAROLD ROBERTS were alpha-male types from N.W. and S.E. Washington, respectively.

A year before Skip came to prison, Timmy was in the boxing gym of Maryland Penitentiary, raining death blows on the heavy bag that Mike Tyson may not have withstood, not in his best days! Timmy was a knockout artist: 6'1", two hundred thirty pounds of raw testosterone. At twenty-seven years old, he was in his prime, so much so, no one would get in the ring with him. The undisputed heavyweight champion of the Maryland prison system, and everybody knew it.

The recreation coordinator "Rice" worked in conjunction with Mack Lewis of Mack Lewis Gym in East Baltimore to bring talented fighters from in and around Baltimore, specifically heavyweights, to spar with the big bruiser from the District.

Doing "life" this time for a robbery gone bad, he was on his second bit. Even though the target of the robbery shot and killed his partner, this didn't matter when the case went to court – under Maryland law, he was charged with the murder.

The four sports he played in prison he excelled in to the maximal level; football, basketball, handball, and boxing. He was a domineering and driven force. The flag/tackle football team he played linebacker for, "Stonewall," were the reigning champs going into the third year when Skip came into the Pen in 1984. Although a talented group, they were big, played dirty, and were bullied into reaching their full potential by an overly aggressive middle linebacker. Their front line, combined, easily weighed a ton.

Someone once said, "I am more afraid of one hundred sheep being led by a lion than one hundred lions led by a sheep."

Not that the teams Timmy led were a bunch of sheep by any means, but he was undoubtedly the lion.

A devout Sunni Muslim, his Muslim brothers called him Abu-Bakr, after the Prophet Muhammad's closest companion and father-in-law. He went to *Jumu'ah* (Friday Islamic service) every week he was not on lockup. He read Arabic from the *Qur'an*, attended the Islamic study classes, and knew more about Islam than any subject he ever learned in school.

Harold Roberts, aka Big Reds, was from S.E. too, although not the Anacostia area, but a low-income section off East Capitol Street on 56th. He was also a light-complexioned black man, standing a few inches taller than Skip at 6'3" and two hundred twenty pounds. When Big Reds wasn't on one of his drug binges, he was on a heavily regimented workout routine, making him cut up as a bag of dope (physically well-defined) with lightning-fast hands.

Though he had ring experience, unlike Timmy Poole, he was mainly a street fighter, whose knuckles were legendary throughout the District, especially in Lorton Prison in Virginia (before it was shut down), the Maryland prison system, and (since 2000, to date) the federal systems of Lewisburg and in Atlanta. Timmy hit harder, but Big Reds was faster; that the two got along as well as they did was a godsend. They had a mutual reserved respect for one another, and were pretty much cut from the same cloth.

Compared to Big Reds, Skip was a choir boy. By the time Skip came to prison in '82, Big Reds was already accredited with four successful escapes; from the D.C. jail, Upper Marlboro, and one of the jails in Hagerstown, Maryland. One of them he escaped twice from; either D.C. jail or Upper Marlboro.

He had an extremely calculating and dangerous mind, in as well as out of prison. During his reign of terror on one of his escapes, he'd wreaked so much havoc upon the hustlers and drug dealers on the strips that the big boys and kingpins put out a bounty on his head. There was only one legitimate "Big Reds," so there was no mistaken identity problem, he was well known throughout the criminal and hustler worlds. When one of his crew members was asked why he carried a hatchet, the response was, "In case somebody got on a ring and claims they can't get it off."

Big Reds, also called "Biggums" by some of his convict cronies, was straight up old school; if he was with you, or he went for you like that, he was with you ride or die. He might "rough-off" an associate on a loan, or walk off with something that you couldn't stand to lose.

Shortly after Skip landed the job in the crisis clinic, "Biggums" approached him with a favor. He wanted to know if Skip had a good "stash spot" on the premises of his worksite, because it would be a personal favor to he and Butch if they could leave…"something" on ice for a couple weeks.

"What is it, Biggums?"

"Hacksaw blades."

Skip was amused. He smiled and told Biggums it wasn't a problem. "Just get 'em to me before I leave out the annex for work." Two days later, Biggums brought Skip what looked to be a stack of seven or eight neatly taped-together blades. Skip knew from the stories around Upper Marlboro that the blades his homeboys preferred were not the average blades. They were some type of diamond-edged; also a jeweler's rope was a hot item amongst escape paraphernalia. Where or how they were getting this stuff, Skip had no idea and he didn't want to know. He knew one thing for sure, if anything happened to these blades while they were in his care…well, "My bad" wouldn't do, that was for damn sure. Biggums asked Skip was he tryin' to roll with them when the time came. If it was not for Skip already signing up to be transferred to the "Patuxent Institution" in Jessup, he would've seriously considered the escape plan with his big homeboy and Butch.

However, the Patuxent Institution was a treatment facility, not part of the Department of Corrections, but its own discrete unit for guys with minor to medical emotional and psychological disorders. When a person was fortunate enough to be admitted into Patuxent's program, that individual didn't have the amount of time the courts sentenced, but his release was more predicated on the doctor's recommendations. It was a five-hundred-bed facility with two hundred or so on the receiving tiers, waiting to gain entry into the programs. If Skip was accepted; it was highly likely that an eight or ten-year parole would be probable. Besides, he desperately wanted out of the Maryland Penitentiary. The place was a mad house! Buggs had made it into the program while Skip was at Upper Marlboro; he was also out of Biggums crew from way back. Skip knew the gesture to accompany them on the escape was more an act of gratitude for stashing the blades then it was genuineness. Skip appreciated it none the less.

Madoo sent her favorite grandson the newest model twelve-inch black-and-white TV Not many people had color sets back then, and if you did, you were like the guy on the block whose family's car was a Cadillac. Skip was not watching much TV on the streets, aside from a little late night with J. Marie, and the Redskins. Surely, he wasn't watching it like that in prison; however, one was a blessing to have nevertheless. "Better to have one and don't need it, than need one and don't have it." Years later, he'd say the same thing about having a "joint" (a knife).

On one of Madoo's visits with Connie, she wore a slick shirt and jacket set, eggshell or cream colored, with a long slit up the front. After the initial hug and kiss from his grandma Skip commented how jazzy Madoo looked, at which point she began avertedly looking over his shoulder at an older fifty-something bubbled-eyed man Skip knew as Eggie. Madoo told her grandson, "Skip I don't mean no harm, but, baby, I'm looking for a boyfriend."

"I'll see what I can do, but not him. That dude messes with faggies, punks…"

"Oh! Lord have mercy, don't tell me!"

Madoo could be a funny old gal when she wanted to be; Skip and her laughed for the rest of the visit about a little of everything. She pulled out some crumpled bills from somewhere down in the front of her blouse but Skip didn't want to risk getting caught. He thanked her for the TV, and told her and Connie how much he really loved seeing them. Skip explained to Madoo how the guys went about getting stuff they were not supposed to have. Her and Connie seemed to get a big kick out of it while Connie put her mom down with passing off contraband in the visiting room.

Connie had gotten to be a professional at passing stuff off to her son; she'd fold up a ten- or twenty-dollar bill real tiny, slip it into a balloon, then tie the balloon off just as small, cut it off, and toss it over the countertop. Sometimes she would palm it to pass it to Skip as she held his hands upon first arrival; they all would. J. Marie and Carlyn would bring him marijuana the same way, and once, Carlyn slipped him a gold rope. Skip kept it in his mouth. The balloons, the guys would have to swallow, which could be retrieved in one of two ways. Some guys could regurgitate it immediately after getting back to their cell, others waited for it to pass through the gastrointestinal tract, that took up to three days sometime, when the money or drugs finally passed through the bowels, it would then have to be fished from the toilet. It had a funky smell but still spent, and the reefer was just as potent, just a little stinky.

In C-dorm, annex one, Skip learned most all he needed to know about jailhouse distilling from C-dorm's most accomplished winemaking old heads; Tomboy, Soldier Dent, Big Niles, and from his homeboy, Short Legs – who also guided him right as far as doing a prison bit amongst Maryland and D.C.'s most corrupted rogues and cutthroats.

Since his Upper Marlboro days, he'd been listening to the tidbits of information imparted upon him. His most beneficial indoctrination, however, came from his first year in the penitentiary. He'd pass the days thinking of ways to help keep his sanity intact, in addition to a couple of his favorite past times – working-out and reading. His reading material changed somewhat. Most of the Harold Robbins, Jackie Collins, Sydney

Sheldon collection he'd completed. Now he was into espionage real heavy, Robert Ludlum. The K.G.B. and all that. He was familiarizing himself with words from the dictionary, and even reading a passage or two from the Bible.

Every Saturday afternoon, he and Soldier had an unofficial standing engagement to run a few games of chess over a quart-sized jug of Solder's specially blended raisin brandy.

After two weeks, Big Reds (Biggums) told Skip to bring "that" to him, and asked once more if Skip was trying to roll with them, again Skip declined the offer. Skip found out how to get an outside phone line from the crisis clinic, and every now and then would sneak out a call to J. Marie, Tawanna (her youngest sister), Carlyn or whomever, either way, he went to the well a little too often. One day while Skip was kicked back in the head psychologist's chair, Officer Lee walked in on him; not only did she make a big deal out of the incident but called the "level" on him. Within minutes, three officers plus a lieutenant escorted him, in handcuffs, though the main yard to south-wing lockup.

It dawned on Skip after a couple days of being on the hammer how much of a good thing it was Biggums got those hacksaw blades when he did. Skip got thirty days for the infraction, but was more thankful he didn't have to contend with Biggums about the loss of those blades… *Whew!* he thought, *there really is a God.*

Skip was on the same tier he was when on receiving, first coming into the Pen. All of south wing was lockup now. His thirty days was almost up; two guys who were also on lockup committed suicide in the south wing. One guy Skip knew from the boxing gym, who also lifted weights - T.C. – slept just next door to Skip on the second tier. He hung himself. Outlaw was one of the best artists in the pen. He followed suit – two suicides in south wing, one in A-block, all in the same day. The third man was "Edward Mann." This guy was charged with the murders at the IBM plant in one of two Maryland counties, either Prince George's or

Montgomery, in 1983. He was given something like six life sentences plus one thousand years, or some ridiculous sentence. Skip guessed he'd given up hope of ever seeing life on the street again, via the courts. Still, there's always the possibility of absconding somehow some way. He could've checked with Biggums, Larry Wallace, Rudiseal, these guys between them had over a dozen successful escapes to their credit. The only problem with each of them was they couldn't stay out!

Skip kept his workout routine going while on the hammer; his same lockup calisthenics he did whenever he couldn't get to the gym: Pushups, bend and reaches, crunches and sit-ups, and a little running in place. When Skip came off lockup, although he was able to move back to C-dormitory, there were no open bunks in annex one. He had to go into a cell on the fourth tier with a homeboy named Mack-Bey, whom came through Upper Marlboro approximately the same time as Skip, however, in another section of the jail.

Herbert Mack-Bey was a dark-skinned stocky-built guy, five years younger than Skip. He came from the same neighborhood as Biggums, in fact, his older sister went to school with "Harold," as she called him. Skip wondered what happened with the escape plan. Neither Biggums nor Butch were on the scene. They weren't in population. Skip figured they were on lockup, or at the new super-maximum facility the Division of Corrections just opened up just across the street. Mack-Bey and Skip got along well in 414, like old friends. The cell was set up like a little apartment. A curtain was fixed over a push broom stick to drop down to the floor. It separated the toilet and sink area, where one could have a degree of privacy if he so chose. Mack-Bey kept the place neat with a fresh scent in the air of the "oil" Muslims wear, or he'd twist some cinnamon inside a square of toilet tissue, light it, then blow it out. Skip knew convicts to be some of the most innovative dudes in the world. They could fashion a switch blade from a sardine can, a full-course meal from the measliest amount of food, and cardboard into a cooler. Skip and Mack-Bey both smoked, so they had their clothes in plastic bags while on the hangers, just to keep the smell of smoke minimized.

Skip was not the neatest guy around, but he wasn't a complete slob either, although J. Marie would beg to differ, he was sure. Both men shared the responsibility of keeping the cell clean, as well as being mindful of the cell door being closed and locked while they were out. "Opportunity makes the thief" was the mantra Skip grew up on. It was with him now that he was in prison more than ever.

Skip found out the "Bey" attached to his new friend's name had something to do with the religion he was involved with, "The Moorish Science Temple of America." All the men and women had either "Bey or El" attached to their last name. Since 1913 this nationalistic group founded by Drew Ali from North Carolina exalted the African American race. They don't eat pork, attempt to adhere to many of the Islamic doctrine, and would tell you they were Moslems oppose to Muslims. They believed Drew Ali to be a prophet and messenger sent by Allah, regardless of what the Qur'an says, that Muhammad is the last and final Prophet (see Chapter 33, verse 40).

Mack-Bey was in the College program that held classes in the penitentiary. Through the Pell Grant, Coppin State College offered an opportunity for the prisoners to enter into the bachelor's program. Mack-Bey was majoring in Business Administration. He encouraged Skip to sign up, especially since, "You're going to be a minute and you already have your high school equivalency."

Skip needed a job. As it stood, he was getting financial help from family and friends on the street, especially Connie, Aunt Lucy and Jennie. Lou would hit him and Kenny off occasionally too. J. Marie he knew was struggling, and if anything, he'd try to hustle up something to send to her, instead of taking food out the kid's mouths.

While on the fourth tier, Skip met an older guy working in the main dining hall that he would give a pack of cigarettes to every few days to bring back cold milk and four pieces of toast with his peanut butter and jelly sandwiches. Willie Donaldson was a good worker for the dining room officers. They looked out for him. Donaldson had pretty much carte blanche to bring out what he wanted from the kitchen. When they had pancakes or French toast, Donaldson would bring Skip stacks of the stuff, wrapped up in Reynold's wrap, with a cup of syrup. Donaldson soon lent out the cigarettes Skip paid him with (2 for 1) until, before long, he had a steady clientele of guys borrowing and paying him back twenty or thirty packs. He trusted Skip to the utmost, and would bring Skip money to hold for him, cigarettes, jewelry that someone may have had in hock or whatever. He told Skip to feel free to use what he needed as long as he let him know what he used.

Dunmore and Chick were regulars with the letters, as was Joan Penn, the realtor that sold him and J. Marie the house. Wee-Wee and

Dunmore, were now the parents of twin girls, Patricia and Patrice. Their birth date was the same as Candie cane's, the day of Kwanza (December 26). Candie was two years older than the twins, and happily preferred her birthday to be on Kwanza's first day rather than Christmas. Skip told her the story of Angela Davis, how she was a light-complexioned revolutionary black woman in the late 60s and early 70s that had strong ties to George Jackson and his younger brother Johnathan. About his attempted assist in helping his older brother escape, the Soledad brothers and all that black revolutionary history. Skip felt proud his daughter did a term paper for class on the subject. Candie was a very precocious girl coming up, defiant to a degree, and one could see early on she'd be handful for…somebody, someday. He began drawing big red candy canes on her letters since she was two and would start her letters off with "Hi Candie, I love you…" She learned to read those few words early on, if no others. Michael D'Angelo and Candie both, as most children, loved receiving letters in the mail addressed to them.

J. Marie once informed her husband of how, one evening, she went in their son's bedroom, and he was in there asleep with all the letters he'd received from Skip spread out all over his bed, as well as on himself. Apparently, he'd been reading them just before falling off to sleep. Skip was deeply touched by the scene he visualized.

Halfway through the summer, Mack-Bey got into it with one of the officers at the school about something. One thing led to another, and the next thing Mack-Bey knew, he was in handcuffs on his way back to the cell to pack up his belongings, preparing to make that trip to south wing.

Skip wasn't in the cell alone not a day before he was given another cellmate. James Minor, aka Frog, was a small-framed seasoned convict from West Baltimore, gold eye-tooth cap and all. He was a substance abuser from way back; he had fourteen years in on life, and was a naturally convivial, easy-to-get-along-with guy. Frog was like many old-school convicts, gave respect when it was due, or when it was reciprocated. If reefer was on the scene, he'd smoke it, wine, he'd drink it, and if smack was the drug of choice, then give him a set of tools and he'd shoot it. All this was okay with Skip, as long as he didn't leave bloody syringes lying around, and cleaned the blood off the toilet. He told Skip, "If I go out" (from an overdose) don't waste time trying to revive me, get help, and tell the officers or nurse what took place – plain and simple. All that went without saying, because Skip had never in his life brought anyone back around from anything, nor was he about to start.

The first weekend the two were in the cell, Carlyn brought Skip a fat balloon filled with reefer on a visit, Frog went down the tier and copped a half gallon of potato wine from a homeboy of his; they already had plenty cigarettes. Frog also had in his property an old record player with a stack of albums just as old. Needless to say, after the last count for the evening, 10pm, the two relatively new cellies got twisted! – as they say, "They were tore up! From the floor up!" Frog was a hilarious dude when he had that sauce in him; it was like one big party in cell 414.

The next morning, Skip was up and out of the cell when the door was unlocked, just after count cleared and the next shift came on. That was Skip's practice, up early, on with the day ahead, the weight room or library, maybe a phone call in G-building, or a few games of chess. He wasn't about lying in the bed half the day; that was for guys that weren't used to maintaining jobs, for the most part. Skip learned that many of the guys in prison never held down regular jobs on the outside, and came out mainly at night, like vampires or something. Their cells were the same likeness; dark like caves during the daylight hours, but as the sun began to decline, they were revitalized and invigorated.

Later that week, Skip watched Frog put up a batch of jump steady. This time they were going all out. They, or rather Frog, used the five-gallon bucket all the guys had in their cells, a bag of instant potatoes, yeast, and about three pounds of sand (sugar). The rest filled with water, and in no more than four days tops, the fermentation process should be completed. Frog would probably sell half to make back the money for the ingredients, plus have a few dollars extra. All Skip wanted was about a half G to kick back with. By the second day, the sauce was beginning to smell like alcohol, it was starting to ferment. The men on the tier were dropping subtle hints, so Skip and Frog took turns every few hours, or at least three times a day, washing the place down with ammonia, bleach, or lighting incense to throw off the scent.

On the third day, during what seemed like a random cell search (shakedown), two officers entered into cell 414 on the hunt. "Ah, what we got over here, boys?" one officer said to the cell's occupants. Frog told him it was some of his laundry water. The officer already knew what it was; the question was more rhetorical than anything else. Skip was a good sport about it, he tried to take the charge himself. "It's mines, officer. That's my bucket."

Skip and Frog both were given tickets for the bucket of fermented juices that, just for the record, weren't quite all the way fermented. For the next couple of days, they decided to try fighting the allegations against them, regardless of the officer's statement, and despite Skip attempting to fess up. They both were in the "bad category" as far as prisoner's status went – meaning, it was not long ago since their last institutional adjustment. Just about any kind of ticket, if it stuck, would send them back on to the hammer again, so neither of them really gave a rat's ass. Finally, after what must've been a week, Skip and Frog were called to the adjustment office in south wing. The hearing officer read the charges, then asked how they chose to plead. "Not guilty," both men said.

After a lengthy explanation and futile attempt to justify a bucket of quasi rut-gut/dirty laundry water, the hearing officer seemed to mumble something about – this time, or maybe he said the next time – either way, they got up when the hearing officer finished talking, heading to the door. The sergeant in the room asked, "Where the hell you think you're going? Turn around, put your hands behind your back. Didn't you hear him say thirty days' segregation?"

Most of the lockup cells this time were doubled up due to overcrowding. His cell mate was a white guy named "Nick Kosmo." He was over there with a year for escape, paraphernalia, as well as other associated violations. He was about to be shipped out to the brand-new super-maximum facility that was about to open up across the street on Madison. The only real problem Skip had with lockup was that the visits were behind a half-inch- to one-inch Plexiglas partition, with a telephone for talking to your guest. Skip couldn't get the hugs from his family; he couldn't kiss and feel up J. Marie. Michael D'Angelo and Candie got a real treat when their father was kissing mama. They would smile, and sometimes count to see if this time was longer than the last. During the first ten days into the lockup bit, there was a terrible commotion going on upstairs on one of the other tiers. Skip and Nick figured it was probably two cellies fighting, or guys rumbling while on their hour walk.

Guys in prison, especially lockup, could wind up fighting anywhere; in the shower – the visiting room, dining hall, school, wherever, whenever. Suddenly a woman's horrifying scream resonated throughout the building, and then it sounded like she was sobbing. The sound of more than one person running with keys, and boots or heavy shoes stumping the catwalk were now on the stairwell landing. More bumping. It was drawing near until the inmates began sticking their little broken "peeping mirrors" through the bars to see the end of the tier where the stairs were. A sea of blue uniforms could be seen dragging, punching, and kicking a lone inmate. Within minutes the news of the multiple stabbing circulated over the building and into the entire population. The prison was now on lockdown status.

Three officers were stabbed, one fatal. Officer Henry Toulsen died from wounds he'd received. Another was in critical condition; that was Big George, a CO II that was like an enforcer. His girlfriend CO II Shirley Anderson was the screamer. The last officer hurt was treated then released for non-life-threatening wounds.

The assailant was a mid to late twenties guy that had enough and couldn't take any more of Toulsen's and Big George's crap. Timothy Applebee's life was about to change forever. The administration took the stabbings of the officers out on the residents of south-wing lockup. For the next week rations were cut to two meals a day. One morning, pretty close to lunchtime, they were given a sour milk and two mini-doughnuts that was to last until the next day.

When the last week of Skip's lockup bit came to its end, his paper work to be transferred to the Patuxent Institute came through. He was told to pack up his belongings and report to the receiving room. At approximately 6:00 pm that evening, the long dark-blue specially constructed prison bus (aka the Blue Bird) pulled up in front of the Patuxent Institute in Jessup, Maryland. It dropped seven transfers at the front entrance. Skip couldn't have been happier to be one of them. The possibility of being accepted into the program, and not having to do the next ten years or so in the hellhole of a jail in Baltimore, overwhelmed him.

He had accumulated a few items from the Pen that were not admissible property at the Patuxent Institute, so he had to have the property shipped home or it would be destroyed. Among the items was a weight lifter's belt he bought off Nick Kosmo. He sent it home for Michael D'Angelo to put away for him until he returned…*if* he returned.

Skip's new cellie that he was assigned on the receiving tier was a guy about his own age from Baltimore named Barksdale. Patuxent was only half the distance from the District that Maryland Pen was. Skip was glad to be able to save his family travel time, as well as the few dollars they'd save on gas money. The visiting room had a long stainless-steel countertop, as opposed to the horse-shoe-shaped wooden one of the Pen, where inmates would come from a lower level to suddenly appear up the stair in the middle of the semi-circle to meet their guest.

There were several men on the tier Skip knew from the Pen that had been there for weeks and even moths before Skip arrived. Unlike the Pen, everything at Patuxent was on the inside. The only thing one had to leave the building for was outside recreation during the warmer months. Skip thought he could easily get used to this place. The food was better, the officers more humane; they walked like they were inspired or motivated and less combative over trifles. For the most part, Skip surmised the inmates knew this was an ideal opportunity to do a short peaceful bit; they weren't trying to blow it.

It would be another three months before Skip could actually begin therapeutic sessions with the counselors assigned to each unit. Depending on the unit you were assigned – 1, 2, 3, or 4 – you would be part of a group setting of anywhere from twenty-five to thirty-five guys to see where your head was; were you a good person that made this one mistake? Were you abused as a child or teen, and this is why you've acted out against others? Maybe you were just an evil, vile individual that the program wouldn't help, and needed to complete the duration of your incarceration amongst others like you in the "Division of Corruption."

In these group settings, as well as the one-on-one session with your social worker or doctor, the inmates at Patuxent were expected to talk about the charge(s) they were accused of, in detail.

Skip was glad he didn't have one of those charges that would embarrass and humiliate him. One of those shameful, disgusting, perverted child-molesting or rape cases that would eventually circulate all over the prison and every prison you went to later. Unlike "Vegas," what happened or was talked about, supposedly in confidentiality at Patuxent, didn't stay at Patuxent. Skip's case was a typical run-of-the mill street-thug mentality, ego-tripped-out, revenge homicide. Months later, when the time came for him to take the "hot seat" before the group, he felt nor showed none of the regret the doctors and social workers were looking for as he narrated his story.

Connie knew all about the program. She'd told him about showing remorse. She said, "Baby you got to at least appear sorry for what you did in front of those people. Life can be like a game sometimes, boy." Skip thought about the song, by The Fantastic Four entitled "The Whole World is a Stage" …and everybody's playing a part… Connie put on a heck of a spectacle during his sentencing hearing before Judge Blackwell in '82 – the tears, snot, the crinkled-up hanky, the rosary beads, and the whole nine. She knew her oldest boy was one of the bad ones. When the State smashed him, it was simply a case of "the chickens comin' home to roost."

Whether because of his youth or failing reproaching self, Skip just wasn't feeling it. He was not repentant by any means. As he replayed the scenario before the group, Skip could see the empathy amongst his peers; however, the unit staff was implacable. While Skip was there, he was hoping to run into his older mentor Buggs, but once again he missed him. He was informed Sam Buggs was shipped out to the Maryland House of Correction, known also by "The Cutt." It too was in Jessup, Maryland, and just down the road a ways, in the vicinity of the women's prison and the Maryland Correctional Institution (in Jessup), or M.C.I.-J.

Skip did however get to see Horacio Sails from his days in Upper Marlboro. Ray, as he was called, was already accepted into the program. He'd caught a tremendous break by the courts considering his charges. He, along with four others, his brother Brain, Shorty-T, Roger West-Bey, and Ronald "Cadillac" Drake, had knocked over Kay Jewelers in Iverson Mall back in late '81 or early '82.

An off-duty police officer was killed when he tried to intervene. The robbers got away with an undetermined amount of jewels and cash. They were apprehended days later, all but West-Bey, who was still on the run. Skip remembered the case well. It was during the cold season. Skip was making frequent trips down on the strip (14th Street corridor, N.W.) to "cop." He thought of asking around while down there on his next trip to try purchasing something from the heist for J. Marie. Later, after his arrest, he was on the same cell block with Shorty-T. The two had become close, prompting Skip to confide that he'd still like to get his wife something if they had a few pieces available. Shorty-T just laughed and told Skip what was not already sold/fenced was not available…at this time.

Horacio caught a huge break, not only was he accepted into Patuxent's Program, but while the others were given life plus, Ray was given fifty years.

Meanwhile Skip had more group sessions and one-on-ones with one of the unit's psychologist to help determine eligibility. Skip was interested in the behavior of people. He wondered about himself. While talking with the psychologist and social worker(s), he paid particular attention to their manner, the eye contact, when they wrote information down. Of the psychologist's interactions, he noticed a technique, he guessed, was that when posed certain questions as to your own behavior, the response would usually be redirected to you in the form of the same question.

Skip asked once why the psychologist thought he didn't cry when his father died. The psychologist responded with, "Why do you think you didn't cry?" – "What do you think it is?" "Who do you think is responsible?"

Skip realized, for the most part, people have an underlying knowledge why they feel certain emotions, and impulses, whether they care to be true to themselves and admit it or not. Deep down, Skip knew why he didn't cry, although during the funeral he felt a twisted tightening in his chest (that's when Connie pulled his head to her shoulder). He wondered how in the world she could sense something going on in his chest when he was sure he didn't exhibit any outward signs of distress.

Skip had by now been in Patuxent close to a year, it was time for the evaluation process to conclude. He was notified he was not eligible for the program, that he could try again in three years. Within the week, he was stepping off the big "Blue Bird" again into the Maryland Penitentiary. This time, as he walked through the Pen's compound on his way to C-dormitory there were quite a few guys to greet him back. His new cell was on the second tier. Cell 205 was in the back. As he pushed his boxes along the tier, he heard several familiar voices call out – "What cell you in Skip?" "Have you seen Kenny O, yet?" When he first glanced in the cell, before the escorting officer unlocked the cell door, he thought it was vacant, and he'd have the spot to himself for a day or so before he was given a cell mate. On closer observation, he realized there was a sheet haphazardly covering the mattress, and under the bunk, there was a lone box. Ordinarily one would not, at any cost, go into another man's property, but in this case, Skip needed clarification. He pulled out the box and lifted the flap to see a couple what looked like dingy T-Shirts, a pair of tattered sweatpants, and some magazines.

The cell was practically void of anything remotely resembling human occupancy. Skip stepped out of the cell upon hearing voices on the tier to see Kenny and one of his walking buddies, "Butter." All parties were genuinely glad to see one another. Kenny was still in annex one, and Butter slept just four doors down from Skip's new cell. Skip asked Butter what was up with his cellie, was the dude cool? "Mitchell's, alright.

He's from out P.G. County. He works in the kitchen with your man Donaldson. He should be in late this evening, you'll see."

Later on, Skip met his new cellie. He didn't have much of anything except time. Mitchell Moore had three life sentences, and little or no help from home. After Skip got re-established, he started looking out for his cellie as best he could. Mitchell loved the Redskins, so Skip gave him one of the two Redskin's jersey/shirts he'd acquired, which Mitchell wore religiously. Donaldson would tease and joke with him about his extremely dark complexion and lips that had less pigmentation, so that they had pink flesh spreading over beyond what one would normally see when a person's mouth was closed.

Skip began to realize how important family and friends were, and that he had people on the outside truly caring about his health and well-being. He knew many people since coming to prison who were not blessed with such a loving and supportive family as was he. Skip was grateful. Some people in prison, men as well as the women down in Jessup at the women's jail, had mothers who didn't deal with them, because of their past street activities or for whatever reason. Skip couldn't imagine such a thing. He recognized the importance of large families. He wished again he would have spent more time with his younger brothers and Carlyn instead of running the streets as he did.

His old kitchen-worker friend Donaldson had "blown up" (financially), from the few packs he got from Skip for his food services, since Skip was at Patuxent; Donaldson turned them over and over, until accumulating a hundred or so packs of cigarettes. Currently, they were on loan throughout the population, after which they would be "flipped" again and again for more packs, or even cash. He, like Skip's old cellie and friend Mack-Bey, were entrepreneurs. Mack-Bey was running a profitable jail-house store now, selling cookies, chips, sodas, and candy bars, two for one; meaning, he'd give you whatever you wanted from his store, but come state payday, when you made commissary, you would pay him double what you borrowed. Mack-Bey and Donaldson both would give Skip what he wanted without having to pay back the going rate. Skip would hit Mack up for cookies from time to time but wouldn't abuse the courtesy.

Donaldson trusted Skip to hold twenty or thirty packs, because he couldn't keep so many in his possession. Each inmate could only have twenty packs at one time.

Skip was beginning to amalgamate himself into the population. This time he knew he had to try doing a better job staying off lockup. Kenny pulled him to the side one day telling him what he already knew to be good advice, that he'd never make an early parole at the rate he was going. He still had some of the negative vices he had on the streets, vices he had to begin to rectify. Skip was lifting weights on a regular basis now. The weights kept him hungry. With a weight lifter's appetite, he was up to a solid two hundred fifteen pounds, the most he'd ever weighed. Mo-El noticed Skip in the weight room, and thought his homeboy from the District could be an asset to his football team – the Bears.

Chapter 14

Although Skip hadn't played any organized sports since his little-league-playing days for Fort Stanton, he'd played several pick-up baseball and football games since then, albeit nothing to compare with prison flag/tackle football. Without question, men prisoners participating in sports are the most aggressive, dirtiest, pugnacious athletes ever! Skip wasn't by any means the fastest dude on the Bears team, but he had big hands that held on to the ball when it was catchable, and he knew how to get open.

Out of six football teams in the Maryland Penitentiary, four were serious contender for a possible championship; Timmy Poole's "Stonewall" were the reigning champs. Others were the Sandtown Steelers, the Bears, and the Vikings. The recreation department allowed a budget for each team to have different color sweatsuits or at least jerseys of the designated team. All the players got one: Stonewall's was red, Sandtown Steelers – gold, The Vikings – green, and the Bears were black. Two other teams that never advanced were the Cowboys – blue, and Tampa Bay – orange. These two were sort of the "Detroit Lions" of the Pen.

Earl Crump (Big Crump) was an offensive and defensive throwback lineman from the 1960s and 70s out of West Baltimore's Red Shield Boys Club. In 1985, three years after his criminal activities were cut short, compliments of the Baltimore city detective's bureau, he brought his skills to the playing fields of the Maryland Penitentiary. Big Crump was a powerful football strategist, who knew what man would be best suited at what position. At 6'3" and two hundred eight pounds, he, along with Jack Cowen at three hundred forty-five pounds, were the nucleus of the Penitentiary's Viking's front line. When their present quarterback, Michael Cherry, was transferred, Crump knew he had some configuring to do. He moved Frye, who was a wide out, to QB, and had him run drills on weekdays with his new primary receiver, stop-and-change-directions-on-the-dime-quick Shorty-T. Along with a group of underachieving misfits, some on medication, like Barkley, they were pushed to maximize their fullest potential.

Games were scheduled on weekends during football season; during the week, team members can practice wherever and whenever they could, up until 1986, the primary recreation yards accessible to the inmate population was four-yard, which was on the south side of the prison where the infirmary was. There was a basketball court directly in front of C-dorm, and, just recently, a yard converted from where F-building used to be.

The main city street bordering this area of the prison was Madison Street. One-yard was seventy percent hard-packed dirt, thirty percent asphalt. Large buildings or thirty-foot granite stone walls kept an impenetrable barrier separating a society within a society from the rest of world.

Four-yard was positioned just outside of the administrative level where the warden's office, visiting room, adjustment hearing rooms, and a passageway that led to the south wing lockup were. All this was a part of, but separated from A and B housing wings. One-yard was all concrete with only basketball racks and a wall for a single game of hand ball; its bordering main streets separating it from society were Eager and Forrest Streets.

Skip's first game was at defensive end. His job was simply to put pressure on the quarterback and make sure he did not over pursue, enabling the runner free reign of the inside. He wasn't exactly Lawrence Taylor (LT) at the position, and was run on and over twice by the highly praised "Sandtown (Steeler) Sweep." He was too light in the rear to withstand such a devastating onslaught by the Steelers' pulling guards. Although the Bears team was fast, they needed more beef if they wanted to contend that year. With the loss of the first game of the new season, practice was scheduled every day the following week on up until the next week of their game against Big Crump's Vikings. Skip had an awesome three days of pass rushing. He was racking up sacks on the QB (grabbing flags), jamming the run out the backfield, you name it. He was all over the place, so much so that the offense began doubling up the blocks on him. The offensive line coach couldn't believe Skip was still making his way to the quarterback for the flag; the linemen didn't like being shown up, and on the next play, a third man somehow got his foot tangled with Skip's. Then end result was Skip's fibula bone in his right leg snapping like a number-two pencil.

Skip walked the twenty or so yards from the playing field to the dispensary to get it checked out. Ms. Lowry, the resident X-Ray technician, told Skip about the break and that he would have to be sent out to the University of Maryland Hospital. All the inmates welcomed trips for any reason, for a ride through downtown Baltimore, which was for one or two reasons only: court trips or to the hospital. He was escorted by two officers from the Pen. He arrived at Maryland University Hospital's security entrance that afternoon, in shackles. Skip hobbled with the one crutch the Pen afforded him for the trip to a prisoner's holding bullpen. After twenty or so minutes he was taken to an orthopedist to have the broken bone set for a cast. Skip was in his environment. He loved the hospital setting with sparkling floors, the smell of antiseptic, the professionalism, the nurses.

Another thing about these trips in town he enjoyed, or rather found amusing, was the attention from pedestrians convicts' received. Some guys lived up to the hardened scowl-faced mug, broken-down stereotype society deems fitting. Most convicts being ushered through pedestrian walkways derive tacit pleasure at seeing people scurrying to clear a path for the escorting officers, or marshals in some cases, at his expense. A parent will quickly place themselves in between their child and harm's way; women nervously fidget with their purse or neckline when suddenly confronted with a man in chains; however, some thrill seekers welcome advances from the captured. Walking through the halls of the hospital with escorting officers on each side, Skip had on his best celeb face. He smiled at the ladies, and nodded to the dudes looking on.

He was reminded of what he told to Michael D'Angelo when his son began first grade. "Son, you're going to meet a lot of girls from now until you're a big boy, and you should be nice to them, son, the fat ones, skinny ones, black and white ones, the pretty ones, as well as, and especially, the not so pretty ones, because one day they all might grow into someone who may be able to help you out, or they may grow into a beautiful or pretty girl that will remember, if nothing else, that you were nice to them." As his son got older and further along in school, Skip would ask Mike D'Angelo, "Son, you still being nice to the girls out there?" His son would always give his dad the same response: "Yeah Dad, even the ugly ones."

Skip welcomed the attention from the hospital attendants, especially the girl who was charged with wrapping the cast around his leg. Her name was Martie. She was no J. Marie, but a beautiful young lady nonetheless. She knew Skip was in no rush returning to the prison, and prolonged his treatment and cast wrap as long as she could. Indulging him in conversation was an act of kindness Skip truly appreciated. He was glad to think he still had the magic. Finally, not being able to delay his journey any longer, Martie started wrapping things up, literally. Skip was thankful the escorting officers chose to wait outside the office, in the hall, or wherever they were – Skip hadn't a clue.

When she was completed, he had a cast from just beyond his arch to the middle of his thigh. Another attendant, a guy this time, showed him the proper way to use the crutches.

Back at the Pen, he was now assigned a bed on the third floor of the hospital. One of C-dormitory's tier workers brought his clothes and other property in a large cart. On the second day of his stay, J. Marie was granted a visit with him at the end of the hall, near the elevator lobby by the window. She seemed a bit more reserved than usual in her persona. Otherwise she looked great and was soft as drug-store cotton.

The kids were at Lou's. They were asking about their daddy. Michael D'Angelo had gotten into a fight at school but was okay. Her job at the hospital was so-so, and she was having car troubles, again. Skip didn't know it at the time, didn't recognize it, but the two of them were drifting apart after all the time and love they once shared.

Much later, Skip would come to understand something of their separation. It didn't have so much to do with anything at the present time per se (J. Marie's word), as it did Skip failing to prepare them for what lay ahead.

"Prior planning prevents poor performance," as G. Gordon Liddy, the Watergate conspirator, once said.

It's an "art" to keeping a wife, or your mate through a lengthy prison sentence. Skip didn't exactly know how to "bit" himself, not all the ramification and details anyway, let alone know how to guide J. Marie through this debacle. Some marriages last for the duration of a couple's incarceration adjustment, while most others falter and then fail shortly after court proceedings, or the first few years. A lot depends upon what bond it is anchoring the union, whether it be children they have together, the time invested, or in some cases, a shared secret. Skip had all three in his favor, but failed to manipulate this leverage into a workable game plan. Skip, unfortunately was new at this, and ignorant to the unwritten rules regulating the dos and don'ts of a protracted incarceration.

While they were teenagers, talking on the grounds of Taft, or on one of the long walks from the school to J. Marie's house on 12th Street, they talked of, among other things, a possible future life together. The two agreed, whatever happened midway through their life wasn't as important as the end years; they would somehow grow old together, or so they thought.

In 1987 Actor Danny DeVito filmed a scene just off Madison Street in East Baltimore for his new movie *Silver Bullet*. The set was in clear view of Skip's third-floor window at the Pen's hospital. He got to see the actor several times, and enjoyed scoping out all the old cars used for that particular scene.

Other than that, and his roommate and homeboy, Dallas, trying to kill himself from a drug overdose (because of an incurable disease), Skip was ready to get the heck out of there and back into the inmate population.

He had been a patient for three weeks when, finally, a single cell on the "flats" of C-dormitory became available. With his leg in the cast, and one of the hospital workers pushing his belongings in one of the institutional cars, he hobbled across four-yard. The "flats" on any cell-block is usually a sweet set up, with the only inconvenience being the busyness and noise level during late evenings rec time when the yards are closed. Skip knew, for the most part, when the cast was removed, and someone else needed a ground-level cell, he would have to relinquish his housing arrangement; until then, however, he would make the best of it.

His friends and teammates visited often, especially during late evening rec periods. At first he was prodded and kidded about getting his leg broken – at practice. After a while, he was watching his teammates finish out the remainder of the season from the sidelines. Two more games were left to be played when Skip was taken back to Maryland University Hospital to have the cast removed. His leg set well. All he needed was a single crutch for support with instructions to take things easy for the next few days. The physical therapist told him he should gradually redistribute the weight of his body off the crutch and on the rehabilitated leg. His team, the Bears, were shorthanded but otherwise still being competitive. Skip wanted to play, more so from ego than from sound judgment. That Skip played really didn't make much difference… He was "on the half," and really couldn't be much of a contribution, limping up and down the scrimmage line as he was. The Bears missed the playoff that year, leaving Timmy Poole's "Stonewall" team the victory over Big Crumps green machine – Vikings. The beef between these two titans would become legendary, as far as prison sports competition went.

The most exciting matchups, melodramatic finishes – until Skip left the Pen to move throughout the system, from 1987 thru '93 – to epitomize the Prison sports circuit would be between Stonewall and the Vikings. The medical staff was on alert when they played because undoubtedly somebody or "bodies" would be carried to the hospital. Extra guards were put in four-yard by the officer in charge (OIC), because fights were surely to erupt. Not that the player(s) involved would be taken on the hammer, but to make sure a full-scale team brawl didn't ensue.

Once, while Timmy was in position at linebacker, he caught Moore-El from the Bears running a slant across "his middle" for a quick pass. Timmy unloaded all of his two hundred thirty-one pounds at the time on Moore-El's one hundred ninety-five. The collision was unquestionably one of the most devastating hits of the day, and dropped Mo' on the spot. After regaining most of his consciousness and willing himself to his feet, Mo broke across four-yard to C-dorm, where he slept, to retrieve his knife. Timmy, realizing the potential unnecessary drama about to unfold, ran after him, catching up with him at the locked grill of the housing unit. He attempted to soothe and calm his opponent, commenting that, "Man, we coming to this about a football game!?"

To Timmy it was just the way he competed in sports, relentlessly and violent at times, well, most times. However, to Moore-El it was a matter of pride, personal integrity, and also an equivalent to attempted murder on his life. That was the closest Timmy would come to an apology, so Mo resigned to settle for it. Both men moved on. Next year – Crump vowed to his battered and beaten team – would be a different ball game. It was something they already knew, because of the intensity of the way they played today. This would be the last agonizing defeat the Vikings had for a lot of years to come.

That summer on the flats of C-dormitory, Skip was enjoying his single-cell life. He'd positioned one of the flats' large industrial fans that cooled the cell to blow where he would have a steady gust of air 24-7. Because Skip's attitude level and lack of discipline and patience was yet to be subdued, he was about to bring upon himself a dramatic inconvenience. When the flats worker, because of his need to mop the waxed concrete floor, repositioned the fan away from Skip's cell, Skip hollered out to him from his locked cell, "to put that damn fan back like it was!" The dude vociferously responded in a way Skip deemed unacceptable. Skip would have to "straighten it." If, but for no other reason than because he cursed Skip in an aggressive tone, and besides that, "Aaron" was a faggy. And in prison, homosexual men have a tenuous line they must cautiously travel upon when addressing men.

Because of Skip's laid-back demeanor, Aaron had no way of knowing Skip had a latent and intermittent explosive personality disorder. Later that evening when the cell doors were opened for evening recreation, Skip stealthily entered Aaron's cell, which was several doors down. Before Aaron had time to register what was happening, he was assailed with a barrage of blows. Keys jingling overhead on the second tier snapped Skip out of his retaliatory mindset. Several minutes later, while Skip sat at one of the game tables on the flats, Aaron exited his cell with a bloodstained shirt and looking like the elephant man. He was pulled up by the officer working the flat's rec area and asked about his condition. Skip knew "what time it was" – that this wasn't good. The officer immediately got on the telephone. Within minutes, an escorting crew had entered C-dorm and headed in Skip's direction. One had a set of cuffs in his hand. Skip was given ninety days lockup time for "category I," assault on another inmate; worse, however, was the punk was pressing charges. Skip thought, *Damn, has he no shame?!* In addition to lockup time, Skip might get additional time behind this, if it stuck.

J. Marie, Michael D'Angelo, and Candie were always in good spirits visiting Skip. He only hated that their visit was once again behind the glass. J. Marie's good spirits and enthusiasm rubbed off on the children. Those two were some of the best-raised kids Skip could've ever imagined to call his own. She was doing a tremendous job with them, he thought. When Connie or one of his relatives would write or visit, they'd always comment how well behaved the children were, about what a beautiful family he had and all that. Skip was again thankful and appreciative, again realizing what an excellent mother J. Marie truly was. A natural child rearer with gifted maternal instincts. The four of them were a happy group spending the hour sessions in each other's company.

Skip only remembered having to sternly discipline his son once, let alone spanking him, and that was because J. Marie made him. Skip and his son were so connected. Mike D'Angelo was such a good little dude that Skip had only to tell him once that he should not do a thing and remarkably Mike D'Angelo would take heed to the warning. The one time Skip spanked his son was when he was about six; the sitter, Ms. Lindsey told J. Marie Mike D'Angelo got smart about a matter. That evening J. Marie informed Skip that, "Skip you have to spank him for this. I can't be the only one getting after him about things."

Skip didn't like the job of causing his main man pain, and maybe even tears! He shuttered at the mere thought. All the while, as his beloved J. Marie was talking, he looked upon her somewhat baffled, and wondered if she may have been speaking in a foreign language, maybe it was Chinese…

"Skip!...go on."

Skip reluctantly walked to his son's room down the short hallway, calling out to him, "Michael D'Angelo!"

"What's up, Dad?"

"Main Man, Ms. Lindsey said you got smart with her when she kept you in from going outside today; you shouldn't have done that. Now Mama says I got to…ahh…spank you." Now Mike D'Angelo was looking baffled, so Skip pulled off his belt. His son only looked at his dad, seemingly to see how far he was going with this new twist in their relationship.

"Mike D'Angelo…man I…" Skip broke it off in midsentence, and swung the strap, catching his son down low, feeling the pain his son should've felt. Mike D'Angelo barely flinched, instead took a double take at his father like he wasn't believing what was happening. Skip knew his son was supposed to be crying at this point, or at least hollering out, so Skip hit him again. This time, when he hollered out, Skip hollered out too. Tears welled up in Skip's eyes and suddenly he was angry with J. Marie. He left his son's room, heading back to where his wife was in the kitchen. Skip wanted to hit her with the belt; instead, he walked pass her to stand on the back porch. Later, after a minute or so, he came back inside and patched things up with his son. From then on, every time he heard the old saying "This is going to hurt me more than it does you" – he believed it, and thought of Michael D'Angelo.

True that, J. Marie was doing a fantastic job with the children; however, his son needed him on the scene to show and explain some things his mother wouldn't naturally think of, the same goes with daughters. There would be a thing or two Skip could point out to Candie as she matured that most woman don't impulsively impart upon their girls. Skip hated it that he'd made them all statistics, another single-parent-led home. Candie was still the prettiest little girl he'd ever seen. He questioned himself if he was just saying it because she was his own.

Skip would inwardly laugh when he thought of having to fix her hair the times J. Marie pulled weekend mornings at the hospital. Candie was anywhere from a year old to eighteen months, and Skip knew nothing at all about parting and braiding little girls' hair. He'd do his best to keep Candie presentable while she was in his care. After helping to raise three brothers and a sister, Skip knew a thing or another about what foods, activities, and attention toddlers and young children were safe with.

Skip would often walk around with Candie seated around his neck, on his shoulders, when they weren't driving. As the time drew near 4:00 pm, Skip would announce, "Time to go pick up Mama, kids." They enjoyed that short phrase more than "Let's go to Kennedy playground!" (No one used car seats or seat belts then, as they did later through the years, and the little ones would clamber over the seat, playing with toys like the car itself was a play area.) Picking up mama from work was the highlight of the day. Candie's face would brighten with joy, and her eyes would seem to say what her mouth could not: "Finally! Thank God."

Seeing what Skip had done with Candie's hair each weekend was like a whole new adventure; J. Marie would be torn between laughter and tears. Skip could never get the part straight down the center of his daughter's head no matter how even he thought he had it. And he knew the little plastic barrettes, or "boe-rets" as he called them, were supposed to go on her head…somewhere.

Skip pretty much kicked his smoking habit whilst on the hammer this time. When he went on lockup, he was holding forty-two packs for Donaldson. He'd gone three days clean before catching the ninety days lockup. Now, since he had a lengthy stretch, he figured he may as well kick back with a pack of Kool longs. As soon as he lit one up, Skip wasn't feeling the peace he usually felt. After halfway down, he stubbed it out, sent the remainder of the pack to his friend Silk (Andre Minor), and he never looked back – except for one relapse; it was a one night thing, and what a night that was.

Back on the second tier of C-dormitory, coming out of lockup for the third time, Skip landed a job in the main hospital. After four years, the administration either forgot he was once locked up for security breach in the crisis clinic, or apparently, they didn't care. Nevertheless, he was working on the third floor, which, because of the AIDS pandemic sweeping the country – the ward was now established by the Maryland Division of Corrections as the "AIDS ward." At the onset, the Maryland DOC took pride in being the forerunners of the campaign to combat the AIDS problem in prison.

By 1988, the quandary reached astronomical proportions, far beyond what Health and Human Services as well as the world expected. One night, Skip had a dream one of the nurses (a little rug rat from East Baltimore) working the floor was coming out of an AIDS patient's room with an infected needle carelessly pointing out as she exited the room. Skip miraculously turned his body away at the last second, avoiding the death prick. He bolted upright on his bunk, breathing heavy, and frightened over the catastrophic nightmare. He'd had these near miss dreams before, dreams of bullets and knife attacks. He was thankful he only had one or two dreams of his experience working the morgue. None of killing George and Gerald Hayes, and none of the monkey and baboon brains he'd removed while working with Dr. Silva in the research department at Veterans. Every night, Skip slept it was like he was starring in a movie. He had almost total recall of his entire dream. Some nights he even looked forward to going to sleep, just for the excitement in the dreams.

Later that week, one of Skip's coworkers on the third floor, "Fat Blunt," was up to what had to be one of the most deplorable and horrific hustles in Maryland prison history. Instead of boxing up the contaminated syringes, then placing them in the red "hazardous waste" containers, Blunt was collecting some of them to wash out (with bleach), then selling them to drug users throughout the inmate population. By sheer accident, Skip stumbled upon what was almost his own HIV death sentence. Blunt was in the elevator lobby on the AIDS ward, out of view form the unsuspecting nursing staff; he was carefully plucking out, then cuffing the least bloodied needles. After observing the opened box and Blunt making no effort to seal it, but instead conspicuously looking at Skip, Skip asked, "What's up!" at the same time bending over the box, and carefully moving a strategically placed paper towel. Blunt never tried to warn Skip of the infected 50-gauge syringe pointed upward. Skip never should have reached in the box in the first place, for any reason. It was surely by the grace and mercy of God Skip wasn't pricked with the protruding needle when he moved the paper towel.

Skip was temporarily in shock at the thought of coming so close to becoming infected. He thought about the dream he had the previous week. Though he wasn't one hundred percent sure of Blunts intentions, he was sure of the carelessness on both their parts. He simply told Blunt, "Man you need to seal this box up," and left the floor. Skip spread the word to the guys in the population, those he knew or thought were intravenous drug users, not to buy any "works" from Blunt nor anyone he affiliated with.

Skip was holding so many of Donaldson's cigarettes, he could hardly keep count. It was over four hundred packs easy, plus a little cash sometime, and marijuana. Donaldson trusted Skip, and by now, Skip was beginning to make a reputation for himself. His latest assault victim was Merv. Skip let Merv look at an "East Bay" tennis shoe catalogue. Merv brought the book back an hour later with a page torn out, the page Skip wanted to send to his brother M.G. to show him what style "Nikes" he wanted. When Skip looked through the book and saw the page torn out, he decked Merv on the spot, right on the second tier in front of several witnesses. He knew Merv to be a cruddy and duplicitous character who had to be checked forthwith without delay. For the next few days, Skip was "on point." He thought once Merv's crew found out about Skip banging out their homeboy and friend there may be repercussions. Only one of his boys confronted Skip about the situation; that Merv, by now had a black eye didn't help matters either.

The confrontation happened in C-dorm's shower. John (Harvey) stepped in front of Skip with several of his boys looking on, and told Skip, "You ain't have to do that to my man." Skip told John, "And you ain't got to be this close to my face telling me this shit." It was over that fast. John didn't really want to risk getting a black eye like his friend, and Skip didn't really want to have to give him one. Everyone in the jail knew Merv was wrong, and that Skip didn't go out his way to start any drama. Besides, there were no weapons involved; it was a fair fight. Well, it wasn't actually a fight.

Skip's new cellie was a dusty hippie-type throwback that would've been fine if he never showered, cleaned the cell, or brushed his teeth. Skip would've given him walking papers from week one had he not landed a job in the prison's library. As it stood, John Trout, a long-haired white boy about five years older than Skip's thirty years, suited Skip's purpose for a while. He stole black-oriented books from the library, the ones Skip had begun developing an interest in: J.A. Rogers's collection of *Sex and Race*, Chancellor Williams's *Destruction of Black Civilization*, along with a new espionage novel *From Time to Time*. After Skip read and digested them, he'd send them out to Michael D'Angelo to start his own little black history library. The worst thing about Trout was he seemed to think there were alligators in the showers, or maybe someone was "leaning on him" for his manhood down there. Skip wanted to know what the problem was that his cellie was not taking showers. If someone was leaning on him, Skip would get the dude(s) off his back. "Look Trout, we'll get along just fine as long as you get your dusty ass in the shower, at least twice a week, and when you have to talk to me, man please turn your head away, because your breath smells like raw sewage! Homeboy do you ever brush your teeth?"

All in all, things were tolerable between the two cell mates. When they had to be locked in during count time, or the jail was on lockdown, Trout and Skip played chess or scrabble. Skip's spelling had come a long way since Catholic School, and "Lucy Ellen Moten" Elementary. He was enrolled in the College program again, plus working in the hospital. His days were filled with positive and beneficial endeavors – other than an occasional sip of "sauce."

If his cellie was out of cigarettes, Skip would give him a pack from Donaldson's stash telling him to give it back on "State day" (pay day for all inmates from their assigned jobs).

One night before crashing for the evening, Skip glanced upon Trout's overhead shelf to see if his cellie had any smokes for himself. He didn't. Skip figured he give him a pack on the house. Skip did that sometimes. He'd give it to him in the morning before leaving out for work. However, the next morning, Skip noticed a fresh pack on Trout's shelf with a couple taken out. Skip thought, *Maybe I'd better take inventory to see where the count is.*

He'd be a little late showing up for work this morning, because something was stinking around here and it just wasn't the stench from his cellie's unbathed body. While his cellie feigned sleep, Skip went through all the spots where he had Donaldson's four hundred sixty packs of cigarette stashed throughout the cell. Not that he could actually hide so many packs; the objective wasn't to hide them; it was more so creating an "illusion" that there weren't so many. By strategically spreading them around fifty to seventy a clip, an unsuspecting rookie officer would not think to keep count, and by the time it dawned on him or her "Wait, I just saw about sixty packs under the bunk in the little box, and how many was that laid out under those boxers and T-shirts?" they didn't want to begin counting all over again. With a two man cell you were good with as many as forty, maybe even a hundred depending on the officers shaking you down. Sometimes a CO that smoked and was about out, he'd take you off for a couple packs.

Skip had four hundred sixty. He didn't know exactly how the officers would play it if they came in on him one day. Living on the edge was the order of the day for Skip, besides, they weren't his in the first place. He was doing someone a favor.

Meanwhile, right now, he had to see what kind of games his cellie was playing. After ten minutes, Skip concluded he was down five packs from what he was supposed to have, not counting the six he himself used earlier that week. Yes, without a doubt, his cellmate roughed him off for at least five. Skip put everything like it was and left the cell as if he was going to work.

Each morning, when the shift changed, the morning shift would manually unlock each cell door, so the inmates could go to their jobs, school, and recreation yard, whatever. If a guy wanted his door locked back as he exited his cell, he'd tell the officer to "dead lock my door" on his way going off the tier. Skip slid the door closed and stepped a few paces down the tier…waiting… Within seconds, Trout jumped from the top bunk and was exiting the cell, no brushing his teeth, no water on the face, let alone washing his hands after that first wake-up piss – that's just how trifling this joker was. As soon as he closed the door shut, Skip was up in his grill. "Cellie, how many packs you owe me? Where're we at now? Things had unraveled way too fast for Trout to think up a good line so quick. Skip intentionally wanted to catch him off guard.

If he would've added the packs he stole to the ones Skip lent him to replace later, Skip would've accepted that. Instead, he gave the count of what was lent to him which was three. As soon as "…Ahh… three" came out of Trout's mouth, Skip gave him the same treatment he gave Aaron on the flats of C-dorm a year ago. He overwhelmed him with a barrage of blows to the face. Unlike Aaron, however, Trout at least tried fighting back. He swung wildly when Skip let up, which made Skip remember something his old childhood friend Dunmore told him – "Step up into him with a straight right hand and aim for the back of his head, because aiming only as far as the face will cut your punches short, zapping them of force. You understand what I'm saying, Skip?"

A couple years later, Skip tried it out on "Nooks," one of his Fort Stanton friends he was fighting with while the two were teenagers. It was a good piece of advice then, as it was now. Trout literally walked right into it. Skip almost felt sorry for him. *But he shouldn't have played me for a chump, or a fool, by stealing from me*, Skip thought. Nevertheless, "There is no honor in defeating the weak." As with Merv, this time there was no going to lockup, only an inquiry by the shift commander, Major Thomas, that afternoon. Since it was Saturday, after the beating, Trout went to the movie with a couple of his friends up to the auditorium. On the way back, an officer observed and questioned him about the lacerations to his face, and a busted lip. Apparently not buying Trout's story about falling face first from his bunk onto the sink, he wrote up an incident report. Meanwhile Skip was treated at work for a fractured right pinky finger, for the third time in his life. Each time for connecting to the head with his fist not properly closed. The first time was on the street, fighting up at the church's Saturday night function against the boys down Morris Road. As a result of Skip's finger never being properly set, by now, it was crooked as a cork screw.

Major Thomas asked Skip about his hand, and was reluctantly resolved to accept the injured-in-the-weight-room scenario. After a few more minutes interrogating the two cellies, the major had Trout sign a "body waiver," freeing the administration of liabilities from any future damages to his…"person"…just in case.

Continuing to live in a cell with a man you'd just beat the daylights out of is not only stupid, reckless, and dangerous, but an egregious error, as far as the unwritten prisoners' code goes. That evening, in the cell, the two men talked about what unfolded earlier. Trout vowed to put back the missing packs. Skip didn't apologize, only told his cellie he'd split the difference. He hoped he felt better, and did he want something to eat. The inside of Trout's mouth was a wreck. Skip doubted if he could've eaten anything.

Skip was naturally a light sleeper, other than the time he fell asleep after one of his marijuana-induced hazes at his mother's house with Mike D'Angelo in the bedroom. Connie and M.G. knew the two were in the room. Mike D'Angelo was not quite a year old and couldn't reach the door knob let alone unlock the latch as Skip lay semi-comatose. M.G. finally unbolted the door knob from the outside, gaining entry, to see Skip sleeping through it all. Connie was furious that Skip wouldn't awaken with the door locked and her grandson in there; J. Marie may have killed him. That was one of the only times Skip had trouble awakening. Skip wouldn't accept any food that wasn't sealed from his cellie either. He didn't know what kind of stunt Trout might have pulled given the opportunity.

Shortly afterwards, an open bunk became available in annex one, and designated for Skip specifically. Skip jumped at the chance to be back in the open twenty-five-man-dorm setting. Kenny O had been transferred to another prison, a lesser security facility. With Skip's help to clear him of the charges, he was making progress with the courts. Skip moved his belongings to the east corner aisle spot within the hour. The corner aisle was the only three-bunk area in the dorm, because of a double bunk up against the wall. Skip shared the aisle with Big Earl Crump and Black Battle, who he knew from his Upper Marlboro days. Battle was one of the lyingest, dirty rottenest scoundrels to ever come out of Seat Pleasant, Maryland. Crump and Battle, as contrary as they were – were the nucleus of the Vikings football team. Both had exceptional knowledge of the game, with a combination of strategic maneuverability from Crump, who was also a playing coach, and the strong-arm aggression and disciplinarian style of Battle. As different as the three of them were, they came together harmoniously for the sake of getting along with their current living arrangement. Crump and Battle both had jobs in the main dining hall. Skip was contented in the hospital setting with access to the officers' dining hall for an occasional meal. Sometimes Skip would bring back leftovers, enough to feed half the dorm. With Crump and Battle working and bringing food and other hustled up items to the aisle, and Skip bringing provisions from the hospital – things in the east corner aisle were sweet.

Chapter 15

As Skip looked out of the second-floor window of the officers' dining room, overlooking four-yard, at no one in particular that July afternoon, he saw a small band of men running from the upper end of the compound toward where he was in the hospital. A few began splintering off as they passed G-building. He could see aggravated and violent scuffling going on within the guards' shack. Moments later a black thirty-something-year-old correctional officer from Baltimore County named Baysmore stood in the opened doorway of the small structure and then collapsed onto the concrete outside.

Whatever meeting twenty plus "hoppers" (young guys) previously had on the third floor of A-building this day prior to the assault was about to peak. Whatever order the leader of this group issued, it was on! There was a guy in the weight room passing out Z-bars (short bars used for curling dead weight), three others had bats they'd pick up off the baseball diamond that carelessly lay against the backstop, while others, because of sheer numbers, used their fists and state issued boots to viciously beat and stomp any and all officers within their scope. Whether the blue shirts were black, white, Hispanic, young, old, male, or female, no one was exempt. Skip saw it all. He saw the young female officer Acree trying to scramble over the twenty-foot automatic access entry gate, before the tower guard saw it was safe to open it for her. Officer Biddle, the fire extinguisher inspector, wasn't as fortunate; that he was in his late

50s and was cool and well liked didn't matter to this pack of renegades. They caught him strolling down from "the level" (administrative offices); before he realized there were "code 13s" going on everywhere on the compound (officers needing assistance) the packs were on him like a swarm of killer bees. After the dust cleared Officer Biddle lay moribund, a motionless heap in the dirt. That he was not killed after sustaining such a beating was nothing short of a miracle.

There was a rookie Skip remembered seeing in the main dining hall a couple months ago when the officer first started working the prison. Skip commented to a guy going through the chow line with him that if anything ever kicked off in this joint that little fellow might have problems.

Officer Atkins was only 5'8", about one twenty pounds soaking wet. He could easily pass for a minor. One of those unfortunate officers assigned to four-yard that day whose post was to patrol the area by the newly constructed school building adjacent the hospital and crisis clinic. Atkins was one of the beat victims, and there was nothing much he could've done to save himself from the angry man swinging the short fifteen-pound weight bar at his head. In defense, he threw up his celery stalk size forearms that were no match for the force and weight of the bar as it crushed them like…well…celery stalks. (Atkin's coworkers would visit him the next day at the hospital. He was in a half-body cast with broken arms; he also sustained two black eyes.)

As Skip and other hospital employees stood at the window of the ODR stunned, Skip was beginning to feel in a precarious position. He was the only inmate in the room among the outside staff, including two correctional officers.

If there were one hundred ten women employed at the MD Penitentiary in whatever capacity, thirty of them were having inappropriate contact or conversation with inmates in the population; ten of the thirty were having sex straight out.

CO II White on the four to twelve shift kept a safety pin holding together a carefully torn rip in the crotch of her uniform pants. For fifty dollars, she would unfasten the pin and let an inmate "get his man," doggy style, wherever the coast was clear. Usually it would have to be in one of the three annexes or on one of the higher up tiers like four or five. Her coworker and friend, Officer Hendrix, was pregnant with the Puerto Rican Chico's baby. Her husband thought it was his until the two had a fight and Chico called him at home one evening during phone time, threatening him if he did anything to harm "his" baby....

Then there was the penitentiary's resident Picasso, Sam Pathmore; he was an artist with exceptional skills. He had paintings hanging in the visiting room, sold them throughout the institution to the inmates to mail home, and was commissioned to do a mural in the dental clinic of the hospital, where he caught the eye of a beautiful dentist. There was also CO II Warlow. She was a gorgeous petite young woman whose pants looked like they'd been poured on her. She had an hour-glass figure and was being hit on daily by no less than thirty guys, not including her coworkers, all thinking they had a shot at reaching "The Promised Land." None however was more convinced than inmate Blake; the body building rapper/preacher/ Casanova was on her like bad breath. He'd been dogging her trail from day one. Stony Blake had convinced himself she wanted him as well, only she was playing hard to get. Sometimes she was only trying to make him jealous by letting all them lames hang around her; deep down she knew what she and he had. Stony knew in his heart of hearts they were meant to be. It was their destiny. *Maybe I'll write her another poem,* he thought. He had her schedule down pat. He knew what days she was off; what post she was assigned, as well as who his competition was. He and Lil Stevie were her most adamant convict suitors. They vied daily for her favors, which were never more than a smile and minor exchanges of pleasantries.

Stony and Lil Stevie's rivalry came to a head one morning in front of B-block, each accusing the other of being a stalker and cockblocking. Stony outweighed Lil Stevie by fifty pounds, but Stevie was game, and was determined not to let the big bammer get out on him. They tussled until the "10-10" code was called, and they were quickly ushered over to south wing lockup. No one was seriously hurt, but they were given forty-five days for fighting, nothing more than a cooling-down period. Officer Warlow had been off on leave when Stony was done with his lock up bit. He'd thought about her, continuing his twisted fantasies, for the entire time he was on the hammer, longing to see her, to smell her perfume; in his delusional mindset, he assured himself the feelings he felt for her were mutual.

The morning of the four-yard riot, Stony learned his possible future children's mother was assigned to the crisis clinic. *This is perfect!* he thought. He cleaned himself up in his best gear, put on a splash of the Muslim oil he had gotten from Rasheed, and was on his way down the yard when all hell broke loose.

Stony Blake, like many convicts, had an alter ego. His name was "Jack," and Jack was whispering to him now, telling him Warlow wanted him to take her. *Man, she's in there waiting for you to save her before someone else gets to her. The time is now!*

In the midst of anarchy and debauchery going on all around him, Stony's eyes and mindset were zeroed in on the door just thirty yards before him. As he walked, he contemplated how he'd get her to open the door. Most convicts that have spent years deprived of female companionship, much less sex, dream of or envision riot scenarios where the prison is taken over, allowing them the release of the demons within them. The female officers and employees are terrified of such a day ever existing. It's their most dreaded nightmare, some of them. Jack new he couldn't do it alone. He'd need accomplices, but Warlow was his. Jack was tired of playing mind games with this broad.

His break came when one of the unsuspecting prison psychologists entered through the first-floor hospital lobby en route to the crisis clinic. Word of the four-yard riot hadn't reached all post, so he was allowed to walk through, past the opened sally-port area, past the medication window – as soon as he was spotted, the inmates rushed across the yard to accost him. He recognized and assessed the situation, then made a mad dash to the crisis clinic door, banging frantically. The female officer quickly tried to allow the doctor's entry, but couldn't get the door behind him closed and secured fast enough. Jack caught up to the inmate assailants as they entered. This was his fantasy come true! He couldn't believe his luck. He thought of kissing and fondling her, but he would have to be quick about it, he knew his time with her would be cut short, with maybe a window of about two minutes tops! And there wouldn't be any privacy.

Meanwhile, in the main hospital's ODR, Skip didn't like the vibe he was getting from the staff. He was thinking any moment these people might direct the enmity of what they felt for the rioters toward him, especially since several of their comrades lay bleeding and battered in the yard.

Skip saw Stony, Man-Man, Hugo, and others rush the opened crisis clinic door. He knew Stony's intentions were seeking out Ms. Warlow, but he was in for a rude awakening. Warlow was in the ODR with some of the other staff taking her break, and the woman relieving her was Ms. Felder, another CO II. Warlow was physically shaken at what she was seeing. When she saw the men rush the opened door of the crisis clinic where she'd just left, her face broke out in hives. She was horrified. Skip, on the other hand, was seeing the writing on the wall. He knew without a doubt as soon as order was restored the prison would definitely be on lockdown status. Some of the inmates would be beaten, some would get charged, possibly getting more time, and all that witnessed it would remember it for the rest of their lives.

Skip began bagging up leftovers from the afternoon lunch meal to take back to the annex. He didn't know if he'd make it across the yard with the large plastic bag filled with the fried chicken livers, a stack of cheese, and forty pieces of cake, but surely he'd try his hand. Suddenly the sound of gunshots. Actually, to Skip it sounded more like the ashecans and M-80s he used to ignite as a kid, in defiance of his parents, that resonated throughout the compound. While the inmates ransacked the crisis clinic, and assailed the staff, the alerted remaining correctional officers regrouped and assembled in the wagon yard area just outside the back emergency door.

The inmates were oblivious to the contingency plan their once overwhelmed captors had formulated. Nor were they aware of a back door to the place they ruthlessly inhabited, and they certainly didn't figure on the surviving officers drawing weapons, as they continued to pillage and maim. "Jack" was no longer present in the idled mind of Stony Blake. Reality, in the form of keys jingling outside a door he previously thought inaccessible, was now warning him. Temporarily shocked into immobility, fear now gripped the inmates in the crisis clinic.

Pellets from the first blast of the twelve-gauge slashed a crease in the side of Man-Man's head, spinning him to the floor amongst the files and trash tossed over the floor. The next fallen soldier would be Hugo, who caught the second blast over his neck and shoulder. As the officers rushed through the back door, firing, no questions asked, the rioters broke for the front leading back to four-yard, leaving their comrades to whatever fate befell them. Now, it was every man for himself.

The viewers in the hospital windows, after the shots rang out, saw inmates breaking across the yard from the crisis clinic, literally running for their lives. In pursuit was a sea of gun- and black-jack-wielding blue shirts, rounding up and beating as many of the perpetrators as they could before the camera and video crew arrived. The innocent and/or casual observing inmate population, those in school, shops, and the hospital, were ordered to their respective housing locations. What seemed an eternity was over in less than ten minutes. The Maryland Penitentiary was officially on lockdown status.

Skip never saw so many blue shirts together in one place as he saw in four-yard after control was restored. A gauntlet was formed from the hospital and school to C-dormitory for the inmates not involved in the turmoil. He dreaded leaving the sanctity of his haven in the hospital and was the very last one on the compound to be locked in. He was allowed to leave with the extra-large-sized grab bag to feed him and his friends in the annex for a few days, only after he did a little post-riot work in the hospital's dispensary and in the crisis clinic. For starters, he had to lug one of the industrial-sized fans from the store room to the clinic to help clear out the smoke from the burning records and inmate psychological files. He also had to use bleach to get up all the blood, from officers that came through the infirmary, as well as inmates, although, the officers were rushed out to local hospitals in downtown Baltimore.

Skip did what he could for his fallen convict cronies in the infirmary, but had to be discreet about helping them, because they were all hated or loathed by the guards now. The guards wanted them to feel whatever pain and discomfort they bore. By mid-afternoon, Skip was carrying a plastic trash bag full of provisions to C-dormitory, specifically to the annex. He spread all of what he had on the annex's card table for the men he shared the open dorm with. The lockdown lasted two weeks, in which visits were canceled, work was halted, shops and schools/classes were closed, and tension between the guards and inmates was higher than normal. The meals, like when Officer Henry Toulsen was killed, were carted to the cells by the officers. Also like when he was killed, the inmates were hesitant to eat food they were served for fear of it being spiked.

Man-Man and Hugo were among those having charges brought against them, despite being shot during the melee. Hugo was sent across the street to the super-maximum facility with several others. Those inmates not charged or sent to super max were transferred to other facilities throughout Maryland, including Stony, who when he saw Warlow wasn't working the crisis clinic, aborted his mission or rather abated it. Fortunate for him he sort of slipped through the cracks of those found responsible and involved. He was later transferred.

Midway through the 1988 football season, Skip was again sent to Patuxent Institution. This time it wasn't so much him attempting entry into the program as it was him wanting a vacation from the penitentiary. (This was during the time one could sign up to be evaluated for Patuxent's program once every three years, so in '88 Skip was again eligible.) Before he left, he would make up for the year he broke his leg in a real big way with his Bears team. Larry T was coaching, and deemed Skip better at tight end than as a defensive end. It proved to be the most prudent of his decisions ever. Skip scored at least one touchdown in all the five games he played before being shipped out. He had exceptional hands, and knew how to sell the play off as someone else being a receiver before sneaking off the line to the opened area of the field and recovering the ball himself. He also played on kickoffs, spearing in on the receiver to the flag. The Sandtown Steelers leading returner, Shorty Crock, would argue to the officials that Skip was jumping count. He was coming off the line too fast, and before the snap, or lining up in the neutral zone.

Eventually teams began putting double blockers on him to prevent him from getting down field.

Tight ends are multitaskers at their position; it's not all about running patterns and catching the ball, like wide outs. Tight ends most difficult job is blocking the usually much larger and stronger defensive end. There were three DEs while Skip was in the Pen that gave him the most trouble when he wasn't going out for a pass and had to stay back to block – Big Moon, Jehu, and worse of all, Kevin Lattisaw. At 6'5", two hundred seventy pounds, this Goliath had the size and strength of a bona fide second-string NFL player. Skip was thankful that the dude didn't have the speed. Big Moon, on the other hand was just as tall, not as strong, but quicker. He played with Timmy's Poole's "Stonewall," and was one of the dirtiest players Skip competed against, ever!

In the fall of 1988, the trip back to the Patuxent Institution was a most inviting change for Skip and the Lucas family, again. This time, the change of venue wasn't only about proximity but those things in his life more intimate and mundane. For one, Skip was growing a bit spiritually cognizant. He always believed in a supreme creator. He went to a religious service or two specifically Catholic. He even read the Bible every so often, despite his evil and debauched lifestyle, in as well as when he wasn't in prison.

There weren't many jobs available for men who were not admitted into Patuxent's program and newly arrived. Again, he was resigned to working in the main dining room, and it was there he noticed Gordon Pack, originally from Florida. He'd moved to Baltimore, MD, with his family when he was thirteen. Gordon, or Pack as he was called, had been in prison since he was fifteen. Now, at twenty-five, he was the Imam (spiritual leader) of the Muslim community at the Patuxent Institution. Early each morning, Pack would lead a group of ten to fifteen Muslims in prayer. They didn't call it praying, but it was "Salah." The only encounter

Skip had with this strange lifestyle was when he would go to Shabazz Bakery on Martin Luther King, Jr. Avenue in S.E. Washington. Connie would sometimes buy whiting fish from the "brothers," as the Nation of Islam would send out men from the local mosque they occupied in the early 70s. Skip had gone there a few times too.

While going to the little Edgewood Terrace mini-mart one morning for breakfast food for him and J. Marie, he saw an old Douglas Jr. High School classmate (William Ford). He and Ford were real cool in the seventh grade, until Ford stole his almost girlfriend Joyce. Skip had not seen him in five or so years, and now Ford was wearing this funny looking little beanie-type cap, and trying to tell him about the "Islamic Movement." Skip was definitely not trying to hear about a way of life to deprive him of intoxicants, illicit sexual intercourse with J. Marie, and driving around in slick stolen cars, nor all types of other immoral and scandalous behavior. He was a rogue and wanted to stay a rogue. He wasn't quite finished destroying himself.

Afterward, he felt bad about the way he brushed Ford off. Skip treated him as if he had the plague. There was the incident at the District Building in D.C., when the Sunni Muslims killed a radio announcer for "WOL." They'd even held at gunpoint the then D.C. councilman, Marion Barry. Kareem Abdul-Jabbar had recently converted to Islam. His previous name was Lou Alcindor, and he owned a fine home in upper-northwest Washington's gold coast. Several people were killed in the home.

It was this second trip to Patuxent when Skip and J. Marie's tenure took a turn for the worse. After close to seven years hanging out with Skip through the prison scene, J. Marie's patience and tolerance of his demands were beginning to take a toll on her. It was bad enough he would accept money from her, but now he expected, in addition, to see her when he wanted to see her, on his time. He received a twenty-dollar money order in the mail from her one evening at mail call; because he'd not seen her in a few weeks, in anger, he sent it back with a brief disparaging note.

Keeping a cool head and algorithms to solve his problems was not one of Skip's strong suits. He was slowly but surely digging a hole for himself, and driving a wedge between he and J. Marie. Something Lou told him as a teenager at her apartment in Edgewood came back. he wasn't sure just what she expected him to draw from it, though he had an idea, nor was he certain what prompted her to say it in the first place. "It's but a sorry rat that only has one hole," she said.

Skip wasn't hard pressed for money orders. He was getting by. He did want a woman to holler out to on a regular basis. J. Marie's enthusiasm was dwindling; that he was sure of. He needed a "plan B." Skip couldn't blame her. If the shoe were on the other foot, he figured he'd have bounced on her years ago, or at least he'd have one or two honeys to holler at. He was a wreck!

Meanwhile, if he and J. Marie were reaching the end of their road, then he needed to begin construction on a new highway.

A few of the women from the VA would write friendly correspondences from time to time. Skip never was one to burn down the bridges he'd crossed, always writing back anyone that wrote. Convicts are like that for the most part; hard pressed for rap from the bricks, and loving attention from women in their lives. He thought about Donna, her family's house was still in Fort Stanton, just around the corner from Connie's, down a few doors from Tommy's. He quickly calculated the addresses, counting up from the "Samuels" because theirs was the exact same as Connie's, only on the next street over…09, 11, 13, 15, hah! Wherever she was, someone living there would forward the letter to her. The message was brief, to the point, without a whole lotta fluff. A page and a half would due, just simply "Hi, I was hoping all was well with you. Say hi to the family," and so forth and so on… Oh, and "Keep me in your prayers" – Skip always included that little piece with spiritually oriented people. It was a nice touch.

The old adage of "The Lord works in mysterious ways" rung ever so true. A week later he was called in from the recreation yard for an emergency phone call in the captain's office. The woman's voice on the other end said that she'd told them she was about to go out of the country and it was imperative she spoke with Mr. Lucas before leaving. Donna was resourceful that way, and although Skip hadn't dealt with this "femme fatale" in ten years, he knew what kind of time she was on. He'd even read about her embezzlement scheme in the *Washington Post* while working at the district's water company one year as he sat in his cell at the Pen. She was a looker, and she had chutzpah. Somehow, he felt partly responsible. During the years they were kids, he'd spoiled her rotten with money and other trinkets he swiped. She grew up under the impression dudes were for getting money from, and the world was her oyster.

After the over the phone pleasantries, she told Skip as soon as she read his letter she dumped her boyfriend and couldn't think of anything else but seeing him. It was music to his ears. "Have my name placed on your visitors list, and as soon as I get back in town next week, I'll be there." Donna didn't ask the visitation days, nor the hours during which she could visit. If she could pull off getting him on the phone in the captain's office, then finding out the prison's operation and location was a walk in the park.

Connie was no different than any other mother in regards to wanting and seeking out a means of procuring their imprisoned son's wants. If it was money they needed for a lawyer, clothes or food from the commissary – they'd keep a few dollars in his spending account; when Connie could help Skip academically, she would send articles from magazines, the newspaper, or books, and when she suspected her daughter-in-law was "going south" on her oldest boy, for whatever reason, well, Connie would do her best to make sure Skip had replacements.

Whatever reason Skip's youngest brother, Paul, had for harboring enmity for Donna was never thoroughly affirmed or investigated. Paul knew something about her he found unsettling, to say the least. Deep down, Skip knew his childhood belle wasn't shooting straight. She had issues that could prove detrimental. To name a few, she was a liar and a crook, among other things. He'd been hooked on this broad since he was six. She was now his nymphet in waiting. Skip was certain she would have rolled with him during his crime spree in the 70s, back in the day, because living on the edge was how she got down. She was promiscuous, dirty, rotten, and lowdown, but he wanted her anyway.

Connie always greeted Skip with a big ole genuine smile upon first seeing him. This time it seemed her grin was even more pronounced. Donna was dead on her heels, greeting Skip with a big hug and kiss on his cheek. Damn! Skip thought she hadn't changed a bit; he never noticed before how large her breasts were, like J. Marie's. Connie was happy to be able to accommodate her son in this way. After the first half hour into the visit, she left Skip alone with his old friend. Skip knew mothers could be the greatest pimps sons could have. He'd heard stories through the years of mother's petitioning girls on buses, at the markets, and in the malls to write or engage in some type of correspondence with their sons in the joint. They'd show the son's photograph around their work place, in the church services, and all that.

There is a lot of truth said in a joke or in a joking way. When Skip use to tell J. Marie if she ever got another guy, "The dude better be able to handle his business (on the physical level), because I'm coming straight at him, just 'cause I can." They'd both laugh, not dwelling on that part of their unforeseeable future, though knowing it was well within Skip's range of doing things. It wouldn't be the first time or second time he'd addressed a matter when it came to someone interfering in his future with J. Marie. J. Marie, by now, had a "friend" too, as she called him. Though Skip didn't like it, he knew this was what prison and separation did to relationships, sooner or later. Skip and J. Marie had long since set boundaries on whom they would not have intimate relations with; it couldn't be someone they both knew. Although, J. Marie knew Donna (she'd met her once), technically Skip's relationship with her wasn't breaching the covenant between them, because Skip couldn't actually be with her, in the sexual sense.

The two finding solace in someone else was bound to become catastrophic to their marriage. Eventually Donna would visit once a month. She'd write letters to Skip and occasionally call him via the shift commander's office. She was wearing him down and showing all the enthusiasm J. Marie used to have, until Skip figured the best thing to do was release his resilient wife from her marital obligations. No point in them being married yet not behaving as married people are presumed to. On Skip's phone night, he called her to say divorce would be their best recourse, considering the way things were going with them lately. She agreed.

Sadly enough, no one ever spoke with Skip and J. Marie about cognitive therapy, talking things out, communicating their grievances before disaster struck, on a personal level. Neither had a father to sit back to "kick it" with; a serious shot caller they could seek counsel from. One they felt comfortable talking with who could seriously relate and perhaps expound upon the latest calamity or thrill. A take-charge-type of guy to put a teenager and /or young adult on point.

Skip was unmindful to the part of relationships that required a couple to try working things out. He and J. Marie never saw their parents, aunt and uncles, or grandparents steeped in a meaningful and harmonious dialogue, one truly and respectfully listening to the other.

Meanwhile, on the Eastern Shore, a parolee from the Eastern Shore Correctional Facility stumbled upon a young couple out for a light stroll. John Thanos was a psychologically confused and unstable substance abuser with a majestic smile, and charm enough to win a nomination for an Oscar. The parole board bought his act, hook, line, and sinker, so in 1989 they cut him loose from the Division of Corrections. Thanos was a closet lunatic of the highest degree; to think this miscreant could be reformed was a costly mistake on behalf of the parole board. The thought of a man like this on the prowl with a gun possibly confronting your attractive daughter is a father's nightmare. Needless to say, the first convenient opportunity he got to confront a defenseless attractive woman, regardless of her traveling companion, he'd take full advantage of.

The sheriff's deputy received a call over his cruiser radio that a suspected killer was on foot in his area, medium-build white male, early to mid-thirties. After a brief chase, John Thanos was being held by the deputy for confirmation; unbeknownst to the deputy, the man he now held in custody had just brutally killed his daughter and her boyfriend.

Kevin Jones-Boone was Skip's cellmate on his second Patuxent Institution trip. At fifteen, Kevin and two other geniuses were the perpetrators of a robbery gone badly, and bad would be an understatement. They killed a Baltimore city priest. However, Kevin, being only fifteen, caught a huge break from the judge. Instead of a life sentence, the judge was lenient, and found him guilty of second degree murder, and gave him the maximum sentence given in the State of Maryland, thirty years.

A gangly youth, who's only experience of the world was what he saw from the back seat of stolen cars, and what his mom Cookie said it was. He never actually knew his father, who was imprisoned most of his and Kevin's life. The cellmates, though from different cities and age ranges, got to know how to make their union work. At sixteen, Kevin was inquisitive, sometimes easily influenced by several of his older homeboys, but he learned life's lessons well.

Intellectually, at thirty-two, Skip still had a ways to go to catch up to an intelligence level he deemed appropriate or adequate for where he thought he should be. He and J. Marie were pretty much cut from the same cloth. Perhaps it's why they clicked so well together early on. Skip once mentioned to Lou, in front of J. Marie, that J. Marie wasn't where she should be at her age. At the time, she was just out of high school, and unbeknownst to Skip, she was only a reflection of himself. So, if she was lacking and/or deficient in some scholarly aptitude, he was partly to blame. Nevertheless, Skip wasn't much help when it came to imparting neither any wise and viable life plans to J. Marie, nor his young cellie Kevin. In fact, it would be Kevin, by now sixteen, who reacquainted Skip with his own enlightenment, spiritually. Among Kevin's mentors was a halfway slick fully corrupted guy named Al. Al was also one of Kevin's homeboys from B-more, with gold caps and crowns on his teeth, the whole nine.

He began to explain to his young and impressionable protégé the rudiments of the Islamic way of life, as he knew it. Each Friday afternoon he and several others left off the tier going to the Muslims weekly worship service called "Jumu'ah." Occasionally, Kevin would attend, he'd come back to the cell he and Skip shared attempting to sway Skip away from his current practice of Catholicism. Satisfied totally with where he was in his religious preference, Skip became even more diligent in his conviction. He'd say the rosary each night, and before football games (he was playing tier flag football), he also went to Sunday morning church service. Since he and J. Marie were unofficially disjoined, he began thinking long and hard about her replacement, who would fill the void. Being Catholic seemed to work for him, after all, wasn't the proof his old belle Donna Hutchinson coming back in his life, and in a real big way? After J. Marie, Skip was a lonely man, and a dude in jail with no girl to holler out to can be a miserable wreck. That's if he's used to bitting with one in his life. So when J. Marie split, he prayed God would deliver unto him a woman to holler out to from time to time. Donna popped into his mind, and alas, believe it or not, a miracle was manifested to the poor sinner. That was months ago, since then, she'd been to see him with enthusiastic hugs, wet sloppy kisses, and breast flashes for him, whew! Yes, Skip was contented where he was with his religious lifestyle. Although he couldn't explain clearly the Father, Son, and Holy Ghost concept; be that as it was, if Kevin wanted to risk corrupting his own soul, well, it was his choice, but don't bring that crazy talk to me. "Do you; I'll do me," he told Kevin when the latter attempted to push his Islamic indoctrination off on him.

One day Kevin came into the cell after Jumu'ah service explaining to Skip about the need for him to begin making "salat" (a formal prayer ritual), and could Skip remove his family photos from the cell wall because of the "angels" or something or the other. Skip looked at Kevin as though he was crazy; maybe he'd fallen and hit his head. No! Skip told him. That was the end of it. He never did see Kevin attempting to perform salat, but two days later Skip showed him a piece of cloth that if he wanted to cover up the few pictures in the small frame (he'd fashioned from a plastic tray to hold pics of Connie, J. Marie, and the kids), *well, just until you complete the prayer then take it off.*

Because of the Thanos case and Patuxent's release of Robert Angel, who went on a killing spree while on leave status, a directive was issued from the Commissioner of Maryland Department of Public and Safety ordering the immediate return of those inmates sent to the Patuxent

Institute from the Maryland Penitentiary, which was the only maximum security facility open at the time.

By the summer of 1990, it was as though Skip never left on the second Patuxent trip. He had his old job in the prison's hospital. Although, now, he was officially assigned to the officers' dining room. Each morning, it was his responsibility to report to the hospital's ODR, pick up the mobile heated food cart, push it through the back gate to the main kitchen, stock it with the lunch meal, and whatever else he could gather of provisions, then push it back down the yard to the hospital. Once in the ODR Skip was like a street vendor. He'd "set up shop". It was one of the sweetest jobs in the prison. He pretty much controlled what foods he served the officers, nurses, inmate workers, and other staff. He ran the little dinette area and left early to go to the library, weight room or wherever. As long as everyone was fed that was entitled to eat off the cart and the place was thoroughly cleaned, Skip was good to go. The only drawback, which Skip wouldn't find out until years later, was he was not getting the maximum amount of "good credit days" (10) that would have pushed him closer to a release date.

He was in the aisle he previously shared with Big Crump and Battle, and thanks to a couple new women in his life, he wasn't sweating the loss of J. Marie, not much. Donna had proved suitable for that which he most needed her; however, she wasn't built for the long haul. The funny thing was, when Skip realized Donna was about as stable as a house of cards, and his mom was swearing the bitch stole ten dollars from her purse, he thought to patch things up with J. Marie before it was too late. The phone conversation between the two left Skip optimistic that he could reconcile what differences he created with his wife before she became his ex-wife. Over the telephone, she was a formidable combatant, but not totally immutable Skip thought.

"Look, Phats, come on up this weekend to see me. We'll talk. If you still feel the same way – hey, I can dig it."

"Okay, Skip, but it won't do any good. You said you thought a divorce was best thing and I think we should go with it. I'll see you Saturday."

"Okay, bye, baby…"

"Click."

"Ha! Got her."

Chapter 16

Skip was confident that once he had J. Marie sitting before him face-to-face, he could work his magic. He'd utilize all the skills in his 70s young player's arsenal to get them back on track. He'd flash that dazzling Skip smile, he'd let his hazel eyes water up a bit, and she'd soften like Georgia cotton.

The following Saturday, true to her word, J. Marie arrived at the Maryland Penitentiary's visitors' check-in desk. Skip got a call shouted up from the guard's booth on C-dormitory's flats. "LUCAS, VISIT!"

The curtain was finally going up for Skip. He had prepared for this scene with J. Marie all week. In his head, he'd gone over how the dialogue might play out; he checked out his facial expressions in the large mirror in the annex's bathroom, in C-dorm, lowering and shaking his head for dramatic effects. Skip was sporting the baldhead look these days due to genetics and earlier stressors. He was more comfortable shaving it all off, as opposed to looking like Larry on *The Three Stooges* or Roscoe Lee Browne. He wore a full beard with a pierced earring J. Marie slipped him on a visit several years ago while at one the prison "functions" in the main dining hall.

This visiting day, Skip wore a pair of AJ's designer jeans, and grey polo three button shirt, freshly showered and scented. One would've thought he was going to court, or had a parole hearing. He didn't realize how much he'd missed J. Marie as the two briefly embraced and brushed cheeks. Skip thought of the old B.B. King recording of "The Thrill Is Gone," but after today it'll be all good.

Yeah, he was feeling on top of his game this morning!

"Hi, Baby!"

"Hi."

Skip did most of, if not all, the talking through the visit, all the way near close to its end. He was cool with it, because he was on a roll, momentarily pausing for effect and to ruminate in his own feelings of importance. He had to admit, he was "on" this day! Barry White in his heyday, Luther Vandross, even the youngin' Keith Sweat had nothing on him today. Skip was hitting J. Marie with some of his best old-school stuff. The whole time Skip was running it off, he noticed her slouched and leaning a little to the left like she did when she rode shotgun with him in one of the Mark III's he pushed back in the day. That was fifteen years ago, this new J. Marie wasn't hearing him, she'd been doing it without him for seven years now and had gotten harder, she was implacable. During Skip's last pitch, she slowly began to shake her head, then finally uttered... "No, Skip."

Skip wasn't finished though. This time, he lowered his head to the wooden countertop with his face resting on his forearm, when he brought his head back up, a few seconds later, tears filled the edges of his eyes, threatening to spill over. "Phats, the kids deserve better than to be brought up like you and I were, with little or no love between their parents." Skip's last play was the tears along with the "kids card." It didn't matter though. It didn't matter what card Skip played, because J. Marie was having none of it. This was her time. When Skip dug the move, he attempted to regain control; now he was angry at himself, but more so with J. Marie. He got a grip on himself and flipped on her.

"Well, got dammit, hurry up and get the paperwork together, go on! Get the hell outta here!"

That ending visiting room scene a few days ago was a devastating blow to Skip's psyche. Whatever feelings of grandiloquence he may have had of himself in the past were abased in the last minutes of his wife's visit. He was pissed off with himself, disgusted for "going out the way he did." Months later, when he told his mother-in-law about it, while adding his humorous and descriptive commentaries, Lou was hysterical with laughter. Skip was glad to be able to give her a good laugh. Although it was via telephone, he knew she had tears in her eyes from laughter. That's how Lou was. She relished a good joke or a laugh, at anyone's expense.

Although J. Marie and Skip no longer shared their previous connection, she brought the children to see their father, and spoke well of him around the house. Once towards the end of a visit, Skip instructed J. Marie to head to the door, leaving their son with him for the last fifteen minutes. It was a great fifteen minutes Skip had with his son, in which he was able to impart upon Mike D'Angelo a few words he thought essential in a young man's life. Though his son was only thirteen, and not legally supposed to be left in the visiting room without being accompanied by the visiting adult for these last few minutes, no one (the guards) would be paying that much attention.

Among the things he told Mike D'Angelo, other than he loved and missed their time together, and that he should be patient, and the "adversity introduces a man to himself" speech, he also told him to "Never, never, ever, never ever, let a girl break you down, where you're going all to pieces and carrying on. Main Man, don't forget what I told you about being nice to them, respectful, and it's even okay to show them compassion and what not. Be straight up and honest, keep your composure and your dignity dealing with people, especially your girl.

"Now your mom and I won't be hanging out like we used to, but I love her, and that's my girl, since she was only fourteen. You understand most of what I'm saying, Main Man?"

"Yeah, Dad"

Skip thought about a term Connie used to warn him about, "graveyard love." She explained it to him when Connie Adams from around the corner used to get beat up real bad by her boyfriend, and then eventually blew her brains out in the bowling alley parking lot across from Eastover Shopping Center. His mom used to say that it was when you had crazy love for a mate, so bad that if you couldn't have them – then nobody could. Skip wondered if he and J. Marie never got back together, and she moved on to another guy, could he accept it and let her go. *Man!* he thought, *love is a powerful and dominating emotion, it can also be dangerous.*

Skip wanted to know if Mike D'Angelo's uncles were spending quality time with their only nephew in his absence. "Main Man, is everything cool at home, except for me not being there, and at school?"

"Your uncle's spending time with you and telling you some good things?"

"Yeah, Dad, everything's alright."

The female visiting room officer, Ms. Streeter was cool with father and son having a little alone time. She saw J. Marie take Candie out, and knew Mike D'Angelo wasn't old enough to be in the visiting room without the adult that brought him there. She wasn't sweatin' it though. She knew the boy was in good hands with the man that worked the officers' dining room in the prison's hospital, and nevertheless, it was time for the visit to end. Father and son said their good-byes. They took a long and warmhearted embrace. Skip was sure to let his son see strength and pride in his old man as the two parted. He caught a glimpse of J.

Marie and Candie through the glass separating the visiting room and the lobby. They all waved good-byes until the next time.

J. Marie! Skip sat up on his bunk. Damn! Another dream. He was disgusted for not catching himself in the dream before hollering out. He looked around, everyone was sound sleep. Good, no one heard him, or at least acknowledged it. It was close to 1 am. The downside of sleeping in an open-dormitory setting was that guys tormented in their sleep, plagued by night terrors and demons, sooner or later exhibit these innermost thoughts for all to bear witness.

Dreams were an every night occurrence for Skip. His imagination was off the chart; he looked forward to sleeping at night because it was like he was an actor starring in his own roles. Most of his dreams were descriptive. The next morning, he'd have a full account of the details. Mostly about particular cars he'd be driving, shootouts where he was about to be gunned down. He'd dream about pastries, and about J. Marie, Mike D'Angelo, and Candie cane. He never dreamed about the people he victimized, the murders, or the bodies in the morgue he worked in, all except once. He opened the refrigerated box where the bodies were kept and saw his old childhood friend Steve lyin' on the slab, not cut open, but just lyin' there, cold and dead.

As Skip moved through the next day, he reflected over the previous dream of J. Marie, and realized he had to get an agenda. He needed other thoughts to occupy the inner-most nooks and crannies of his mind.

Later that evening, after returning from work and settling down in his aisle with one of the many books he had begun to accumulate, Skip read over one of J.A. Rodgers books on sex and race. He sent several to Michael D'Angelo on topics of race, and other books to educate him as he grew older.

Recreation had already started in the big yard, as one could hear the noise filtering in through the annex windows. Most of the guys that slept in annex one were outside taking advantage of the warm summer evening. When something was about to go down, a ghastly quiet would blanket the area about to become affected. In this case, it was four-yard. It's an instinct most develop without precursors, the men just… know.

Skip was hearing it now while concluding volume 1 or rather he wasn't hearing it. In any event he decided to rest his eyes and stretch his legs…he'd step outside for a moment. As he stepped through the opened grill, then out C-dormitory's door leading to the courtyard, he heard Sargent Rizeeka shouting to the four-yard tower guard to "Shoot him!" Any second Skip expected shots to ring out, filling the air with the "crack" of gun fire. The scene had all the makings of a set straight outta the convict's desert island book *"Blood in My Eye"* when George Jackson was gunned down in the yard of California's infamous San Quentin Prison. Thankfully, there was a moment of indecision, and the tower guard, rifle in hand, didn't squeeze off a round or two at the man standing in the middle of the Viet Nam court. Blood covered his face from one of several head wounds he received earlier. One would've thought he was on attack mode, but he was clearly on defensive alert. Blood and sweat ran down his arms, and the hand tightly gripping a violation of category 1, rule 105 (possession of a weapon or articles modified into a weapon).

Tracy Bennett and his brother Faddy had been beefing with Hakim's younger brother "Kid," and his sidekick Francis since way before Skip came into the penitentiary, and it was Tracy now with severe blunt-force trauma to the head, holding the big rusty knife.

Several years later, Skip would write a story for one of the prison's newsletters in which he described the account as such: "So when I came out the door from C-dorm… Whoa!!! Scene three is being played out, act two, which puts a lone desperado standing in the middle of the court (center stage, you dig) with a big, sharpened, rusty-looking blade in his hand. He's about to make the 6:00 news and ring the death tally up to five for the Pen that year, because they were gonna light him up and that's a fact…victim or not. And here come I, on the set, late as usual, and I'm like Bob's frozen custard, I freeze… 'Cause ain't nothing on stage moving except this blue-shirt three striper waving his arms frantically and barking orders to the tower. Now, all eyes on me, my eyes were on the cat with the big rusty rule no. 105, category I violation clutched ever so tightly. I'm hoping and praying that blood running down his face into his eyes ain't clouding his vision, and I get mistaken for the other red dude he's beefin' with. I'm hoping he's reading his lines right and knows that I'm no threat to him. Thank God he was! So now his eyes are back on the two amigos responsible for his all of a sudden deteriorating health, and now I can backpedal my way to that from which I came with the quickness… So why am I still hanging around?

"I can tell he's not totally oblivious to these pernicious orders from the sergeant to the tower, but this was subsequent to the immediate threat. I figured he had a rough enough day as it was, so my next look was to the tower guard. Now this guy (the tower guard) was caught between a rock and a hard place, a sure 'nough catch twenty-two, doggone if you do and doggone if you don't. One can usually detect when a fellow man is not completely sold on a course of action, when the person doesn't really want to do a thing, you dig… Well, I could tell this tower guard wasn't wholeheartedly bent on following through on the orders of his maniac superior to bang off on Tracy, just because he was bloody and had a joint in his hand. The guard needed an out, another seemingly sound mind at the time to urge him into lightening that trigger finger, so I figured what the heck do I got to lose. I shook my head in the negative and gave a long 'nooo!'

"What do you know, it registered. I guess it was what all parties needed to change the atmosphere or the setting. As I looked around, although I missed scenes one and two, while preoccupied with my book on sex and race, it didn't take a Rhodes scholar to read into the scenario. After all, the stage wasn't totally cleared off from the last act.

"**Exhibit A**: the bottom part, of the heavy end of a push-broom lying off to the side with a clump of hair wedged in splintered cracks, and that red stuff I'm betting ain't beet juice.

"**Exhibit B**: would be the yougin' "Chestnut" stretched out on the pavement looking like Emmett Till after they pulled his young body from the Tallahatchie River. Big Rock would carry his beaten and battered body to the infirmary.

"Last but not least, were the two amigos, 'Dastardly Deeds Incorporated,' waiting to go in for the coup de grâce if an opportunity presented itself. It wouldn't…this time. Maybe they were just lyin' in the gap waiting, watching the curtain to close out the final act like the rest of us. They would then start off yet another stretch on the hammer and be out of everyone's hair for a few more months, or years.

"I'm sure it had to be a reality check for everyone. The sergeant was able to resurvey the battlefield, calm down some, and realize this wasn't "Hanoi" after all, or "Attica, N.Y." Thankfully the tower guard didn't have an itchy trigger finger. The wounded soldier, as well as his foe, were at a stalemate, and by right, shouldn't have been allowed off the hammer in the first place, mortal and avowed enemies as they were. They should not have been cleared to roam the compound together, not at the same time. The administration and every mother's son knew what the odds were, who'd go down, who would be the one. They knew which one would take the fall when all was said and done. Now they were all surrounded, ordered to drop the homemade weapons, and to put their hands behind their backs. To lockup they'd be steppin'. And it's just another day of trying to keep the beast away, in this jungle where I live."

Skip wrote several articles and a few poems with story lines to amuse the population, specifically for the men on lockup, some of whom were not in the habit of reading. They needed that blood and guts stuff to hold their interest. Now in his sophomore year of the Penitentiary's Coppin State College program, he was digesting various history books on the plight of African Americans, from slavery to freedom. He read of ships containing human cargo from Africa harboring along the Southern American seaports of the Carolinas and Georgia. Because in 1650, according to something he read, there was no North and South Carolina, only "The Carolinas" (see, *Slave Trade and Slavery* pg. 38, by John Henry Clark and Vincent Harding). The Carolinas is where Skip's entire maternal side of his family was from; he knew that Connie's mother (his grandma Madoo) was from Spartanburg, South Carolina, and Connie's grandma Lucy Howard-Smith lived in Wilmington, North Carolina. He read most of the slaves taken from Africa had an Islamic indoctrination, because the Islamic excursion swept all through Northern and Central Africa on around to Morocco in West Africa. It was highly likely his forefathers were not Christian but Muslim, at least on his mother's side. On his father's side, the Lucases, he only knew what his granddad told him, straight Anacostians outta South East Washington. His grandfather once showed him the house he was raised in on the Old Nichols Avenue across the street from "Barry Farms Projects!" His brother Anthony later told him some earlier generations of Lucas's were from Danbury, Virginia.

During the next few days, Skip's time was spent more productively than it had been in years. He devoured any and all material he found on the slaves capture and trade, on the Muslim expedition, and conquest of "The Shams" (Northeastern parts of the African coast and Asia) and West Africa. Skip diligently studied the dictionary to increase his limited vocabulary. His main reason was so a wise guy couldn't call themselves "getting out on him" with words, or people couldn't talk over his head. The average person in his realm couldn't do it during conversations of generalities – between college courses, independent study of race and religion, vocabulary, exercising, and courting two women who made themselves available, his days were satiated with details and obligations. Annette Parsons was one of the medication girls whose job was to dispense medication to the inmates at pill call. She hand carried a basket-like tray to serve the guys in south wing, under the watchful eye of an escorting officer. Annette was a big-boned, dark-complexion thirty-something girl from West Baltimore's Edmondson Village, with a twin brother serving twenty years in Jessup for a drug violation. An affable college-educated woman with a ready smile, killer hips, and voluptuous breasts like J. Marie's; although, she was not a looker by any stretch of the imagination. It didn't matter to Skip, though, because these days he was hardly afforded the luxury of being choosey. Like the other girls Skip served off the heated lunch cart, she thought the brighter her smile and more pleasant her disposition, the better her chance for any preferential treatment Skip might care to bestow upon her. She knew Skip had additional provisions not on the hospital menu, food only he and a selected few were privy to. Skip learned from old Mr. Ty how to use the cart as a grill. The microwave was his own personal oven. Before long, on the weekends when things were slow on the administrative floor, Skip would prepare a special breakfast meal for him and his...ah... date. They'd sit at one of the tables overlooking four-yard, eating and talking like they'd known each other for years, totally oblivious to the reality of the prison scene. For that epoch in time, Skip was uptown, at Florida Avenue Grill, or Ben's Chilly Bowl on U Street.

Garnetta Lokken was an old friend from the Veterans hospital that kept the communication lines open since the third or fourth year of Skip's incarceration. At first, it was two or three times out of the year he'd get a few lines from her, or a "Thinking of You" card; though after J. Marie's departure Skip put the press on. Garnetta was a supervisor in the

VA's chemistry department, who knew her stuff; twice divorced, white, middle-aged mother of two adults – a lawyer son and a daughter who was a nurse. The kids knew of the ex-coworker friend of their promiscuous mother, and were cool their mom had an old friend sending her innocent, friendly poems, and just being a nice guy, even if he was in prison for a double homicide.

For the most part, Skip thought he was covering his bases fairly well. He resigned to not let himself worry about what was going on with J. Marie and the kids, because after all, as she so infelicitously put it, "What could you do about it if we weren't doing okay?" She hurt Skip bad with that one, real bad. He thought it was the most insensitive thing she'd ever said to him in their entire life together. What made it even more caustic was he didn't have a sustainable answer.

Meanwhile, Skip was wrestling with his conscience over this new-found information concerning his spiritual persuasion. He needed to talk with someone, a theologian maybe, someone knowledgeable in the religion he himself came up on, Catholicism. One afternoon while Skip contemplated and walked from four-yard, he saw the resident vicar, Pastor Rose, heading towards him. This was excellent, now he'd have a heart to heart with someone he figured sure 'nough knew the score, and would help settle his mind in the religious and spiritual sense. Actually, Rose was a pseudo-priest in training but would have to do.

"Vicar Rose! Man am I glad to see you, I need…"

Rose was walking too fast, headed in the direction of the prison's hospital. He gave Skip a quick "Don't have the time right now."

Skip was taken aback. *How dare him!* Skip humorously thought, still under the impression everything and everybody had to comply with his schedule. Nevertheless, he took the brush off as a chance to make inquiries. A day or so later he spoke with a guy known to attend Islamic services. The two of them were at a table together in the main dining room (MDR) during the dinner meal.

"Wali." (Pronounced Wha-lee.)

"What's happening, Skip"

"Man I wanted to check out that service you go to. What I got to do?"

"Just come up to the third floor of A-building when count clears for afternoon activities. It starts at 1:00 pm every Friday.

That was Tuesday. On Thursday that night on the flats of C-dorm, Skip saw Big Preston, who played defensive linemen for his football team. He noticed, however, certain guys called him "Baseer," and that he was also in one of the Islamic groups, though Skip was not exactly sure which one. He told Baseer, "Man I'm supposed to attend service Friday in A-building where y'all meet."

"That's good, Skip. I'll see you then."

The next day Skip broke down the lunch cart early. He told the officer in charge (OIC) of the hospital he had an appointment. Skip was pretty much a permanent fixture at the hospital by now. He wouldn't likely be harassed on the compound by the officers, and wouldn't get sweated during shakedowns in the aisle he shared, not much. He once loaded a wicker chair from the hospital's third-floor lounge on a cart, telling the first-floor grill officer he was taking it to get it repaired. He took it to the annex and in the aisle he shared with Crump and Battle. By then Battle was working in the hospital too. It was the worse hiring mistake the OIC made as far as hiring inmate workers.

Skip bagged up the leftover fish squares; half of sheet pan of cake, a few milks, then proceeded to annex one. Like always, once back at the dorm, he took his share off the top, placing the remainder on the table for the others. Next, he showered, cleaned up, and prepared to leave for his engagement at A-building's third floor with the Muslims. Skip set off across three-yard, in route; once there on the third floor, he was faced with a dilemma he hadn't foreseen. There were five rooms on the third floor, four of which had services going on, all supposedly Islamic gatherings. These groups, for all intents and purposes, were just that –"under the guise" – all but one. Skip failed to take into account and no one told him exactly which room was specifically catering to the needs he sought. After bending the corner at the top of the stairwell, he stared down the corridor uncertain which of the four rooms to enter. Two rooms were out of contention from Jump Street: the Moorish Science Temple of America, or Moorish Science Resurrection, whichever of the two it was. Skip wasn't trying to go that way.

They were more about nationalism and exalting blackness. Skip didn't see them much in the way of spiritual enlightenment, nor a strong adherence toward God consciousness. In the other room, to his immediate left, he could see "Big Preston," aka Baseer, through the glass panes in the door, and "Harlow," aka Brain Sails, one of the Sails Brothers from the 1982 Iverson Mall Kay Jewelry store holdup that resulted in the execution-style killing of an off duty police officer. They both (Baseer and Sails) had on white shirts and Red bowties. He now knew they were in the Nation of Islam (NOI), not only were they nationalist, but offensively conspicuous toward whites. He knew all about "The Nation" from going to the temple on M.L.K. Avenue, S.E., back in the 70s. With two rooms left, the next algorithm was easy, it was Skip's practice to always go right. Since he was a kid running the grounds of Parkland, on through adulthood, whenever faced with a seemingly equivalent option, he'd always take the course to his right. When Dawelda Rogers brought J. Marie with her that day (on the third floor of Taft Jr. High.) J. Marie was to his right. However, that day it really didn't matter where J. Marie was standing. This afternoon, true to form, Skip stepped in the small classroom-sized carpeted room to his right.

Because of the direction the room's occupants faced, the door Skip entered designedly placed him in the back of the room. There were four to five rows of men, all sitting crossed legged on the brown plush carpet, in stocking feet, a few were barefooted, all were facing the front. As soon as Skip removed his shoes to sit in the last row, an older convict Skip knew from the weight room and boxing gym approached him. Farrakhan-Bey was an older version of Mr. T, without the Mohawk and all the gold. He and his rap buddy "Shamsu-deen" were from Savannah, Georgia, penitentiary solders who'd been in the joint and practicing Islam before Skip knew there was a Penitentiary in Baltimore City for the worst of Maryland's worst. Farrakhan-Bey began to set Skip straight on a few particulars. Pulling Skip just outside the door of the prayer service room, Farrakhan-Bey proceeded briefly to explain, in his own rough, off-handed manner, what was going on here, some of what this group of men were all about. With his face contorted in a scowl, which was usually his permanent look, he told Skip, "This is the more Orthodox practice of Islam. We believe in the One True God Allah, and follow His last Prophet and Messenger, Muhammad, who was an Arab living in Mecca over 1400 years ago, not Elijah Muhammad who died in 1975, and we are serious about this thing here."

Skip told him, "Okay, then this where I'm tryin' to be." The two men went back in, sat on the thick carpet, and waited, for what, Skip didn't know, but after a few minutes, a tall slender man got up from the front row, or from somewhere off from the side, Skip wasn't exactly sure where he came from all of a sudden. Nevertheless, he took his place behind the podium with several sheets of paper in his hand. He greeted the crowd with the Islamic greeting of "As-Salamu-Alaykum." The group responded back with another term Skip was familiar with from hearing on the compound amongst some of the men, "Wa-Alaykumu-As-Salam!"

Immediately following that, another man stood up. This guy was definitely off the front row. He placed both hands up open wide by his ears, palms facing frontward, then half sang half chanted a call of sorts. It lasted for about a minute and a half, then he sat back down on the floor. A guy Skip would later learn was named "Rasheed", the group's Imam (pronounced E'mam), the spiritual leader of the Sunni Muslims, gave a five- to ten-minute oration, all in Arabic. Skip wondered was he the only one who didn't understand a word of it. Rasheed then stooped down beside the podium, mumbling something, stood up, then said he would translate what he'd previously said. He also added some information concerning the affairs and actions they should be mindful of, not just while in the population, but in the privacy of their cells too, because Allah, the Most High, sees and hears all that you think is hidden. This speech, Skip learned, was called a "Khutbah." It took all of a half hour, then the group stood up in perfectly straight rows and followed Rasheed in a timed and well-orchestrated prayer ritual. Skip followed along too, taking his cue of movements from the guys on his right and left sides. The positioning of hands, the bowing and prostrations too, until the prayers ended, which was the last spreading of the "salaams" (peace) to the right and left sides.

That was the conclusion of the services. The men stood around talking and shaking hands. Farrakhan-Bey gave Skip a small book he said Skip should read. It was entitled "Kitaab Al-Iman" (The Book of Faith). Skip stalled around a few moments so not to just abruptly leave, meanwhile he noticed several of the men, the "Brothers" he recognized from the population but had no idea they were Muslim. Like the big bruiser, Timmy Poole, and his sidekick Oscar (Abu), also there was the guy Hightower who was instrumental in getting the fighters into the prison from the street through the outside recreations liaison Mr. Rice; though Hightower didn't like being called that anymore, but insisted on being called "Nuri," with emphasis on the long "e" sound at the end. Also Wali Aquil from C-dormitory was up there. Skip didn't know him personally, but he always seemed busy. If he wasn't exercising or practicing marital arts, he was reading something. Other members Skip would come to know were now on the hammer, but were some good stand-up type dudes. Overall, the Sunni Muslim community was well respected throughout the population, as there were many enforcer types in the group that went hard and were not to be taken lightly.

Skip wasn't a Muslim, and, for the next three weeks, he only went to Friday Service (Jumu'ah service, it was called). During the second week, he saw the booklet Farrakhan-Bey gave him to read. He figured he'd at least read something out of it in case the brother quizzed him on something from it. In the first few pages, after the introduction, he saw three questions asked: What is Islam? What is Iman? What is a Muslim? Well, he thought, I may as well start with the basics. This was perfect, as far as information goes, because just last year, not long before leaving the Patuxent Institution, he heard a guy that supposedly knew a thing or two about the religion of Islam ask another "What is a Muslim?"

After the answerer stumbled unsuccessfully to find a comprehensive response, the questioner (his name was Westclock), apparently not satisfied, proceeded to answer it himself. Afterwards, Skip was still uncertain "What a Muslim was." Neither man gave a definitive response he could grasp. Now however, in this book (Kitaab Al-Iman) he found an answer he could work with. It said, "A Muslim was one who observed the Pillars of Islam…" He read that Islam was submission to Allah – total submission. Furthermore, he found Islam was not only total submission to Allah, but that it was built upon five "Pillars." These Pillars are:

The Shahadatain (to testify that none has the right to be worshipped but Allah)

Salat (prayer 5 times a day at prescribed times)

Zakat (a poor rate or charity paid annually – 2.5%)

Saum (fasting in the month of Ramadhan)

Hajj (a pilgrimage to Mecca to perform the necessary rituals at least once in your life, provide you have the means)

And that "Iman" was the Arabic word for faith, and it too meant more than just that. It also meant a certain belief you accepted (for instance, Allah is the True God of the worlds and all that exists); belief in the angels (that man or woman cannot see); belief in the books (the last one being the Qur'an); belief in the Prophets (Muhammad ibn Abdullah, who was an Arab, was the last and final one); belief in the Resurrection, and in the Divine Decree.

Skip had a lot of reflecting to do; he didn't find the Islamic lifestyle particularly difficult. He figured much of what was expected were those things morally correct or righteous anyway, that the sacrifices he'd be making to outwardly come into conformity with the practice would somehow be a benefit. Besides that, keeping his mind occupied and spending his time wisely helped to keep his thoughts off the breakup with J. Marie.

The book his old cellie swiped from his job at the library helped him in a most profound way – *The Autobiography of Malcolm X* by Alex Haley kept him very busy these days. He saw three transitional periods in Malcolm's life; from hustler/con man and all around hoodlum to autodidactic educator and representative of a nationalistic movement he truly believed in, and then finally, to the man he was when he was gunned down while giving a speech in 1965 inside New York's Audubon Ballroom. He was a man believing God looked not to one's color, but the heart of the individual. Now he was following the more orthodox, traditional practices of Islam, the sunnah.

Skip was cool with the external expressions Islam put forth for mankind, to include organized praying, studying to learn about this way of life he was now leaning towards, and attending "Jumu'ah" every Friday (no excuses short of being gravely ill or court appearances). He could deal with the prohibitions against drinking and drugs, pork, cursing, gambling, and sex outside of wedlock. He'd given up cigarettes several months before on his last lockup bit, so that wasn't a problem now. The only thing he did have a problem with was "internal strife"; his heart was still inclined towards the indoctrination he held as a child, that Jesus was the son of God.

In surah (chapter) Al-Fatihah (1) of the Qur'an, ayat 6 reads:

"Guide us to the Seeratal Mustaqeem (straight way)."

Guidance is of two kinds, the Islamic jurists have said; Guidance of Taufiq – this is when Allah opens one's heart to receive the truth (from disbelief or being non-Muslim to belief in Islamic Monotheism). And Guidance of Irshad – this is through preaching by Allah's Messengers and pious preachers who preach the truth, i.e. Islamic Monotheism, that there is none worthy of worship except Allah. No one amongst the inmate population ever approached Skip about Islam…

Chapter 17

By 1990, the penitentiary's boxing gym had been relocated twice, from the dining hall to the second floor of A-building, to its present location, in an out of the way dilapidated storage building near the laundry and power house. This latest spot was straight out of *Rocky III*'s "Eye of the Tiger." It was damp, poorly lit, low hanging pipes dripping in some places, with paint peeling off the walls, reeking of sweat and mildew, and an animus crowd. Skip was sure if anyone had foreknowledge of the structure before entering into the compound, they never would have agreed to fight in this place. Yet, at the behest of his longtime friend and sparring partner, now a convict friend of Skip's, Derrick Holmes, Sugar Ray Leonard was gloved up, climbing into the boxing ring to go a couple minutes with several of the Maryland Penitentiary's most promising welterweight and middleweight contenders. Derrick himself, once an aspiring fighter from Prince George's County, was, shortly after Skip, convicted of a robbery gone bad (gone bad meaning someone was shot) and was doing thirty slices. Of course, Ray put all of his challengers down handily. However, between the four of them; Satch, Morgan, Louis Medley, and Al Brown, there was much fanfare, and even accolades given by the ex-champ himself. All of them went the distance with only minor damages to their reputation. The most serious perhaps was Al. Morgan did receive a modest or rather complimentary pat on the head by Ray, but the highlight clip belonged to Skip's homeboy Lou, for better or for worse.

For the first minute, Lou was being as careful as he could be. After all, this was Sugar Ray Leonard. Lou wasn't taking any unnecessary chances. They traded complimentary jabs, then Ray let Lou get in a shot to his chin to give Lou confidence, which it did; it went straight to his head. Lou took the shot and ran with it. Though Ray literally shook it off, taking it as to help the brother out, within the next trade of jabs, Lou threw caution to the wind. Deciding to take it to him, Lou went all out. Miraculously, Lou connected with two jabs from a flurry of combinations, nothing heavy, but enough to get a roar from the crowd especially the D.C. boys. Perhaps had not the crowd made such a big deal out of the minor achievement Ray would have carried the exchange longer, as it now stood, however, the former champ was a bit agitated. It wasn't so much Ray mind being tagged, but he was a showman, and it was time to shine for old time's sake.

Ray peppered Lou with a few lefts, then the right came like a flash, a left uppercut that rocked Lou's head back, followed by, what looked like to the crowd, no less than a fifteen piece up and down the challenger's head and body. The crowd went wild with excitement, never mind one of their own was the recipient of the onslaught. When Ray was done, Lou was out on his feet. Ray rushed to catch him before he would have fallen head first to the canvas tarpaulin, and walked him to his corner. Derrick and his rap buddy (on his current charge), Napoleon, were the corner men for the Pen's challengers. They quickly climbed through the ropes to help get Lou seated.

Skip noted this to be a most memorable time, as far as Penitentiary sports activities went. None so memorable, however, or remarkable as the time "Reggie Gross" from Baltimore came in, when the gym was still on the second floor of A-building, the same Reggie Gross that fought mad Mike Tyson for the heavyweight title. Unlike with Ray Leonard, there weren't a handful of contenders for Gross, and now it was only

Timmy Poole to glove up with him, whom Skip called by his Muslim Name "Abu Bakr" after the second Caliph, and father-in-law of the Prophet Muhammad (P.B.U.H.). This two-round spar could've surely gone either way, and if you ever saw the fight scene in *Let's Do It Again*, where Bootney Farnsworth (Jimmy Walker) and Fortieth Street Black swung deep right haymakers at the same time, then it's similar to what happened with Abu Bakr and Reggie – only the punches were straight right hands, with Reggie's landing a second before the big boy from N.W. Washington's. Getting your bell rung in a fight can be a very humbling experience. Skip never saw his Muslim brother so humble, if only for a little while. Abu Bakr was not one to be mitigated very long. He was his old irrepressible self within the week.

Skip's conversion to Islam was yet another feather in the cap, or rather the "kufee" of the Muslim community in the Penitentiary. Most people by now knew him to be a fair dealing and affable guy, that just so happened would deal with you, nine times out of ten, should you cross the line. The Muslims welcomed another standup-type brother in faith (who would now be called "Mustafa," which meant chosen). Some were uncertain as to his motives; after all, "Ramadhan" (the month of Fasting) was only a couple months away. They thought perhaps he was only doing it for the feast at the conclusion of Ramadhan.

He was still in the three-man corner aisle of annex one with Big Crump and Black Battle. They themselves weren't sure how far their friend was going with this "Muslim thing." They, like many others, including his family now, would just have to wait for time to tell the seriousness of his conviction. One thing the men in the population could say for sure, you could set your watch by him, because sure enough, every Friday afternoon, he would come outta that hospital where he worked the ODR, carrying a laundry bag full of the day's leftover rations. Either

Mustafa would stop off at the dorm to take a shower and don his best clothes for Jumu'ah service, or head straight across three-yard.

Time was, he would bring all the leftovers back to divvy up with his twenty-plus roommates in annex one. Now, suddenly he was taking it with him to feed those Muslim brothers of his, for an after Jumu'ah service feast of sorts, and everyone knew Friday's meals; lunch and dinner were usually fish and pizza for the main course. However, on Friday's service day (Jumu'ah), Mustafa would scrounge as much as he could from the main dining room to extend to the brothers. It would often include a sheet pan of the rich pink icing cake, one hundred plus slices of cheese off the block, a couple loaves of bread, all distributed amongst the brothers to feast on.

The days following his conversion to Islam found Mustafa busy like he'd not been since his early days at the VA Medical Center. This was back when he painted on the weekends with Scruggs, Phil, or Dunmore; he'd even taken Lil Mike D'Angelo on a couple jobs to give the boy his first feel of a paint brush. Mustafa was taking "mortuary science" courses at Washington Technical Institute, and still finding a night or two to run with a crime partner to break law. The old adage of "idle hands are the devil's workshop," he found to be a true bill.

The Summer of 1991 favored Mustafa with enough positive aspirations that he would think often that there weren't enough hours in the day to do all that needed his attention. In the morning, until breaking the meals-on-wheels cart down at the hospital (around 1:30), he would study Islamic lessons, as well as those lessons for school, then he'd stop off at the weight room on his way to C-dormitory's annex one. He'd then shower and go to whatever college class he had that day, or write Mike D'Angelo, Candie, or Garneta. He made a point to learn all the basic Islamic information there was, and transmitted this new-found knowledge to his son, as best he could.

Some of the money he got from Garneta, he'd send to J. Marie to help out with the children, or he'd send some directly to them. He had a carpenter friend design a jewelry box for Candie with her name engraved in cursive block letters; Mustafa thought it was beautiful, he was sure his daughter would love it. Roosevelt did an excellent job on the project, despite having to take two weeks longer than the expected completion date due to cutting off the tip of a finger while working on it. Mustafa was starting to spend money recklessly, and told Garneta to only send fifty dollars each month. He still wasn't very good managing it, let alone saving anything.

Garneta had cake ($). She sent Islamic books to help him learn more about the way of life he'd chosen, clothing and food packages to make his stay comfortable, and visited semi-monthly, like clockwork, come rain, sleet, hail, or snow, she was at 954 Forrest Street. The black girls hated it, to see this classy long-haired white woman depleting their already drained pool of African American men. Mustafa himself wasn't exempt from the daggers their eyes cast, but he didn't care in the least; not a one of them buff-head broads would kick out like Garneta, not time, money, or tolerance. Mustafa was doing him; he still had one of the honeys to holler at in the hospital, and these friendly preoccupations all contributed to making his time run fast and smooth.

However, all good things soon come to an end; they run their course, eventually, that is except Paradise, or as the Muslims call it "Jannah." Johnny Reynolds was a sneaky drug-using thief and crud-ball that was returned to the Pen's population after a two year stint at the super max, and was on a mission to get back on his feet. Johnny was an opportunist from way back, a chunky, medium-height, bookish early-thirties black man looking for a mark. When he was assigned a cell on C-dormitory's fourth tier, a few cells down from "Hasan," an opportunity presented itself he couldn't pass up regardless that it was by way of a member of the Sunni Muslim community. Hasan was a small low-key older brother that kept the books straight as best he could, helped out with classes, and mostly kept the main means of commence, the exchange, for the Sunni community (cigarettes).

Somehow finding out, perhaps through observation, that Hasan kept cigarettes for the Sunni Muslim's, Johnny decided to throw caution to the wind one day, and slipped into Hasan's cell before the CO locked the tier down. He stole over twenty packs. How Hasan found out Johnny was the culprit was unknown. Nevertheless, he took the information to certain representatives in the community. Mustafa didn't know Johnny, let alone that he was the perpetrator, not until leaving C-dorm for work one morning only to find a dozen or so of the Muslim brethren gathered in three-yard around a lone individual – this would be Johnny.

Listening in as an observer, Mustafa wondered what the "protocol" in these type of situations was, if there was a such a protocol. Mustafa had heard of guys being placed in these circles of Muslims, and the outcome was never favorable for the one encircled; this was the first time he was legitimately allowed a bird's-eye view. Just when he felt something was about to kick off, Captain Purnell, a blatant homosexual senior staff, turned the corner coming from the administration level. His presence was just enough to disrupt the tempo; while he stood off to the side pretending to be engaged in conversation with another inmate – Johnny took advantage of the opportunity to excuse himself from his quasi-captors. He definitely got a reprieve; perhaps it was best, due to an administrative official on the scene. For the rest of the day Johnny was as elusive as a running greased pig, a frightened running greased pig. His temporary relief wouldn't last long, Iman Rashid, though not present at the three-yard hearing that morning, made it clear the integrity of the community was breached, and this situation must be rectified… forthwith!

Mustafa knew, just like when he came to prison eight years ago, when someone threatens the stability of your existence in this place, you have to address it head-on, no ifs, ands, or buts about it. This dude had called the Muslims' hand, and everyone knew it, even if he would bring forth what was taken, he'd still have some form of punishment meted out. Now, a message must be sent to the inmate population that the repercussions of stealing from the Muslims would be detrimental to your health. Mustafa wondered whose responsibility it was to carry out the task. More than likely it would or it should be someone from C-dormitory since that was where the offense occurred. Later that day, Mustafa evaluated the nature and character of each individual Muslim in C-dorm. He discerned that, although there were a handful of Muslims there more than capable, no one had yet expressed any predilections of dealing with it.

When Mustafa was very young, Connie told him a word he'd never heard before, "procrastination." She said it was the thief of time, that it meant putting something off for tomorrow what you could do today. She said, "Skippá, when you have something you know needs doing – do it! And when something in your mind warns you against something, that's your conscience, not no damn little bird. It's your conscience, so you should listen to it." This dude had to be dealt with and Mustafa knew it. Someone had to take care of Johnny before morning, as soon as the count cleared, and the doors opened. Mustafa would "suit up", put his biggest knife in his "dip", go up to Johnny's tier to his cell and kill him. As Mustafa lay down to sleep in annex one that night, he replayed the scene over and over in his mind; from his dress gear and the joint securely stashed in his dip to leaving the bloodied body on the tier floor.

The cells on the flats were usually the first ones opened, then annex one, since it was just off the second-tier landing. Another officer would be topside to unlock the fourth and fifth tiers, but first they had to open up the other two annexes (two and three). Mustafa was in his aisle, waiting anxiously for the sound of keys at the door, dressed in his hoodie, sweatpants, and tennis shoes, all black – he figured black would hide the blood he knew was bound to spill. As soon as the door opened, Mustafa waited a few seconds for the CO to proceed on to his next assignment, on the second tier, then bounded up the stairwell. Mustafa pulled up the hood as he reached the fourth-tier landing. He saw Abu Bakr and big Omar as he was about to enter on to the tier. They were coming out of annex two. Omar was 6'3" and four hundred pounds, and was now, like Abu Bakr, aka Timmy Poole, Mustafa's Muslim brother. They both looked at Mustafa knowing his sudden appearance was not a social call for whomever he was seeing, so they stood at the entrance of the tier to see what their newest brother was up to.

Mustafa was on the tier before all the cells were opened by the CO, as he was working his way towards the front. He'd began unlocking from the back, and now he was at Johnny's cell. Soon as he stepped out of his cell, just like Mustafa did his old cellie a year ago, Mustafa would get him. It would've been disrespectful to Johnny's cellmate for Mustafa to run into the cell to carry out the assault. About ten doors down, a lone hooded figure was mixed with the hustle and bustle of departing inmates about to begin their daily routines. Mustafa thought the situation couldn't have been sweeter. The officer had just exited the tier, and now Johnny was exiting his cell. He took a quick look to the right, and Mustafa didn't think he'd seen him, even as he was making his way through the crowd towards him. He must've seen him, because Johnny quickly shut his cell door and jetted left to exit the tier.

Mustafa was glad the two giants (Abu Bakr and Omar) didn't interfere. He thought it would be superfluous. He wanted to handle this on the solo tip. Johnny was gone again. He'd gotten away. *This one was on me.* He stayed out of C-dorm all morning, but he had to return eventually, and Mustafa would be waiting…somewhere. Several times throughout each of the prisons three shifts, "head count" is conducted, where each inmate is no longer able to roam about the compound, but must be accountable in a designated location. At 11:00 am, before the afternoon lunch line begins, the inmates in the MD Penitentiary are locked in their sleeping quarters, whether it be one of the three annexes or a cell, to be counted. So wherever Johnny was, come hell or high water, at 11:00 AM he'd be making his way up the stairwell to the fourth tier. Also wherever he was, he was confiding in someone about his last few days escapades, and if he had any sense, he was trying to procure for himself a "joint," if he didn't already have one.

After Johnny's escape that morning, Mustafa went back to annex one to post up in one of the windows overlooking three-yard, the route from the west wing, and the immediate vicinity of C-dorm's entrance. He figured when his prey returned, he'd see him on his way to the building, then jam him up on one of the upper levels in between the tiers, or the stairwell. Exactly how Mustafa managed to excuse himself from his job at the hospital this day wasn't quite clear. What was clear was he stayed on a "stakeout" of sorts, and at approximately 10:55, Johnny was with the last wave of men to clear the yard. Mustafa spotted him about fifty yards out, so he left his position to casually make his way upstairs. From the fourth tier, if one looked straight down the stairwell, they could see where the stairs first began, as well as who embarked upon them. Johnny was taking a long time, Mustafa thought. That lame must've stopped to talk with someone just before or after entering C-dorm.

Finally he appeared at the bottom of the stairs. Mustafa could now only see his hand on the rail traveling upward. He passed the second tier. His hand was still on the railing up onto, and now past, the third tier. Now Mustafa was making his move – he pulled the big homemade knife from his front waistband under the hooded sweatshirt, timing it just so when his mark turned the corner of the stairs, just after the midway point of three and four, he'd meet him head-on.

Mustafa had the knife overhead, bringing it down to plunge it into his victim's chest, but it wasn't Johnny about to be hit – it was Hasan, the keeper of the "Baitulmal" (the community wealth), the one that had his cell burglarized. Hasan threw his hands up to block the knife, but Mustafa had already realized who it was, and as he brought the joint down, he cuffed it to his side – Johnny was right behind Hasan and realized the almost fatal mistake.

Mustafa was angry, confused, and agitated – how in the world had his Muslim brother gotten in front of the intended victim? And now, with his hands still raised to ward off an attack, was hurriedly attempting to explain how everything was fixed, or settled. "It's been taken care of," he said. Mustafa continued down the stairs, brushing past the two. Johnny's eyes were wide with terror and looking at his would-be assassin.

Just after count was cleared Hasan came to annex one's door, explaining first how he wound up ahead of Johnny on the stairwell, then how he'd gotten the reprieve. He mentioned how they approached the base of the stairwell together. Johnny apparently didn't trust Hasan behind him, so he allowed Hasan to go first. And as far as the reprieve, it came from Imam Rasheed that they were to meet with this joker in the prayer area of A-building that afternoon, and you (Mustafa) should be present. As always, Mustafa was prompt when he had somewhere to be. It went back to his meeting with J. Marie after school, and picking her up from her various jobs. With several Muslim brothers, they were there minutes earlier than Johnny to discuss things, Mustafa was anxious to hear how this situation was…fixed.

The "Majlis-ash-Shura" (the governing board of the Muslim community) in the penitentiary, at the behest of Imam Rasheed, were to meet with Johnny that afternoon. That was one of the places he went that morning, A-Block, where Rasheed slept to try to smooth things over. Rasheed hadn't known exactly how far Mustafa was going until Johnny told him of the attempt on the fourth tier that morning. Now the Imam of the Muslims knew that the newest member of their community was too extreme; the punishment didn't fit the crime. At most, Johnny could only have his hand cut off. Rasheed told the brothers he was only to be beaten up; thus began Mustafa's objectionable career as the Muslims' troubleshooter. He was at the door to let Johnny in the room, to be seated on the rug with the brothers. With his back to the door, he sat to begin whatever discussion or ultimatum that was so imposed, which was all a farce. Within minutes, without cue, Mustafa left the door, came up behind Johnny, and in all but fifteen seconds "L'd" him out. Unconscious, he was beaten, stripped down to his shorts, which turned up a knife, and disarmed. Mustafa didn't know a lot about punishment in Islam, but read somewhere the thief's hand is to be amputated. He contemplated stabbing his hand to shreds, but settled on breaking the fingers on his right hand, one by one, all but the thumb.

Before the hostage taking that summer, there were other problems the small community or "Jamaat" faced, which needed someone's appropriate attention. For reasons Imam Rasheed and others deemed warranted, Mustafa was elevated to position of "Wazir" (an overseer of affairs and special assistant to the Imam), replacing a senior brother that didn't appreciate losing his place to the new loose cannon. Nevertheless, Mustafa was learning fast. He was diligent in his studies. He walked the walk, and he had moxie. He soon won over the doubters who thought he was only a flash in the pan, and Big Crump, Battle, and a few of his homies who though he was in it for the big feast after the Islamic month of Ramadhan.

Abdul Haqq had been down a few years longer than Mustafa. He'd been a good practicing Muslim longer too, and had history with Imam

Rasheed that involved gunplay while participants in a foiled escape attempt. When Abdul-Haqq went on the hammer for a situation he got into with "Cadillac's" hot little CO girlfriend in the west wing, a couple brothers pulled Cadillac up to talk to her to squash the ticket she wrote sending Abdul-Haqq to south wing. It seemed to the brothers 'Lac was dragging things along and playing games. Rasheed mentioned, to no one in particular, that "This joker needs a fire lit under his tail to accelerate things."

The very next day, the men in three-yard, and those looking out of C-dorm's annex window saw their first drive-by…uhhh…"run-by" hit. Cadillac was able to make it to the infirmary with the help of a friend, receiving only a few stitches to his head. The following day, Purnell, who was now 'Security Chief Purnell," summoned Mustafa to his office on the level. Mustafa was allowed immediate entry to see the chief. Purnell read from a note in his hand stating, "Skip hit Cadillac in the head with the big rock." Mustafa's instinct was to snatch the note to see who wrote it. That's what the faggy wanted him to do. Purnell had no problem with putting a snitcher "out there." When Mustafa failed to react fast enough, the note was lowered and put in his top drawer. Next, he warned Mustafa that "The next time your name comes up in something, your red ass is outta here" (meaning sent to another jail).

Purnell was not the only one agitated by the assault on Cadillac. Many of the guys 'Lac had an allegiance with from the District weren't particularly thrilled either, including his rap buddies from the Kay Jewelry store holdup. All in all, a lot of homies went for the young ex-player and thought Mustafa went against the grain on this one. They didn't like it, but couldn't do much, if anything about it.

In the second week of July, 1991, Mustafa and Big Crump were sitting in their aisle, kicked back like you don't ordinarily see convicts living in a state facility kicked back. It was 8:30 pm, the yard was closed, everyone was supposedly locked down, and Mustafa was reclining in a wicker chair unlawfully procured from the hospital. With his feet up on a padded milk crate that was now a foot rest, dunking duplex cookies in a cup of cold milk, looking at one of the color TVs, as comfortable as he was, he felt an unusual sense of ambivalence. He expressed his feelings to Crump, "Man, prison ain't supposed to be this laid back… look at us!" Crump only smiled as if to say, "Fool, won't you just accept these blessings our Lord has bestowed upon us, for crying out loud!" No sooner had Mustafa gotten the words out of his mouth, waiting for Crump's response – Geronimo appeared at the opened annex door.

Two things were wrong with Geronimo's appearance at the anex door; first of all, there was no jingling sound that was the usual precursor for the opened door. The next violation was the missing blue-shirted CO that was supposed to be accompanying him. Instead 'Ronimo stood in the doorway alone. What came from his mouth was even more anomalous. "Come out, y'all. We got C-dorm."

It was as though 'Ronimo had spoken a foreign language, and then he was gone. The nine or ten guys closest to the door who heard him only stared, not totally clear what was implied. Mustafa looked at Crump as if his big friend could further elaborate, now his face was serious and reflective. "What the hell is he talking about, Crump?"

"I don't know, but I 'spect someone should go find out." What Mustafa saw when he looked off the landing to the flats left him awestruck. When he didn't come back inside after a minute or so, Crump and several others went to see why he hadn't returned. Now over half the men from each of the annexes were standing on their respective landings staring down on the flats – at Corrections Officer Barnes sitting in a straight-back metal chair with his hands cuffed behind his back. Anwar was behind him with a small-caliber handgun to his head. A few other men were in the guards' office tussling with on duty Lieutenant Pitts, while others subdued the hard nose "K-9" (they called him that because of his duties with the dogs).

In all, there were supposedly five correctional officers working C-dormitory that night, four men and one woman. Lieutenant Pitts and K-9 were white, CO II Aunsby was a black early-thirties woman, the dark and lovely type that wore her pants too tight to be working in a men's prison, way too tight. Even before it was certain the inmates had control of the wing, the hunt for Ms. Aunsby began. "Oh, shit," someone behind Mustafa said. After assessing the situation, Mustafa left the men on the landing. He knew exactly what he had to do. First, change into the proper gear, and for starters he got both his knives. He purposely put the biggest one in the front of his dip in plain view, while putting the other in the short pants pocket under his sweats. Next, he put on his "kufee" while leaving out to make his rounds, checking on all the Muslims he knew to be housed in C-dormitory.

Bedlam, confusion, and destruction were everywhere. A band of renegade "hoppers" (young guys under twenty-five) were in possession of all the guards keys. They were opening certain cells to rob, beat, and pillage, whether the occupants were in them or not. Those guys that ran personal stores were targeted first, all but Mustafa's old cellie and homeboy Mack-Bey, and Geronimo. Others were taking the opportunity to settle vendettas. If a man had a beef with someone, now was the time to settle it without interference from the officers.

Then there were those still on the hunt for Officer Aunsby. "Aunsby! I know you're in here," Mustafa heard some of the men hollering out. *God help her*, he thought, *if those sick, demented heathens find her.* He wondered would he try to help her if faced with a predicament; he wouldn't assault her, at least he was 99.9% sure he wouldn't. He shook his head to clear his mind from thinking about the dirty pictures he was imagining.

Mustafa wasn't the only one walking around strapped. He thought the place reminded him of the wild west, where gunslingers wore their sidearms at the ready, in plain view. There was no need going down on the flats, no Muslims slept there, and it appeared everyone that was housed there was hanging out; Geronimo was posted up – observing. He ran one of the stores in C-dorm, and was well known throughout West Baltimore for drug dealing, but mostly for the shootout with Baltimore police in 1983. In hot pursuit from Pennsylvania Avenue on through the Murphy Homes Projects, Baltimore's police shot and seriously injured Roland "Geronimo" Bell. He was now confined to a single crutch, sometimes a wheelchair.

Anwar, one of Mustafa's Muslim brothers that had one of the guns during the hostage taking, was one of Ronimo's lieutenants in the early 80s. He was struggling with his Islamic commitment(s), and Mustafa understood it wasn't easy coming from twenty- or thirty-plus years as a hoodlum and thug to suddenly do a 180-degrees turn around. Mustafa was still struggling with certain particulars of his "Deen" (Islamic lifestyle) too, only it wasn't as obvious as with some Muslims.

The second tier was fairly peaceful, except for the pillage of Romaz's (R.C.'s) store. At the escalation of the riot/hostage taking, inmates were given the option of leaving the building with no fear of reprisals, or staying and rolling with whatever the situation brought. R.C. left with not so much of a word to Greg (his cellie). Now Greg had to make sure the looters knew not to bother his stuff from that belongings of R.C.'s. They took R.C.'s photo album, amongst the food stuff, with an 8" x 10" photo of his correctional officer girlfriend (Fat Payton). They taped it up on the screen of the flats rec area TV for all to see. (This would cost Payton her job after authorities took back control of C-dormitory.)

There were only about five men from C-dorm opting to exclude themselves from the revolt. They were standing outside to be escorted to a safe housing location. Many others would wish they were among them before the next day.

On the third tier, Mustafa ran into one of the groups of hoppers with the ring of keys they took from one of the officers. They were letting themselves in and out of people's cells. Right now, they were gathered outside of a cell being looted. Wali Aquil was housed on the third tier, Mustafa considered him one of the more pious Muslims in the community. Most of his family was Muslim, his children were in Islamic schools, and he could read and recite Arabic better than anyone Mustafa knew. He was standing outside his cell just hangin' out, but on point. Just who let him out, Mustafa didn't know, and he seemed glad to see his new brother looking to be on patrol. After their initial greetings of salaams, Wali expressed concern about the hoppers not making the best decisions with their control of the keys. Mustafa was the Wazir of the Sunni Muslim community, and by right was in charge of the Muslims' affairs in C-dormitory, because the Imam (Rasheed) slept on the other side of the compound. Mustafa was by nature a take-charge-type dude, and anyone that knows how Muslims are in the joint knows they are always attempting to run something. That's just the way they are.

If Mustafa wasn't known throughout the jail by now, he was most certainly known in C-dormitory. After Mustafa finished talking with Wali, on his way towards the hoppers, he saw the first one to acknowledge he was coming, only to see them look away in disgust. They all knew him to be on "serious time." Even before his conversion to Islam, he'd given their friend and homeboy a black eye about a torn page out of a tennis-shoe book, he broke Johnny's fingers, and was just barely still in population about the Cadillac incident. Nevertheless, he was fair about his dealings, and his word was good, so when he approached them about turning over the keys to the cells and some of the store rooms, though he was greatly outnumbered, no one objected. That he had a rusty handle of a joint sticking out of his waistband wasn't lost on the group. Mustafa never looked in the cell to see what had attracted their attention, what they were stealing, or who they were assaulting. If it was something that had to be stopped or the degree lessened, then Wali would've mentioned it. He knew it wasn't anything to do with Aunsby, because fortunately for her, Mustafa found out her boyfriend, Butchie, put her down that "Something's jumpin' off around here of an extremely serious and dangerous nature." Instead of reporting it, she had to just find an excuse to punch out early, and had it not been for Geronimo's intervention, a couple guys that found out that he put Aunsby down were going to deal with Butchie.

Since he was already on the third tier, Mustafa proceeded to unlock the remaining cell doors, he did the same on four. On four, he almost bypassed his main man Herbert Mack-Bey's cell. It was funny to see the expression on several of the men's faces as he unlocked their doors. They were like… "What the Hell!" Some didn't know all of what was going on and didn't want to know; they were contented to be locked in where they assumed would be a safe haven. One of his older homeboys and Muslim brothers, Shareef, aka "Short Legs," hollered up on the tier from annex one landing, "Mustafa, you doing that…man you" (then he simulated putting on a mask, he didn't care to holler that part out), but it was way too late for that. Mustafa acknowledged the admonition nevertheless.

There were several cells he purposely left locked, because the occupant(s) simply didn't want to mix in with the rioters, nor be amidst the chaos, or as in the case with "Hot Larry," it was best he didn't see all that was going on. Besides, when Mustafa peered in his cell on the fifth tier, it was dark and appeared empty. Hot Larry was hiding in his locker. All the cells on the fifth tier were single units. One of the two remaining guards was held there. The other, Barnes, was somewhere Mustafa wasn't sure of. The men ordered them out of their uniforms and into street clothes to look like inmates, one of the better ideas someone came up with yet.

It was rumored the smooth-talking Clarence Mouzon got his trick (CO II White) to bring in two handguns, so aside from prostituting on the four-to-twelve shift, she was now an accessory before the fact to a prison hostage taking – among other things. How the hacksaw blades got in this time was unknown, but it all went for naught, because this diabolical escape plot failed when too many of the blades were used up cutting through the wrought-iron cage holding the blower that took air from, or into, the wing from the outside.

Some genius thought once cutting through the cage then removing the large blower there would be this big hole in the building leading to the street. Even if they did manage to remove the blower, there were still additional bars separating the street side of the blower from Madison Street, and those bars were as thick as a small child's wrist. Whoever designed this set-up did their homework, sure 'nough! After it was clear the escape plot was a bust, despite the guns and blades, Clarence thought of saving himself. Before anyone realized what was happening, Clarence took K-9 out the dormitory door to the secured area outside; where or how Lieutenant Pitts got out even before that was a mystery. Mustafa's priorities weren't so much on the hostages or the escape as they were on the plight of the Muslim body in C-dormitory, as well as his own safety.

Someone reminded him there were still people on the second tier locked in, some of them wanted to be out amongst the people. On two, while opening the remainder of the cell doors, he began hearing what sounded like a sledge hammer striking concrete coming from somewhere overhead. Curiosity led him to follow the sound. Back up to the fifth tier he went, out through the back landing, which was normally only accessible to the COs, through the landing off to the side. In another auxiliary area of sorts he saw a small group of white boys attempting to plough through the wall the old-fashioned way. With a large, heavy steel pipe, these cats were slugging away. Though it was tedious work, concrete and brick bits were flying off the wall like bark from a lumberjack's axe. They took turns in between taking swigs from a jug of wine. One of them raised the jug to Mustafa when they saw him admiring their efforts. Mustafa waved it off, shouted a few words of encouragement, and shook his head, smiling as he headed back to annex one. He knew at this point it was a hopeless endeavor, but no way would he rain on their parade. After what must've been two or three hours from the onset of the siege, and as Mustafa was just about to enter onto the landing of the annex, someone spotted figures outside C-dorm where the bleachers were. In fact, they were standing on the bleachers, peering in, at the corner by the hospital. Flashlights darting around could also be seen. Someone else shouted, "They're out there!" The banging from the makeshift sledgehammer halted. "You'd better not run up in here with that dumb shit. We got guns and hostages!" Another yelled. C-dormitory was now totally surrounded.

Chapter 18

ABU BAKR, AS FAR AS Mustafa knew, had never carried a joint. His legendary hands had served him well through the years and were all the weapons he ever needed…other than during his crime spree, committing armed robberies and the like. Though he was Mustafa's brother in Islam, and followed the sunnah, he too was struggling in some areas of his conduct and overall way of life to make himself a better Muslim. As far as maintaining order in the Sunni community, no one could equal his art of persuasion when and if he so chose. There were only a handful of Abu Bakr's Muslim brothers he'd take admonishments from, and even then, the admonisher or "suggester" should come right, or not come at all. For Mustafa and any conscious Muslim, they'd always start off with "Bismillahir-Rahmanir-Raheem" (with Allah's name the Merciful, the Bestower of Mercy), then perhaps something from the Prophet Muhammad (S.A.W.) and, lastly, standing firm on the conviction or admonition.

Mustafa didn't know where Abu Bakr was during the turmoil, but hoped he was staying out of trouble, wherever he was. The last he saw of his big go-hard brother was on the fourth tier with Big Reds, Big Head Dave, and a couple other ignoble characters. While Mustafa was gone, annex one had become the unofficial base of operations; it'd become an extremely busy and high-traffic area. C-dormitory held approximately three hundred men, now that the annexes were cut in half. Those that were holding any sort of narcotics or sauce (wine) were making it available for consumption. The standard order or rule now was "If you don't use it, you gonna' lose it," so besides the stabbings and rapes, the men (most of them) were also drunk or high off something.

Crump was sitting up on two stacked milk crates about to nod on to the concrete floor, Battle's eyes were glazing like two honey-dipped doughnuts, and the others just gave Mustafa some of the stupidest-looking smiles he'd ever seen. Those not indulging in narcotics had cups or plastic bottles of wine in their hands.

"Don't mind me, men. I'm just passing through, but….damn!"

Back in the partial seclusion of his aisle, Mustafa allowed the big weight lifter Lloyd to hide out and waste his time with a lot of trivials. Like many others, Lloyd left his cell abandoned to be pillaged by the rioters, not willing to risk their lives defending it. Size and strength doesn't always mean a man or woman is exempt from transgressions, not on the street and not in the joint. A lot of it has to do with being recognized, connected, or having made one's "bones" early on in the neighborhood, on the streets, or in the prison system.

Meanwhile, Mustafa was trying to guess the next move of the authorities just outside C-dorm, but more so the move of headquarters, because at this stage that's where the major decisions were coming from.

Black Battle came to the aisle calmly saying, "You better go check on your man. They trying to get him."

"Who!?"

"Go on the landing and look down on the flats."

Mustafa excused himself to look down on the flats as Battle suggested. In all the confusion, he'd totally forgotten his financial backer, Donaldson, aka Pitt Bull. Mustafa observed several hoppers trying to coerce him from his cell with threats. They even set papers on fire and stuffed them through the bars of his cell. Though his cell was unlocked, he had the foresightedness to place a padlock on the bar closest to the rear when things first jumped off, rendering the door incapable of sliding open. No one could get in or out without first removing the lock.

Mustafa hadn't been down on the flats, and saw for the first time the stairwell leading from the flats up the first set of stairs was barricaded. Mustafa was in shape, so it wasn't a problem maneuvering through the furniture and rubble strewn about the stairwell. Without a word to the men gathered in front of his old friend's cell, he began pulling the burning newspapers off the cell door, and telling the men to hold up!

Jim-Jim spoke for the group. He was holding a pair of handcuffs in his hand, clicking them the way some police do when their hands are idle. He said, "We know that's your man and everything, but he got to kick out that money and cigarettes." Mustafa had two foot lockers under his bunk in the annex belonging to Pitt. He wasn't exactly sure what was in them.

"Alright, come on out, Pitt. I got you. We going to the annex to let these dudes have this crap."

"No, No, they gonna kill me."

"Pitt, I got you, man, come on out."

Pitt continued his refusal, until Battle shouted down from the landing for Mustafa to give Pitt his word that if he came out nothing would happen to him. Big Crump and a couple other men from the annex were on the landing as well, observing the dilemma. Mustafa knew it was a tall order, considering the circumstances, that a whole lotta folk, not just in C-dormitory, but half the entire population, didn't like the way Pitt conducted business. He could be an annoying pest when a dude was late with a payment. Mustafa found it all amusing. The old country sayings he would spit out to a dude when the guy was late or short some of Pitt's money. He was famous for telling a dude, "Man, you paying me like a bear shits in the woods – a spot here and a spot there," or "Man, you treating me like the damn paperboy – come back later."

Now some of these guys or friends of them had Pitt, and they'd make him pay, with interest! Nevertheless, Mustafa gave his old friend his word that nothing would happen to him. Mustafa looked back at the group, told them to chill out, and that the stuff in the cell…Mustafa waved it off, saying with the motion what they understood. The only property of value Pitt had in his cell was a color TV, a modest-sized boom box, a watch, and several CDs. He unlocked the padlock, Mustafa slid open the cell door from behind his back as he faced the group, pulling Pitt out, and keeping him in between himself and the other cells, lest someone try to take a cheap shot at him.

For some reason, all Pitt had on was his robe. Mustafa figured he probably slept in the raw, and when the crap hit the fan, he was awakened and disoriented. Pitt had some strange habits. Someone once said the craziest or weirdest dudes in prison were those that had big bits and were Vietnam veterans. Pitt was a good candidate to be eligible for a case study, or something on that.

He stumbled and fell. Jim-Jim tried to cuff his wrist. Mustafa pushed him away and picked Pitt up then ushered him towards the stairwell. The mob didn't waste time taking possession of the spoils, but Pitt was a shrewd business man and would eventually recoup his losses. Mustafa helped him climb the barricade and on up the remaining stairs, then, inside annex one, said, "Come on, old timer." There were mixed emotions amongst the men in the small dorm where Mustafa slept. Some felt Pitt got what his hand called for and it was poetic justice, or something along those lines. Others, like Battle, Crump, and those that at one time or another worked in the main dining hall with him sympathized. They knew he was Mustafa's own personal bank if he needed the scratch, whenever and however much.

Now there were two men using the corner aisle for their sanctuary. Mustafa put Pitt in his own bed and told him to rest up, look at the TV if you're up to it, or get yourself something to eat out the locker. Usually Mustafa would've used Stonewall's speedy running back's crutch phrase, "It ain't heavy." Croxsell would say that, no matter what, but now wasn't the time because this situation was indeed heavy.

While Pitt lay on his bunk, Mustafa sat in the chair right next to him, on guard. People still thought he had money stashed somewhere, and it seemed like this would be a long night. Ten minutes hadn't past when the halfway-slick old-school head from D.C. appeared at the aisle's entrance.

"Mustafa, let me holler at you a minute, home!" It was Herman Davis, an old hustler and con man outta D.C.

Donaldson was sitting up now.

"What's happening? Who is that?"

"Nothin', Pitt. Just relax yourself. I got it."

Big Head Dave was just outside the aisle when Mustafa stepped to them. Dave did the talking after Mustafa brushed Herman's request and comments off.

"Mustafa, man, this dude got some money, I know it!"

"You don't know nothin', 'cause he don't have nothin'. He don't even have on clothes, and y'all been all in his house!"

"He got it in his ass," Dave said.

Mustafa was getting irritated and got louder. "He don't man. He got nothing!" Mustafa's raised voice brought Shareef (Short Legs) from his aisle. Shareef was like family to Mustafa. His cousin Ann had a baby by Mustafa's youngest brother, Paul.

"Something wrong, Mustafa?"

"Nar man, I got it."

With that, Dave and Herman bounced.

Donaldson was only a shout away from hysteria for the second time that evening. He was a bundle of nerves. Another intrusion might surely send him over the edge, and if it was going to happen, then his next visitor put him on the brink.

Big Reds showed up just after Mustafa tucked his joint under his folded arms. He told Mustafa he only wanted to holler at Pitt for a minute. Pitt got up, stepped out of the aisle, and could be seen shaking his head and spreading his arms. He knew Big Reds was perhaps one the most dangerous and cruddiest men known, not just amongst the prison population, but in the state! If that weren't enough, it was rumored he had not a knife but a hatchet. Mustafa truly believed the rumor, though he hadn't spoken with anyone who'd actually seen it.

Pitt apparently convinced Biggums he was broke. Perhaps he swore he'd just sent all his money out and lent out all the cigarettes. Mustafa was on point nevertheless, and half expected a hatchet to come sailing past him into Pitt's skull any minute. Mustafa imagined a direct route to Big Reds' stomach with the knife he held folded in his crossed arms, should it come to it. He prayed to Allah it wouldn't. Mustafa didn't fool himself for a minute; he knew despite him being "strapped," if Big Reds had the like for it, and truly thought Pitt had money, the knife Mustafa held wouldn't deter him in the least. Biggum had been in way more combat situations than Mustafa, on the street, in prison, with knives, guns, and especially his fists.

The only deterrent that did carry weight with Biggums was Abu Bakr. "Lucky," as Biggum called him, who was now Mustafa's people.

On the third tier, another vendetta was being carried out. This one against Curly, a kitchen worker a few guys were hating on in part because he had a few women. Sometimes he was arrogant, and also he'd get out on you verbally, but couldn't demonstrate on the physical tip like that.

He wasn't a people person, more the loner type, and needless to say he was not "connected."

One of the errors on Mustafa's part may have been to open the cell doors without first asking the occupants present. Some guys would've been contented to be locked in with their light off in the dark until the authorities restored order, but even this was no guarantee for safety.

Someone Curly angered at one time or another stabbed him in the stomach. As he lay on his bunk bleeding, his cellie and neighbors tried unsuccessfully to encourage him to let them take him to the front grill of C-dorm. So far, this was the protocol for the injured. They'd be laid between the two grills at C-dorm's entrance, a caller would announce, "Got one for the hospital!" The injured would be picked up and carried by stretcher to the infirmary for treatment. Two men were sent to get Mustafa. When he arrived, the bottom half of Curly's shirt was soaked through with blood, some had ran off onto the white sheets.

"Hi, Curly, main man, we got to get you outta here and to the hospital. You don't want to lie here bleeding. You'll die."

"No, Mustafa, they'll think I'm telling!"

"No they won't. They'll think you needed to get fixed up. Let's go."

Mustafa and one of the men that retrieved him attempted to get Curly off the bunk while he struggled and resisted as much as his weakened body allowed. All the while protesting that Mustafa should let him stay, which wasn't open to discussion, because Mustafa would bring him out of there by choice or force. Curly was left at the dorm's entrance on a couple blankets while the fifth emergency call of the night was made. "Got one for the hospital!" Suddenly, Diggs was nowhere to be found.

At or around midnight, the major medical emergencies were handled, and the threats of physical harm to various individuals had been abated. Now that there were no clear feasible plans for an escape and the thieves and looters had captured most of the spoils, all that was left were negotiations for the hostages.

Mustafa didn't expect any action from the authorities until daybreak, then maybe there would be tear-gas canisters coming through the windows, followed by someone, he didn't know who, storming the joint, crackin' heads, and maybe shooting – like Attica, New York (1971).

Well, the first part of Mustafa's premise rung true. The National Guardsmen were everywhere when the men awoke. They'd replaced local authorities. They were lining the walls, on roof tops, and throughout the yards. A makeshift committee was formed to discuss things, first being the two remaining guards. Marando (Anwar) was chosen to walk one of them up to the administrative level to turn him over in exchange for a list of demands and grievances. The men had partied, looted, and raised hell all night; now was the dawning of a new day. Clear, expedient, and prudent decisions would have to be made.

Usually, by 8:00 am the men would have had breakfast two to four hours ago, but now there would be no breakfast line for C-dormitory and no meals-on-wheels cart brought from the main dining room. Most of the men fortunate enough to have food in their lockers from the commissary or from their prisoner's personal "survival kit" (peanut butter, honey, and a few noodles) shared with a friend. Mustafa enjoyed food just for the pleasure of it. He always had his homeboy, ex-cellie, and store man, H. Mack-Bey. Mack-Bey always had something held down for his friend with a high concentration of glucose.

After a person is used to doing certain things at a prescribe time, when the cycle breaks, it can create mental, physical, and/or emotional havoc. This hostage and riotous scene took its toll on C-dorm's inhabitants. Now that it had wound down, the men were drained, hungry, and restless. With Marando leaving out to negotiate, they were expectant of good things to come. After all, they had bargaining chips. They were back at the windows, watching as he exited C-dorm, up past the side of the main dining hall, and then disappearing down the slope where the level was.

Mustafa heard some of what the committee compiled to be presented, and thought the request for "pizza" typical. He wondered what was it about pizza that seemed to always make its way on a captor's list of demands. The TV was showing C-dorm on the news, a picture of annex one's windows, and several men with masked faces. They were getting airtime. Shareef was the first one to notice the red dot on Smooth Talker's forehead; one of the happy-go-lucky, perhaps itchy-trigger-fingered National Guardsmen was playing games, or was waiting for the go-ahead to send a message.

One of the men suddenly snatched him away, out of harm's way. Big Hollywood warned his little buddy, "Keep on showing your face in that window and Mrs. Harris gonna be making funeral arrangements for that dusty ass. You niggas just got to be in the spotlight."

When Marando came back, he didn't even have a promise. They took the guard and carried Marando like the amateur negotiator he was. They gave up zilch, nada – no comprende, hombre negro. What they did, however, was took Imam Rasheed and Hakeem (Dennis Wise) off lockdown, escorted them to C-dorm, then let them holler up to the windows to try to bring closure to the seeming impasse. The administration figured they were covering all the bases by sending Rasheed and Dennis to stand before the men; Rasheed because he was the Inmate Advisory Council President (I.A.C.) and leader of the Muslims. Abu Bakr (Timmy Poole as they knew him) was housed in C-dorm, and one of the few people he was obligated to obey was his Imam, Rasheed.

They teamed him up with Hakeem (Dennis Wise) because he was looked upon as a bona fide shot caller amongst the youth, as well as some of the senior convicts. Actually, the men were already willing to throw in the towel. Rasheed's and Dennis's presence gave them the nudge needed to relinquish their position. At a little past 1:00 pm, Warden Sewall Smith was allowed entry into C-dormitory to assess the situation and heroically bring out the last hostage.

On the fifth tier, the last held officer was in civilian clothes under Taymulla's bunk. Big Reds was watching him. When the time came, he slapped the officer's ankle. "Let's go." However something was wrong with him. Biggums had seen this type of subtle response before coming from one who has been abused, sexually. The guy was timid and spiritless. Maybe he was just tired of the ordeal, he hoped.

For now, Biggums had to deliver him to Warden Smith who was waiting in annex one. Smith had him immediately taken to the infirmary to await transport to the nearest civilian hospital (University of Maryland or Johns Hopkins), where a team of doctors would thoroughly examine him. Meanwhile, the authorities were preparing to receive the approximately three hundred ousted inmates.

In single file, the men were instructed to exit the building with only the clothes on their backs, and they were to have nothing in their hands or pockets except ID. At 6:00 pm Mustafa threw his prayer rug over his shoulder, grabbed a small book he'd been reading, entitled *Morals and Manners in Islam*, and left with the others.

National Guardsmen, state and local law enforcement, and some administrative personal formed a human passageway. He was surprised the men weren't made to strip at least down to their shorts; even more surprised no one said anything about the rug and book. The passageway directed them into three-yard, where the gate was locked. The guardsmen and officers then were positioned outside the fence facing the now disarmed and vanquished. The men were strip searched in G-building before entering three-yard.

Nightfall swiftly fell upon them with each man or group of men finding their own area of three-yard in which to seclude himself. On the bare ground, Mustafa and Wali Aquil found themselves resting their heads on a partially upraised wall left from the destruction of the old automotive repair shop. They were glad the rug was allowed on the exodus to keep their heads off the bare cinderblock. Looking up, they saw the star filled July sky, a panoramic masterpiece, and what could surely be a testament to what the Prophet Muhammad (S.A.A.W) said in his authentic ahadeeth (narration): "The stars were created for three reasons: to decorate the heavens, as a guide for the travelers, and missiles against the Shaytan (devils), and for those who seek out more, they only waste time. Mustafa and Wali Aquil looked into the heavens counting stars, as many as each one could until sleep overtook them. They made Isha salat about midnight, and the fair prayer (early morning salat) shortly before the flatbed truck pulled into the compound with five thirty-man tents. After they were erected, the men had a choice of sleeping in or staying out. Most chose to be inside the tents for the camaraderie.

Throughout the first two to five days, men began to hear their names called to report to the back entry gate where they were received by a small squad of officers. These men had direct, violent involvement in the takeover. Their names were anonymously placed in an accessible mailbox, compliments of Security Chief Purnell. He knew the snitchers couldn't wait to seize an opportunity to drop a few names.

The days in three-yard, Mustafa thought, just had to be the hottest days so far all summer. Several men were having physical and emotional breakdowns. They were taken to the infirmary. A few of the white boys were so sun-burned they looked like cooked lobsters – they were taken out as well. The fifteen Muslims stayed close, most slept in the same tent. They made all the congregational prayers together, and Mustafa was allowed to lead them several times. It was the first time he had led such a large group; however, Wali Aquil led mostly, because he was one of the best at recitation, and knew the most Qur'an.

Mail call was the brightest spot in the day, after congregation salat. Mustafa would get his, then take it to a private shady grass area around by the laundry where the buildings block the sun. An officer that usually worked the hospital that was assigned patrol of that particular area knew Mustafa to be a hard worker and straight-up guy, so he allowed him the out-of-the-way space, even though it was a borderline area. Mail is real big to convicts and guys or gals away from loved ones. Mustafa deeply enjoyed the shout outs he received, especially the occasional money orders.

Men were still being swept-up, supposedly under investigation. The few female officers involved were fired for their part, whatever it was. What criminal charges were brought against the parties involved wasn't known yet, and Mustafa was questioned about a set of missing keys.

Food was being brought on carts to the entry gate by the kitchen. By the fifth or sixth day, the rest of the population was off lockdown. Items were beginning to make their way to the men in the yard by all methods known. Some stuff, particularly food, was dropped from the side windows of the kitchen. Small items, along with personal things, could be slid under one of the fans.

On the ninth day, the penitentiary's administrators began making housing arrangements for the remaining two hundred plus men. A heavy thunderstorm was forecast to hit the Baltimore area. The commissioner of public safety wanted the men out of the yard. Some were moved to A and B blocks, and while they all were initially headed in that direction, certain ones were snatched out of the groups to be detoured to south-wing lockup. Mustafa was in that group. Assigned a cell on the yard side of south wing, on the flats, news quickly spread Mustafa was on the hammer.

Big Reds, who was in the first group snatched out of three-yard hollered down to him from somewhere up on the second tier.

"I'm glad to know you joined us, boy!"

"Yeah, homeboy, you know how these jokers play. Ain't nobody exempt for real." Mustafa knew exactly what Big Reds meant by his statement, and was glad in a paradoxical sort of way he'd joined those implicated in the uprising.

In all, there were approximately forty men placed on lockup, with ten sent to the infirmary for one thing or another. By the third day Mustafa learned he was being held for having institutional keys, aiding in escape (by letting the men out), and reportedly armed with a knife. These were very serious accusations that carried detrimental repercussions. The Muslims from C-dorm, Donaldson, and many others, if not every inmate in the housing unit, knew the real story.

Loads of food were sent to him from guys all throughout the population to hold him down. He gratefully appreciated it. He had more food stuff than he needed, and felt obliged to hit several guys off not as fortunate. He continued making all five prayers, reading the translation of the Qur'an, and continuing with his readings and letter writing. Farrakhan-Bey was on lockup too on the other end of the flats. Every two days, when they ran shower, he was able to spend a few moments at his cell door, where he'd leave off a pack of cookies or two, and read one of the volumes of ahadeeth (Sahih Muslim).

One night, Mustafa was awakened by the sound of packages rattling. Someone or something had intruded upon him in his domain. He knew about the rats and mice coming in the cells, specifically on the flats. He prayed it wasn't a rat. He saw the small gray creature scurrying as he flicked the overhead light on, so he stayed up half the night hanging the food on lines hanging from the clothes line and up on the porthole over the cell door. Mustafa found out mice were some of the most daring and acrobatic rodents he'd ever seen. This one began tight roping the line to the tied-up cookies and chips. Eventually, Mustafa started sending most of his food to the Muslims and some friends on the hammer. He kept only enough that he could easily place it out of reach from his nighttime burglar.

The thief stealing his food stuff reminded him of the ahadeeth (narration) by Abu Huraira about what the Prophet Muhammad said of Shaytan's knowledge of Ayatul Kursi (the Verse of the Throne).

After thirty-plus days, the men from C-dormitory, black and white, Muslim and non-Muslim, sent letters and pulled Security Chief Purnell up on the compound, petitioning for Mustafa's release. He was exonerated of all charges and sent back to C-dorm, on the third tier this time, with a younger Muslim brother named Bilal, nicknamed "Easy." Bilal began teaching Mustafa the Arabic letters – identification, pronunciation, and linking them up to make small words. The penitentiary cells were too small for the two to stand side by side; however, they still reaped the benefits of praying in congregation by lining up one behind the other.

During the weeks following the siege, confusion set in over the confiscation of the men's property by the officers. "Boot camp" was assigned the task of carting out everything from C-dorm not nailed/bolted down, other than the bunks. Men lost clothes, appliances, TVs etc. The loose stuff was cast into a dumpster. The boys from boot camp were exchanging their tennis shoes or boots for the men's. The officers were welcoming themselves to whatever food and drinks (sodas) were left by the store runners. Mustafa's color TV was missing, but it wasn't heavy; he didn't have ownership papers anyway. It was a gift from a friend that was transferred out last year.

A meeting was held by the warden, some of his assistants, the I.A.C. president (Rasheed), and Mustafa was Rasheed's (sort of) personal assistant, so he was invited to attend also. For one thing, Mustafa was pissed because of the way the officers went into the cells and annexes throwing stuff out, slamming it into boxes, and allowed those jokers from boot camp to help themselves with whatever they thought they could get away with – besides, his TV was M.I.A.

Midway through the meeting, Mustafa got up out of his chair to hurl accusations at Warden Smith, who rose from his chair to face Mustafa with a just as aggressive rebuttal. The two men were shouting now with Imam/ I.A.C. President Rasheed pulling his Wazir toward his seat next to him.

Imam Rasheed had savvy. In his early thirties, he was prudent and he knew how to handle people. He believed all fifty-something men in "Jamatul Khalid bin Abdul Al-Walid" had their specific stations, and it was his responsibility to recognize these positions and bring out the best in that individual. He knew all along there was a strong possibility his new Wazir (Mustafa Lucas) would ruffle feathers at this meeting, but unlike Abu Bakr (Timmy) he was not borderline irrepressible. Mustafa could easily be quelled. Though he was a good one for maintaining order in "The House," he'd need work on his tact and diplomacy in these situations. The meeting ended shortly afterwards, with Rasheed smoothing things out with the Warden and his staff.

Outside he looked at Mustafa, staring at and seriously considering his brother. Mustafa thought he was in trouble with the Imam and was about to catch hell when Rasheed's face suddenly broke into a grin and he placed his arm around his shoulders briefly as they walked out of the rotunda. Things had worked out exactly the way he'd planned, but for "Surely Allah is the best of planners." (Qur'an, Surah 8:30)

Two weeks after the meeting with the Warden, the crooked Lieutenant Donnell took his break in the main dining room of the Pen's hospital to enjoy the view overlooking four-yard. So, many of the officers and staff did this while stopping to grab a bite in Mustafa's work place.

Mustafa figured this was a most opportune time to inquire about his missing TV, since the lieutenant had the inside scoop on practically everything that went on inside the walls. Not only did he know about the TV, but attempted to exploit the situation by extorting twenty dollars, because as he put it, "I know you're doing alright for yourself around here, Lucas. Man, I tell you what – just give me a dime." Mustafa couldn't believe the nerve of this lame! The worst part was that Mustafa wasn't even doing all that swell. He wasn't hustling the extra rations off the food cart, nor smuggling stuff from the kitchen. He was giving it away to whomsoever was hungry, especially his Muslim brothers. He'd told Garneta to cut the one hundred dollars down to fifty a month, and when he could, he was sending money home to J. Marie for the kids. It wasn't a lot, but hey---

"Ten dollars! Man, I ain't got it like that… You know what? Man take that TV and stick it up your ass."

It was the first-time Mustafa purposely cursed since he'd been Muslim.

Donnell only gave a faint laugh and stayed focused out on four-yard. Mustafa knew he could get out on Donnell this time because he had tried to extort him.

In the later part of that year, Donnell and CO II Joyce (a hot little redbone from Brooklyn, N.Y.) were fired and charged with stealing tech, Officer Willie's check.

In October, 1991, a work strike was organized and put into effect, whether by the Inmate Advisory Council or not. For three days the inmates didn't report for their job assignments and those six that did were threatened with physical harm. The jail was on another lockdown status; since Imam Rasheed was also the I.A.C. president, he got the charge. As Mustafa and his cellie Bilal sat in the cell kickin' it about everything, a little, and nothin', someone called him from out on the tier.

"Ralph Lucas!"

Mustafa assumed someone he had close ties with was playing games, because only a few guys knew his government name.

Mustafa stuck his little "peeper mirror" through the bars to look down the tier. He saw what looked to be ten riot-gear dressed officers, complete with shields. One was videotaping everything as the spokesperson of the group ordered Mustafa to back out of the cell with his hands behind him when the door opened. He quickly put on his combat and traveling clothes – shorts under the sweatpants, double sweatshirts, double socks, and shoes with the best traction. He didn't know exactly what these guys had on their minds, but he'd be Red-Cross ready. Besides, there was no telling when or if he'd ever get his property, so he would at least have a different outfit. Once out of the cell, he was shackled with the division of correction transportation's own traveling outfit (leg irons, waist chains, and the black cuff box) and escorted to the receiving area of B-block. He saw Imam Rasheed, Tahya Sabir, Mu'tazz, Abdullah, Harrison, and another younger brother. Mustafa wasn't quite sure of his name. They all were shackled up and awaiting all the files the Maryland Penitentiary had on them, to be transferred out of the institution; with the first stop being just across the street at the super max on Madison Street. There, they dropped off Rasheed and Yahya. The remaining five were taken to the newly opened Penitentiary Annex in Jessup, Maryland.

Mustafa was somewhat familiar with the area; it was down the road from the Patuxent Institution, and directly behind the Maryland House of Corrections (aka the Cutt). Mustafa had heard stories about the Cutt when he was at the Diagnostic Center, before being classified to the Pen. It was supposedly a high-medium-security-facility joint, not maximum like the penitentiary. This new joint, although maximum, had a twenty-foot fence, instead of the thirty-foot wall at the Pen.

Chapter 19

The van pulled up in front of A-building in the late evening. A-building was lockup and administrative segregation. B-building was for the general population, where most of the guys from the first wave of ship outs from the Pen were. Abu Bakr, Big Reds, Abdul Haqq, and about twenty-five of the wild renegade hoppers that were involved in the takeover during the summer. Many were in the super max, however, only two buildings were opened in the new spot. Five others would open in the years to come. Each building had four wings spilling off an elevated central control booth where the officers could look on to all four tiers.

Fortunately for the men, their property came along with them. They were placed on administrative segregation pending investigation. The "jacket" that Chief of Security Purnell documented, or rather "concocted," along with an emergency classification board, portrayed Mustafa as a threat to the population and staff. When Mustafa got his copy of the document, he couldn't believe the state's attorney's office sanctioned it. Yet there was the stamp and signature. Had this occurred seven years later the Division of Corrections would have undoubtedly sent him out of state as they did Hakeem (Dennis) Wise to Arizona, Clarence Mouzon to Boston, Kerwin (Truck) Epps to Florida, Darnell Roberts to El Paso, Texas, Rob Boyd to Florida then Atlanta, and Malik, from the Nation of Islam, to New Mexico, just to name a few.

The news of the newest arrivals quickly spread throughout the Pen Annex, or "Out Back," as it would come to be known, because it was in the back of the Cutt. Mustafa and the others stayed on administrative segregation on through to mid-January 1992, then they were assigned cells in B-building with the rest of the population.

Mu'tazz was elected inmate Imam. Jumu'ah service was held each Friday on any available recreation area in A-building. They were only a group of forty, and like the community at the penitentiary, fairly easy to maintain. The outside Muslim coordinator, who also was responsible for the Muslims across the yard at the Cutt, was an affable early-forties Muslim brother from Philly, Kareem Muhammad. Kareem was a hands-on coordinator who did good overseeing the affairs and education of the Muslims for the past three years.

The more senior of the Muslims from the Pen took issue to some of the information, and some minor changes Kareem began to implement. Kareem brought them the "Haqq" (truth) as best he knew it, and had the proofs to back it up. He traveled in the company of some pretty heavy hitters in the Muslim world, as far as the men from the Pen were accustomed to, like Shaykh Muhammad Saad Adly, Dhiyauddin bin Yaya, and his main man and friend from Newark, NJ, Dawud Adib. Dawud Adib was a knowledgeable, fiery, and charismatic orator, that at first glance looked like Eddie Murphy; however, he didn't like to hear that, because that was likening him to a "Kaafir" (a disbeliever in the oneness of Allah the Most High). Dawud was also much taller, and had a very deep voice. He was a strong adherent to the sunnah of the Prophet Muhammad (S.A.A.W.), and committed most of his life calling people to the correct Islamic teachings. Dawud made "Hajj" (the Pilgrimage to the Holy City of Mecca), and studied overseas too. Mustafa knew he wanted to make Hajj, like Malik Shabazz aka Malcolm X, Dawud, Kareem Muhammad, and all the more serious Muslims. In fact, he knew it to be one of the five Pillars of Islam. It was an obligation on every Muslim that had the means (i.e. money and health).

Mustafa's brother M.G. (Big Mike, as the family was known to call him, so as not to confuse someone into thinking it was Mike D'Angelo) had been in the Philippines, and also stationed in Kuwait with the Air Force, and sent Mustafa a beautiful tan suede-like tapestry of a Qur'anic verse in black calligraphy. Mustafa wasn't reading Arabic very well yet, but took the tapestry to Islamic class one night, where Kareem informed him it was "Ayatul-Kursi". Ayatul-Kursi, Mustafa knew was the Arabic name for the Verse of the Throne (or Footstool), and it was the verse that reminded him of the story of the thief that was stealing when the mouse was coming into his cell when he was locked up in south wing after the hostage taking. Subhanallah! (Glory to Allah) Mustafa said, then dedicated time to learn this most popular and greatest verse in the Qur'an, in Arabic, Surah Al-Baqarah (2), verse 255.

The new Pen Annex, Out Back, had yet to have a visitors' room; it had no main dining hall, nor an infirmary. The men had to go next door to the Cutt if they were ill. For the past five years, Mustafa had been wearing glasses for reading, and every couple years it seemed he needed the lenses recalibrated. This time, to get his eyes checked, he was escorted in shackles to the back part of the Cutt where the hospital area was. This setup wasn't like the Pen, construction-wise, everything looked to be on one floor. Still in handcuffs (the black travel box and leg irons were removed) he was shown a seat until the optometrist was ready to receive him. It was close to lunchtime, "feed-up." Suddenly he saw the meals-on-wheels cart rolling his way. The cart was an exact replica of the one he handled at the Pen's hospital ODR. The guy pushing this one, however, was sharply dressed, as far as prison standards went. Mustafa thought he was a bit over the top. This young brother had on pressed clean white shirt and pants, with the shirt tucked in, a red bow-tie, and white usher's cap like the Nation of Islam wore during special affairs. Upon closer observation, the cap had "F.O.I." on it, neatly stenciled. Mustafa knew F.O.I was a security detail within the "Nation." It stood for Fruit of Islam. Mustafa knew this guy. It was "Byron Smoot" who Moore-el used to holler at from four-yard to the third floor of the Pen's hospital.

"Smoot, Alhamdulillah! What's happening?"

Smoot got along well with most anyone. He was a people person with a ready smile, a fast pace to his gait, and he could carry a conversation with the best of them. There was always a "project" he was working on, or something in his hand to read or study. He didn't know Mustafa personally but had seen him around through the years at one spot or another, especially around the Muslims.

"Hey, Brother. All's well. Just trying to stay under the radar till I bounce next month."

Mustafa didn't attempt to stretch the dialogue out. He knew Smoot had work to do, setting up the cart to make ready for the lunch line. A year later (1993), Mustafa was transferred to the Cutt, and was working in the hospital, not in food service, but as the new sanitation man. It really didn't matter in what capacity he worked there, just as long as he got his foot in the door. It wasn't so much about the nurses, but in the summertime, the hospitals were the coolest place in the jail, aside from the Warden's and his secretary's office. The way this entire ordeal transpired, he thought, had to be nothing short of divine intervention, again.

Warden James "Three Fingers" Smith was the warden of the Maryland House of Corrections. He and his assistant warden, Ronald Hutchinson, and Security Chief Singletary ran the Cutt, and didn't do too bad a job. Aside from a mass escape in '91 (seven from the recreation yard), things ran pretty smooth. The body count was down, and they kept a lot of bad ink from spilling into the newspapers. Three Fingers Smith and Sewall Smith from the Maryland Pen weren't related; in fact, Three Fingers didn't much care for his fellow warden. It may have had its origin in the fact Sewall was put in command of the new joint in Three Fingers own back yard. The men from "Out Back" were using his jail for everything except sleeping, that they were of maximum-security status should not have been a factor as far as he was concerned.

Pulling Mustafa over to the Cutt and from under Sewalls authority was just as much personal with Three Fingers as it was to help Mustafa out, even though he certainly admired the young man's leadership qualities. He only hoped this tier representative "Lucas" would exercise the same enthusiasm to help the I.A.C. board and administration/inmate population relations as he'd attempted to do in the new prison. That was last year, when Abu Bakr took Mustafa with him to sit in on an I.A.C. meeting, which the warden of the Maryland House of Corrections and a few of his staff set up to try to establish better communication lines with this supposedly rogue and displaced group from the Old Pen. Warden James Smith (Smitty as he was also called) took notice of Mustafa when he took control of what could have escalated into a "situation" between one of the Old Pen guys and his lieutenant.

Two weeks after the I.A.C. meeting, on a Friday right before Jumu'ah service, Mustafa's tier officer told him to report to the major's office (in A-building). Mustafa couldn't figure out what it could be for. Usually when a guy was asked to report to the major's office or the chaplain it was because of a family crisis. He hoped Connie was alright; after all, she was getting on in years. He quickly calculated her age on his way to the next building, she was sixty-five. When he entered the major's office, the major dialed a number, spoke into the receiver briefly then handed him the phone.

"Lucas, this is Warden Smith at 'The House.'"

Mustafa knew "The House" was short for The Maryland House of Corrections.

"How ya doing, Warden Smith. What's happening?"

"Son, how would you like to take housing over here at the House?"

"Yes, sir. I'm pretty sure I'd like that. When?"

"Right now, today."

"Warden Smith, I'd appreciate that, man, but I'm scheduled to give the Khutbah sermon at Jumu'ah this afternoon. How 'bout tomorrow?"

Mustafa heard light laughter over the phone.

Warden James "Three Fingers" Smith thought this guy had nerve.

"Alright, I'll get you here tomorrow. Be ready in the morning."

"Thanks, Warden Smith. Take it easy."

"Click."

Chapter 20

J. Marie was thoughtful enough to bring the children to visit every couple months. He was calling them too. He knew the telephone could be expensive and J. Marie was struggling, so he did more writing. The children would take pictures with their dad and seemed to understand why he and Mama wouldn't share in the long kisses they used to. He'd still hug her, however, with an occasional seemingly innocent brush across the side of her breast when he released her, until, one time, J. Marie drew back from him, or his hand rather. That gesture blew Mustafa away. He was more shocked than hurt, and the anger would come later. He never tried that move again. Mustafa thought later that she was indeed a good woman, for whatever dude she was with; still it was a devastating blow against their history. Even though Garneta was kicking the doors in to the visiting room every other weekend, he missed J. Marie and wanted her back. He thought about what a guy at the Diagnostic Center in Baltimore told him, this was in '83 and he and J. Marie were still a loving couple. Goldsmith was a black guy from Baltimore and had done a bit or two before. He told Mustafa how a guy's woman could be like the steel ball in a pin-ball machine. Then he began simulating how that ball bounces from post to post, off the cushions and the sides, but when it runs itself out eventually, that ball's gonna drop in the hole. Mustafa liked that analogy and reflected on it often through the years, but for now, he wanted to beat that nigga with a baseball bat, whomever the coon-booger was, Mustafa wanted to kill 'em!

He continued writing the children, occasionally he'd get letters from them too, especially when Candie started learning to use the school's computers. He still pressed her and J. Marie to locate and send the photo of her and he on the hill of "Our Lady of Perpetual Help" overlooking the city next to J. Marie's red Mustang. It was his favorite picture of he and Candie together. She couldn't have been more then fifteen months old. Three months later he was in prison. She looked more like her ole dad than of J. Marie. Mustafa liked that. Mike D'Angelo, on the other hand, favored his mom. All in all, Mustafa reflected over how blessed he was, and thankful Allah bestowed upon him such a beautiful family.

Mike D'Angelo started playing little league football several years ago. Now he was one of Gwynn Park High's star running backs, and a good kick returner too. Mustafa was looking at his stats in the sports section of the *Washington Post*. Mike was scoring touchdowns and racking up yardage. Channel 50 showed highlights on Sunday evenings. It was a most exciting time for Mustafa to see his boy on TV, running the ball. Mike D'Angelo, Mustafa reflected, was an all-around good dude, and the relatives had only good things to say about him. At the rate he was going, he might even be eligible for a sports scholarship next year out of high school. Still, Mustafa encouraged both children to aspire towards high and tangible academic ideals. He'd explain about the influence Islam had on the slaves brought from Africa to the seaports of the Southern states; that's where Connie's side was from. The Lucas's were four generations out of S.E. Anacostia, though later Grandaddy Lucas moved to 10th and Maryland Ave., N.E., then on to the house up on North Capital and W streets, N.W., where he died. J. Marie never talked about her roots, where the Williams's came from, or Lou's side; he suspected somebody somewhere had something to do with an Asian because of J. Marie's semi-slanted eyes. Something real strange was going on in that gene pool, and Mustafa convinced himself, half-jokingly, a Chinese was involved. He put Candie down with "Angela Davis." Because of her light complexion, he'd let her identify with Angela coming up. Mustafa knew growing up fair-skinned had its cons as well as its pros.

The same way Mustafa was escorted on foot when he had to report to the hospital, so was it the next morning. He was given three large boxes early that morning, in which he placed all his belonging, then into a laundry cart. He'd miss several brothers he'd gotten extremely close to at the Pen's annex, especially Abdul-Haqq and Abu Bakr, who he knew from the Old Pen, and also his cellie Hasan Salis. He was glad he was able to pay Abdul-Haqq the money he promised to pay him for breaking his TV the previous month. Mustafa was thankful Garneta was "caked up" as she was; she sent Abdul-Haqq a hundred-dollar money order within the week. He'd (Mustafa) already had forty dollars or so in his account, and gave Abdul-Haqq the rest in commissary. The story, although it set him back a few dollars, was funny as hell, and got laughs every time he told it. How, while on a chair trying to adjust the antenna, the chair began sliding out beneath him, and he and the TV crashed to the floor. Mustafa landed on his back with his head hitting the floor next. He was temporarily unconscious.

He arrived at the Cutt by 9:00 that morning. While waiting in "center hall," he saw several familiar faces, some thought he was packed up to go home or to "camp". This was a strange phenomenon to be thought "going home." Where he'd been over the past ten years, no one went home, because maximum security inmates had too much time. Several Muslims passed by, checking him out. They greeted him with "salaams." He returned the greetings. It was the proper etiquette of the Muslim's mannerism. The wait in center hall to be assigned a cell or dormitory bed could be a precursor for the grave. Any and every one walked by in route to the main dining hall to get medication as well as hospital affairs; and/

or speak with the "brass" about one thing or another. You're on display for all to see, so if you've had a beef with a guy in another jail and now you're here; well, now everybody and their mama knows it. They also know you will be leaving center hall shortly to get to your new sleeping quarters. He'll wait for you from some covert observation place. This joint was over eighty years old and filled with out-of-the-way corners, cubby holes, poorly lit areas, and outright blind spots. The Cutt was an assassin's paradise.

After the clerk gave Mustafa his pass with his assigned cell, a couple Muslims were there helping him carry his property as well as to provide their own personal escort. He was assigned housing on the kitchen workers' tier, F-2; all the cells in the Cutt were single units. As small as they were, Mustafa wondered how they could be anything but. The average-sized man could extend his arms and touch both walls. Hakeem (D. Wise) was on f-4, two tiers upstairs. He was working in the college office with Mu'meen, who was running the college program's entry office. Mustafa was added on the list to begin classes for the spring semester. He had about ninety credits and needed thirty more before obtaining a degree in psychology.

The Cutt was wide open; that is to say, it was like the Pen. As far as going from point A to point B uncontested by an officer, it was unlike the Pen; however, everything was inside, and the only thing a man had to go outside for was for gym and yard. Of course, to get to the gym, one had to go through the yard. Mustafa arrived in The Cutt during the month of "Ramadhan." The Muslims all over the world were fasting from sun up till sundown. This evening, he went on a special "count out" for the Sunni Muslims in the kitchen, where he met all the brothers on the location. He met the Imam, another brother Rasheed (in his mid-forties), spoke briefly with Hakeem, and was surprised to learn Hakeem was not only following the sunnah, but was the Wazir and assistant

Imam. Alhamdulillah Hakeem had learned more of the fundamentals and regulations of the Deen (religion) of Islam; he was showing strong signs of adherence. Mustafa saw Nuri too, who used to help set up fights through the recreation department while in the Pen through Mack Lewis's gym. Nuri was the treasurer of this community. He and another brother name Mustafa (Alexander). They took care of the donations and money vouchers. This was a seemingly very organized group of Muslims to be so large a Jamaat (community). There were about one hundred.

Mustafa found out many of the brothers slept in the "back dorms," of which there were four: H-annex, H-dorm, I-dorm, and J-dorm. H,I, and J dorms held one hundred four beds. H-annex was like an honor dorm that only held about twenty-five. This was the most laid back of all the dorm-like settings, perhaps in the entire Division of Corrections. Imam Rasheed slept in I-dorm; they called it "Little Mecca" because there were so many Muslims sleeping in it. The back dorms could be very dangerous, because they were the farthest away from center hall and had a low officer presence. Most of the Muslims at the Cutt knew of Mustafa Lucas. They'd heard of some of his leadership qualities and escapades, as well as his adherence and diligence to the Deen while he was Out Back. They heard some of the tales through the prison grapevine all the way in Baltimore while at the Pen. Kareem Muhammad, the outside coordinator, had words with Mustafa last year during Ramadhan. Mustafa accused Kareem of being insensitive to their needs and not doing for them (the Muslims Out Back) as he was for those at the Cutt. Mustafa's new Imam Rasheed convinced Mustafa to try getting moved from F-2 to the back dorms with them.

Instead of I-dorm, Mustafa was sent to H; Rasheed thought he could help restore a degree of order there; H-dorm Muslims were "off the hizzy!" They listened to loud music, some were getting high, profanity was used in regular conversation, and they had no respect for the Muslim Amir (leader for the dorm), because he was a part of it too. Despite Mustafa's controlling nature, he opted to lay back as best he could, gradually amalgamating himself into the group. His presence toned them down some, but nowhere near an acceptable lifestyle for the more conscience of Muslims.

Moore-El was in H-dorm too, so was Davis-El, who was nicknamed "Peacemaker." they had a strong presence in their community (the Moorish Science Temple). Moore-El was one of Mustafa's teammates in the Pen. He and Davis-el were transferred out before the hostage taking and before Cadillac had his head cracked in three-yard. Moore-El was another one that wasn't particularly pleased Mustafa assaulted their homeboy on behalf of the Muslims. Like the others, he too had to let it go, because, for one, Mustafa was now too big in the Muslim community to risk reprisals, the second reason was, though 'Lac was cool, he still had that cloud hanging over his head from the aftermath of the Jewelry store robbery. It wasn't long before Mustafa settled into a routine that kept him out of the dorm for most of the day. Working the hospital during the day and college classes afterwards, the days seemed to pass quickly because he was staying busy.

In the morning, just before sunrise, he'd make the rounds in the dorm, waking the brothers up for the morning salat. Though he'd only been Muslim for three years, he knew more Qur'an and hadith than the others. Besides, the men accepted that perhaps his character was better than theirs. All this is according to the criterion of who's most worthy to lead salat, or be Imam. As always, Mustafa attended all Islamic study classes and tried hard to maintain a high standard of good conduct. He was still learning about the Islamic way of life, about the Qur'an, about the ways of the Prophet Muhammad, and interacting with his Muslim brothers according to the Qur'an and the sunnah. A brother he'd met for the first time named "Umar" (Leon Mason) informed him one day, while the two were at the gym, that unless he was married to Garneta, he should not be kissing her during her visits.

In the two years and few months she'd followed him from the various jails, no one had imparted this information upon him. Not his first Imam (Rasheed), not Mu'tazz or Wali Aquil, nor other Muslims that had seen him in the visiting rooms with her through the years. The next time he encountered her, he'd have to explain it as best he could. He quickly shot out a letter to Garneta that night to prepare her, so there wouldn't be that awkward time before or after the embrace. During the visit they talked about it. She didn't like it, but like Candie when he told her he wouldn't be sending Christmas and birthday cards, she understood. The kissing was out, but that didn't stop Mustafa from the subtle breast and rear-end brushes during the hugs, until Umar mentioned it a few weeks later.

Mustafa wondered how the hell he was finding all this information out about his visiting room activities – were there spies in the lurk?

He said, "Mustafa…brother…you don't understand. Unless a woman is your wife, you cannot have that type of contact with her. There are no girlfriends in Islam." Of course Umar was absolutely unequivocally right. He was in accord with the information on intermingling found in the sunnah of the Prophet Muhammad, and better yet the Qur'an. When Mustafa broke the news to Garneta the following visit, she was apoplectic.

"If you don't want to be bothered with me anymore, just say so. You don't need to play these games with me!"

"Garneta, I'm just finding this information out. I'm not playing games with you…" The two went on, back and forth, for several exchanges, until Mustafa tired of it, finally telling her that this was Islam. It's different from the life of doing basically whatever turns you on, and that's the way it is.

This was the first time Mustafa came close to remarrying after J. Marie. Garneta wanted it, but Mustafa knew he had a ways yet to go before his release, and didn't want her "on hold" that long. Connie was pissed too that her son wouldn't even give Garneta hugs now. "As good as she's been to you, Skippá, damn. The least you could do is…"

Mustafa told Connie (respectfully of course), "Look, Ma, you know I'll ride with you on everything else, but this is my way of life. It's Islam! I don't have to kiss or hug a woman to let her know I appreciate her kindness, especially if it's going against Islam." And that was that.

The Cutt's Imam, also named Rasheed, was the most learned Muslim inmate Mustafa ever met. He was more knowledgeable about the Deen than some Muslim chaplains/coordinators. He had a vast Islamic vocabulary with keen insight into the grammatical structure of Arabic sentences. He also knew "Tajweed" (the correct pronunciation and beautifying of the Qur'anic recitation). He oversaw the class setting and curriculum.

Rasheed gave Mustafa basic Islamic literature to read, as well as cassette tapes of lectures recorded from Muslim scholars, and "Shaikhs" to listen to. Mustafa got his first introduction to an obligatory concept every Muslim should know about called "Aqeedah," the belief system, or creed of the Muslims, male and female. In the reformer Muhammad ibn Abdul-Wahhab's famous book *Kitabul ul Tawheed*, it is defined as "a religious tenet upon which the heart and mind are settled, and to which one holds and adheres." Under it are many subheadings or topics that Muslims must know about and implement or refrained from daily. The Muslims Aqeedah is built upon or based on "Tawheed" – maintaining the belief that Allah is the only true God worthy of worship, and that He is "The true and only Rabb (Lord), the maintainer of everything." The opposite of Tawheed is "Shirk."

The first thing Mustafa told Michael D'Angelo and Candi cane when he came into the correct Islamic understanding, and when they were of the age of discernment, was what Luqman the Wise told his son, when he said to his son while instructing him, "O my dear son…" (he told Candie, "…my dear daughter") "do not associate anything/ no partners with Allah…" (don't commit Shirk). "This is a great wrong." Qur'an- Surah Luqman (31) verse 13

Before Rasheed was released to go home in 1994, and while Mustafa was housed in I-dorm, he asked him who he thought would make for the best Imam after he left. Rasheed already knew his personal selection for the leader upon his departure, but was curious who Mustafa had in mind. At the time, there was another Muslim whose name was also Mustafa that knew more surahs (chapters) from the Qur'an, he knew more ahadeeth (narrations by the Prophet), more of the grammar, etc. However, the people didn't care for him. They thought he was arrogant and egotistical among other things. Needless to say – the Jamaat may not have had a healthy transition. Mustafa said, "Saleem, I think, would be the best Imam after you, Akhi" (Akhi: my brother). Rasheed was pleased with Mustafa's selection. He too had decided in favor of Saleem. And that the other Mustafa would be best helping out with individual Islamic tutoring.

Pete Collins was a thug that grew up in West Baltimore's Gilmore Home Projects. By nineteen he was convicted of a double homicide and sentenced to two life sentences to run consecutive. Perhaps the lengthy sentence was because the homicides were in commission of a felony, and also a poor effort on behalf of his court-appointed attorney. Either way, Ms. Juanita's son would be laid down a while. He'd had a rough bout with drugs on the street and was battling it in prison up until 1992, just before Mustafa came from Out Back.

During his earlier years in the Pen, he'd joined the Nation of Islam, and was quickly promoted to captain of the F.O.I. He was 6'3", aggressive, and an imposing force. During the late 70s, after Elijah Muhammad's death, many members in the Nation left to begin practicing the true Islamic lifestyle, that of the sunnah. Though Saleem was not the most knowledgeable Muslim in the Jamaat he was by far the best qualified to lead the prison community. He'd earned a dual degree from college, and he was definitely a people person. Saleem wasn't just "liked," he was genuinely loved by the prison population – Muslim and Kaafirs (non-Muslims) alike. Mustafa thought Saleem could be one the funniest guys he'd ever met, and would often mention to Saleem to be more serious. At which his new Imam would only look at him, then take on an exaggeratedly serious expression, causing Mustafa to laugh, shaking his head while walking away in a mock disgust.

Saleem's more personal comrade and assistant for "special affairs," Hakeem, also possessed exceptionally unique leadership skills. Perhaps Saleem was more committed at the time to doing right by Islamic standards, and right now, Rasheed needed not just a good or great leader to replace him, but one walking the walk with the knowledge of the Deen.

It's said that great leaders wouldn't be so great were it not for the competent people around them. Saleem had an excellent group of men to assist him and help him run the affairs of the Jamaat. Mustafa was honored to be counted among them. Hakeem was the official problem solver. That's what he did, and he was good at it, and everybody knew it, including the administration. His knack for manipulating situations were legendary, so much so that Mustafa would often hear of a situation in the Muslim community and not feel slighted in the least when Saleem and Hakeem took council, only allowing him amongst them as an observer.

Mustafa would wonder how Hakeem would deal with the problem, then mentally document his tactics. Though Hakeem was older now, and his days of proving himself were far behind him, it was known, at 6'1" and carrying two hundred forty pounds these days, he was capable of handling things. In the old days, his psychotic, paranoid, delusional younger brother Bruce would seek out his older brother's stressor, and, sometime shortly there afterwards, a "10-10" would be called for an assault…somewhere. If for some reason Bruce was unavailable, usually because of lockup, then Hakeem would grease a palm or two with drugs or cash. The next thing one knew there was no longer a problem. Mustafa saw only one occasion when Hakeem got physical with someone. He removed "Kent" (Later Kent would become Jamal, one of Mustafa's closest companions) from the main dining hall of the Cutt for going back and forth with Kareem Muhammad in a heated verbal exchange during one Ramadhan. The most awe inspired Mustafa ever was with Hakeem's presence and intervention was in '95 when Mustafa was charged with a category 1, rule 102 (assault or battery on an inmate) and 105 (possession of a weapon or any article modified into a weapon).

It was because an old Penitentiary associate, "Big Rock" (the same Big Rock that carried young Chestnut to the Pen's infirmary after getting his head split down to the white meat for being caught in the middle of the beef with Tracy Bennett and that dastardly duo, Bruce and Francis). Apparently there was a discrepancy about a call Brother Nuri made during a flag football game that Rock took a vociferous stance against. He banged Nuri in the mouth, busting his chops till his grill was covered in blood. It was never mentioned whether there were Muslims in the courtyard observing it all – if there were, then they should've dealt with Rock on the spot. It shouldn't have fallen in Imam Saleem's hands to call a shot; nevertheless, after it was all laid out how it went down and that

Rock wasn't even playing in the game, Saleem sent a few brothers to his cell with an ultimatum.

Nuri wasn't a big dude, not a fighter, or out that mob by any sense of the word. He couldn't really hurt the big bully, and Rock should have gone for the "strike for strike sanction," instead he was arrogant and hostile. He told the brothers sent that "Ump, ain't nobody doing a motha F'in' thing to me!" Mustafa was sitting in an obscured position on the stairwell but could hear the exchange. Rock's walking buddy, "G," was with him. This attack on Nuri couldn't have been executed at a worse time by a Kaafir (non-Muslim). Saleem was the incoming Imam and had to let it be known this sort of transgression would not be tolerated while he was "holding it down."

Had Rock had just a little bit of an inkling of foresightedness, his impulsive nature would have been suppressed long enough to see outside the box, the bigger picture.

That despite Nuri being arrogant and snobbish towards some people, he was, for the most part, in very good standing with the Sunni Muslim community. As far as Mustafa was concerned, the retaliation against his old associate was for the sake of Islam, and he would've carried out the hit regardless of who the Kaafir was, anytime, anywhere. He knew he would have, because when Sewall Smith's goon squad slammed and roughed up Abdul-Haqq and Clarence in the property room not too long after the hostage taking, Mustafa and Clarence's cousin Michael (Malik) laid in wait for Warden Smith on his route from the level…strapped. Imam Rasheed knew nothing about this personal hit on the warden, the less he knew the better. Fortunately for all parties involved, Warden Smith didn't leave his office until the shift changed.

Mustafa fashioned a joint shortly after moving into H-dorm. It wasn't much, but it was his, and it sufficed. Before the sun came up the following day, another assault would occur, a "10-10" would be called.

By the time lunch was called, Mustafa was ready to leave on his mission. It wasn't uncommon for the Muslims sleeping in the back dorms to roll to the main dining hall together. They had peanut butter and apple jelly for lunch that day in silence. Rock was nowhere to be seen; maybe he'd catch up with him at the dinner meal.

Mustafa hated dragging stuff like this out; he wanted it over and done with. As they stacked the empty trays in the rack to leave – lo and behold, there the big fella was, posted up against the wall that headed out to the "slot area." He had on a slick black-and-grey pullover Coogi sweater, styling like he hadn't a care in the world, totally at ease as Mustafa approached him with an affable greeting. No sooner had Mustafa completed the salutation, he flipped his wrist up, which held the stiletto, catching Rock off guard with the first strike in the neck. The follow-ups were partially blocked before he took off running through the packed kitchen with Mustafa on his heels.

Of the five to seven COs on the scene, none intervened, nor did the two guys Rock was talking to before Mustafa approached him. After running a short way, to Mustafa's surprise, he stopped, spun, and came in low on his pursuer for the old Cheltenham-bust (scoop). Had Mustafa thought fast enough or anticipated this counter by Rock, he could have caught him in the face with the hard knee. As it stood, his only feasible option was to headlock him with his free arm, while continuing to plunge the knife into this raging bull's ribs and soft tissue on the sides.

Big Rock was in excellent shape for a guy of 6'3", cut up and strong as an ox. He was able to raise himself with Mustafa still locked onto his neck, shedding the sweater all the while, until that's all Mustafa was left with – an empty sweater. He was off again, running towards the back kitchen grill, leading to the cooking area where the cooks were with their big pot-stirring paddles, where mop wringers were, and maybe even a pan of hot grease he could use to throw. With Mustafa on his heels again, he slipped at the grill before getting it opened. Mustafa was on him with all fours stabbing at his neck, face, and chest. Rock was fighting desperately to defend himself, but Mustafa was pretty strong too. He was in excellent shape, and with a knife in his hand, he was frightening.

Finally, the officers felt they could safely disengage the two without themselves getting hurt. With the AIDS epidemic spreading throughout the prison system the way it was since '82, and hepatitis, no one was in a great hurry to be anywhere near an enraged bloody-knife-wielding convict. The officers were able to safely grab Mustafa, while he recognized one of them as being friendly towards him throughout his time there. Both men were escorted from the kitchen. Rock was showing fatigue from the punctured lung. He was taken to the Cutt's infirmary to await an outside emergency vehicle to University Hospital. Mustafa was examined too, then taken to a cell on lockup to await the disposition hearing.

For the next few days, the jail rang with the buzz of whispering and convoluted tales of the account; news of this magnitude not only circulates throughout the jail where it happened, but throughout the entire D.O.C. (Division of Corrections). Some guys in prison live just to be a part of jail-house history, and war stories. Just to be able to one day say, "I was there, nigga!" And then they'll add their own spin or twist to it to make it sound more exciting. Everybody has to embellish these narrations a little more than the person he or she heard it from.

At the time, Mustafa was writing a girl down at the women's jail, in Jessup also. Sharon Jones was at a Jumu'ah service Kareem Muhammad gave there a few weeks after the incident in the kitchen, where, for whatever reason, it came up, and right there in the midst of the Khutbah, after a brief gloss over of the account, she said, "Yeah, Mustafa." Kareem later mentioned it to Mustafa.

Meanwhile Saleem, Hakeem, and others made sure Mustafa was well taken care of. He had all the sweets he wanted, and some. Again, he was able to send something of his provisions to other Muslims on the hammer not so fortunate. Whenever he had to be escorted from the lockup wing for one thing or another – Jihad (Vandervall) was around to help provide the Muslims private detail. Traveling through the jail cuffed from the back can prove very dangerous, and it's when a man is most vulnerable.

Mustafa was housed on the flats. Rock returned from University a week later and was placed in a cell just above on two. He was transferred out to another jail just days before Mustafa was taken up for the infraction to face charges. This was a very serious charge; he could possibly be given more time added to his sentence. He knew if that happened, he'd have to keep it from Connie somehow. She'd have a fit if she found out he'd received more time. Hakeem was sent to represent him. Mustafa was glad to see him - not that the dearly respected brother and friend could do any more that what Allah decreed, but, nevertheless, grateful beyond words.

The two couldn't have been seated more than five minutes before the hearing officer, who knew Hakeem, exchanged small and subtle pleasantries, and then took on a more serious tone as she read the accusations. She began making comments like "Not sufficient evidence," and "I don't see where…" and then "I don't read where Mr. Lucas actually assaulted the victim, only there was a disturbance, and he was removed from the scene," and then about something being vague.

The next thing Mustafa knew, she said, "I'm going to have to dismiss the charges for lacking specificities in their allegations, and, and… (so forth and so on). Mustafa heard…"The conclusion of this hearing…" at which Hakeem didn't waste time with any thank yous or good looking outs, or none-a-that. He just backhand Mustafa's arm and said, "Let's go."

In Mustafa's mind, as well as those of the more spiritually conscious Muslims, the exoneration was again the outcome of what could only be described as divine intervention. Without a doubt, Allah had decreed what He will, and His will was done. The sergeant that wrote the infraction about the stabbing wrote it in a way to give Mustafa an out. Also, Three Fingers (Warden Smith), his assistant Warden Hutchinson, and Security Chief Singletary, for whatever reason, went for Mustafa in a real big way. Warden Smith caught Mustafa in passing one day, pulling him aside briefly, long enough to imply Rock was a damn bully and got what he deserved.

In 1995 Mustafa bumped heads with a long-standing inmate hospital worker at his job site named Sylvester. A three hundred plus pound "Tom" in every sense of the word. His younger brother Irving played on the Bears team with Mustafa at the Pen, and they'd gotten close, so Mustafa decided against going with thoughts of splitting his head at the job one afternoon. Warden Smith got Mustafa the job not long after he was sent from Out Back, and it would've surely been a slap in Three Fingers' face, so he quit.

For three months Mustafa idly waited for an opening in Wood Shop I. Finally, he got the call. Sometimes, he resigned, "You gotta take one on the chin for the greater good."

Another group of Muslims would soon become Mustafa's sahaba (companions), though he'd never forget nor sever the ties he forged in the Pen and Out Back in the Pen's annex. These were Muslims who within the past two years he'd come to love as his own mother's sons, even more so in some regards, because these brothers worshipped and knew Allah. They loved Islam; unlike his fornicating, "Khamra" (intoxicant) consuming, gambling, mushrik (one who associates partners with Allah) brothers – though he loved M.G., Anthony, Paul, and Carlyn dearly.

The Muslims' bond can easily become tighter than biological bonds, especially outside one's immediate family. Mustafa now had a corner aisle directly across from Imam Saleem. He was working in the spray room out in the wood shop, and about to graduate from the college program.

Two of the closer relationships Mustafa formed were with Dave Jacobs and Lemuel McGlone. Dave, whom also was called "Clean," was the son of legendary boxing trainer Dave Jacobs, Sr. Mr. Jacobs was one of the first, if not the first, trainers of Sugar Ray Leonard. The families, including the McGlones, all knew Ray, and watched him through the years. Dave Jacobs, Sr. was a devotedly religious Christian, who, when Mike Tyson, aka Malik Abdul Aziz, was released from prison had him in his camp. However, this union was short lived, because Mr. Jacobs didn't approve of the ex-champ's lifestyle, his consistent profanity, as well as other irreligious activities.

Clean also boxed. He trained some of the youngsters in the courtyard as well as in the dorm. He was a better trainer than he was a boxer in his day. Lemuel, whose Muslim name was Furqan, was married to Clean's sister Dianne. One usually found Furqan working on his case, trying to find a loophole, or studying the Arabic grammar, or exercising with weights and the heavy bag at the Cutt's gym. Though the Muslims in I-dorm, as well as in the entire Jamaat, were like family, most of the times, like family, they too would fuss and sometimes come close to throwing blows. Mustafa had a few close calls with Muslims fighting, which is a horrendous atrocity, once, even with Furqan and his son Ibn. Furqan's oldest son Lil Lem unfortunately got caught up on the streets of Landover, Prince George's County, Maryland, and was sentenced to the Division of Corrections.

While housed at the Maryland Correctional Institution in Jessup (M.C.I-J), he roughed a guy off for the guy's phone time and paid the price. Most stabbing victims in the joint (Maryland) are transferred; Little Lemuel was transferred to the Cutt. Not long afterwards, Furqan got him moved to I-dorm. By Allah's will, Little Lem, who actually wasn't little at all, but the same height as his old man (5'10"), only about forty pounds lighter, entered into Islam. The fruit doesn't fall far from the tree; they were a lot alike in many ways. They both had an infectious sense of humor. Lil Lem, who was now called Ibn, was more athletically gifted, and he could also fight. Mustafa took to Ibn and several of his hopper friends instantly. Ibn had heard a few tales of Mustafa's reckless adventures, and figured he wasn't the Jamaat's troubleshooter for nothing.

Graduation day was one of the proudest events Connie had ever been to for her oldest son. Probably more so than when he came home in his Class A's from boot camp, or when he and J. Marie gave her and Paul their first grandchild. Until now, Connie was the only one in the entire clan to earn a bachelor's degree, except her father. Now Mustafa had successfully completed the necessary requirements. He was in the 1995 graduating class of Coppin State College, along with Furqan, James "Turtle" Wells, and about twenty others. Furqan's family was there too, his mom, other son, Lemuel was there as a worker, with Clean, who also was Muslim now, Alhamdulillah!

Connie was there with all her children and Michael D'Angelo, not Candie because her and Mustafa were beefin', and he didn't want her spoiling his day. J. Marie was livid! In a phone conversation she had with him before the graduation, she attacked him verbally, insulting him relentlessly. "You 'spose to be a Muslim," and, "that degree don't mean nothing!" "That's your daughter; how you think it makes her feel?" She even said something disparaging about his mother! She covered all her bases; everything dear to Mustafa, J. Marie hit it and attacked it. They went back and forth for several minutes, until he barely got the "goodbye" out when he heard the phone slam. She was pissed, But Mustafa hardly cared. He and Candie would carry this feud for years. He would be so angry with her, he once told someone, "Man if I could sell that little vixen into the Asian slave market for two G's, they could have her." One day she'd hung up on him three times in a row. Though J. Marie gave her the tongue lashing of her young life and Michael D'Angelo got on her as well, Mustafa was so hot with her, his nose bled. He knew he'd have choked her out if he could just get his hands on her. It was amazing; here it was he was getting more respect from murderers, kidnappers, rapist, and thieves than he was his fifteen-year-old daughter.

He didn't have to wonder where it began unraveling. He definitely knew; he'd almost predicted as much a couple years ago. For years, they'd been communicating wonderfully, on the phone and in letters; Mustafa had even made her a beautifully constructed mahogany stained and glossed heart-shaped lockbox. Candie loved it. One day, while kickin' it with her over the phone while he was still in the hospital, Mustafa told her how it was so cool they were close now. She was only about twelve or thirteen when he explained he was afraid they'd not be as close, and he might even lose her for some years when she became interested in boys, and she saw they were just as interested in her. He told her he might lose her to them for several years, but "You'll be back," he told her. "When you find out them dudes are after one thing – eventually you'll be back, Candie, because my love is unconditional. I'll always be here for you, whether it's here in prison or I'm on the street by then."

Sure enough, when Candie got about thirteen, Mustafa could tell she was hurrying their conversation over the phone. Occasionally, Mustafa would ask, "Candie…do you have some place to go?"

The only other time he saw her after that within the next two years was when J. Marie brought her to see her father several months before he was carried out from the Cutt en route to University Hospital in an assassination attempt. Candie used to visit her cousins in Congress Heights in S.E., and would often babysit, Shakira (Cindy's granddaughter).

This visiting session with Mustafa, she brought her along, which caused her to be distracted and preoccupied, no matter how hard he tried making amends. In his own awkward way, Mustafa tried to soothe the tension between them, but Candie was implacable and defiant in some exchanges, until, finally, he couldn't take it anymore. He leaned over the visitors' counter from his seated position and, up close, told her, "Don't make me jump over this counter and stomp your ears together."

"That's why I don't come to see you now!" She hysterically screamed out, enough to draw attention from the other visitors.

Mustafa looked to J. Marie asking, "Who she talking to!"

"She's talking to you!"

Mustafa knew damn well who she was talking to. The question was more rhetorical than anything else.

Candie was upset and crying a little. Shakira, who was only a year or so old, seemed fidgety, reacting to the outburst. Mustafa sensed she was agitated that the ruckus upset her big cousin and keeper. Needless to say, the visit was a disaster. Moments later, the girls parted with little more than a mumble as they walked to the exit.

Back in the dorm, several brothers saw Mustafa was vexed as he made his way to the back where the majority of the Muslims slept. The greetings of "salaams" is always a tension breaker when a Muslim is ill at ease, and it's congratulatory when he or she is jubilant. Mustafa greeted the brothers with "As-Salaamu Alaikum," then went and pressed his bunk, fully-dressed with his boots still on.

Saleem El-Amin came over after a while like he was looking for a book out of Mustafa's vast library of Islamic literature, seeing his brother's eyes weren't shut but looking to the ceiling. He knew for the past year his friend was going through something heavy with Candie. The two, Furqan and Clean, whose name was "Jamal" now often made light of it all. Clean, or Jamal rather, had a daughter several years younger than Candie, and Mustafa often reflected back when his and Candie's relationship was as loving and open as Jamal's and Shayla's.

Saleem could be a riot sometimes in the mist of trying to cheer Mustafa up.

"Is everything alright, Akhi?" the Imam asked.

(Akhi is Arabic for 'my brother.')

"That was J. Marie, and that doggone Candie."

Saleem smiled, "What color was her hair today?" He was referring to Candie changing her hair color during her defiant period to a blondish-orange, which, seeing it, had left Mustafa stupefied.

Mustafa told his brothers about the visit as they sat around laughing. It was perhaps the same one he told, in his most humorous storytelling voice, of how, once, as father and daughter, while exchanging information, Candie used the phrase "Back in the day," referring to three years ago. "Back in the day, huh?" Mustafa couldn't hide the sarcasm. Though he knew his daughter was intelligent, he thought this maxim she used was both funny and disrespectful to an older person. As if she were actually a part of some serious "old-head" history.

Mustafa laughingly told his small audience, "Man if she wasn't making her rounds through here half-way regularly, I'd have put the big hand on her." Mustafa tightened his lips, bringing his open hand as if to slap someone, until the brothers all rolled with laughter.

Saleem knew these were now tumultuous times for father and daughter. Not just for him, but a girl growing up without a father on the scene is no picnic either. He and his own sisters had come up under similar conditions, also there was the book Jonetta Rose-Burruss wrote *Whatever Happened to Daddy's Little Girl?*, where she described a condition girls can go through that she explained as "fatherless daughter syndrome."

Everyone knew, despite Mustafa's rough exterior and not having her at his graduation ceremony, that he truly loved her. These dudes, Muslims included, had desensitized this clearly respected and loved brother to a degree. Saleem and Hakeem talked about their own take of Mustafa, that they should speak with him about taking some of this stuff with a grain of salt. They feared he would someday get additional time for seriously hurting someone before he got out. Ultimately causing him to receive more time and winding up growing very old in the joint like so many others that ran their bits up – eventually dying here.

Saleem and Hakeem both knew what they were talking about. They themselves often reflected upon a similar fate. Saleem had double life for felony murders, and Hakeem life for contract murder. Governor Parris Glendening had a press release in front of the Maryland House of Corrections that year stating life meant just that…"life," and that unless you were old or terminally ill, you weren't going anywhere. He'd even went so far as to pull in all the lifers that were out in the camps and on work release.

All this because the straw that broke that proverbial "camel's back:" one of Mustafa's old workout partners and fellow hospital worker (Rodney Stokes) made pre-release status, cut into a secretary, and couldn't handle the rejection when she dumped him. He shot her in the head and then turned the gun on himself. "Graveyard Love." Connie use to call it – "If I can't have you nobody will!"

Islamically, Mustafa was doing most all the things good conscious Muslims attempt to do. Amongst other things, he was fasting three days each month (on the Islamic calendar), enjoining the good upon the people, and calling them away from the bad. He'd make the late-night prayer called "Qiyyamul Lail" (the night standing).

This would be each night when everyone else was asleep, in the very early hours. On Tuesdays, he would awaken Saleem to pray the individual salat too, and on Wednesdays he'd shake Jawad's bunk.

He once read in a book of ahadeeth where The Prophet's (S.A.A.W) youngest wife Aisesha (R.A.) and daughter of his closest companion "Abu Bakr" (R.A.) sprinkled water on the face of Prophet Muhammad sometimes to awaken him. Mustafa use this on Imam Saleem whenever he didn't respond to the second call to rise. Mustafa thought it was so funny to see the big brother slapping at his face thinking perhaps an insect was accosting him. After several seconds, he'd open his eyes to see Mustafa smiling at him, or extending the salaams quietly as he walked back to his own aisle.

None of the Muslims wanted to be touched directly when being awakened, but instead preferred to simply be called, or, at most, have the bunk tapped. Mustafa and Joe (Yusuf Jennifer) were the easiest to arouse. All one had to do was call their name once, and their eyes would pop open. With Mustafa, he'd bolt straight up in bed, shake his head, and say the salaams and "What's up?" He was adamant about no one ever putting their hands on him to awaken him – "Not unless you can get J. Marie up in here," he'd joke.

He had no less than five specially made "joints" in his aisle – spread out in various places – that he'd personally fashioned at the woodshop. Actually, no one wanted to enter his aisle, much less put their hands on him whilst he slept.

Chapter 21

KEVIN REYNOLDS AND MUSTAFA WENT back to their Patuxent Institution days in the mid to late 80s. They'd been cool for years despite the separation from jails. He was short-statured, with a real slick bebop 1960s-something walk. He was outta the worst streets of West Baltimore. He didn't bother anybody and nobody bothered him. He had a crew that went for him in a real big way and they all looked out for one another like "family." When Ibn (Lil Lem) was at M.C.I.-J. it was Kevin's phone time he roughed off, in which he was ultimately stabbed, resulting in his move to the Cutt. Now, Ibn wasn't exactly sure but could swear one of the new transfers into the house (the Cutt) was the guy. Two days had passed when Ibn got back to Furqan, telling his dad he needed to square this thing, that Kev was one of the guys that hit him up.

It was agreed via mediators the two would fight head-up on Saturday morning in the gym's bathroom. The rules were just that no weapons could be brought and no one was to stop it no matter who was on the receiving end of the beat down. Mustafa figured Lil Kev agreed to it not necessarily thinking he could take Ibn, but because he had heart and was a stand-up dude. Kevin thought win, lose, or draw, this would bring closure to an unfortunate situation.

When Saturday came they all met at the gym as if they were to work out. Too many people in the bathroom would definitely draw a tip to the gym officers, so the two would go in alone, or so it was said. Mustafa definitely didn't need to go in there, so he sat off on the other side of the gym's basketball court, where he could see blurs of people and the fighting through the bubbled six-inch frosted glass. Furqan was inside with Ibn, and Lil Pizza and another of Kev's homies were inside on Kev's behalf. Several others stood in the doorway, spilling outside the bathroom's anteroom. From his position Mustafa could see the usual movements for a fight and anticipated in a few moments Ibn would bloody Kevin's face or drop him, and that'd be it. Suddenly there was unanticipated movement not conducive to the usual everyday prison-type punching. He recognized Furqan's form through the frosted glass and that he was reacting to something down low, as were the other men. Mustafa broke to the door; not surprisingly, no officers were alerted. When he pushed through the crowd Ibn had Kevin pinned face up and was pummeling him. If that wasn't enough he snatched a pair of hair clippers from a barber standing by and proceeded to jab Kevin in the face. As would be expected, that's when "Pizza," Kevin's friend, intervened, and that's what drew Furqan into it; the only thing left for anyone else to do was observe. After all four men were disengaged Pizza began a vociferous tirade of insults complete with death threats to Furqan and Ibn: "You motha-fu– are dead, dead!"

Pizza and Mustafa were never on more than just tolerable terms. Shorty used to practice Islam; he'd go to Jumu'ah service on Fridays, classes occasionally, and would lead the brothers of H-dorm in salah. Struggling is a major part of Islam, that's what "Jihad" means; to struggle or strive. Some Muslims too easily give in to their desires – Pizza was one of those and when his home-boy Roper moved into H-dorm, when Mustafa (the Sheriff, as some called him) went to I-dorm, H-dorm soon became a haven for the worst of the Muslims. Pizza began openly getting high, didn't fast the following Ramadhan, and abandoned the five obligatory prayers. It was obvious he wasn't practicing Islam; eventually he went on the hammer for dirty urine. When he came off he was moved and temporarily placed in I-dorm just until a bed became available with his cronies in H-dorm.

When Mustafa heard him threaten the lives of Muslims, red flags and lights were waving and going off. He wasn't 100% certain whether Pizza was speaking just out of the side of his neck and only motivated by anger or whether he was hell-bent on following through with the proclamation. The crowd dispersed from the gym to the courtyard; the participants and spectators went their separate ways. Mustafa wasn't sure who went where; he himself went to sit on the bleachers, to reflect.

A short time later two old Penitentiary pals approached to lessen the severity of their friend's threat. Mustafa was only half listening; he remembered fragments of their intercession. Mustafa thought he remembered hearing something about "We got him," or "We'll take care of him"? When the yard closed for morning rec, Mustafa walked through I-dorm to his bunk area; Pizza slept a few bunks down. He had all intentions of letting things go, at least until Saleem or Hakeem mentioned otherwise or until receiving what he perceived as a direct threat. No sooner had the thought of the direct threat entered his mind when he heard something hit the floor where Pizza was bending down fumbling under his bunk. Without giving further thought to other possibilities, Mustafa assumed he was getting his joint to bring the McGlones a move, one or both.

Mustafa's mind was definitely playing tricks on him, and it was perhaps the whispering of "The Shaytan" inciting him to do evil. He snatched up one of his joints and quickly made his way to Shorty's aisle, raising the knife overhead and coming down. Mustafa remembered the look in his victim's eyes being the same as that of the Hayes brothers just before shooting them in the head. Pizza threw up his hands to try warding off the downward thrust but was overpowered by strength and repetition until he collapsed to the floor in a puddle of his blood. Mustafa went down with him to finish him before the dorm officer was alerted by the deadly silence, a sure indication all was not well in a dorm setting. Mustafa plunged the blade into his head as far as he could, all the while looking to see if the CO was on the catwalk; he was. Mustafa quickly left the bloodied body to make his way to the shower before the dorm was swarmed with blue shirts. After grabbing his shower grip and throwing his clothing in the trash, he was in the shower for only a few minutes before an authoritative command ordered him out and to report to the front day room area. The body had already been removed by the time he grabbed up fresh clothes to put on. There was a blood trail leading to the front day room with a large puddle that everyone had to sidestep before entering it. Mustafa took his place amongst the ten or so men already awaiting further instructions. The ten to twelve awaiting officers had everyone remove their shirts and show their hands before they were allowed back in the bunk area. The COs were looking for signs of a fight or blood.

Mustafa regretted not clearing things with the Imam, too bad he had been asleep.. Though Saleem didn't say anything you could tell he was disturbed. The tension throughout the jail that afternoon on through the evening was as thick as Pompeian ash. Around 5:00 pm Mustafa was summoned to center hall, where an investigator from the police barracks was waiting to ask questions. Mustafa had been investigated earlier that year for a knife-manufacturing charge. Someone dropped a note on him and the investigating lieutenant with two COs came out to apprehend him directly from the wood shop. The investigation started there; they searched his locker, then took him inside the jail straight to administrative segregation. That's where they dropped the ball, because on lockup Mustafa sent word by the tier runner to get one of the brothers to get three of the joints out of the aisle – these were the ones he hadn't stashed in good out-of-the-way spots. The other two or three were cool; they'd never find them. One was in his big radio; for the other two they'd have to flip the large metal cabinet completely over. He had others stashed in various places throughout the prison – even one out in the courtyard under the bleachers near the horse-shoe pit. One was in the false bottom of the specially constructed shoe bin in the musalla (prayer area); he even had Mu'meen put one around the school. The shake-down crew not only missed the obvious but failed to recognize knife-making paraphernalia in his aisle. They didn't make the connection with the black electrical tape, duct tape wound around a pencil, sandpaper, and even the flat stone doubling as a pet or art; they missed it all.

He stayed on the hammer with that one for three weeks, until Warden Smith's assistant came off vacation and found they didn't have anything on him. Mustafa was allowed to go back to work, where the plant manager, mindful of the implications, told him, "As long as your work is satisfactory I don't care what goes on inside the jail."

Now Mustafa had an outside police investigator asking a bunch of questions he had to know Mustafa wasn't giving a truthful answer to, other than "Do you know the victim?" These investigators don't actually expect anyone involved in a prison stabbing to confess. It's all a formality for the report they must turn in – obviously someone dropped a note on him. An hour later leaving center hall he decided to drop by H-dorm to see Pizza's people. Without a joint he threw caution to the wind to get whatever these dudes had in store for him over with.

"Allahumma anzil nasraka" (O Allah send down your help)

The back dorm's entry grill was just newly reconstructed to be a "double" grill, each five feet from the other. There now was a small cell-like space to wait in before getting access into the front rec area part of the dorm, where the phone bank, hot pot, ping-pong, and a pool table was. However, if the first grill was opened one could walk up to the second one to talk through the bars/grills to communicate with whoever was in the rec area. The dorm officer was just off to the side behind a fenced-in catwalk; from there he operated both grills and could patrol the dorm without actually coming into it. The catwalk encircled the entire dorm's sleeping quarters.

When Mustafa approached, the first grill was open, allowing him to talk with whoever was on the other side in the rec area. Kevin was the first one to the grill; he didn't look too bad from the fight with Ibn earlier that morning. Two others joined him as he and Mustafa spoke.

"Kevin, I did that to Shorty, nobody else was involved. You know he and I were never on the best of terms. I know y'all don't like it but that's the way it is, so when you bring it – bring it to me, nobody else."

"Nobody else was involved, Mustafa?"

"Nope, just me."

By now there were seven of Pizza's boys listening in; one signaled the officer at the desk to let him out. As the grill began closing behind Mustafa so that the one separating him from the guys in the rec hall could be opened, he missed it. Mustafa was so engrossed in conversation he failed to recognize what was unfolding before him. He failed to make the connection of one grill being closed and the other opening until he saw Michael Grey, or Melvin's, hand coming towards his head with something shiny in it. Reflectively, he put up his left arm to ward it off and threw a right to his assailant's face, which knocked him back, but the floodgate was opened for the others that poured into the cubical on him. He noticed they all had something in their hand, something shiny with a sharpened side or a point. Mustafa backed up to the wall, and for the next sixty to ninety seconds, threw no fewer than two hundred lefts and rights, straight right hands, and uppercuts, at his attackers, some at the air and some finding flesh.

There were so many men trying to get at Mustafa they were getting in each other's way. Pee-Wee went down to try taking his legs from him but only managed to get one, which left Mustafa hopping on one leg, but still flicking out jabs. Ironically, once while Saleem observed Mustafa's workout routine, he'd mentioned the "one-legged hop" for balance. Now it came in handy, but Mustafa hardly had time to think about it. Though he was feeling several stabs, after the initial two or three the rest only felt like thorn pricks. It helped that he had his back to the wall and that they seemed more fearful of his jabs than he was of the knives.

Finally, the officer must have realized if Mustafa went down or died on his watch or post he'd have some explaining to do. After what seemed an eternity for Mustafa, the young CO began closing the grill. Now the group had a choice to make: stay in between the two closed grills to try to finish what they started, or bail back into the rec hall. After the grill closed the first one opened, allowing Mustafa to get the hell outta there; before he left, however, he looked down and picked up his kufee, which had been knocked off his head during the melee. Mustafa also saw a slick watch on the ground, obviously belonging to one of his attackers, and he pocketed it. "To the victor go the spoils" he remembered reading somewhere, "Alhamdulillah!" (All the Praise and Thanks be unto Allah) he said, for allowing him to walk away from it.

Though not unscathed, he knew he needed to get to the infirmary. There were too many body hits for something vital not to be affected. He first headed to the hospital, but after a few steps down B-flats he decided against it, opting instead to beat it up to I-dorm; maybe the brothers could patch him up and maybe it wasn't as bad as he thought. He was able to check himself in the security mirror just outside I-dorm. Aside from the blood running from a head wound, he appeared at first glance to be okay. There were small and a few large holes all over the black long-sleeved shirt from the knives; it looked like the shirt was dry-rotting or full of machine-gun spray.

One thing Mustafa picked up from his father if he didn't pick up anything else was to always, ALWAYS, keep a napkin or something for wiping a snotty or a bloody nose. Now, at forty, he was never without one of the brown state paper towels in his pocket or folded up in his sock. He quickly pulled it out, spit on it, and wiped off as much of the blood from his head and face as he could; just good enough to get past the dorm officer. He put on the kufee to help conceal the wound and slow the blood from running down to his face.

Inside the dorm he greeted the officer with a smile though his side hurt like hell, and suddenly he was having problems catching his breath. The CO nodded in return while Mustafa quickened his step to the back before the blood ran again. Walking fast past several Muslims' bunks, including Imam Saleem's, on his way to the back showers, he only said, "They got me, come fix me up."

They quickly followed him into the large open shower, where he sat on the bench allowing himself to be helped out of his shirt. The last thing he remembered before going unconscious was a look in Saleem's eyes that said, "Man, I don't know where to start." This crew, these brothers of Mustafa's, weren't doctors but he was in good hands – prison "cut men" and jailhouse surgeons have been known to stitch up many a stab wound without alerting the officers. However, this was too tall an order. They had to get him outta there before he died. Mustafa was unconscious now; someone snatched Saleem's wooden bed board from under his mattress to use as a stretcher. He was then rushed to the front of the dorm, where someone yelled, "Open the damn grill, CO, we need to get him to the infirmary!"

The officer saw the bloodied man on the board he knew as Lucas, but he'd just passed by. The officer now thought maybe Lucas had been hit when he'd gone in the back of the dorm just now. Nevertheless, he didn't hesitate to let the men out. He'd get to the bottom of it later, or better yet the investigators would have to come back. *Man!* he thought, *What's going on around this camp all of a sudden?*

Once inside the infirmary the Muslims were directed to place their fallen brother on the table inside treatment room #2 and told by the physician's assistant they'd have to leave. The P.A. proceeded to stop as much of the bleeding as he could by stitching up the larger wounds until the emergency vehicle arrived, which, surprisingly enough, was only ten minutes or so after he was brought in.

He began reciting "Al Kalima Shahadatayn" (The testament of faith) over and over again.

"La ilaha illallah, wa anna Muhammadar – Rasulullah" (There is no god except Allah (none worthy of worship except Allah) and Muhammad is the Messenger of Allah).

"La ilaha illallah, wa anna Muhammadar Rasulullah."

"La ilaha illallah, wa anna Muhammadar Rasulullah."

When the emergency technicians arrived, a man and woman, Mustafa's recitation of al-Kalima was only a little more than a whisper. They rolled him out to the back entrance, then outside to the awaiting ambulance. He began to feel rain beating down on his face. The rain was refreshing to him, it was cool and pleasant, but the Kalima was only a mumble until the woman riding in the back with him told Mustafa, "Keep talking, baby. Keep on saying that thing you were saying."

Suddenly he became more alert and picked up the chant more strongly, clearly, and loudly than before. He looked at her; she was smiling at him and nodding her head.

This time he didn't get to enjoy the ride into the city as he usually did while going to court, or like when Richard X (Basir) and Jackson-El broke his leg at football practice back at the Penitentiary. The next time he came to from unconsciousness, he remembered being in what his mind could only conceive of as a surgery or operating room. Someone was fooling around with his side, he could barely breathe, and then something was forcibly jammed in between his ribs, causing him to cry out in excruciating pain; then he was out again.

After the last stabbing incident, the shift commander had no other recourse but to place the Cutt on lockdown status, at least for the remainder of the evening. The next day news of the stabbings were on the channels: "Ralph Lucas and Robert Nedd were in serious but stable condition with multiple stab wounds at an area hospital…" Jamal (Clean) took it upon himself to contact Connie to inform her of Mustafa's plight. That she was to call the prison to find out more information about her son.

The assassination attempt was a devastating blow to the Muslim community throughout the Maryland Prison system. That the "Kufar" (non-Muslims) would have the nerve to hit and bring down a pillar of the Muslim community was unfathomable. Once thought to be untouchable, Mustafa's strike sent shock waves around jails and sent a message that neither Mustafa nor anyone else was beyond reprisal.

When the lockdown status was lifted, any and every one who'd ever had a beef with a Muslim and still harbored animosity were on board, siding with the retaliators. They posted up aligning B-flats to let it be known, "Here we are…what's up?" Hakeem was sent to H-dorm to try to squash any further bloodshed. News reached the Muslim community at M.C.I.-J., where Wali Aquil was. The two had camped out under the stars after the hostage-taking five years ago. Now his friend and brother was in a very bad way. He encouraged the brothers to make "du'a" for Mustafa.

Abdul Haqq was still in the Pen's Annex (Out Back). The last time he saw Mustafa was when the Muslims in the annex had a problem with the new Muslim chaplain, Sauddiq, they were considering bringing him a move because they thought he was working for the Feds, conspiring against them. Hakeem, Saleem El-Amin, and Mustafa were all escorted from the Cutt to meet with them at Jumu'ah. This was unprecedented; never in the history of Maryland's prison system had inmates been taken from one prison to another to calm a potentially volatile situation, but here they were, attending Jumu'ah service, then afterward talking to the brothers about resolving the matter, without killing Sauddiq. That was Mustafa for you, he thought, always some Islamic issue to resolve, he was always where the main body of Muslims were. So how could this have happened, so many wanted to know…

The bottom line was, it was Allah's Decree (His Qadr), and though Mustafa supplied the armament for the Jamaat and kept no less than five serious ones (joints) in his aisle at all times, he didn't have one on him when he needed it most. That was Allah's Qadr; for whatever reason He allowed it to happen. "Kun-faya-kun" (Be and it is), He says in Surah Al-Ghafir, aya (verse): 68 of the Qur'an.

It had been two days since Mustafa was carried away. No one knew much about his condition throughout the inmate population except the Muslim chaplain, Kareem Muhammad, and his information was fragmented. As usual, all types of rumors and fictitious tales circulated around the institutions.

When he came to, on the third day on the intensive care ward, he had five tubes or lines running from his body. The most aggravating was the fat one coming from the hole in his side, seeming to be pumping out dirty blood from his collapsed lung. He also wondered who the heck attached the small line in the hole of his penis, for urinating. He was a little embarrassed when the chubby brown-skinned nurse came to see how he was. He figured she was the culprit fooling around with him while he lay unconscious. After a brief exchange of greetings and the discomfort of the tubes and lines he asked for a small container of water. To her surprise it wasn't for drinking – he began a washing ritual, "Wudu," he called it, because he had to pray.

Later that afternoon he had visitors, Connie, M.G., who had been in the Air Force for several years, and Anthony, who wasn't long out of the Navy. At first he wondered why his family was suited up in protective or contamination-proof gowns complete with plastic face masks. Mustafa then remembered during his years working in the morgue he'd contracted a positive testing for T.B., although the X-rays were negative. It only meant he was once exposed to T.B.; he didn't actually have it. This was the first time Connie had seen one of her children in such a bad way since M.G. got his head split open playing in the basement with Skippá.

Despite the circumstances, it was a good visit for Mustafa; maybe not so much for Connie. He could see she was concerned and figured her pressure was up. In the future his closest Muslim brothers would be instructed to never under any circumstances get word to his mother or family about his injuries, ever! He did, however, get to impart upon his ole ma a noteworthy piece of information. As always if he had a sensitive topic to discuss with her, unless it was an emergency, he'd wait for her to "open the door." This time it was pertaining to children supposing to outlive the parent(s). "Ma, with all due respect, baby, it ain't etched in stone that I or any of your grandchildren are going to outlive you and if you think for a minute we all are – you're in for a rude awakening. Allah/God is the only one who knows *when* our lives will end, or *where* they will end. You might very well outlive not just some of your children but some of your grandchildren, too!"

A few days later Mustafa was discharged from the University of Maryland Hospital. For two days he'd be kept in the brand-new isolation ward at the Cutt's (Out Back) hospital facility. Because he had been in a wheelchair rumor spread he was paralyzed from the waist down. That was the last the Cutt would ever see of Mustafa Lucas. For the next six and half years, by the Grace and Mercy of Allah, the Most High; he would be granted 100% recovery and lead the Muslim body of "the Maryland Correctional Training Center" (M.C.T.C., or the new jail as it was called) as "Imam Mustafa."

His greatest fear when he first came into the "new jail" was that this new group of Muslims, all but a few, didn't really know him enough to look out for him while he was recovering. He couldn't even defend himself if things got thick. It wasn't that he didn't have the strength but that his stomach wasn't yet bound back together. He prayed Allah would strengthen him and spare him a humiliating and violent end. He was sure somewhere along the way he must've angered his Lord and that Allah had sent him here in the green rolling pastures of this large complex that looked like a college campus to die. He prayed each day the du'a (supplication) "Allahumma anzil nasraka" (O Allah send down your help).

The staples were removed after three weeks by the P.A. Sometimes while he sat on the rug during Jumu'ah service the wound would leak fluids from where the skin had yet to close completely. He had fresh stitches in his head, shoulder, and sides where one could tell he'd been in a battle. In two months he got to where he could fast-walk around the yard; later he'd do the skip-walk he used to do keeping up with Paul through Parkland and Shipley Terrace in S.E. Then he began to slow-jog and do pull-ups and light dumbbell presses with two younger Muslim brothers that had taken a liking to the older convict and brother; and besides, he knew a little something about Islam and practiced what he preached.

During the last few weeks of '96, Mustafa noticed before and after service a few brothers passing out football pool slips; furthermore, the Imam was running this operation. He had various brothers assisting him in this "Haram" (prohibited) gambling venture, distributing tickets to all seven housing units, including the huts, where he slept. When Mustafa saw all there was as evidence against the resident Imam, he pulled him up. "Say, I say, Brother Imam! You know you running this football pool is haram and you have to stop."

Of course Mustafa greeted him with salaams first, and then said a word straight to the point. And that was that, no more football pool, at least not amongst the Muslims at Jumu'ah.

In early '97 the Imam was granted a transfer to lesser security and Mustafa was elected the New Imam. He was fully recovered and had been Imam for about six months when two brothers from Housing Unit 3 told him a young guy that had just come into the jail on their tier was asking a lot of questions about Mustafa; questions that made Mustafa uncomfortable especially after coming out of that situation at the Cutt, which all of the Jamaat knew about. Mustafa began asking a few questions himself and when it was clear this young guy was not known to Imam Mustafa, he had no choice but to discourage him from inquiries. Three Muslim brothers caught him that afternoon in the shower stabbing him over twenty times; no one was charged. Mustafa sent a message with his own signature for all coming into the jail asking a bunch of dumb questions. It was unfortunate what had happened to the young guy, who perhaps had just heard the stories or maybe only wanted to meet the Imam. Then again, maybe he had another motive, and in that case he got what his hand called for.

Imam Mustafa ruled with an iron fist in a titanium glove; his first Imam (Rasheed) from the Pen and Abu Bakr would've been proud. Some referred to him as a tyrant because he wasn't taking any shorts. Delivering Khutbahs on Fridays he wore the traditional Islamic garb, called a jallibiyya or thawb, usually with a kufee to match. A newly arriving Muslim inmate that didn't know him would think he was an outside guest. During his second year as Imam, the outside Muslim body coordinator/chaplain was fired, leaving the body without a liaison to the administration. From the warden on down they soon recognized Mustafa as running the affairs of the Muslim community and since he was working in the chapel anyway, they'd occasionally allow him to utilize the former coordinator's office, without the telephone of course.

For one year Mustafa governed Islamic affairs with the skill and application of an outside chaplain. For the time he spent successfully leading the Muslims, he would first and foremost attribute it to Allah's help and that He'd sent to His slave/servant a capable body of Muslims to assist him. When he found out two Muslims conspired to take advantage (sexually) of a younger brother he gave them the "Ta'zir" punishment. Which could be anything from fines, excommunication, ostracizing the individuals, or ten lashes or less. He enacted the full extent of the lashing, and did it himself.

His young adopted nephew Ibn joined him from Roxbury Correctional Institution, after beefing with some gang boys. Gordon Pack (Abdullah) was on board from Patuxent, as was Big Hamza. Shakir, Mujaahid (Blue), Larry Wallace (Shareef), Big Yahya and Little Abdul-Wadood were all on the Shura board by the time the new outside coordinator was hired. Isma'il Ibraheem was from New York and had brought his wife and small children to the Hagerstown area of Maryland. The new chaplain had studied extensively in Saudi, and knew the rules of grammar and Tajweed (the correct pronunciation of Qur'anic Arabic). He gave structure to the classes as a qualified instructor like the brothers were in a "madrasa" (Islamic school). He was clearly the most knowledgeable Muslim there, if not in most of Western Maryland. Mustafa was happy to let his new mentor take the lead in areas of educating the Jamaat. Mustafa and his Shura board still enforced the discipline needed to maintain the moral and/or ethical code of the

Muslim body. The new Imam, Isma'il (Mustafa now referred to himself as an "amir") found out Mustafa was giving lashes for various offenses and told him only, "You should get someone else to do it." He designated his old friend and reformer "Abu Fatwa" aka Jamal or Kent.

Everyone was in place in "Jamatul-Jihad." There were even brothers whose main focus was to intervene in Muslim/gang conflicts. They kept peace and had verbal agreements from all the leaders of the existing gangs (Black Guerilla Family (B.G.F.), Bloods, and Crips) that whenever there was a problem serious enough where there was the strong likelihood of bloodshed, they would confer with the Muslim leadership, if it was at all possible.

In 2002 Mustafa was ready to "take his act on the road" as he'd be fond of saying. He put the wheels in motion for a transfer. After a year on the transfer list it became obvious the current administration wasn't willing to be rid of inmate Lucas – why would they, when he and his crew of roughneck Muslim security force and educators were doing such a tremendous job with their group, for better or for worse?

The worse or one of the worst clearly being once when another brother named Abdullah from Housing Unit 1 gave him a small but thick lockup-type note (a kite) with the name Mustafa on it. Mustafa was in the gym on a Sunday morning at the time, making ready to go out with the Muslim football team, of which Big Hamza (Garnell Carter) had made him defensive coach. Ibn was star running back and kick returner. The young fella, who was now much heavier from lifting weights, and stronger, had exceptional athletic abilities. After being out all morning running up and down the sidelines, finally Mustafa emptied the contents of his pockets to prepare for a shower. Remembering the kite, he opened it, to his dismay discovered fifteen to twenty small packets of white powder he believed to be heroin. Enraged, he immediately flushed it and saw Abdullah about it the following day. Mustafa had no choice but take Abdullah at his word that someone had given the kite to him to give to Mustafa. As there were three Mustafas in the community, he gave it to the former Imam, now first Amir, as he was used to receiving such notes from guys on lockup. Fortunately, Amir Mustafa couldn't punish anyone, as he wasn't sure which Mustafa was involved with this haram activity. It was all water under the bridge now. It would for a long time be one of the many thrilling stories Mustafa would tell and laugh about. Subhanallah! (Glory to Allah)

From his days Out Back (the Pen Annex), until 2002, Mustafa had numerous women friends that helped him along, either visiting, sending letters, or helping with his cash flow. He was almost married three times; two to Muslim sisters and once almost to Garneta. Each time he called off the engagement, feeling he wasn't being fair to them, nor to himself. He knew he was only "settling" because he was pressed and lonely for female companionship kicking in the visiting room doors. And he was pretty sure had he been out of prison he could do a lot better; that was the reason most people in prison get married. Presently he was seeing Helen, a slightly older woman who was the mother of one of his Muslim brothers. After Garneta she was perhaps his biggest financial contributor, buying his word processor, sending in a monthly stipend and letters, not to mention an occasional visit. This went on for five years; he liked her a lot and probably would've married her had he an idea of how much longer a bit he had. They all would say they'd wait, but Mustafa knew that was more easily said than done.

Candie had even come back on the scene by now, albeit with a daughter, but hollering at her old dad nevertheless. The two, father and daughter, were back on track; just like he'd told her they would be years ago, before she nutted up on him leaving him "illin'."

Mustafa and J. Marie had two grandchildren now, and they were beautiful. A boy named after his father, Michael D'Angelo, whom

Mustafa called Malik, and a girl (Candie's daughter) named Kennedie Marie, whom Mustafa called by her last name (Futrell), "Miss Futrell," respectfully. J. Marie accompanied Candie and Miss Futrell on a visit one weekend, posing for a family photo in the visiting room. As they were leaving at the end of the visit, she headed for the door and surprisingly came back to kiss Mustafa on the cheek – she fit into the grandmother role beautifully, though only forty-five.

Mustafa was curious as to who his granddaughter's father was. All he knew was that his name was Juan and for the most part he wasn't fulfilling his fatherly role as far as financial support. He'd caught a young bitt recently but neither Candie nor J. Marie would tell Mustafa which institution he was in. They thought Mustafa would perhaps try to acquaint himself with the young man or, worse, send someone else to. Although he knew how a young man and woman's urges led them to one thing or another, he still had ill feelings about some joker deflowering his little princess.

By 2003 Mustafa was definitely ready to leave M.C.T.C. He and Mo Darryl, the leader of the Moorish Science Temple, discussed their displeasure openly at the run of the institution one morning at work in the bakery. It was a long shot, but they thought they could get enough guys talking, eventually leading them toward a peaceful demonstration. No one would go to dinner that Sunday, which was easily accepted because there was only meatloaf and green Jell-O. They were protesting the shoddy medical treatment resulting in three deaths, beatings of inmates by the racist officers, and the exorbitant commissary prices. Although Warden J. Michael Stouffer knew Mustafa was behind it all, he didn't have a problem with the men peacefully expressing themselves. Mustafa got word via Captain Webb per Warden Stouffer that should anything go wrong (violent) he'd regret it.

Mustafa got the message loud and clear. He knew Warden Stouffer was acting deputy commissioner when he authorized the state police and the Correctional Institution Technical (CIT) squad to sweep through the Cutt in 1999. The result was Hakeem was sent to Arizona State Prison, and hundreds of others relocated, a few others out of state. The strike was a textbook example of a peaceful kitchen set-out. The strikers achieved some of their objectives; medical personnel were fired or transferred to other facilities, the food in the dining room was better prepared, for a while, and apparently someone spoke to the officers because there was an obvious change in their attitudes. Despite the peacefulness of it all Mustafa was sent to the Maryland Correctional Institution in Hagerstown (MCI-H) just up the road from where he'd been at M.C.T.C.

Gordon Pack (Abdullah) was now the first Amir as Mustafa requested and Shakir was next in command, an excellent choice. At the "old jail"/MCI-H Mustafa was on the tier with his friend Jamal, aka Abu Fatwa; several days later they were cellmates to forge an even closer bond. The two eventually moved down in the jail's tunnel area where there were eight twenty-five-man small dorms. Mustafa was in H-dorm and Jamal was next door in G-dorm, where the Imam was. The Imam for the Muslims on this location was Rafeeki, a country boy from Alabama that had a fantastic rapport with the Muslim community, and who the good-old-boy hillbilly administration was truly comfortable with. Mustafa saw others brothers he'd not seen in years, at the Cutt or penitentiary in Baltimore. One was Rauf, who also knew Debbie, whom Mustafa had cut into while she visited family in Southeast over thirty-five years ago. Debbie was his homegirl, but he didn't know her as well as Brother Jihad (Turtle Wells) who at one time was her man.

Mustafa also ran into Rasheed ibn Bennett, whom he hadn't seen since he, Saleem, and Hakeem had to straighten out a situation in

C-dorm where Rasheed slept. Rasheed was no more the skinny kid with a lot of heart; now he was big from lifting heavy weights and quite knowledgeable in the Deen. Rasheed was the "troubleshooter" for the Jamaat at the old jail, but not to the extent he was while in Cumberland, where he and a young rambunctious brother named Saleem bin Alston from P.G. County cracked a few blue-shirts' heads, running the big young kid's bitt up. Now Saleem too was in the old jail and he and Mustafa were walking companions to the chow hall. Saleem was the Imam for a little while in the Cutt when most all the old heads were gone and a new breed of Muslims had an agenda.

Mustafa stayed in contact with many of the brothers through the years, even when Maryland prisons stopped direct inmate-to-inmate letter writing. Connie was his go-between, or Carlyn and Anthony too; his family was a tremendous help through the years. He wrote Hakeem out in Arizona, Saleem El Amin, whom was the Imam at the Roxbury facility, also in Hagerstown, Wali Aquil, and Furqan. Others he'd send word to like Abu Bakr, who was now at the Eastern Shore (ECI) facility with Lil Glen (Hasan) and Big Taymullah. Mustafa was extending salaams to the Imam down at the Pen's Annex (Out Back), Imam Mosi. Though he'd never met him, Mustafa had heard a lot of good things through the years about him. He'd studied under Shaykh Talib, who was the coordinator down there. Mustafa knew personally most all the inmate Imams, as well as the coordinators throughout most of the Maryland system, as far away as the Eastern Correctional Institution, on the Eastern Shore.

Chapter 22

Like in all jails, there are good people regardless of a previous charge that landed them there, as there are bad ones, too, who truly need not be back among society, maybe never. Muslims are no different as far as behavior goes – Christians, Jews, Seventh Day Adventist, and Jehovah Witnesses, none of them. There are good and bad amongst them; prison is a big melting pot of races and religious preferences.

For the most part the behavior of the Muslims in H-dorm was so-so. Out of the eight or nine, half were up to par as far as never using profanity, lowering their gaze when scantily clad women appeared, not listening to music, let alone buying it or going out borrowing CDs or cassettes, and knowing the basics of the Deen of Islam.

They'd all by now heard Mustafa was a no-nonsense type of brother that called to the righteous conduct and forbade the wrongdoing. For the most part they tried not to give him a reason to "check" them, at first. Mustafa, however, was growing old and getting a little tired, or more laid back in his admonishments, unless the action was out-in-the-open blatantly haram. Young Saleem use to tell his older brother how he would've liked to be on the scene with him years ago when he was aggressive with his admonishments. Mustafa would only smile, telling his young protégé, "Things change, Akhi, I'm getting kind of tired of beating these 'fasiqs' (evil and foul livers and doers) down so much these days."

One afternoon while two brothers were going back and forth, it was clear the exchange would have a bad ending. Mustafa tried his best to quell the insults being hurled. It was obvious the one brother, who had boxed professionally, was baiting the other in; he was setting him up to be slaughtered. Neither man was taking heed of the warnings so Mustafa tired and went to his bunk area. When the inevitable happened and the ex-boxer had his victim's shoulders pinned while pummeling him and telling him, "This is what I do, nigga!" Mustafa ignored them, while young Saleem rushed out of his own aisle to pull the one off the other.

That Friday at Jumu'ah Mustafa and Saleem narrated the scenario to Imam Rafeeki and Wazir Rasheed bin Bennett. Mustafa had been placed on the "Majlis-as-Shura" (the Muslim advisory board), despite his protest to be on it. He explained he had – if Allah wills – a solution in accordance with the Sunna of The Prophet Muhammad (S.A.A.W.). Rasheed bin Bennett, who usually handled these things, conceded to the Imam to allow Mustafa free rein to deal with this travesty.

With the matter decided immediately after the two rakat Jumu'ah prayer, Mustafa hastily made his way to the auditorium's stage. After getting everyone's attention, he called for the following brothers to quickly join and for no one else to leave. Abu Bakr, Bobby Grimes, Big Moon, Jabbar, and Wali Aquil were now in the old jail too, just transferred from M.C.I-J. These men, all but Jabbar, had been with Mustafa, on his team, for years and knew of his policies. They trusted his calls for the most part no matter how extreme or unorthodox. He briefly told them he had a situation to deal with involving a couple brothers transgressing against one another. He told them to keep the perimeter clear, Insha Allah, this won't take long.

This private detail spaced themselves and stretched the length of the stage. He then, in a loud and commanding voice, called for "Abdullah and Abdul-Qawi from H-annex"; then, in a lower, almost humorous tone, with a taint of sarcasm, he said, "Ikhwan (brothers) please join me on the stage." He was wearing the black-and-silver embroidered vest Connie made for him while he was in M.C.T.C. He had his boots on and his old half-broken glasses, setting a visual psychological perception.

Sidebar conversations faded out and most of the hundred-plus worshippers' eyes were now on the two brothers making their way to the stage. He knew from experience the way of successfully pulling this off in this spirit of the moment, quickly, without a lotta hoopla, was to overwhelm the guilty or suspected party before they had time to think about what was happening. He simply told them, "Look, you know what you did; it was out of order, dead wrong. I'm going to give you both a 'ta'zir' punishment – strikes under ten lashes." While talking he removed his glasses, tossed them in a chair, and retrieved an oversized shower shoe from his back pocket. He wasn't waiting for a nod from them of acceptance, nor anticipating words of acknowledgement. This execution of punishment was non-negotiable. Mustafa used the shoe to point to the wall on a partially blind spot of the stage with direct eye contact. The presence of Abu Bakr, Bobby, Big Moon, and Wali Aquil wasn't lost on the two; they knew they all had a history in the Old Pen and that they had an immutable allegiance to Mustafa.

He gave them both nine strikes that resonated throughout the assembly like the cracks from a taskmaster's whip. Afterward Mustafa sought Allah's forgiveness (astaghfirullah) and told them to make "taubah" (repentance), said "Masha-Allah…" (what pleases Allah) "As-Salamu alaykum."

Rafeeki was released that year and Rasheed was now the Imam of the Muslims of the Maryland Correctional Institute, in Hagerstown (MCI-H). The year was 2005. Mustafa and young Saleem had by then put three more brothers to the lash for varying offenses. Everyone wasn't satisfied with these methods for deterring the blatant haram and transgressions. The masaajid (plural for Masjid) was contacted uptown and so was Da'wud Adib. A directive came back from the street in the form of a sanction informing Rasheed in no uncertain terms they had achieved their objective, but should now desist from further punishments of this nature.

Michael D'Angelo's wife Serena had another baby, a cute Asian-looking girl they named Madison Alexandra. Of course Granddad Mustafa had his own name for her; he called her China Doll because she had Chinese-looking eyes. Serena would write her father-in-law occasionally; she told him in one letter that Madison had to get the eyes from J. Marie.

Candie was driving up to see her father a couple times a year now; she'd always bring Miss Futrell, and the three would always take a picture together, except once when Miss Futrell was angry her mother wouldn't allow her to stand on the bench to take a picture, causing her to pout, messing the flick up. The following week when Granddad got the picture he sent one to her mom and the other to her with a note saying no more pictures until next year. Candie had met an older man at work and was being wined and dined. This cat from Philly was even taking her and Miss Futrell to Hawaii, almost as often as her father changed jails. Mustafa couldn't have been happier for her – too bad his parents weren't as pleased. J. Marie would make her own cameo appearances about once a year as of late, or when Mustafa would be transferred she'd visit the new spot.

Upon greeting Mustafa, she would always start off with, "What's happening, how you doing?"

Mustafa would likewise have the same standard comeback line; he'd give her a most confused look while repeating, "What's happening? I'm lonely, that's how I'm doing… What's up?"

She'd laugh because she knew where her ex was going with it. She also knew he still loved her and wanted her. Mustafa hated the game but this time around if there was a second act it would be on her time, her rules. He'd often compare her to his relationship with the Orioles baseball team. As soon as he thought he could cut them off and be rid of them, they'd come around with some spectacular play, causing him to want to stay on board. The few times they saw one another in the last few years had been pleasant. She was beginning to remind him more and more of their grandmothers (Madoo and Tia). She even wore the Indian turquoise bracelets worn by Madoo and all her daughters, except he wasn't sure about Toni. He never heard from his youngest aunt; the one time was back in 1982 when she and her then-husband Bruce put up a grand to help with legal fees. He'd written his aunt since then several times, all to no avail. He often wondered whether she had been holding a grudge since they were kids. He'd snatched a necklace off her neck in the heat of an argument and they both watched her entire string of fake pearls bounce and roll down Campbell Drive.

Mustafa figured he'd eventually wear J. Marie down, he'd win her over, but he wanted his cake now! J. Marie, on the other hand, wanted to see if this new and supposedly improved Skip was in fact the real deal before she let him all the way in the gate. He'd been in prison almost twenty-five slices! Whew! It was no telling how he'd changed, or what he'd changed into. The fact that she'd never remarried was a testament to Mustafa in itself. He often wondered about the pact they'd made while they were fourteen; they vowed to each other that "no matter what happens in the middle of our union, as long as we grow old together... it's all about the ending."

The thing that bothered Mustafa the most about J. Marie was her still smoking. He knew from extensive reading that there was no better way to kill yourself in middle age than to smoke. It was hard for her to stop, he knew this, but she couldn't have been thinking of all those children who'd surely miss her if she died before they learned to understand death. Not to mention how much he too would miss her. J. Marie also showed signs of believing in karma. She was of the mindset that Mustafa having dealt unlawfully with cars in every way was the reason she was having car troubles (also someone had stolen Candies car). If this was indeed her indoctrination, then may Allah forbid that one of the children, Mike D'Angelo or Candie, died while she was still alive. Who's the one in jail for murder? Who's the one with the street assaults? Robberies, attempted murders? Mustafa didn't need that held over his head for the rest of his life. Maybe it was best he moved on. *Damn, J. Marie!* he thought. *Where'd you get this crap from?*

Anthony Trusty – Brother Luqman, aka Lo-Lo – had a tongue that spit out sarcasm like darts. He could be the rudest, most insulting man you could ever talk to, unless, for whatever reason, he respected or admired something in you, and then perhaps you'd be spared. He knew sports as well as half the columnist in any town's news office. He and Mustafa were the same age, and used to have a good time working in the Pen's hospital years ago. Luqman still had sharp fighting skills and would bury that blade in a dude if need be. Mustafa bore witness to both exhibitions first hand.

So when an overzealous rookie officer waited until he was handcuffed one evening after a discrepancy about Luqman not getting to his cell quick enough, and then punched him in the face, the hit within itself wasn't heavy for the old veteran con. No matter how long it took, Luqman vowed to himself, "I'll catch up with the lame." They locked Luqman up that night, by the next afternoon word had spread throughout the old jail about the details of the event. A lotta people liked Luqman, especially the new Imam Rasheed and his now-right-hand man Mustafa. That evening during rec in the big yard, the two walked to discuss the matter. Something would be done to the young rookie officer, that part was clear, insha'Allah.

It'd been years since Mustafa had taken on an assignment this big. What made this one so momentous was he had to get away with it. Assaulting a corrections officer had laid a many a convict down, for decades. He had a similar charge when he first entered the system while at the Diagnostic Center in '83, fortunately it appeared to look like an accident; he was only given thirty days lockup time.

On this trip, he made the two "rakat" sunnah for the "Istikharah" prayer (prayer for seeking Allah's advice), and he'd need, in addition, two vital entities to pull it off. Mustafa wanted a young, trustworthy, knows-how-to-keep-his-mouth-shut, non-descript brother, not overly familiar with many guys in the population. He wanted to train him as a student of sorts in multitasking within Jamaat affairs, because, at fifty, although years of exercising and studying the basics of the Deen had kept him fairly well balanced (physically, mentally and spiritually), he was showing signs of winding down.

Mustafa was one of the few old heads around that still kept a joint. He had two, one for traveling that he'd never under any circumstances lend out (it'd withstood numerous shakedowns, even though the officers on several occasions had it in their possession without knowing it). He wouldn't use one for the rookie officer, however. He had some other tragic fate in store for this punk. Mustafa needed to know who he was, let alone his itinerary; he did not know him from a can of paint. Yeah, Mustafa decided or realized rather, the prison Jamaat needed another "Mustafa" on the scene. *Insha'Allah* (if Allah wills) *I'll be "uptown"* (on the bricks) *in less than a nickel.*

In early 2006 H-annex had a vicious spider infestation of a massive proportion. This, along with a falling out with Abu Bakr, compelled Mustafa to move from the annex to E-tier into a cell. His old friend

Yahya bin Childs wound up being his cellie sometime later. Yahya knew nothing of the conspiracy against the rookie officer. The day before the hit, Mustafa's cell was thoroughly searched. The two cops went through everything, or so it appeared. They weren't just looking for a joint, but they were also looking for incriminating notes too.

The entire time, they had Mustafa handcuffed on the tier he "dhikred" (remembered Allah with praises and supplication). He had two joints in his cell, one, he wasn't particularly concerned about, but the biggest one, up in the slot designed for the radiator pipes, well… "Allahumma-anzil-nasrika" (O Allah! Send down your help), over and over and over again Mustafa's lips mumbled this, until the Kaafir left, and then "Alhamdulillah!"

After failing to turn up anything they could make an issue of, he was escorted to Captain Ridenhour's office. Captain Ridenhour had a few of his comrades there with him. Lt. "Bull Dog Face" Smith did most of the talking. This was all about the Luqman assault; when it was all said and done, all Mustafa could attest to was, "No, the Sunni Muslim community isn't particularly cool about your officer taxing Trusty, but I don't plan on doing anything to him about it. As for the rest of the community – I can't speak for them."

Mustafa thought how the people placed in authority over him could ask some of the stupidest most asinine questions sometime. After about a half-hour session of trivialities, he was directed to pack his property and report to the property room, because he was being placed on administrative segregation. On the administration-segregation tier, among others Mustafa hadn't seen in weeks or months, were Abu Bakr, and of course Luqman. They both wanted to know what ill-fated circumstance brought him there. Knowing Mustafa as they did, they were 99.9% sure it had something to do with Islam. Luqman wasn't sure he was happy, proud, or grieved his old friend was there on his account.

Mustafa told him something of the exchange between him and the brass that afternoon. He was just beginning to get into his lockup workout routine when, after three days, the administration shipped him out. This time he was sent to the third of the prison tri-factors in Hillbilly Hills – The Roxbury Correctional Institution (RCI) in Hagerstown, MD.

He was sent to housing unit one, in a cell with a Muslim he remembered from his first few years at M.C.T.C. – the new jail. Malik Colbert was a friend with his daughter's soon-to-be ex-boyfriend, Shaheed.

Mustafa had met Shaheed while the two dined over lunch one day. The nice young fella knew Mustafa was the Imam of the Muslim community, and knew more about Mustafa than the Imam knew about him. He introduced himself as knowing Candie, and figured Mustafa put together they were friends. Mustafa empathized with him when he asked, "Imam Mustafa, why is it that some girls won't wait for dudes when they come to jail." Mustafa only smiled as the young man confided in him before running it all down. He remembered explaining to his daughter about guys who started out much like himself that were "jail prone." She knew all about those type dudes, yet still got involved with one, but Mustafa wouldn't trade his granddaughter in for all the bricks in Fort Knox.

Mustafa and his new cellie at RCI hit it off well. They made salat together, and he helped Malik learn the rest of his prayer; the part that so many Muslims neglect, the "Tashahhud." He had a great reunion at Jumu'ah that Friday with his old friend and Imam, Saleem El-Amin. A lot of the brothers on this new location, especially the younger ones, were anxious to see the two old heads meet up again for the first time in so many years. The guy spoken of, sometimes in hush tones, around the jails as Saleem's lieutenant down at the Cutt in Jessup. This guy whose name was, at one time or another, on the lips of so many of the

Maryland Prison systems heavyweights, or so called legends of the time. Saleem looked to be in great shape. He was fifty-three years old, had an Arabic grammar book in the works, and was surrounded by people who loved and respected him. He was housed in A-building next to Mustafa (H.U.J.2). Mustafa considered making the transfer to join him, but decided against it in lieu of something Umar (Leon Mason) told him when he was first sent to MCTC. He wrote Mustafa that, "Allah has spread us all out, the learned, the leaders, and the fasiqs, so there would not be an overwhelming concentration of one group at any location.

Mustafa helped out the tier Amir (leader) where he was – a diligent young street kid they called Stink that Mustafa took an immediate liking to. Except for the name, which Mustafa thought unbefitting a Muslim leader, so he named him "Sultawn," which means ruler or governor of a land. The tier's dayrooms had several tables the men used. Each gang had a table. At first the brothers only had access to a table three times a week, but after a few weeks Mustafa established a table the Muslims would always use, all three rec periods.

At around the end of '06, there was a big gang melee, where the Crips coordinated a timed assault against the resident Bloods. Spilled blood smeared the floor and walls, and the stench of mace lingered until the next morning. The jail went on lockdown status for two weeks, until all the Blood members were segregated or transferred out. During the lockdown, or shortly afterwards, Rasheed ibn Bennett from the old jail was transferred to Roxbury, under duress. He too had not seen Saleem El-Amin in a very long time. When Rasheed left the Cutt in '94 he was sent to "Cumberland, MD." Now he was wiser, more diligent in the Deen. He'd matured and was on a serious campaign to rid the Roxbury Jamaat of the deep gang infiltration. Saleem gave Rasheed free reign to begin the purification of the ranks.

The outside coordinator was a good old-school brother from Denver, Colorado. Rasheed and Mustafa first met him at one of the annual seminars at the old jail. Abdul-Mateen had come up through the "Nation of Islam," and, like Isma'ill Ibraheem at MCTC, studied formerly in Saudi Arabia. Abdul-Mateen was the kind of guy one could hang out with on the street, as long as your activities were lawful. He was very much in touch with what the Muslims faced out of prison. They'd both made Hajj to Mecca, and given khutbas to educate, remind, and admonish the brothers on Yaumul Jumu'ah (the day of Friday). Chaplain Mateen conducted Arabic grammar classes, brought in an occasional outside guest speaker, and was an exceptional counselor when one of the men needed "naseeha" (counseling).

Another brother Mustafa hadn't seen in years showed up not long after Mustafa and Rasheed, Jihad "Turtle" Wells went back with El-Amin way before Mustafa; he was a few years older than El Amin. He'd written and had published three books, and probably forgotten more about jailing than Mustafa would ever know. He and Debbie, (Mustafa's summer of 1967 childhood heartthrob) had a history in Baltimore for years as she grew older. Rauf Matten, Kareem Hasan, and Rafiq (Sip) all knew Debbie. She was their home girl. They'd often kid Mustafa about the two of them hookin' up one day; Jihad even gave Mustafa a few flicks of Debbie, back in the day and more recent. She'd recently married, and, at one time, had a bout with substance abuse. Mustafa wanted to see her just for old time's sake, not that he wanted anything to come of it, or so he said.

In late 2007, Kareem Saleem El-Amin was transferred to the Patuxent Institution. He left his first Amir (Hasan) to be the Imam, although actually it was a recommendation, and the shurah had to confirm it. Rasheed didn't want the Imam position though he was most qualified, Mustafa definitely didn't want it, as he was saying these days, "Man,

I'm on some laid back time." He'd even gave his traveling joint to one of the new young soldiers in the Jamaat at Roxbury he took a liken to. They, along with the shurah board, vowed to help Hasan to the best of their ability run the Jamaat at Roxbury. After just a few months as Imam, the good brother Hasan felt he was in over his head, and also had the foresight to recognize Rasheed was better qualified to deal with the bunch of renegades that comprised the Jamaat. Surely this was a rough mob, unlike what Rasheed and Mustafa had ever witnessed. Mustafa had put the shoe on the backs of more brothers at Roxbury than at MCTC and the old jail combined, and still these brothers were hell bent on doing it (practicing Islam) their way!

Somewhere along the way (around 1998), the administration at MCTC tagged Mustafa a gang member or affiliate, not just him, but his once assistant Imam Abdullah Muhsin bin Pack. Abdullah was no longer the Imam or first Amir of MCTC, because of a fiery khutba about "assisting your brother/coming to his aid, etc. etc." whether it's a blue shirt (CO) involved or not. The administration took issue about it; it's not clear how they found out about the Friday sermon. Nevertheless, they shipped him out to Cumberland's North Branch maximum-security facility.

Imam Rasheed had been tagged as well, as a Crip, BGF, or Blood member, let alone the Sunni community was labeled a gang – at least by the good-ole-boy network of Hagerstown. When in all actuality, the Hagerstown and Cumberland Correctional Officers were the biggest gang in Western Maryland, without a doubt. Through the last ten or twelve years there, several men throughout those prisons had gone above and beyond the call of duty to keep peace. Because they would, by necessity, have to interact with the gangs' leaders or representatives to quell a potential volatile situation, the administration of Western Maryland took that the wrong way.

The administration at the Roxbury facility had Mustafa so deep in the gang saga that every time the jail was on lockdown status his name was "flagged," preventing him from going to work. He addressed this matter several years ago while at MCTC before Captain Webb. Webb informed him this "tag" had followed him from the Cutt in Jessup. Mustafa knew this was a lie, and, if anything, information from the Cutt was misconstrued. Making matters worse, the jail's gang task force officer (Lt. Dickens) brought in a special terrorist agent from the FBI to investigate potential threats from soon to be released prisoners throughout the United States.

Special Agent Rosario was allowed a meeting with Mustafa, in which he was asked about the contents of the khutba (Friday sermon), what masjid he planned to attend upon release, and were there any Muslims that, through the years, he'd known to express sentiments of a subversive agenda towards the United States government. By nature, Mustafa was a "participatory listener" – he got it from Connie. His and Connie's talks would be some of the most disrupted, rudest, and breaking all the rules governing conversational courtesies ever. However, this time Mustafa remained silent, even though insulted and highly offended the "Kaafir" would approach him about these affairs. He understood it was perhaps now a government protocol for the Division of Corrections to do their job in the "Homeland Security" forum.

When agent Rosario finished, Mustafa told him, "Man, you've got to be kidding. These guys in this system – half of them – won't even be practicing Islam to an acceptance level, let alone on a suicide-bombing plot. Maybe if you checked out some of the brothers in the feds in New York or New Jersey, but here in these Maryland joints?! ... Nar."

"Mr. Lucas if you did know of anyone of a potential threat of this nature would you inform the appropriate authorities?"

"Probably not."

Imam Rasheed was spoken to also, so were others in the Jamaat, and it wasn't just at RCI. This thing was statewide. In fact, prison Islamic communities all over the country were being infiltrated, being closely monitored for signs of subversive activities, and having their accounts dismantled, classes discontinued, and so forth.

Mustafa was settled in at doing special sanitation on the main dining room floor until something better came along. Most jobs in the Maryland prison system pay anywhere from $.90 to $1.05 a day, and it's been that way for over thirty years, regardless that the prices in the commissary continue to climb, inflation, etc… However, some guys are hired by the "Maryland Enterprise Corporation," which used to be "State Use Industries" (SUI), earning anywhere from sixty to two hundred dollars a month. In the mid 90s Mustafa was earning a hundred dollars while working in the wood shop, but these days none of the "shop" plant managers wanted to touch him, leaving him relegated to the lesser-paying jobs around the jail(s). Mustafa's side hustle for the last three years (since Helen cut him off) was sewing workout shorts for the guys at four or five dollars. He'd also do alterations and other tailoring jobs. He was in demand, and very skilled at what he did. It was relaxing to him. Sewing was therapeutic, and he knew it was something he inherited from Connie – same as Carlyn. He couldn't wait to go by the house on 18th Place when he got out to try his hand on her old sewing machine. She wasn't using it these days because of her arthritis.

Mustafa was biding his time with the one-hour-a-morning job. It was sweet with a few perks – it was all about the snacks to him. A lot of the older guys, it seemed, had developed a sweet tooth these days. He ate lunch while at work, and occasionally was able to smuggle back something to tide him over a few days, without actually "stealing" it. After all, he was Muslim, and everybody knows Muslims don't steal. The job he had his sights on was the kitchen-laundry-man detail, but first he had to wait until old Clay's transfer came through for minimum security (in about seven months).

In his last year before he himself was eligible for minimum, he'd planned to get in the "office technology" class to learn computer and other necessary skills to compliment the degree he held. Meanwhile, he was working out hard, and was perhaps in the best shape of his life. He'd recently come in third place in the one-mile forty-and-over race for the entire jail. While in the "new jail" (MCTC), he and three others would win the forty-and-over 880 relay four out of the six and a half years he was there. He strategically placed each man where he was best suited, placing himself on the third leg, because he was the slowest of the group. Each year, it was like free money for them. It was as much about each of them winning the six dollars pocket change as it was about bragging rights.

In 2006, at fifty years old, he was perhaps in the top five of being in the best overall shape among his fifty-and-over peers. Among them, and in better shape than he was, were his friends Wali Aquil, Sonny Jackson – and Briscoe wasn't no slouch either. Big Earl, who was actually a little guy, and Mo Darryl Johnson-Bey too. Mustafa's only medical maladies were his high cholesterol and enlarged prostate. He began joking with his grandson Maleek (Lil Mike D'Angelo), who was a star wide out on his little league football team, that he could beat him running, and his daddy too! Michael D'Angelo senior was getting heavy these days. Mustafa didn't know what Serena was feeding him, but granddad definitely planned to check out his daughter-in-law's cooking just as soon as the state of Maryland was done with him, insha'Allah!

Candie Cane married Dr. Robert Alfred Copeland in 2008. On a visit she had with him just after the wedding, he thought she may have been pregnant. She had that look. Father and daughter were having a great time enjoying one another's company. They'd come a long way since the time when Mustafa would've sold her into the Asian slave market.

Mustafa was fifty-two years old, and had had his fill with Western Maryland. Though he was comfortable in his new laundry-man job for the M.D.R., he was hearing news of guys being sent down to the Jessup region. Jihad had gone, Tray, Piggy, and even Shakkir, and 6'9" (Muhammad) were there. Besides, Connie and them had trekked up to these hills to see him for twelve years now; he wanted to give them a break. They'd been putting their old junk heaps on the road for a lotta years – all but Carlyn. She was pushin' a Benz these days (in way over her pretty little head). The next time he went up for annual review, he cracked for a transfer. There were only two jails left in Maryland they could send him – "Out Back," now named JCI for Jessup Correctional Institute, and ECI (Eastern Shore). He'd make "du'a" that Allah would soften the Kaafir hearts and try his hand.

In the main dining hall, he was working with one of his closest friends. Abdullah Muhsin bin Pack had been sent down from "Cumberland," finally. He wasn't working directly with Mustafa, but in the back of the kitchen on segregation bags. His old aisle buddy and friend Big Earl Crump was there also. He was his adopted nephew and understudy J.B. made sure Mustafa fit into his new position without any glitches. They knew he was still on sweets, and made sure to put him "on," more often than not, with his favorite chocolate chip cookies, bananas, and even an occasional pumpkin pie, or perhaps it was sweet potato. Mustafa really couldn't much tell the difference.

After a year or so in the cell with Malik, Mustafa was made to move onto A-tier, which was for men fifty years old and over. He didn't mind much because as he was fond of saying these days, "Man I'm on some laid back stuff now, and ain't so fast to jump out there for most of these fly-by-night-type dudes." A-tier had on it old heads up till about eighty years old, guys the Division of Corrections could clearly release, guys that weren't a threat to no one anymore. Some of the old dudes couldn't get around without canes; they'd forget sometimes what tier they were on and where they were in a conversation.

One weekend, Mustafa's cellie, old Joe Parker, moved onto the honor tier where Imam Rasheed and his assistant Hasan were. Mustafa was in the cell by himself all of two days when someone told him of an old gray-headed fat guy standing in the foyer with boxes like he was moving on A-tier. By the grace of God, Mustafa had been fortunate as far as cellies went. Now, since this apparent new cellie was described as "fat" – more than likely Mustafa would have to give up his bottom bunk to move up top. Most fat or obese guys have a hard time jumping on and off prison top bunks. Mustafa preferred the top. He didn't mind the hopping up and down for one, and, two, because he'd fart a lot when he ate sweets, and the smell wasn't as offensive to the man on the bottom, or so it seemed.

Good cellies, like good prison jobs, weren't always easily procured. A person, man or woman, will tell you that having a good cellie and a good job you don't mind going to is half your bit done right there!" Nothin' could've prepared Mustafa for what was coming, not in a hundred years. When the cell door opened, he was looking at the Redskins about to drop another one in the fourth quarter and only half-way looking at the new guy. As long as it wasn't a homosexual moving in, there wasn't an immediate problem, besides if it was one, he would've been forewarned. One could've knocked him over with a feather when he recognized his new cellie. It was Buggs! But Mustafa had his head half turned towards the TV (compliments of Anthony back in '99 or 2000), so Buggs couldn't clearly see his face, and, after all, it had been over thirty years since he'd seen his young student. Mustafa decided to have a little fun with his old mentor. "Don't worry 'bout unpacking, Pops, you ain't gonna be here long."

"Main Man, I ain't just start bittin', you startin' this thing off all wrong, homes – oh hell! Skip???

"Yeah man, you old buzzard son of a gun. My man!"

When Mustafa first saw Big Crump after getting to Roxbury, it'd been fifteen years. Coach Crump had already been at the jail for about nine years. It'd been ten years since Mustafa had seen Saleem. They were great reunions amongst old friends. Now, as for Sam Buggs, he'd not seen him since four or five years before he was locked up, in about '78! They had a lot of catching up to do, that they were in the same cell was serendipitous.

Buggs, like Mustafa, was on the tail end of his bit. Mustafa didn't sweat him about calling him by the Muslim name he'd chosen. The only ones, other than family, that were not calling him Mustafa were those men that had known him long before he was going by Mustafa.

The two reminisced until 2 am, any later and Mustafa would've had serious trouble getting up for the "fajr" salat (early morning prayer). Buggs told him about his daughter's mother dying of AIDS, which happened to be Ibn's mom. Ibn and Buggs's daughter were half brother and sister. It all came back to Mustafa, back when he and Ibn were at MCTC, and Ibn was saddened beyond words over the loss of his mom. Mustafa, half-jokingly and to lighten the moment, asked Ibn did he need a hug. Ibn needed one for real, however, and Mustafa was so glad to be there for his adopted nephew.

They talked about the Ali vs. Jimmy Young fight at the Capital Centre when Buggs thought he saw him and some fine redbone down close to ringside. Mustafa told him about meeting J. Marie when Connie threatened him with Cedar Knolls or Training School. They talked about their children and grandchildren, about as much as they could get in the first night. The two rekindled a newer and stronger bond now since they were older. Eventually, Buggs got a job in the kitchen too; he began working out and taking better care of himself. Buggs was stabbed in the head while doing a bit down Lorton before the authorities shut it down. A piece of metal fragment was still lodged in his head, which sometimes caused him to blackout. Buggs was having nightmares too. One night he was wrestling in his sleep when suddenly Mustafa heard something hit the floor. Mustafa awakened and looked down to see Buggs lying on his back, hands and knees up, and eyes wide with terror. After making sure he wasn't hurt, they both broke out laughing. The next morning, Mustafa told him how glad he should be that he wasn't sleeping on the top bunk.

Buggs was a good cellie, except he was a vicious snorer. It was thunderous, even worse than Jamal's (Kent), and he had three levels like Jamal's, only louder. Buggs and Mustafa worked out a system so the snoring wouldn't cause the two friends to become unbenefited. As long as Mustafa went to sleep first, everything was cool, so Buggs agreed to give him a ten to fifteen minute jump before he himself crashed.

Though their hometown football team blew yet another season – like most diehard fans, they still enjoyed watching and rooting for then. They were overjoyed Obama won the presidency. They would remind one another of the larger picture when one or the other was distraught or agitated over something gone wrong in the jail, or with an individual. Mustafa was often prone to expressing his feelings of not fitting in with this "New Jack" inmate population as he once did. Sadly enough, some of his own Muslim brethren appalled him; in a khutba he gave at Jumu'ah, he openly called the lot of them a bunch of disobedient "fasiqs" (evil livers and doers). Every jail these days was infected and infested with gangs. Several of the jails had his own homeboys caught up on more of a geographical clique than anything else – "Murder Inc.," which some

Muslims were even secretly in. One of the bright spots in his life now was his children continuing to strive and prosper. Candie had twin boys sometime mid-January, and Michael D'Angelo added an edition to his family – they both had two boys and a girl.

In the first week of March, 2009, Mustafa's case manager sent for him. It was time for his annual review. Alderton had been Mustafa's case manager since the later part of last year. Up until now, Mustafa only spoke with him in passing. There was no other reason he needed to see him. He'd sent him a change to his visitors' card to delete a few names to make room for Aunt Jennie and Duke, and to change Candi's last name to Copeland. On this day, however, it was time for that old "Skip charm" that worked so well for him in the 70s. He found Alderton very easy to talk to. Mustafa chalked it up to two reasons; because they were about the same age, and because Alderton perceived Mustafa as someone with a degree of social and academic aptness.

They talked about the youth stigmatizing themselves with tattoos all over themselves, to include their necks, faces, and hands. Then about the influx of gangs throughout the prisons these days, and about taking advantage of educating oneself. Mustafa's degree came up, and how he'd like to take it a step further, perhaps acquiring a master's degree in… something. Mustafa thought Alderton must've had free time on his hands to spend this time to kick it this way.

Finally, Mustafa didn't want to waste any more time, and began steering the conversation to respecting authority, the elderly, healthcare, and then *Bam!* He broadsided him with his mom, and how he'd like to make things easier on her. How she'd been trekking up to the area for over twelve years. At eighty-one years old, it was taking its toll, and "I'm sure trying to make it easier on her." He further explained there were only two jails left in the DOC that were medium and would take him – Jessup, and down on the shore, "And as you know ECI is farther away for her then here."

"Well, Mr. Lucas I can only 'recommend' that you be sent to JCI, but the final decision must come from my supervisor."

"Is that Ms. Liesinger?"

"Yes".

"I'll tell you what, Mr. Alderton. I'm going to write Commissioner Stouffer because I've known him since he was the warden at the new jail (MCTC), and I'll see if he'd mention something in my favor to her. Give me two weeks from today. I'll write him tonight. Maybe he'll give me a letter to send her or something. I'm going to pray on this thing, and if I don't hear from him in two weeks, I'll write you a letter telling you to go on and put me in for the transfer, taking a chance it's to JCI. Put me in for the recommendation. I appreciate it."

"Okay, Mr. Lucas. I'll hold off on the transfer papers till I hear from you."

Mustafa told Buggs that afternoon what transpired between he and Alderton. Later that evening, he drafted the letter to the commissioner of corrections, J. Michael Stouffer.

On March 11, 2009, Mustafa's letter was just one of many brought to the commissioner's office from his secretary. Her job required her, among other things, to briefly scan letters from inmates for pranks, and those filled with vulgarities. After reading through several before getting to Mustafa's, he was glad to get to one where he recognized the author. The last time he saw the one-time Muslim leader of MCTC was at the old jail when he was shortcutting through the main dining hall during the lunch chow line. Lucas had left his table to cut him off at the water fountain just to say "Hi." He thought how he seemed genuinely glad to see his former warden. The two talked for several minutes under the watchful eyes of the guards – they dare not admonish Mustafa for being away from his table for so long a time. Commissioner Stouffer told Mustafa of the day little "Abdul-Wadud" (Anthony Wise) died when he came back on the tier from the gym.

Mustafa reminded him of their encounter, also mentioned a lot about his mom, and how he would appreciate him helping him get to Jessup. Mustafa knew how to keep these type of letters brief and to the point, sometimes with a little humor. Mustafa, on one or two occasions, referred to the commissioner as "man," as he was so prone to do in ordinary conversation. He knew just what he was doing with this. It was in Allah's hands, and whatever He decreed, His will be done.

On the 22nd of March 2009, the seven-am-to-three-pm officer, "Charlesworth," came to Mustafa's door without getting it opened to tell him, through the crack, to pack up, you're scheduled to leave for JCI tomorrow. Just like that. Mustafa said, "Alhamdulillah!" then told Charlesworth, "Thanks for telling me." He and Buggs smiled at each other, the big hug good-bye would come just before leaving the cell for good, tomorrow. The news of Mustafa leaving for Jessup was all over the compound by late that afternoon. Many of the men were happy for him to finally be getting what he'd wanted for years, to be outta Hillbilly Hills, and able to give his family a break from traveling the long distance. At the same time, they were sorry to see such a good man leave their midst. Surely the Sunni Muslim community would feel the loss. Mustafa kept peace throughout the population as far as many of the Muslims were concerned. He was respected by the Muslims, the gang boys, and the officers for the most part. He wasn't naïve enough, however, to think it was unanimous, because he knew for a fact every mother's son didn't love Brother Mustafa, contrary to popular belief. Through the years he'd ruffled some feathers, stepped on some toes (some corns), and everybody ain't always forgiving or ready to move on.

The next day, Mustafa was enjoying the long ride outta Western Maryland to Jessup on the prison van; he was the only one going to JCI. He arrived in Jessup for the first time in twelve years, close to thirteen. It'd been fifteen since he'd been in the Pen Annex or Out Back, now officially Jessup Correctional Institution (JCI). He was assigned housing in D-building on C-tier (DC), most fitting for a guy out of the District. When he left this place, there were only A and B buildings open, and now they were up to "F," and now run by a majority of Africans. Not just correctional officers, but the medical staff as well. It was like Hagerstown in Black. Mustafa couldn't help but to think of the movie *Hotel Rawanda*.

Just as the news of his departure spread around the compound of Roxbury, so was it the case with his arrival back in Jessup. Everyone it seemed wanted to see their old friend and/or Muslim brother. The first familiar face he saw was the infamous, ex-escapee con-man entrepreneur Byron Smoot. As soon as he pushed the cart with his belongings into the building C-tier, Amir Basit and Mustafa's old cellie Hasan bin Salis pulled up the Wing Sargent Lyles to have him moved on their tier.

Two days later, when he was able to make it to the VAC/school building, he visited the outside coordinator, Abdul-Mateen. Mustafa was glad to see the old Shaykh, Abdul-Mateen, looked well, always the pleasant smile. Mustafa didn't think he had much to give as "Sadaqa" (charity), so Alhamdulillah! He put into practice a hadith from the sunnah where the Prophet (S.A.A.W) said what means, "Your smile in the face of your brother is an act of charity." (Sunan at-Tirmidhi.)

Mustafa was saddened to see Abdul-Mateen leave Roxbury as coordinator, and was happy to catch back up with him again. The office a few doors down from Mateen's was where Imam Mosi worked, and where Rasheed (Mustafa's first Imam from the Pen) hung out. It was the office of "Sargent Lynn," who took close notice of the reunion going on in her office amongst old friends. Mustafa was sure, out of respect, to give her "her propers." He'd made it a habit long ago of checking the name tags of officers, especially the brass. He would then, for future usage, address the officer as such. Thanks to Sargent Lynn, by the grace and mercy of Allah, she took the recommendation from several men she respected, including Abdul-Mateen, to recommend Mustafa to the open hospital worker's slot. He'd not been in the prison a month and was already on a payroll and drawing ten days a month going towards his good credit time. The way Allah was raining blessings upon him, he was looking to be "minimum," or back at Connie's, before next year was out. It'd been a long "tour" he'd been on, but now Alhamdulillah! He'd made it back on seemingly friendly and familiar soil. Other than "geese and geese crap" everywhere, things were copasetic.

Connie and Anthony were the first visitors Mustafa had at Jessup Correctional Institution. Since it was his birthday, he wasn't really surprised to see someone on this hot July afternoon. He thought he would see Mike D'Angelo and Candie a few weeks earlier, because of Father's day. She and her brother made previous appearances throughout the years at or around that time. Mustafa suspected his son was somewhat perturbed at the accusations he'd made months ago, last year in fact, about Michael D'Angelo's predisposition to alcoholism. Perhaps he and Serena had construed Mustafa was calling his beloved son an alcoholic. Whether he was drinking everyday (even a beer) or not wasn't the issue; he was only trying to give his son a heads-up like someone should've done him years ago. The fact was, when Mustafa came to prison the Summer of 1982 he wasn't only an alcoholic, but he was a drug abuser too, and no one said a thing. Mustafa remembered being helped from the car into Connie's house while in one of his drunken stupors by Michael D'Angelo, who was only five years old!

Mustafa was thankful he wasn't forced to do a bit, like some guys, with very little if any outside help; a few letters, no financial assistance from anyone, and with only their state pay to rely on, which was usually only from eighteen to about twenty-nine dollars monthly, depending on the institution. One would think it would be enough, considering the state provided food, clothing, and lodging. Surely a man or women incarcerated could make it off something close to that each month, provided they ate the sour, bland, and unimaginative diet plan from JCI's dietary staff. These meals, Mustafa concluded, had to be "in house," because no way were the Division of Corrections big wigs involved in concocting such a horrific menu. Nevertheless, it was possible to make it from year to year without help from home, but it'd be a lot of "doing without."

Connie, Anthony, Big Mike (M.G.), and Chick, when he'd ask, were Mustafa's main financial contributors, especially after Garneta and Helen ran their courses. His Aunts Lucy and Jennie continued to hit him off from time to time as well, and he was making "workout shorts" for the guys from the sweat shirts the state provided. At four or five dollars a pop, a couple pair of shorts a week, he was able to keep himself in the extra food items he'd grown fond of through these last few years. Granola and bran cereals, fish steaks, kippers, and dates. The peanut butter and apple jelly he got from his trips to the main dining hall while picking up the trays for the hospital. Mustafa surely appreciated Sargent Sonja Lynn for putting him in for the "blood spill" assignment – that hit paid him sixty slices a month. Though Lynn put him "in" for the job, his actual supervisor was Sargent Brown, whom he'd known (though not personally) since her rookie days in '94 when she was going by "Anderson." Brown hadn't really changed much, other than picking up ten pounds or so. Her and her first officer, Raylene, ran the hospital during the day like a finely tuned engine. Mustafa liked them both. They were easy to talk to, probably because they were good listeners, something he was just beginning to improve on.

Mustafa was flying under the radar – keeping a "low profile" would be an understatement. Working in prison hospitals gave him time to mentally escape the physical aspects of incarceration. It was an entirely different circuit than the general inmate population. There were twenty-five beds in the Cutt's hospital, even though the jail part (cell blocks, and dorms were no longer holding inmates). Besides handling all the sanitation duties on the late afternoon and evening shift, he served the dinner meal, in which he had to push a cart around to the back of the kitchen to load it with pre-prepared trays of whatever the population was having for dinner, pretty much like what he did at the Pen twenty-plus years ago. This go around, he was learning patient care from the nurses as well. They showed him about the different tubes and lines inserted in the patients for their recovery, like the feeder tube, IV lines, and one that was totally new to him called a "wound vac."

The regional hospital took patients from all the jails in the Jessup area, also including other facilities in the southeastern part of Maryland. Mustafa got to see guys he hadn't seen in several years, decades in some cases. The regional hospital, much like the penitentiary's, was also used as a hospice center/senior citizens home for old and infirmed convicts that couldn't take care of themselves. Mustafa had known some of the men on the wards for over twenty years, like Mr. Gilmore, who was now in his seventies, and just recently had his leg removed from the thigh down, and half his foot amputated on the other leg because of diabetes. Mr. Holly was in another room with Parkinson's, and old Bob (Robert Brantner) was in ward IV, wasting away at sixty-nine. Mustafa would sometimes change his diaper when the nurses allowed it to stay soiled too long because they'd gotten busy. Bob wasn't speaking intelligibly. He could barely be understood. Mustafa started teaching him the alphabets of American Sign Language. And then there was Tracy, who had AIDS, and was drawn up – "retracted" as they called it. He too was bedridden.

There were at least six old men who could've easily been granted "medical paroles." Brother Mateen, aka Juvenile, was only in his twenties, but had terminal cancer, with his kidneys and liver shutting down. Mustafa tried making it easy on them as best he could, and thanked Allah for all the favors the Most High blessed him with. Perhaps he'd work the hospital circuit again, after his release.

Most of the black women throughout the prisons in Maryland wore "fake hair," either wigs or extensions. The African women followed suit, all but a handful. Nurse Dorkas was one of the few to wear her short hair in the old-school cornrowed style. She was mid-thirties, and very conscious to seldom make direct eye contact with the male inmates. She reminded Mustafa of the ayats (verses) in the Qur'an that spoke about Prophet Musa's future wife; how shyly she came back to Musa after he had watered their flock at the well, to fetch him for their father to personally thank. (Surah Al-Qasas: ayat 25)

Nurse Dorkas was from Africa, though Mustafa wasn't sure what part. She walked very fast like Mustafa did when he was traveling by himself throughout the compound.

Prison had come a long way since he'd first entered. There was time before the 80s when the cell-block showers would be filled with rows of wet naked men, and only the Muslims would be the ones showering in their boxers or specially made showering shorts. Nowadays, throughout the prisons, only the most perverted or the exhibitionist were going "butter ball" (naked) while showering. There were not personal fans in the cells when Mustafa started, unlike now, where most of the institutions allowed you to order them (large or small) directly from the commissary. In the Penitentiary and Cutt, practically everyone had their own personal plastic five-gallon bucket, in which he'd hand wash his clothes. Like so many others, Mustafa's fingers on his right hand between the joints were rubbed raw from years of knuckling his clothes. His new cellie was a

Tuskegee University man until his senior year, eventually graduating from Morgan State. Elijah Davis was learned and well informed about some things. He would be known to "keep it real" occasionally – though keeping it real can sometimes go all wrong, as he would later attest.

Each building at JCI had its own small fenced-in asphalt courtyard with two rims for the ballers to hoop. It had a weight-lifting area for the yard boys, and if one wanted to run, they had to do it along the fence. Mustafa very seldom ran, but power walked; he did calisthenics and still lifted weights a little. Keeping his weight down to a ball eighty-five or six caused him to lose a lot of the strength he had in his early years. He was barely pressing two hundred pounds. And was thankful even for that!

The main disturbances were usually gang related. However, every now and then, an isolated fight might kick off from something small or of a more personal nature. With men, it was always about "disrespect," whereas a woman's gripe and main beef, nine out of ten times, would be about "envy or jealousy," though they'd never admit it.

While in the courtyard one Sunday morning, kicking it amongst friends, Abdullah said something that struck Mustafa in a far-reaching and penetrating way. In his "Roscoe Lee Brown" manner of articulating the English language, minus the accent, he expounded upon what Mustafa felt was strictly from the brother's heart. He said, "I would like you esteem colleagues to know it is indeed an honor growing old with you, and although this…" (he then swept his hand expansively around the confines) "is of the most ill-fated of places, I am grateful to Allah for your company. I've never been immured with such worthy and trusted friends…"

"What the hell is immured?" Butter interjected.

"Calm down, brother, let him finish," someone said.

"…however," Abdullah continued after the interruption, "whomsoever you love, you must leave them one day or another."

"Alhamdulillah!" Umar Hajji exclaimed.

Tyrone "Abdullah" Harrell was a dual-degree graduate. Like Mustafa, he began college before coming to prison. Now sixty-one years old, he hardly looked it. Abdullah was with Mustafa walking a few of the tiers during the hostage taking in '91. He too was cast out of C-dorm into three-yard to sleep on the dirt until the tents arrived. This was the Maryland Penitentiary's own "Desert Storm."

Mustafa couldn't think of a better group of men to be around this last year of his incarceration. If Allah willed, these men were as close to him as his own mother's sons. Some had become closer than all of his cousins, uncles, and so called "friends" he'd left on the streets twenty-seven years ago. Friend was a word Mustafa learned to become intimate with through the years in which others hardly knew at all, though they thought they did. They knew some of what it implied and represented, but hadn't a clue as to the literal meaning. How sad it was, he thought, his indelible J. Marie must've forgotten any and all of what it exemplified when it came to him. They had six beautiful grandchildren. They were her life. Mustafa could certainly understand that. She, Mike D'Angelo, Candie, and the little ones had formed a bond that Mustafa longed for. He wanted to be an integral part of the newest additions of the Futrells, Copelands, and Lucases, including his many nephews and nieces; and it was more than just for the sake of genetics. He knew it would take time, years, before he'd establish anything close to the connection J. Marie had with their grandchildren. They'd started off just the two of them, and now by the grace of Allah they were ten deep. The one thing Mustafa learned the last years of his incarceration, if nothing else, was "Sabr." Sabr is the Arabic word for "Patience," loosely translated.

He'd wait for the little crumb snatchers (as Papa Earnest would call children) to come around, and he'd wait on Grandma J. Marie too, at least for a while. Then he'd have to move on…with or without her.

Milton Keynes UK
Ingram Content Group UK Ltd.
UKHW010010310124
436990UK00004B/68/J